IDENTIFYING THE POOR

Voor mijn vader en moeder

Identifying the Poor

Using subjective and consensual measures

KAREL VAN DEN BOSCH
Centre for Social Policy, University of Antwerp (Ufsia)

Ashgate
Aldershot • Burlington USA • Singapore • Sydney

Published by
Ashgate Publishing Limited
Gower House
Croft Road
Aldershot
Hampshire GU11 3HR
England

Ashgate Publishing Company
131 Main Street
Burlington, VT 05401-5600 USA

Ashgate website: http://www.ashgate.com

British Library Cataloguing in Publication Data
Bosch, Karel Van den
Identifying the poor : using subjective and consensual measures
1.Poverty - Research - Evaluation 2.Poor - Identification
3.Cost and standard of living 4.Poverty - Research - Belgium - Case studies
I.Title
305.5'69'072

Library of Congress Control Number: 2001093301

ISBN 0 7546 1836 6

Printed and bound in Great Britain by Antony Rowe Ltd.,
Chippenham, Wiltshire

Contents

List of Figures

List of Tables

Preface

This book is about the question whether and how subjective information can be used for the identification of the poor in social research settings. Usually, the poor are distinguished from the non-poor by means of income thresholds (or thresholds defined for another measure of the standard of living.) There are a number of ways to determine such thresholds. This study focuses on methods where respondents in sample surveys are asked about their views or feelings on the matter. The relevant survey questions can be of two kinds. One can inquire after people's views on the income or consumption needs of families *in general* (the consensual approach), or one can ask how they feel about or evaluate their *own* income situation (the subjective approach). As will be seen, these two approaches involve rather different methodological issues.

This study is motivated by problems encountered while participating in research at the Center for Social Policy, University of Antwerp (UFSIA). In 1986, using the subjective CSP-standard, the Center found that poverty had not increased in Flanders during the period 1976 to 1985. This finding was unexpected and was greeted with some skepticism, not least by ourselves, since the period 1976 to 1985 was one of economic crisis, rising unemployment, falling wages and welfare state curtailment. Understandably, the validity of the CSP-standard was questioned. Would people not adapt their subjective income needs to their more restricted economic circumstances? Would a subjective poverty standard therefore not produce a downwardly biased estimate of real trends in poverty? Later, it was shown on the basis of other poverty standards that poverty had actually *de*creased in the period 1976 to 1985, and explanations for this surprising trend were also found (Cantillon, 1990). Yet, those questions generated an interest in the validity of subjective standards for the measurement of poverty. This book is the final product of that interest.

The research context in which the problem of identifying the poor is approached is that of socio-economic research where the object is to obtain estimates of poverty for the whole population of a country or region, as well as for subgroups within that population. This goal implies that one has to conduct surveys with large samples of households. The scale of these surveys makes it necessary to use standardized questionnaires of limited length with pre-coded answers. Fairly complete information can be gathered about household composition and income, but it is generally not possible to determine the precise living conditions of households in great detail. In other words, any method to identify the poor must not be too information demanding in order to be feasible. In practice, this means that one has to rely on imperfect indicators of the actual standard of living of families.

The focus in this study is on the problem of how to identify the poor, i.e. how to distinguish the poor from the non-poor. Another issue is how to measure the total extent of poverty in a group or population, taking into account not only the number of poor persons, but also how far the poor are below the poverty line. I have given little attention to this issue, since it seems of a somewhat secondary nature, and also because I do not have much to add to the existing literature.

The study is organized as follows. In the first chapter, I present my definition of poverty, which is inspired by the writings of Amartya Sen. Chapters two and three are about two 'consensual' methods: the consensual income method and the consensual standard of living method. The first one uses survey questions about how much income a reference family of a particular type needs to get along or to make ends meet. The second consensual method asks people to indicate which items, of a list of goods and services, they regard as 'necessities', in the sense that no one should have to do without them. Both chapters review the literature, present new empirical evidence for Belgium, and conclude with a discussion of the validity of the methods.

The subject of chapters four, five and six is the income evaluation method. This is treated at greater length than the other methods, as it has been used more often, and also because it's theoretical foundation is stronger. It uses survey questions like the Minimum Income Question, which reads: 'In the circumstances of your family, what would you consider the minimum income to make ends meet?'. In contrast to the consensual questions, it explicitly asks for a respondent's subjective view on his or her own income needs. Chapter four reviews empirical results from the literature on the determinants of the answer to the Minimum Income Question and the more complex Income Evaluation Question, as well as the resulting poverty thresholds and poverty rates. Chapter five presents new empirical results from the Belgian Socio-Economic Panel, concentrating on three issues: the reliability and validity of the method using a psychometric perspective; the empirical determinants of the answers to the income evaluation questions; and the resulting income thresholds and estimates of poverty rates. Chapter six discusses possible interpretations of the method (in particular the claim that it provides a cardinal and interpersonally comparable measure of welfare) and its validity and usefulness in empirical research on poverty.

Chapter seven looks at the income satisfaction method, where people are asked to rate their feelings of income satisfaction on a particular scale (e.g. from 'terrible' to 'delighted'). Again, results from the literature as well as new evidence for Belgium are presented. Although seemingly very similar to the income evaluation approach, the income satisfaction method turns out to produce very different results, in particular as regards the costs of children. A number of possible reasons for the differences are explored.

Finally, chapter eight summarizes the study and draws conclusions regarding the validity of the various methods and their usefulness for empirical research on poverty.

When writing the thesis on which this book is based I considered the following title: 'Everything you ever wanted to know about subjective and consensual measurement of poverty, as well as a great deal more on the same subject'. In the end I dropped this title, if only because the first part would not have been correct. Yet, the study is undeniably rather long and often very detailed. Writing a thesis is one of the few opportunities in an academic career to go into a subject really in depth. Getting this opportunity is no doubt a luxury (for which I am grateful), but I also believe that detailed and sustained analysis is necessary in order to make scientific progress. Writing down the results of such an analysis in full detail is intended as a service to the scientific community.

Yet, many readers will not want to read all of it. The best place to start is probably chapter eight, which summarizes the whole book. With the help of the table of contents, readers should be able to locate chapters and sections that are of interest to them.

This book would not have been finished without the help of many people. First of all, I thank my thesis *promoter*, Prof. Dr. Herman Deleeck, for giving me the opportunity to work on the thesis, and in particular for his continued support and confidence in me. At some stages his confidence was almost foolhardy in the Biblical sense of the word: to an outsider it must have seemed that the thesis would never be finished.

It is often said that writing a work such as this one is a lonely job. This has not been my experience. The Centre for Social Policy (as well as the Department of Sociology and Social Policy generally) has been a constructive and friendly environment in which to work. I thank all my present and former colleagues for contributing to this atmosphere. Special thanks are due to Bert Meulemans, Diane Proost, Filip Van Bourgognie and Rudi Van Dam for creating the BSEP (Belgian Socio-Economic Panel) databases with which I have worked. Bea Cantillon, Ive Marx and Barbara Tan provided helpful comments on earlier versions of parts of this book. As director of the Centre for Social Policy, Bea Cantillon made sure I could spend large parts of my time to work on this book.

Mieke De Becker, José Gabriëls, Lieve Van Bergen, Josiane Van Mele, Ingrid Van Zele and Inge Wouters typed parts of this book. I want to thank in particular Ingrid Van Zele, who efficiently took care of the final layout of this work.

This book has been published with generous financial support from the University of Antwerp (UFSIA).

I owe gratitude to all anonymous respondents in the BSEP, who spent time to answer the survey questions. In many cases, the questions must have seemed tedious, if not impertinent. I hope this book will contribute, albeit in a very limited and indirect way, to better social policies for all people living in Belgium.

1 Defining and Measuring Poverty

1 What is poverty?

What do we mean by the words poor and poverty? I will first state my definition and then present the supporting arguments. I define poverty as a situation where people lack the economic resources to realize a set of basic functionings (cf. Sen, 1985, 1993). Functionings are what a person is or does, e.g. being healthy, visiting friends, or living in a decent home. The definition focuses on what a person is capable of doing or being (given her resources and circumstances), not on the functionings that are actually achieved. A crucial aspect of poverty is that it is enforced. A healthy and able person who is living in squalid circumstances even though she has the means to improve her situation, cannot be considered poor. Moreover, not all situations where basic functionings cannot be realized come under the concept of poverty, but only those where this is due to a lack of economic resources. That is, a person who is unable to visit friends could be considered poor if the reason is that she cannot pay the bus fare, but not if she is connected to a life-support machine or is agoraphobic. Yet, depending on circumstances and abilities, different person's may need different amounts of resources to realize the same set of functionings. Handicapped person's may require a specially adapted and therefore expensive car to visit friends. For healthy and able people the most important variable influencing their resource requirements is probably the size and composition of the household they live in.

The crucial question is, of course, what are the basic functionings that people should be able to realize, or how can they be determined? In my view, the best answer we can give is: whatever people regard as basic functionings. This may seem a bit lame, but as argued in Van den Bosch (1999), attempts to circumscribe basic functionings or basic 'needs' in a more substantive way were not very successful. Some philosophers have tried to define basic needs with reference to the requirements of human flourishing or similar notions (e.g. Miller, 1976; Wiggins, 1987; Doyal and Gough, 1991). At such a high level of abstraction, one can indicate a number of functionings or needs in a general way (e.g. adequate health, some education, some income security), but it is apparently not possible to specify a list at a useful degree of detail. In particular, the important question of *how much* (e.g. income security) is needed cannot be answered. Citizenship theorists say that people are in need (i.e. cannot realize basic functionings) when they lack the means to preserve their status as a full member of the community (Titmuss, 1968; Harris, 1987). This conception of need is more specific but seems to imply a rather homogeneous view of society. Although there are certainly a number of common elements in the various material cultures in a particular society, people living in societies characterized by economic inequality will inevitably participate in those common elements in different degrees, and it is unclear whether there is a point below which people can be described as being 'excluded', either in the sense of being socially isolated, or of being treated as a 'second-class' citizen.

The position taken in this study is that as a matter of fact, some people regard some functionings as basic, i.e. as functionings that no one should have to do without. It is an open question whether in any society at any particular time many people have views on this matter at any level of articulation, and to which extent these views agree or diverge. (This study is partly about this very question.) If there is a reasonable degree of consensus on the set of basic functionings, one could say that persons who are unable to realize those functionings are excluded from a style of life that is regarded as the minimum in the community. However, this is an abstract, latent or invisible kind of exclusion, since it does not necessarily mean that those persons are socially isolated, are treated as second-class citizens, or are otherwise anything else than ordinary members of society. After all, many kinds of deprivation may not be noticed by outsiders, first because they happen 'out of sight' in the privacy of the home, and secondly because even when the condition is visible, it may not be recognized as deprivation. E.g. a family that cannot afford to eat meat regularly may be considered poor, but few of their family and friends may be aware of the fact that they do not. Moreover, many people do not eat meat from choice.

What is the motivation for this definition? The motivation (more fully developed in Van den Bosch, 1999) consists of three parts. First, the concept of poverty is inherently normative, i.e. it is about conditions that are regarded as unacceptable. Poverty definitions and poverty research that disregard this normative dimension run the risk of being irrelevant. Secondly, in order to avoid the arbitrariness of personal values, the definition of poverty should be based on standards and conventions in the community. Thirdly, since the welfare state is the main social institution in the struggle against poverty, it is assumed that it incorporates social concerns about poverty, as well as the associated standards and conventions. This is a kind of revealed preference argument: it is supposed that an institution that in most democratic nations takes up such a large proportion of National Income, will express, in its generic features, the concerns of at least a large part of the electorate. Therefore, the definition of poverty should be consistent with the general and long-term objectives of the welfare state. However, a danger to be avoided is the confusion of what is regarded as desirable with what is regarded as feasible. The concept of poverty should not be identified with the concrete arrangements of the welfare state at a particular moment. For instance, we do not have to assume that the level of income provided by social assistance is necessarily sufficient to escape poverty.

In this study, the focus is on the income transfer branch of the welfare state. The assumption is that one of the objectives of those transfers is to make sure that recipients can enjoy a minimum standard of living, i.e. a set of basic functionings. The choice for this particular part of the welfare state is pragmatic rather than theoretically motivated: investigating health care and public education involves different issues, mainly because the latter services are mostly provided in kind. Income transfers enable people to acquire goods and services in the market with which they can realize a particular set of more or less basic functionings (i.e. being fed, clothed and sheltered, socializing, etc.). Depending on their characteristics (e.g. being handicapped) or their circumstances (e.g. having many dependent children), persons have different abilities to convert income into functionings. Many social income transfers schemes recognize this by granting extra benefits to those persons. Of course, the various branches of the welfare state are not totally independent, since health and education may affect persons' abilities to transfer income into functionings. Yet, I think that the links are sufficiently limited to justify taking those factors as givens in the determination of the income requirements of a set of basic functionings.

A number of features of this definition are worth noting. It is *unidimensional*, since lack of sufficient economic resources is the single crucial characteristic of the poor. It is *relative*, in the first place since people in different societies can have different views on the set of minimum functionings, and also because the requirements in terms of goods and services for a particular functioning may vary across societies. It is *objective* in the sense that a person's individual feelings, values and preferences are not directly relevant for the assessment of poverty. It is *indirect*, since what matters, conceptually, is what people *can* do or be, given their resources and their abilities, not what they actually achieve (except as evidence for the former).

The implications of the definition of poverty and the reasons for its adoption may become clearer by making explicit what poverty is not. First poverty is not a low level of welfare, when welfare is understood as either a mental state (e.g. pleasure or happiness) or as the satisfaction of desires. Philosophers writing on welfare have stressed that the ethical significance of those concepts of welfare is doubtful, since some persons may be harder to please or may have more demanding desires than others (Sen, 1985; Griffin, 1986; Broome, 1991). Also, social income transfers do not seem designed to help people maintain a minimum level of pleasure or happiness. Instead, welfare should be defined in a more objective way, that is, in terms of the availability of goods and conditions deemed important for a good life. However, it seems that the nature of those goods and services can best be clarified by reference to basic functionings.

Poverty is not low status either. A number of writers have put forward concepts of poverty as a certain social position, or as an aspect of social relations: dependence on social assistance, the subculture of poverty, the *underclass* and *social exclusion* (e.g. Simmel, 1904; Lewis, 1968; Vranken, 1977; Murray, 1984; Wilson, 1987; Engbersen, 1991). These concepts (in particular social exclusion) tend to be multidimensional, seeing poverty as deprivation in a number of areas, such as work, health and education. In comparison with the definition proposed here, the low social status concepts of poverty appear to point to situations where a low material standard of living is aggravated by other kinds of deprivation, making the condition both more conspicuous and more difficult to remedy. However, it seems to me that these aggravated forms of poverty are indeed only particular forms of poverty and do not encompass all conditions that income transfers are meant to protect people from. In fact, in many cases income transfers may be ill-suited to shield persons from low social status (which is probably one of the reasons for the disillusionment that some feel about the welfare state).

Figure 1.1 shows the relationships between the various concepts that are relevant in the definition of poverty. The central concept is the set of feasible functionings, which are also called a person's or household's capabilities. The size and composition of this set depends on the person's or household's economic resources and on (dis)abilities and circumstances. From this (usually enormous) set, a particular choice is made of functionings that are realized. This choice reflects a person's or family's preferences. How people feel about their standard of living - i.e. their subjective welfare - depends on the number and nature of the functionings realized, but also on their personal standards and expectations regarding their material life-style.

Poverty has been defined as a situation where the set of feasible functionings does not include a set of basic functionings. But, strictly speaking, a person's poverty status cannot be determined on the basis of the set of realized functionings. It is possible that a person does not realize all of the basic functionings even when these are in his capability set. Yet, the importance of this possibility should not be overrated. It lies in the nature of basic functionings that people will tend to realize those first. From a revealed preference point of view, one might even argue that basic functionings should be defined as those which are chosen before all others.

However, in large-scale socio-economic surveys, it will be practically impossible to gather more or less complete information even about realized functionings. In current empirical work, a person's poverty status is mostly assessed on the basis of her economic resources and her (dis)abilities and circumstances. The problem then is where to draw the income threshold between poor and non-poor, and how to adjust the threshold according to a persons (dis)abilities and circumstances (i.e. how to determine the equivalence scale).

In order to work towards a valid and practical poverty standard we must be able to link a person's resources, (dis)abilities and circumstances to indicators of the extent to which functionings are realized. These indicators need not be perfect. One such measure could be a selection of important functionings. Another could be indicators of subjective welfare. In the latter case, the main problem will be that there is no simple relationship between realized functionings and subjective welfare, but that this is mediated by the personal standards and expectations of individuals. If everyone had the same preferences and there were no differences in standards and expectations, subjective welfare would be a perfect indicator of a person's standard of living. If there was only random variation in standards, a valid index of the standard of living could be formed by relating subjective welfare to economic resources, (dis)abilities and circumstances. Of course, both assumptions are not very realistic.

Figure 1.1
Concepts used in the definition or measurement of poverty

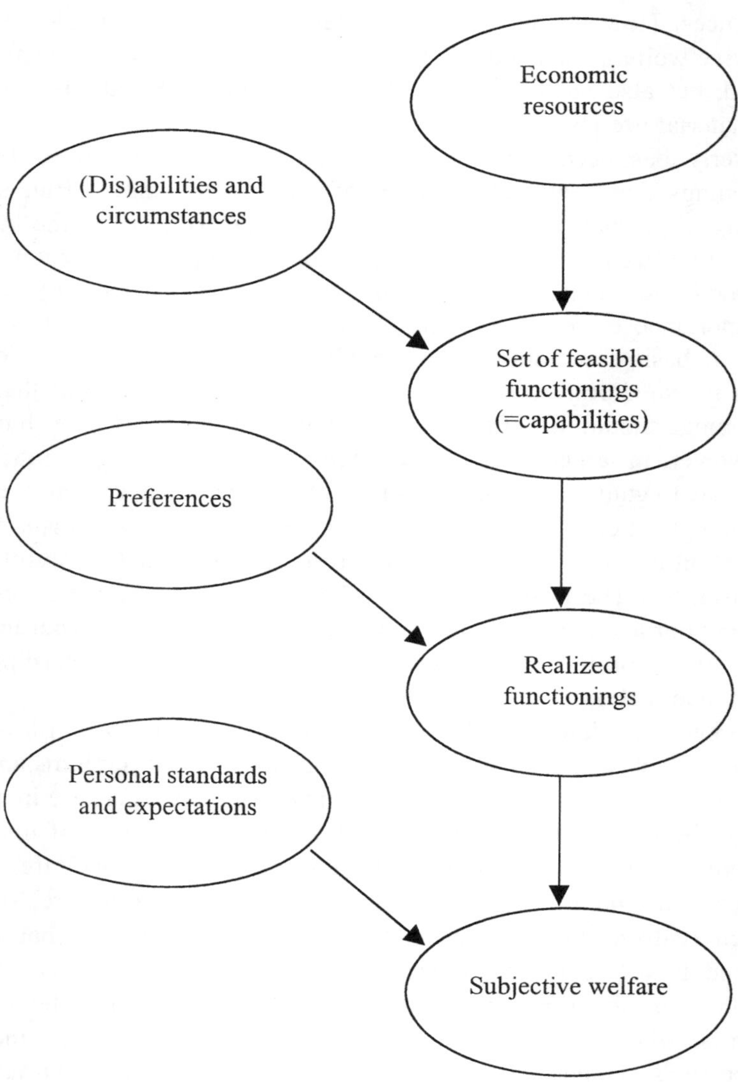

2 Poverty measures currently used in empirical research

Poverty researchers currently use a variety of methods to identify the poor. Income poverty lines can be set by five methods: budget standards, official standards, the food-ratio method, the relative method, and the subjective and consensual methods. Below, I will briefly discuss each of these methods, except of course the consensual and subjective methods, which are the main subject of this study. Following Townsend (1979), poverty can also be measured using the direct or deprivation method, on the basis of a list of items about housing, food consumption, clothing, consumer durables, as well as social activities. (For a review, see Whelan, 1993.) However, researchers using this approach still have to face the problem of where to draw the line between the poor and the non-poor.

Budget standards

A budget standard is a specific basket of goods and services which, when priced, can represent a particular standard of living (Bradshaw, 1993). In principle, using the method to estimate a minimum income standard is very simple: one draws up a list of goods and services that are deemed necessary, estimates their lifetimes, allocates prices and adds up the resulting amounts. In practice, this is of course an enormous and complicated task (or, in the words of Bradshaw, 'a ghastly chore'; Bradshaw, 1993: 236). One must ensure that the budget is complete, one must collect realistic prices for every last item and so on. This requires a team of experts and a lot of time and energy. A variety of sources of information is used in the selection of items: other budgets, expert opinion, actual spending patterns, public opinion, moral judgments.

Budget standards have been used in the pioneering poverty studies by Rowntree (1901) and Rowntree and Lavers (1951). In the sixties and seventies the budget standard approach has been subjected to heavy criticism. The critics' fire was mainly directed at the claim that budget standards provide a way to establish a non-subjective, or 'scientific' subsistence poverty line. Against this, it was maintained that these standards are based on actual patterns of living, and inevitably involve value judgments at several points (Rein 1970; Townsend, 1979). This criticism is certainly justified as far as it goes. But it seems to leave room for drawing up budgets, in which the (partial) dependence on prevailing standards and conventions, and actual patterns of living, is explicitly recognized, and where all value judgments are made explicit. E.g., Bradshaw's team developed 'low cost budgets' using the criteria that any item owned by 75 percent or more of the population, or regarded as a necessity by at least 67 percent, is included in the budget.

The most important advantage of budget standards is that they are very concrete and show exactly to what standard of living the resulting income levels correspond. This makes them appealing to a lay audience. Budget standards are also flexible: items can be taken out or replaced by other ones. This concreteness and flexibility comes at a price, though. The major disadvantage of budget standards (as a method to estimate poverty lines) is that their development and maintenance require a tremendous effort. Also, they are devised for very specific household types (e.g. a couple with two children aged 10 and 4, living in a rented terraced house in York), making the validity of generalizations to other situations uncertain.

Another problem is that budget standards may seem unrealistic when compared with actual expenditures. E.g. the 'modest-but-adequate' clothing budgets of Bradshaw (McCabe and Rose, 1993: 76) are equal to actual expenditure on clothes by households in the upper income groups. This points to what is perhaps the fundamental problem of budget standards: the uneasy mix of expert judgment, actual household spending patterns and public opinion in the selection of items. Choices often seem ad-hoc and arbitrary. (Yet the resulting budget amounts may be less arbitrary than one might expect: an adaptation of Bradshaw's low cost budgets to Belgium for three household types produced results that were rather close to budgets developed totally independently by Flemish social workers; both the total amounts as well as several budget components matched quite well; see Van den Bosch, 1997.) One way to resolve this problem may be through greater involvement of the general public, e.g. using discussion groups where experts and interested laymen and -women talk and reflect about the choices to be made.

Food-ratio poverty lines

Food-ratio poverty lines are based on the assumption that families who spend the same proportion of their income on necessities (such as food, clothing, heating), are equally well off. This method is used by Statistics Canada to construct their so-called Low Income Cut-Offs (LICOs) (Wolfson and Evans, 1989, cf. also Wolfson et al., 1990). The procedure is as follows:

- "determine the proportion of income spent 'on average' by the entire population of families on 'necessities' defined as food, shelter and clothing" from household budget survey data;
- "derive the cut-off proportion to be used to define the LICOs by adding 20 percentage points to this overall average";
- "estimate a mathematical relationship (i.e. fit a curve, log-linear in this case) between spending on food, clothing and shelter on the one hand, and pre-tax income on the other - the 'Engel curve' - taking account of variations in family size, urbanization, and geographic region";
- "given this mathematical relationship, solve for the income levels which correspond to the specified proportion of spending on food, clothing and shelter" (Wolfson and Evans, 1989: 15).

There are a number of technical concerns with the method, extensively reviewed by Wolfson and Evans (1989). The fundamental problem in the context of poverty measurement is, of course, that the cut-off proportion used to define the income thresholds is largely arbitrary. In fact, the main purpose of the method seems to be to estimate equivalence scales, rather than poverty lines. This application can also be criticized. In particular, the assumption that households of different size and composition that spend the same proportion of their incomes on necessities are equally well off, is problematic (Deaton and Muellbauer, 1986: 196). Nevertheless, versions of the food-ratio method have been used quite often to estimate equivalence scales, and the resulting estimates "are generally reasonable", though some aspects "are implausible" (Whiteford, 1985: 49).

A practical but important problem results from the way the LICOs are updated across years. They are recalculated each time new household budget survey data become available (roughly every four years), while in intervening years they are updated on the basis of the Consumer Price Index. "Users have had to make a considerable reappraisal of the incidence of low income when publication of each of the revised series of LICOs began. Indeed, the published series may be said to be revised in fits and starts" (Wolfson and Evans, 1989: 32).

The official poverty line of the USA has been set by a procedure which can be regarded as a hybrid of the food-ratio method and the budget approach. "It is based on the amount needed by families of different size and type to purchase a nutritionally adequate diet on the assumption that no more than a third of the family income is used for food" (Orshansky, 1969: 38). The income needed to purchase an adequate food budget was derived from the Agriculture Department's 'Economy food plan', which gives minimum food needs for an array of household types. Those amounts were multiplied by a factor of three to arrive at the poverty line, because food consumption surveys had shown that the average expenditure for food by all families was about one-third of income. Ever since its inception in 1964, the line has only been updated on the basis of the Consumer Price Index. If at the present moment the original procedure would again be applied, the resulting income thresholds would be very different from the current official poverty line. This is one of the reasons why many observers feel that the latter is rather outdated. Recently, it has been extensively reviewed by an official committee (Citro and Michael, 1995).

Official standards

In the official approach the rate of minimum income support offered by the social security system (or by social assistance) is used as a poverty line. In Belgium, this is the so-called 'Bestaansminimum' or 'Minimex'. The resulting legal or official poverty line has a certain prima-facie plausibility. One might assume that these rates reflect a political consensus (or, at least, a majority view) on the minimum level of income acceptable in a particular society. However, this interpretation is difficult to sustain. The level of minimum income support is generally the result of a historic process, in which many conflicting considerations may have played a role, including the state of government finances and possible repercussions on the labor market (cf. Callan and Nolan, 1991). Indeed, the adequacy, or otherwise, of the minimum income support in social assistance and social security is often the subject of research and debate, and is not something that can be taken for granted.

The guaranteed minimum income in Belgium is a case in point. Apart from regular updating on the basis of the consumer price index, there have been irregular increases in the real level of the minimum income guarantee. Yet, in international perspective, the level remains rather low. Particularly problematic is the absence of a rent subsidy scheme. Many people who depend on the minimum income support have to devote a very large part of their income to the payment of the rent. Many social assistance agencies recognize these problems and provide supplementary benefits, but the level of such assistance is unregulated and can differ strongly between one municipality and another one.

Relative standards

Many comparative studies of poverty use the relative method, where the poverty threshold is set at a certain percentage of average or median disposable or equivalent income in each country (e.g. OECD, 1976; O'Higgins and Jenkins, 1990; Smeeding et al., 1990; Mitchell, 1991). The particular percentage chosen is of course largely arbitrary, but 50 percent seems to be popular. Also imposed is a household equivalence scale. In O'Higgins and Jenkins (1990) and other early studies of poverty in the European Union, the equivalence scale was calculated using the following weights, as recommended by the OECD (1982): 1.0 for the first adult, 0.7 for other adults and 0.5 for children. The resulting scale is rather steep. For this reason, Hagenaars et al. (1992) have proposed the 'modified OECD scale', where the weights are 0.5 for other adults and 0.3 for children. Other studies (e.g. Atkinson et al., 1995) have used the 'square root' scale, where the equivalence factor is equal to the square root of the number of household members. For most households, the modified OECD scale and the square root scale do not differ much.

Since the level of the threshold is completely arbitrary, the relative method appears to have very little face validity as a poverty measure. As many have said, it is a measure of a particular aspect of income inequality, viz. the size of the bottom tail, rather than of poverty. This said, one can argue that for many purposes a measure of low income is more useful than a measure of poverty. The comparative studies where such relative measures are used are (or should be) made with a purpose, e.g. to evaluate how well countries have managed to protect or to improve the situations of the people that are economically the most vulnerable. As Orshansky (1969: 37) has written: "We need benchmarks to distinguish the population group that we want to worry about. A benchmark should neither select a group so small, in relation to all the population, that it hardly seems to deserve a general program, nor so large that a solution to the problem appears impossible." From this perspective, a measure according to which 55 percent of the population is poor in Portugal, while 0.7 percent is poor in Sweden, is not useful. At least for comparisons between countries of the OECD, relative poverty lines have proven to produce plausible results. Nevertheless, relative poverty lines have severe shortcomings as regards the measurement of trends in poverty over time. The results can be particularly perverse in relation to the economic cycle: wage increases during a period of economic upswing may produce a rise in poverty (as measured by relative standards) when pensions and other social transfers lag behind, while, mutatis mutandis, an economic recession may lead to a drop in poverty.

3 Conclusion

I have defined poverty as a situation where people lack the economic resources to realize a set of basic functionings. The identification of basic functionings (or 'needs') is essentially a normative matter. Therefore, the definition of poverty should be based on standards and conventions that exist in the community. I assume that those standards are to some extent incorporated in the welfare state, as the main institution in the struggle against poverty. As income transfers form an important part of the welfare state, this is one reason to focus on income as the measure of economic resources.

Another reason for this focus is the practical but important problem that in large-scale socio-economic surveys which must be used to measure the extent of poverty, it will be practically impossible to gather more or less complete information on realized functionings. In current empirical work, a person's poverty status is therefore mostly assessed on the basis of her current income and her household situation. The problem then is where to draw the income threshold between poor and non-poor, and how to adjust the threshold according to a person's circumstances (i.e. how to determine the equivalence scale).

None of the current methods to set a poverty line are very satisfactory. The level of the relative and food-ratio standards is largely arbitrary. Use of the official standard begs the question whether the statutory minimum income is sufficient to escape poverty. The budget approach is theoretically more promising, but difficult to implement practically.

This situation creates a demand for a method that is both theoretically valid (in terms of the poverty definition proposed above) and practical. The subject of this book is to evaluate whether subjective or consensual measures of poverty constitute that method.

2 Consensual Income Methods

1 Introduction and overview

Consensual methods aim at identifying minimum standards by reference to people's views about the incomes or the possessions and activities of families in the community in general. The consensual method that has been used most often is to ask respondents in sample surveys how much income a family of a give type needs in order to reach a particular level of living. Probably the most well known question of this kind is the so-called 'get-along' question: "What is the smallest amount of money a family of four needs each week to get along in this community?" Another method is to ask respondents to indicate which items on a list of amenities and activities they regard as necessities for all households (this is the subject of the next chapter).

Consensual methods are to be distinguished from what I have called subjective methods, where people are asked questions about their *own* income or standard of living. The latter are sometimes called 'consensual' as well, but, as will be argued in chapter 6, this is misleading. While the consensual methods, at least according to the most straightforward interpretation, presuppose that a social consensus on a minimum income or standard of living exists, this is not true for subjective methods. The distinction between consensual and subjective methods corresponds to the one Barry (1990b: 12-13) makes between privately-oriented and publicly-oriented evaluations. The former have oneself or one's family as their object, while the latter have everyone or a large group such as a country as their object.

It seems to me that one can properly talk about a consensus only in the context of publicly-oriented evaluations, simply because privately-oriented judgments by different persons are about different things. You and I can agree or disagree about what income is needed to make ends meet in our community. If we agree, there is consensus. However, if I state how much income I think I need, while you say how much income you need, then there is neither agreement nor disagreement, because we are talking about different matters. Consequently, in the latter case, it is beside the point to ask whether there is consensus.

An important issue is, of course, whether the distinction between publicly-oriented evaluations and privately-oriented evaluations is actually recognized by respondents when answering consensual or subjective survey questions. While this cannot be ascertained directly, the recorded answers can provide indications. In particular, because publicly-oriented evaluations are to be made with a larger reference group in mind than privately-oriented ones, and thus from a more general point of view, one would expect them to be less influenced by the personal circumstances of respondents. Below we will see whether this is empirically the case.

How can a minimum standard be derived from these answers? If there really is a consensus in the most simple sense that everyone agrees on the same answer, it is of course obvious what the standard should be. But consensus in this strict sense is unlikely to prevail, and what is to be done then? As we will see below, most researchers use the mean or median of the answers as the standard, but they generally do not give much of a reason for this. I think that the use of the median could be justified in the two following ways (there may in addition be other ones).

In the first place, one could argue that many people will not have considered the issue of a minimum income or a minimum standard of living very deeply, and consequently will not have settled views on the matter. The answers they actually give will only be a first approximation. They would be quite likely to change their mind after some reflection or discussion with other people. Quite possibly, if people had a chance to do this, their views on the matter would converge to a consensus. The median of the answers could, then, be interpreted as the best guess as to where that hypothetical consensus point would be located.

Another possible justification of the use of the median does not envisage respondents changing their views, but considers what would happen if people had to vote on a minimum income or a minimum standard of living for the community. In a normal democratic process, the median answer would be the expected outcome. After all, if the minimum income were put at a lower level than the median answer, a majority could be found for increasing it, and, if the minimum income were to be set at a higher level than the median answer, there would be a majority for decreasing it. (This is of course an application of the median voter theorem, cf. Downs, 1957; also Mueller, 1989: 657. A number of assumptions have to be made to get the median result, including the one that voting is not affected by other issues.) It must be noted, though, that the result of such a (hypothetical) voting procedure is not, strictly speaking, a consensus. This need not bother us unduly when views are not very wide apart, but otherwise this interpretation of the median of the answers makes it less convincing as a poverty line. If the views of people on the minimum income or the minimum standard of living really vary quite a lot, many people will not agree with the use of any particular poverty line. This is a disadvantage, even though in that situation one can probably do no better than take the median answer.

To avoid misunderstandings, it may be useful to state what the consensual method does *not* set out to do. Some authors make a rather direct link between the consensual method and what should be done about poverty in policy terms. According to Piachaud (1987: 148) two variants of the consensual approach can be distinguished: "what the public says should be provided at the minimum level", and "what the public is prepared to pay for in taxes as a minimum income." Walker (1987) argues for the latter variant on the grounds that "If the existence of poverty carries with it a moral imperative to do something about it, [...] then an indication of the preparedness of people to act must be incorporated in the measure of poverty. [...] Under a consensual model, [...] poverty exists only to the extent that people are prepared to take action about it" (p. 215).

This argument superficially resembles the position taken in this study (chapter 1), that the poverty concept is inherently normative, and that a situation can only be described as poverty if we, as a community, perceive it as problematical, and would, in principle, want to do something about it. But following Walker's and Piachaud's line of reasoning entails the danger of confusing what is seen as desirable with what is seen as feasible, or, simply, with what is seen as having more priority. There is no inconsistency in saying that a minimum income at level Y should be provided by the government, and not being prepared to pay more taxes for this purpose. One may be of the opinion that the needed money should be reallocated from other government budgets, or that someone else should pay[1]. Nor is it inconsistent to take the position that a family needs at least income Y to escape poverty and that it would be desirable if amount Y were to be provided as a minimum income, but that in present circumstances the latter is not feasible. One may think that this would disrupt the labor market too much, or that other goals (say, third world relief) are now more important. Finally, there is even not necessarily an inconsistency in putting the poverty line at Y, and at the same time regarding it even in principle as undesirable that Y should be provided as a minimum income. One may hold the conviction that income transfers are bad for people's morale, and that the government should fight poverty by creating jobs for everyone instead. The question about the level of the poverty line and the question how much should be provided as a minimum income are different questions, which should be kept clearly distinct (cf. Veit-Wilson, 1987: 202).

This chapter deals with consensual income methods, the next one looks at methods that aim at measuring a consensus about the minimum standard of living. The main question that will be addressed is, of course, whether this method produces a poverty standard that can plausibly be interpreted as reflecting a social consensus on this matter. As argued above, this requires two things. In the first place, there should be indications that respondents take a fairly general point of view when responding to the consensual questions. In particular, the answers to these questions should not be strongly influenced by the personal circumstances of the household of the respondent. Secondly, the views in the population should not be too widely apart, otherwise it would become inappropriate to talk about a consensus. Furthermore, I will discuss a number of perhaps secondary, but nevertheless interesting issues that have been treated in the several studies.

In addition to the assumptions for the consensual approach in general, as set out above, the validity of consensual income methods turns on two additional assumptions. The first is that people are able to understand the meaning of short verbal descriptions like 'getting along' in terms of a particular standard of living, or, even more concretely, a basket of goods and services. These understandings should not be too divergent across the population. Secondly, people should be able to put a price on this consumption packet, i.e. everyone should be able to translate a given standard of living into an income amount. This implies that people should have some idea about the way the standard household lives (whether it rents the dwelling it lives in, or is owner-occupier, whether one or two parents work, etc.), and about the expenses they have to incur to maintain a certain standard of living. Some authors (e.g. Mack and Lansley, 1985: 43) regard the assumption about the pricing abilities of respondents as particularly problematical.

The chapter is organized as follows. The remainder of this introduction is devoted to an overview of the studies that have been carried out, using the consensual income approach. The following sections look at various aspects and results in detail. Section 2 considers the relativity of answers to the consensual income questions with respect to average income in the community. Variation in these answers across respondents is the subject of section 3. Section 4 is about the equivalence scales that can be derived using the consensual method. In section 5 the meaning of the consensual questions is examined further. An analysis of some Belgian data is presented in section 6. In the seventh and final section, the results will be summarized and evaluated.

Overview

The consensual method that has been used most often is to ask respondents in sample surveys how much income a family of a give type needs in order to reach a particular level of living. Probably the best known question of this kind is the so-called 'get-along' question:

> "What is the smallest amount of money a family of four needs each week to get along in this community?"

which has been asked routinely in the Gallup Poll. A similar question, the health-and-decency question, has been asked almost each year since 1945 in the Australian Morgan Gallup Poll. The long time series of average answers has enabled researchers to study the development over time of consensual income thresholds (Rainwater, 1974, 1990; Kilpatrick, 1973; Saunders and Bradbury, 1991; see section 2 below).

The amount of information provided by this single question is, of course, rather limited. Additional 'consensual' income questions were asked in the Boston Social Standards Survey (Rainwater, 1974). Respondents were asked questions about the amounts of money they thought necessary for living at different levels, given different family sizes. This makes it possible to calculate equivalence scales (section 4).

A limited cross-national study has been carried out by Riffault and Rabier (1977) for the Commission of the EC. They have asked samples of adults in each of the then Member States of the EC how much money is needed to enable a family of four persons to live *satisfactorily* in their neighborhood. Respondents were also asked to state what they thought were the *minimum* incomes needed to make ends meet for three different household types.

An alternative method has been introduced by Dubnoff (1985). Instead of asking respondents to give income amounts, they are requested to rate the standard of living of families with varying income levels and varying compositions on a scale with the following points: Poor, Nearly Poor, Just Getting Along, Living Reasonably Comfortably, Living Very Comfortably, and Prosperous.

I also present results from some studies (Aguilar and Gustafsson, 1988, and a study by myself) where respondents were asked what level of income should be provided by social assistance agencies. As argued in the introduction to this chapter, it would be wrong to regard views about the level of social assistance as equivalent to those about a consensual poverty line. At the same time, it would be clearly foolish to think that they are totally unrelated. At least as a working hypothesis, it seems reasonable to assume that many persons' judgments about the minimum income that should be provided by the government will be strongly influenced by what they think is the minimum income to live on.

2 The relativity of the consensual income threshold

The consensual income method is rather unique in that long time series exist for two countries, the USA and Australia. This has enabled analysts to study how the answers to consensual income questions have developed over time, in particular in relation to indicators of the average standard of living. In this section the results of the analysis of these time-series will be discussed for each country in turn.

In the USA, in almost every year from 1946 to 1986, the Gallup Poll has asked the 'get-along' question, or a very similar one, in at least one survey. The answers to this question have been analyzed by Rainwater (1974, 1990) and Kilpatrick (1973). Both authors interpret the amounts stated as indicators of the views of respondents on the poverty line. Kilpatrick (1973) thinks that "most respondents would interpret 'getting along' to represent a higher standard of comfort than the poverty line" (p. 327), but he assumes that the poverty line is a constant proportion of the income needed to get along.

Both authors analyze the elasticity over time of the average get along amount with respect to average income or consumption. Rainwater (1990) has estimated this elasticity with respect to household mean income, as well as per couple consumption, in the period 1950 to 1986, using regression analysis with linear as well as log-linear specifications. He finds that this elasticity is equal to one, if the constant term in the equation is constrained at zero, and only slightly below one, if there is no constraint. This confirms earlier results obtained by Rainwater (1974). The elasticity of one implies that the average get-along amount as a proportion of average income does not fall or increase over time. Rather, it fluctuates in an unsystematic fashion between 70% and 80% of household mean income (calculated from Rainwater, 1990, table 1: 5).

Kilpatrick (1973), on the other hand, finds that the elasticity of the mean get-along amount with respect to both per capita disposable income and median family income is significantly lower than one. His point estimates of these elasticities range from 0.55 to 0.66.

How can the difference between Rainwater's and Kilpatrick's results be explained? Kilpatrick's (1973) data are limited to the period 1957 to 1971, as he regards pre-1957 data as unreliable or incomparable. Furthermore, Rainwater uses nominal data, while Kilpatrick has converted all amounts into constant dollars. A re-analysis of Rainwater's (1990: 5) data shows that in current prices the estimate of the elasticity of the mean get-along amount with respect to household mean income in the period 1957-1971 is only 0.79 (with a standard error of .06). If the amounts are deflated by the consumer price index (U.S. Bureau of the Census, 1987, table 738), the estimate drops to 0.62 (with a standard error of 0.13). This is clearly within the range of estimates that Kilpatrick obtained. The difference between the latter's and Rainwater's estimate of the elasticity at issue is thus due to the more limited period chosen by Kilpatrick, and the fact that he used amounts converted into constant dollars. It is not clear why the elasticity would be lower in the period 1957-1971 than in the complete period 1950-1986. In the mid-sixties, there were some years of very strong growth in real household mean income, and it may have taken some time for people's income standards to have taken up with this. According to Vaughan (1993: 27), there is a noticeable shift in the average Gallup get-along level around 1960: in the preceding period they average 79% of after tax median income of four person families; after 1960, the average across years is 70%.

One might ask the question, at this point, whether it would not be more appropriate to estimate the elasticity using constant dollar amounts, and what effect this would have on the results for the period as a whole. We will take up this question below, after a discussion of some Australian results.

A question similar to the get-along question has been asked regularly since 1945 in the Morgan Gallup Poll, which uses samples of around 2000 Australian households. It reads (Saunders and Bradbury, 1991: 55):

> "In your opinion, what is the smallest amount a family of four - two parents and two children - need a week to keep in health and live decently - the smallest amount for all expenses including rent?"

The series of average responses from 1950 until 1988 has been analyzed by Saunders and Bradbury (1991). They estimate the elasticity of the average health-and-decency amount with respect to three indices of average community income: private final consumption expenditure per capita, household disposable income per capita, as given in the National Accounts, and an index of male average weekly earnings. Across the period as a whole the estimates for the elasticities with respect to the first two income measures are virtually equal to one; with respect to average male earnings the elasticity is 0.91. However, Saunders and Bradbury locate a structural break in the series around 1970. Within the two periods - before and after 1970 - the estimates of the elasticity are around 0.75 for the first two income measures, and 0.63 for average male earnings. It is not clear what has caused the break in the series of average health-and-decency amounts.

On average across years, the mean health-and-decency amount is 86% of household disposable income per capita. (Calculated from results shown in table 2 of Saunders and Bradbury, 1991). In 1987 the mean response was 79% of the average net income of respondents in households consisting of a couple plus two children. These levels seem quite high, and, though the figures are not directly comparable, higher than those found by Rainwater (1990). Indeed, in 1987, 36% of couples with two children had incomes below the mean health-and-decency amount (Saunders and Bradbury, 1991: 67).

The elasticity of consensual income amounts with respect to price changes

As noted above, Rainwater has estimated the elasticity of the get-along amounts in nominal terms while Saunders and Bradbury have deflated all amounts by the price index. Which procedure is to be preferred, and what effect does this have on the results? Rainwater (1990: 7) defends his use of nominal amounts on the ground that "survey respondents are making judgments in terms of the current economy". But this seems somewhat unsatisfactory. Whether the changes in actual income are real or only nominal does seem to make an important difference to how the elasticity of the mean get-along amount is interpreted. Suppose that all incomes increase in line with the rate of inflation, i.e. real incomes remain constant. Then one would expect that the mean get-along amount would grow at the same rate. Otherwise, the real value of the mean get-along amount would fall, and respondents would apparently suffer from a kind of money illusion. But that would seem to imply that the answers to the get-along question could not reliably be used as indicators of a social minimum level of living of some sort. A finding that respondents do not fully discount for price changes in their answers to consensual income questions would seriously undermine the validity of the claim that such questions provide measures of the income needed to reach a certain standard of living. If respondents make systematic, and not just random, errors in "pricing" a certain standard of living, it is at least doubtful whether the mean or the median of the answers to survey questions about standards of living can be interpreted as reflecting a social consensus. In other words, consistency requires that the elasticity of the mean get-along amount with respect to purely nominal changes in income is equal to one. On the other hand, the elasticity of the get-along amounts with respect to *real* changes in income could theoretically vary between zero and one.

In order to get empirical results on this matter, the data used by Rainwater (1990) and by Saunders and Bradbury (1991) were re-analyzed. The average responses to the get-along or health-and-decency questions in *current* prices were regressed on indicators of household income in *constant* prices and an indicator of the price level. Technical details and full results can be found in Appendix 2.1. The results for the American Gallup question are clear: the estimate of the elasticity of the get-along amounts with respect to the price level is 0.99, and the hypothesis that it is equal to one is not rejected by a formal test. On the other hand, the elasticity with respect to changes in real household income is estimated at 0.79, and the hypothesis that it is equal to one is rejected by a formal test. The same is true for the hypothesis that the elasticities with respect to prices and with respect to real household income are equal. Unfortunately, the results for Australia are more ambiguous. The structural break in the health-and-decency series complicates matters. The hypothesis that the elasticity with respect to price changes is equal to one across the whole period 1950-1988, is rejected by a formal test in two instances. Nevertheless, they are fairly close to one. Furthermore, the elasticity with respect to changes in real income is clearly much lower than the elasticity with respect to price changes. The estimates for the former vary between 0.72 and 0.21.

Thus the conclusion seems warranted that respondents in sample surveys are able to distinguish between price changes and real income changes. Price changes are apparently fully discounted for in the answers to the get-along question. This result considerably enhances the validity of the consensual income method. Another result from the re-analysis is that the average get-along amounts are not completely relative with regard to changes in real household income, though the elasticity is quite high.

The relativity of consensual income amounts across countries

The relativity of answers to consensual income questions, not across time, but across countries can be assessed using the data provided by Riffault and Rabier (1977). The median answers to questions about 'satisfactory' income and about 'minimum' income, both referring to four-person households, as a percentage of median income in the sample were:

	Belgium	Denmark	Germany	France	Ireland
satisfactory income	94	105	82	111	106
minimum income	88	96	79	100	101
median income*	562	953	713	610	340
	Italy	**Luxembourg**	**Netherlands**	**UK**	
satisfactory income	125	100	86	101	
minimum income	125	97	84	94	
median income (1)	319	606	656	413	

Note: * median income in ECU per month in sample.
Source: Riffault and Rabier (1977, tables 5 and 9), and own calculations.

The median answer to the satisfactory income question varies between 82% and 125% of actual median income, the median answer to the minimum income question lies between 79% and 125%. There is no clearly discernible pattern across countries. An estimate of the elasticity of the answers to these questions with respect to median income across countries can be obtained by regressing the median answers on median actual income, using a log-log specification. For the satisfactory income amounts the estimate of the elasticity was 0.81 (standard error: 0.12); for the minimum income amounts the estimate of the elasticity was 0.79 (standard error: 0.11). This result suggests that the answers to consensual income questions are as relative across countries as they are across time.

3 Variation in the consensual income amounts

Of course, in any particular year, not every respondent gives the same amount in answer to the get-along or health-and-decency questions. In fact, there is considerable variation in the answers. From data provided by Rainwater (1990: 28-29) it can be derived that in the USA in 1986, when the median answer to the get-along question was $350, the first quartile was situated at $250, and the third quartile at $450. Thus a band of $200 ($10,000 a year, or 57% of median income) contains only 50% of the answers. Over the years the interquartile range has increased considerably: in 1960 it was only $40. In real terms, the increase is of course much smaller, but still significant: about 35%. The same is true for the standard deviation of the get-along amounts. However, if we look at the variation in relative terms, i.e. as a percentage of the average answer, there is no clear trend. If anything, the relative variation in the get-along amounts was higher in the fifties. (This is probably due to the fact that the amounts given by respondents generally are strongly rounded, so that they tended to jump from, say, $50 to $100. In later years, the jumps were relatively smaller.)

Rainwater (1974, 1990) has also investigated with what variables the variation in the answers to the get-along question is correlated, using the Gallup-Poll data for several years. The variable with the greatest impact appears to be family income. Averaging across a number of years, Rainwater (1990: 10) finds that the cross-sectional elasticity of the get-along amounts with respect to family income is 0.157. Family income explains, on average over the years, 7.3% of the variance of the get-along amounts (with a double-log regression equation). The effects of the age of the head of household, and the size of the household, are small, and may be a function of differences in income between age and size classes. Rainwater (1974) reports that for the 1969 Gallup data contextual factors (i.e. mainly the cost of living and relative income in the community) accounted for about 11.5% of the variance in get-along amounts, and family factors (mainly income) for 7% to 8%. Also, the answers of respondents who live in families of four are on average quite close to those of people in other types of families (Rainwater, 1990: 5).

A few more limited studies have provided similar results. Saunders and Bradbury (1991) have analyzed individual responses to the health-and-decency question in the Morgan Gallup Poll of July 1987, in Australia. Although they do not explicitly report any measure of dispersion, it can be calculated from some results they do report (i.e. the R-square and the standard error of regression with income) that the standard deviation of the logs of the amounts given by respondents consisting of a couple plus two children (the type of household to which the question refers) is about 0.30. This would imply that, if the amounts are approximately log-normally distributed, about two-thirds of the answers are located in a band which extends from 74% to 135% of the geometric mean. Saunders and Bradbury (1991) have regressed the answers on income and other variables (double log specification), using data of families of four. The estimate of the elasticity of the health-and-decency amount with respect to family income is 0.25; the effects of other variables - age and working status of husband and wife - are not significant; 11% the variance is explained.

Rainwater (1974: 94-117), in addition to the Gallup Poll data, also reports results from the Boston Social Standards Survey. Among other questions, the get-along question was asked, but now for several family types. Averaged across family types, the "geometric standard deviation" is around 139% (Rainwater, 1974: 96-97), implying that about two-thirds of the answers are located in a band ranging from 72% to 139% of the geometric mean. Again, very little of this variability is accounted for by background characteristics of the respondents.

Dubnoff (1985) has applied an alternative technique. Instead of asking respondents to give income amounts, they are requested to rate the standard of living of families with varying income levels and other characteristics. A scale with the following points was used: Poor, Nearly Poor, Just Getting Along, Living Reasonably Comfortably, Living Very Comfortably, and Prosperous. Respondents were presented with ten stimulus families, randomly chosen from a population of stimulus families, which was constructed by combining eleven family types, ten income levels, and three ages of children.

Dubnoff treats each rating as a single case. Not unexpectedly, the income of the stimulus family is very important for how its living standard is evaluated. In fact, stimulus income explains 55% of the variation in the ratings. (The several ratings had been assigned numerical values of 1 to 6.) Yet this leaves a great deal of variation unexplained. "Just getting along" is the modal response across a fairly wide income band - from $12,600 to $21,000, but within this band, other ratings are also popular. Only part of this variation is accounted for by other stimulus family characteristics: stimulus family size explains a further 3.6%; other characteristics are even less important. About 40% of the variance is thus due to differing ratings of the same situations by different respondents. However, background characteristics of the respondent - income, family size, retirement status and sex - add only about 4% to the explained variance.

Given the relationships estimated in the regression analysis, Dubnoff is able to compute income levels corresponding to various standards of living and family situations. The income amount needed by a family of four to be rated as "Just Getting Along" by the average respondent is $21,435. This amount is quite close to the geometric mean of the answers to the get-along question, which was also asked in the same survey ($22,100).

Aguilar and Gustafsson (1988: 261) have asked respondents in a Swedish survey how much they believe one should get to make ends meet after taxes and housing costs are paid. The context made clear that the question referred to social assistance. The coefficient of variation for the responses referring to single adults or to couples was 31%. If the responses were normally distributed, this would imply that two-thirds of the answers are in a band ranging from 69% to 131% of the mean response. The coefficient of variation for the answers referring to benefits for children was much larger: 46% for children from 0 to 3 years, somewhat less for older children. Despite considerable efforts to find some relationships between the answers and background variables, very few statistically significant relationships were discovered, and those were very weak (R-square of only 0.006 at most). Aguilar and Gustafsson (1988: 272) conclude that "the Swedish population is rather homogeneous with respect to the opinions about the income thresholds governing welfare programs".

Summing up, it seems that all available studies come up with the result that there is considerable variation in the answers to the "get-along" question, and similar questions in the consensual approach. They are equally consistent in the finding that very little of this variation can be explained by such background variables as income, age, and household type.

How, then, should this diversity in answers be interpreted? Rainwater (1974: 59) writes: "Differences in the responses seem to be produced by highly idiosyncratic factors, and probably largely by response error in which respondents have difficulty connecting a number with their underlying understanding of the consumption that enables such a family to 'get along'." This interpretation provides him with a justification for regarding the average get-along amount as a measure of the social consensus on the poverty line. There are two problems with Rainwater's interpretation. In the first place, it is clear that people generally have no very precise idea of the amount of money needed to get along. This is indicated by the fact, for instance, that most respondents in the American Gallup Poll provide an amount that is rounded to a multiple of $100 (more than 70% in 1986; Rainwater, 1990: 29). However, even if differences between respondents are indeed due to response error only, Rainwater must make the further, implicit, assumption that these errors are symmetrically distributed in such a way that they cancel each other out on average. If the errors are not purely random, but are due, for instance, to inaccurate pricing of a minimum basket of goods and services, there is no particular reason why this would be the case. If the average of the errors is non-zero instead, the average get-along amount would be a biased estimate of the minimum level of income that enables a family to 'get along'. A second objection to Rainwater's argument is that the possibility cannot be excluded that people's opinions on the minimum standard of living actually vary considerably. Even assuming that the answers to the 'get-along' question are only accurate to within a range of $100, there is still a great deal of variation left unexplained. Rainwater (1990) and others appear to jump from the finding that differences in views are not correlated with background variables to the conclusion that there are no real differences in views. This is less than completely convincing.

4 Income equivalence

Until this point we have concentrated on the views about the incomes of families consisting of a couple with two children. It is of some interest to examine what these views are for other household types. Unfortunately, the USA Gallup Poll and the Australian Morgan Gallup Poll do not provide such data. But in a number of other, more specialized surveys, questions were asked about a range of household types.

In the Boston Social Standards Survey (cf. above) respondents were asked questions about the amounts of money they thought necessary for living at different levels, given different family sizes. The living levels were poverty, getting along, being comfortable, prosperous and substantial, and rich. Six possible family sizes (couple with zero to five children) were distinguished, but the sample was divided into subsamples, so that each respondent made an estimate for only one family size for each living level.

Rainwater (1974) has computed an equivalence scale for each living level by comparing the geometric means for the several family sizes. It turns out that the scales are rather flat. The equivalence factors of four children families, relative to no-children families, thus computed, are 1.35, 1.44 and 1.30, for the poverty, get along and comfortable living levels respectively, which are most relevant for our purposes. Although the equivalence scale of the get-along amounts seems to be somewhat steeper than the other ones, the difference is probably not statistically significant, given the large variability in the amounts (Rainwater, 1974: 103). A regression analysis across all living levels results in an estimate of 0.312 for the family size elasticity, implying an equivalence factor for four children families of 1.41 (Rainwater, 1974: 99-110).

Dubnoff (1985) has used a procedure somewhat similar to that of Rainwater, but instead of asking for income amounts, he has asked respondents to rate the standard of living of households having a certain composition and a certain income. The results of a regression of these ratings on income and size of the stimulus households (see above) can be used to estimate the income levels which are associated with the various points on the living level scale (i.e. ratings), and from these income levels an equivalence scale can be derived. The resulting equivalence scale is rather flat: a family of six needs only 47% more income than a family of two to achieve the same living level. This scale is very close to the one Rainwater (1974) obtained.

Equivalence factors for three household types haven also been estimated by Riffault and Rabier (1977) in their nine-country study for the EC. They calculated the ratios between the median answers to questions about the minimum income for three household types (a person of 30-50 years living alone, a household of two persons of 30-50 years, and a family of four persons - a man, woman and two children between 10-15 years).

These are as follows, with a two person household as the base:

	Belgium	Denmark	Germany	France	Ireland
single person	64	71	68	64	68
two person household	100	100	100	100	100
four person household	128	131	140	143	139

	Italy	Luxembourg	Netherlands	UK
single person	69	69	76	71
two person household	100	100	100	100
four person household	143	133	124	135

Source: Riffault and Rabier (1977, table 8), and own calculations.

The results are reasonably similar across countries, though in The Netherlands the amounts for the three household types seem closer together than in the other countries. On average across countries, the single person amount is about two-thirds of the two person median answer, while the four person amount is about 35% higher. These equivalence factors are higher than those found by Rainwater and Dubnoff, but still much lower than those conventionally used (such as the scale recommended by the OECD (1982)).

Aguilar and Gustafsson (1988: 262-263) have also used the responses to the question about social assistance support levels to calculate equivalence factors. Their estimates imply that the Swedish public thinks that the needs of single persons are about 59% of those of a couple, while a family with two children aged between 4 and 10 needs 54% more income than a childless couple. Compared with other consensual estimates of equivalence scales, this is a rather steep scale. The authors remark that the equivalence scale derived from the answers is close to the scale incorporated in Swedish welfare programs. It is also close to conventionally used scales, e.g. the OECD one. Note though, that the scales reported by Aguilar and Gustafsson exclude housing costs, where economies of scale may be assumed to be relatively large.

Thus, in general, consensual income methods seem to produce estimates of the equivalence scale that are much flatter than those found in other studies (as Rainwater and Dubnoff both recognize). Why is this the case? Rainwater (1974: 108) suggests that the difference reflects "the consumption value of children to their parents". That is, if traditional scales reflect the incomes that different families need to achieve equal material well-being, then the difference between those scales and the "level of living"-scale is an indicator of the amount of income that a family is willing to forego in order to have another child. I will consider later whether, *if* this interpretation is correct, consensual equivalence scales are appropriate for poverty measurement. Whether it *is* in fact correct, is, with the data at hand, difficult to assess. But it may be noted that Rainwater (1974: 94) was "concerned not to focus the respondent's attention on the family size variable"; both the design of the Boston Social Standards Survey and the way the questions were phrased reflect this concern. No such concern is evident for Dubnoff's (1985) study; but family size was only one among several characteristics of the stimulus family and respondent's minds may have focused on income levels. Although we cannot ascertain to what extent real differences of opinion between European and USA respondents have played a role, it is significant that the equivalence factors found by Riffault and Rabier (1977) and by Aguilar and Gustafsson (1988), where the order of the questions emphasized the household type variable, are considerably steeper than those of Rainwater and Dubnoff.

5 The meaning of "getting along"

Up to this point the question has not been addressed how respondents might have interpreted the phrase "getting along". Of course, we cannot get into the mind of respondents. But two kinds of information are available for clarifying this issue somewhat: first, the relation of 'getting along' to other living levels, and, secondly, qualitative descriptions of what it means to 'get-along' or to live 'in poverty', etc.

In 1989, the Gallup organization has asked respondents in a special survey the following question:

> "People who have an income below a certain level can be considered poor. That level is called the 'poverty line'. What amount of weekly income would you use as a poverty line for a family of four

(husband, wife and two children) in this community?" (O'Hare et al., 1990, quoted in Vaughan, 1993: 25).

The get-along question was administered in another survey, earlier in 1989. After some adjustment for price changes, it turned out that the average answer to the poverty question is 28% below the average get-along amount and slightly less than 50% of median four person family income, while being 23% above the official poverty standard for four person families. The proportion of four person families below these amounts is 10% for the official poverty standard, 13% for the average poverty amount, and 20% for the get-along amount (Vaughan, 1993: 25: 31).

More detailed analysis of a range of living levels has been carried out by Rainwater (1974) and Dubnoff (1985). As described above, in the Boston Social Standards Survey, respondents were asked to state the amounts of money they thought necessary for living at different levels, given different family sizes. Of those living levels, "poverty", "get along" and "comfortable" are the most relevant here. The results, as reported by Rainwater (1974), show that the geometric mean of the get-along amounts is considerably higher than the geometric mean of the poverty amounts. In fact, it is about midway between the poverty and comfortable amounts. This is especially significant, since respondents were asked to give the *highest* income level a family could have and still be considered living in poverty, while for the get-along living level, as well as for the comfortable living level, respondents had to give the *lowest* amount consistent with that living level[2].

Rainwater's results are confirmed by Dubnoff (1985), who has let respondents in another survey rate income levels for a range of household types in terms of living levels (cf. above). The income band where "Just getting along" is the modal (i.e. most frequently occurring) response seems to be halfway between the income bands where "poor" and "comfortably" were the modal responses. The "Near poor" living level seems to be closer to "Poor" than to "Just getting along"[3]. The results of Rainwater (1974) and Dubnoff (1985) suggest, therefore, that in the minds of respondents the living standards associated with 'getting along' and 'just getting along' are at some distance removed from poverty.

Somewhat in contrast with this, Riffault and Rabier (1977: 20) find that the difference between the median answer to the *minimum* income question for four person households is in all countries less than 10%-points below the median answer to the *satisfactory* income question (cf. the results shown in section 2.2). While this result may be interpreted in various ways, it is useful to note that the minimum income question was placed in such a way as to focus respondents' minds on differences between household types, and not on differences between living levels. It is also possible that the word 'minimum' evokes different responses than the words 'poor' or 'poverty'.

In addition to income amounts, Rainwater (1974: 118-135) has also asked respondents in the Boston Social Standards Survey about the images they had of the life lived by families who are "poor", "getting along", "comfortable", etc. Open-ended questions were used, which served more as suggestions to talk freely than as requests for specific information. Because it is the only study, or one of the very few studies, which has explored the meaning people attach to a phrase like "getting along", I think it is worth quoting from the conclusions of Rainwater at some length.

One of the more interesting results is that

> "the imagery offered for getting along is not too different from the one other respondents give for the 'just average' Bostonian. [...] There is a sense that there is not very much leeway between a level of living that is so low that one cannot feel that the family is getting along as a family should, and the level that stands for the most 'middle' of Middle Americans" (pp. 129-130).

What does the life-style of a family that is just getting along look like?

> "It is understood that a few luxuries are required in order to get along, that without them the family cannot feel part of the broad Middle American stream. The imagery offered for family life style at the get-along level involves care, scrimping, and focusing on family activities and family visiting not just for the warmth they bring but because one cannot afford more commercial entertainments. But within this restrained style the family is able to carry out the ordinary activities of all families, maintain a home, rear and educate children, find gratification in one another. This is difficult and sometimes wearing and depressing for the family heads but it is possible, really not all out of the ordinary. The family gets by in this way, but its consumption package does not contain some of the symbolic goods that make for the good life-longer vacations to more distant places, more little luxuries, good clothes, newer cars, better houses" (p. 130).

Getting along seems to be qualitatively different from being in poverty.

> "Poverty is different from getting along in that it is a very special status. Getting along involves being at the low edge of the mainstream, and people understand that getting along shades into just average and mainstream life. Being poor, however, is seen as somehow being removed from that kind of life. If you are poor, it is not that you just have fewer things, but that you do not have important things, things that *every* family should have. One does not have the normal things, and many feel that not having the normal things means not having a normal life. In poverty, the family has to struggle for whatever it has. That struggle is sometimes thought to produce just the bare necessities and at other times not even that" (p. 133).

> "Poverty [...] is also a social and psychological condition in which there are specific effects on how people feel about themselves [...] and on how they behave [...]. [...] The difference between getting along and being poor is the difference between [...] a good chance for things to get better and nothing ever changing" (p. 135).

6 Some results for Belgium

In this section I want to present some results for Belgium from the Socio-Economic Panel, wave 1985. The "get-along" question, or a similar one, was not asked in this survey. Instead, a question was asked about the subsistence minimum income that is guaranteed as of right to every Belgian.

The question asked was the following:

> "I will now name several types of social security benefits. Could you tell me for each type of benefit what amount each person drawing this type of benefit should be able to receive, in your opinion, if he/she is a single person and if he/she has a family to support?"

The types of benefit named were: pensions, disablement benefit, unemployment benefit, and subsistence minimum (welfare).

In the present context, the subsistence minimum is the most interesting. The subsistence minimum is a minimum income guaranteed to all Belgians and to some persons of other nationalities living in Belgium. The amounts provided in 1985 were 14,200 BF per month for a single person and 19,700 BF per month for a couple.

As argued in the introduction to this chapter, it would be wrong to regard views about the guaranteed subsistence minimum income as equivalent to those about a consensual poverty line. At the same time, it would be clearly foolish to think that they are totally unrelated. Many persons' judgments about the minimum income that should be guaranteed to everyone will be strongly influenced by what they think is the minimum income to live on. In Belgium, this is especially likely to be the case because the subsistence minimum is an uncontroversial part of the Belgian welfare state. No political party challenges its continued existence, and there have been very few political worries about its costs (in contrast to the costs of social security as a whole). During the economic crisis period in the beginning of the 1980's, when many benefits were reduced, the subsistence minimum was not affected. It has even increased in real terms (Cantillon et al., 1987: 192). This is probably at least partly due to the low number of people receiving this benefit: only 50,000 persons or 0.5% of the population, in 1989. Consequently, the total expense does not amount to more than 1% of all social security expenditure.

The phrase "a family to support" in the quoted question is somewhat ambiguous. The Belgium social security system provides higher benefits if one has a family to support, and in most cases this refers to a dependent spouse. The presence of children does not generally lead to a further increase in benefits, as their costs are assumed to be covered by child allowances. (There was in fact a further question about the minimum child allowance in the survey.) Therefore it seems most natural to assume that the family amounts given by respondents are in fact amounts for couples with no children, though this may not be true for all respondents.

In order to reduce the possible effect of people who have just mentioned the first amount that came into their head, most of the results presented below are based on answers of respondents that were consistent and cooperative. Consistency involves two conditions. Firstly, for all four types of benefit the family amount should not be below the single-person amount. Secondly, the amounts for a single person should be ranked in the same way as the amounts for a family (ties are allowed). Thus, if the single person amount for benefit A is lower than that for benefit B, than the reverse should not be true for the family amounts[4]. Respondents are regarded as cooperative, if they have provided full information on the incomes of their household. Of 5,439 (84% of the total sample) respondents who provided both subsistence minimum amounts, 374 (7%) were excluded because of inconsistency, and a further 295 (5%) because of uncooperativeness.

The results are presented in table 2.1. It appears that, whatever measure of central tendency is used, and whatever restriction is imposed on the respondents, the average answer to the subsistence minimum questions is 20,000 BF or a little more for single persons, and 30,000 BF or a little less for families. If only consistent answers from cooperative respondents are used, the averages are a little higher; if 204 respondents are excluded who gave amounts of 50,000 BF (the sample median household income) or higher, the averages are somewhat reduced.

In this case also, we find that the answers vary considerably, though apparently somewhat less than in the Swedish sample used by Aguilar and Gustafsson (1988). Using only the answers of consistent and cooperative respondents, reduces the variability only slightly. The interquartile range of 10,000 BF for a couple can be put into perspective if it is realized that the distance between average household income in the first and in the second income decile is 8,600 BF. Though most answers are in a relatively small range, a considerable number of respondents gave rather high amounts. More than one in six (consistent and cooperative) respondents apparently were of the opinion that the subsistence minimum for a family should be 40,000 BF a month or more. This is about the same as income in the fourth decile. (Some of these respondents may have included children in the 'family'.)

Restricting the sample to (consistent and cooperative) *single* people only does not change these results significantly. The mean and median single person amount in this subgroup is 20,000 BF, while the standard deviation of the amounts is 5,362 BF, and the interquartile range increases even to 10,000 BF. Thus, whether the respondent is familiar with the household situation in question or not, does not seem to influence his or her answers.

As in the studies discussed above, I find that the variation in the answers is very weakly related to background characteristics. A regression analysis was carried out with the following independent variables: total household income as estimated by the respondent, age and sex of head of household, number of household members, socio-professional category of head of household (manual workers, lower employees, higher employees, self-employed) and whether or not receiving the subsistence minimum.

Both linear and log-log specifications were tested. Only the answers of consistent and cooperative respondents were used.

In the linear specification, which seemed the most successful one, the independent variables together accounted for 2.9% of the variance of the single-person amounts, and 4.6% of the variance of the family amounts (the R-squares are unadjusted). The most important variable was total household income (the first-order correlations were 0.14 and 0.17, respectively), but the regression coefficients were very low: 0.025 for the single-person minima, and 0.04 for the family minima. (Both estimates correspond to an elasticity of about 0.07 at the mean.) Interestingly, respondents who actually received the subsistence minimum (they numbered 25 in the sample), stated amounts for single persons that were 2,650 BF higher than those of the average respondent, and family amounts that were 4,300 BF higher, in both cases ceteris paribus other factors. These differences are significant at the 5% level.

Is this variation in the answers to the subsistence minimum largely of a random character, or does it reflect real differences of opinion between respondents? This is a question for which there is at present no definitive answer, but there is some circumstantial evidence.

Table 2.1
Public opinion about the level of the subsistence minimum (guaranteed minimum income), Belgium, 1985, monthly amounts

	All respondents		Only consistent and cooperative respondents*, extremes° excluded	
	Single Person	Family	Single Person	Family
Measures of central tendency				
Mean	21,184	30,190	20,808	29,469
Median	20,000	30,000	20,000	30,000
Geometric Mean	20,375	28,905	20,138	28,671
Mode	20,000	30,000	20,000	30,000
(Standard Error Mean)	(77)	(115)	(76)	(99)
Measures of dispersion				
Standard Deviation	5,725	8,568	5,142	6,688
Coefficient of Variation	27	28	24	22
Interquartile Range	7,000	10,000	7,000	10,000
90th percentile-10th percentile	15,000	20,000	12,000	20,000
Minimum	200	500	5,000	10,000
Maximum	60,000	80,000	45,000	48,000
N	5,555	5,590	4,566	4,566

Notes: * see text.

° extremes: values of 50,000 BF or higher.

Source: Belgian SEP, wave 1985.

Secondly, we can look at the consistency of the answers to the eight minimum benefit questions. The fact that only 7% of the respondents who answered both subsistence minimum questions did not conform to fairly restrictive consistency conditions, shows that most respondents did not answer haphazardly, but had at least some structure in their minds[5]. However, a further 145 respondents (3%) said that couples should get the same subsistence minimum benefit as single persons, which is hard to make sense of.

Thirdly, we can look at the ratios of the family amounts relative to the single-person amounts for the various types of benefit. These can be regarded as estimates by the respondent of the equivalence factor of families relative to single person households. It seems reasonable to require that ideally, the estimates of each respondent should be equal for all types of benefit, while these estimates may vary across respondents. On the other hand, if respondents answer the questions with no notion whatever of the appropriate equivalence factor (except that the family amount should be at least as high as the single-person amount), one would expect that there is as much variability in the scales of each respondent separately, as there is across respondents.

In fact, it is found that for consistent and cooperative respondents who answered all eight minimum benefit questions (4456) the variance of the equivalence scales between respondents is 0.0602, while it is only 0.0325 within respondents[6]. From these results it is possible to calculate the intra-class correlation coefficient, which is measure of the homogeneity of the classes (here: respondents) relative to the total variability of the variable (Blalock, 1972: 355)[7]. It is equal to 0.18. However, if 16 cases are removed where the difference between the lowest and the highest factor is greater than one, the intra-class correlation increases to 0.37 (the estimates of the variance between and within classes are 0.0473 and 0.0142 respectively). The correlations of the four equivalence factors vary between 0.72 and 0.88. A factor analysis showed that these correlations are due to a single underlying dimension. Thus, it appears that respondents have a certain conception of the appropriate equivalence scale when answering the minimum benefit questions. At the same time, this conception is not very precise: the standard deviation of the four equivalence factors for the average respondent is 0.12. Incidentally, the average equivalence factor of families relative to single persons is 1.42. This is only slightly lower than the ratio of the mean amounts (1.43, see table 2.1).

The results presented above indicate that many, if not most respondents do not answer the minimum benefit questions, including the subsistence minimum question, haphazardly. On the contrary, respondents are reasonably consistent in their answers.

I think that there are two possible interpretations which can explain both the consistency and the variation. In the first place, it is of course possible that there is simply no consensus in society regarding the level of the subsistence minimum, and that different people have different ideas about the living standard that households dependent on the subsistence minimum should be able to enjoy.

Secondly, it is conceivable that a consensus on the minimum living standard does exist, but that in the minds of different people it corresponds to different amounts of income. Essentially, this hypothesis means that one assumes that people can be mistaken about the price level. Though everyone agrees that the minimum living standard includes, say, eating meat every other day, and a new set or clothes every year, different people have different ideas about what it costs to obtain those goods. (In a country as small as Belgium, regional price variations are not very important, except possibly for housing.)

As a third hypothesis, one could assume that respondents have a set of relativities (between different types of benefit, and between families and single persons) in mind, but do not have a clear conception of the minimum living standard itself. Answering the first minimum benefit question, they state the first reasonably low income level that comes to mind. The other amounts are then derived from the first random one, by applying the set of relativities. Though conceptually different, this hypothesis is indistinguishable from the second one in its empirical implications regarding the answers to the question.

The question whether a consensus exists regarding the minimum standard of living will be examined in the next chapter, when we will be looking at the results of the so-called life-style indicator approach (cf. Mack and Lansley, 1985).

In the meantime, we can consider one possible implication of the hypothesis that a social consensus on the minimum standard of living does exist, and that the variation in the income amounts is mainly due to different estimates of the income that goes with it. If this hypothesis would be true, we would expect that persons whose own actual standard of living is close to the minimum one would make fewer mistakes than other people. Therefore, the variation in the answers to the subsistence minimum question should be relatively low for respondents at that particular income level. That income level - not necessarily equal to the mean or median answer - would reflect the social consensus on the subsistence minimum income.

This hypothesis was tested in two ways. First, a graphical analysis was carried out. Two scatterplots were produced with the single person or family subsistence amounts on the y-axis, and the respondent's estimate of the actual income of the household on the x-axis. Neither plot revealed a point where the variation in the answers was clearly smaller than average. Secondly, a more formal test was performed. The actual income of the household was recoded into 28 intervals. Within each of these intervals, the standard deviation and the coefficient of variation of the single person and family subsistence amounts were calculated. These values were then regressed on actual household income (i.e. the midpoints of the 28 intervals). If the standard deviation and/or the coefficient of variation would be small at a particular point in the income scale, but larger below and above that point, one would expect that a quadratic term in the regression equation (i.e. the square of household income) would be able to capture this effect, at least approximately. However, in all regressions there was only a weak linear relationship, while the estimate for the quadratic term parameter was very small, and very far from statistically significant.

7 Summary and conclusions

In this section I will first summarize the empirical findings reviewed or reported above, and then evaluate the consensual approach to setting a minimum income level.

The long series of surveys in the USA and Australia in which a consensual income question has been asked, has enabled researchers to investigate how the average of the answers to these questions behaves over time. A review of studies by Rainwater (1974, 1990), Kilpatrick (1973), Vaughan (1993) and Saunders and Bradbury (1991), complemented by a re-analysis of the same data, has shown that in both countries the average answer rises strongly when average household income increases. However, the elasticity is clearly less than unity, and appears to have a value of about 0.8 in both countries. A similar estimate is found using cross-country data presented by Riffault and Rabier (1977). On the other hand, both in the USA and in Australia price changes are fully discounted for in the average answer to consensual income questions.

All studies report substantial variation in individual answers in each single survey. Very little of this variation can be explained by background variables of respondents, despite sometimes extensive efforts by researchers to find covariates. Generally, the correlation with household or individual income is the least smallest.

Equivalence scales estimated in American studies by Rainwater (1974) and Dubnoff (1985) are rather flat, compared with most equivalence scales used in research, i.e. the needs of families rise only weakly with size. This result may be partly due to the design of these studies, though. Other researchers using the consensual income approach (Riffault and Rabier, 1977; Aguilar and Gustafsson, 1988, and the present author) have found equivalence scales that are steeper.

Both Rainwater (1974) and Dubnoff (1985) have extended the consensual income approach to a range of different levels of living. For our purposes the most important result is that there is a considerable distance between the income amounts associated with "just getting along" and the upper limit of "poverty". When Americans in 1989 were asked what amount they would use as a poverty line, the average was 28% below the average get-along amount (Vaughan, 1993). This suggests that in people's minds "not getting along" does not necessarily entail that one is living in poverty. This is confirmed by the rather different descriptions people give of the life styles of families who are just getting along, and of families who are living in poverty.

Evaluation

The aim of the consensual income method is to find out what the public thinks are the levels of income a particular kind of family needs in order to achieve a certain standard of living. In the context of poverty measurement, we are particularly interested in what respondents say is the minimum level of income level below which people are unable to get along or to make ends meet. As argued in the introduction, the validity of the consensual income method rests on a number of assumptions. In the first place, respondents should take a general point of view when answering consensual questions. Evidence of such a general point of view would be that the answers are not much influenced by the personal circumstances of respondents. Secondly, in the minds of respondents, phrases like 'getting along' should evoke a fairly concrete image of a particular material standard of living, in terms of what a family has and does. These images should not vary too much across the population. Thirdly, respondents should be able to translate a given standard of living into a cash amount. This means that, implicitly or explicitly, they have to define a standard of living in terms of a concrete basket of goods and services. In a second step, they have to price the basket.

The first condition seems to be well met: responses to consensual income questions correlate hardly or not with background characteristics, indicating that respondents do indeed take the required general point of view. Regarding the other two assumptions, the results are more ambiguous. If all respondents would have the same understanding of the material standard of living corresponding to 'getting by', and would be capable of putting the correct price tag on it, all answers should be nearly the same. The empirical results show clearly that this is not true: the variation in the answers to the get-along question and similar questions is quite large. But it is not at all clear which one, or perhaps both, of these assumptions are violated. According to Rainwater (1974: 59) the variation is mainly due to errors when people translate a standard of living into a cash amount. There can be little doubt that some of the variation is indeed due to this factor. After all, respondents have to perform in a few seconds a task on which teams of home economists spend years of research. Some errors are to be expected. Moreover, the differences are not necessarily always due to pricing errors; respondents may also have varying images of the particular living circumstances of the reference household - whether it owns or rents the house it lives in, for instance.

However, it seems unlikely that respondents all have the same standard of living in mind (implicitly or explicitly), and that the total variation in the answers is generated when this standard of living is translated into a cash amount. Two pieces of evidence support this statement. In the first place, the extent to which amounts are rounded provides an indication of the subjective margin of error of respondents, and this margin or error is much smaller than the overall variation in the amounts. Secondly, a re-analysis of average answers to the Australian 'health-and-decency' question and the American 'get-along' question indicated that, as a collective, respondents are able to distinguish between real and only nominal increases in income. They fully discount for price changes in their answers, while the adjustment in response to real rises in income is only partial. This suggests that the average respondent has adequate knowledge of the overall price level.

There are thus fairly strong indications that not all variation in the answers to consensual income questions represents random error. For the consensual income approach this conclusion is a two-edged sword. On a certain level it obviously enhances the validity of the method and its results. But is has also rather damaging implications for the consensual income approach: if respondents know what they are talking about, and still give widely varying answers to consensual income questions, then there are apparently important real differences of opinion regarding the standard of living corresponding to such notions as 'getting along'.

It may be useful to note that such differences of opinion do not necessarily imply that respondents attach different meanings to phrases like 'getting along'. It is possible that 'getting along' evokes a single and precise image in the minds of respondents, but that this image is not one of a particular material standard of living. For instance, for respondents 'getting along' might refer to a certain level of frustration experienced while trying to make ends meet. This level of frustration may depend on the material standard of living, *and* on a host of other, social and psychological factors, including aspirations and reference groups, which differ across respondents.

If the conclusions reached above are accepted, can we still use the average or median of the answers as an income threshold? As noted in the introduction, even when there are real differences of opinion, providing these are not too large, we might still interpret the median as a kind of convergence point. However, if the average of the answers is used to represent the supposed consensus view, one must not only assume, implicitly or explicitly, that most of this variation is due to random 'mistakes' by respondents, when linking an income amount to a verbal description of a certain standard of living (which, as argued above, is probably not true). In addition one must also make the assumption that these mistakes or differences are symmetrically distributed, such that their average effect is zero. There is no particular reason why this would be the case. Therefore, even if something like a social consensus on the standard of living (defined in terms of goods, services and activities) corresponding to 'getting along' would exist, we cannot be certain that it is adequately represented by the average (median or mean) of the answers to the get-along question.

Alternatively, one could maintain that the average of the amounts stated by respondents is just that: an average view, which may or may not be mistaken, about how much income is needed to reach a certain standard of living. For many research questions, this may be a valid approach, for instance if one is interested only in how public opinion about these matters develops over time. But an average is not a consensus. If there would be real and important disagreements about the material standard of living associated with certain verbal labels (such as "getting along", "near poverty", etc.), it would be inappropriate to use the average amount as an income threshold representing the "community view" about how much income is needed to reach a particular standard of living.

In addition to all this, there is the difficulty that the relation between the standard or standards of living associated with 'getting along' or 'living in health and decency' and the standard of living regarded by respondents as some kind of social minimum is unclear. We have seen that for American respondents 'getting along' evokes something that is closer to the average standard of living than to poverty. Though the minimum standard of living may be higher than the one required to escape poverty, it is therefore likely that it is below the one needed to 'get along'. However, the difficulty is not just that we are unsure about where the minimum standard is located in the hierarchy of living levels from extreme poverty to prosperity. It is also that different persons may locate it at different positions. This may be especially true if, as suggested above, different persons associate phrases like 'getting along' with different material standards of living. Thus, the minimum standard of living may correspond to 'just getting along' for one respondent, and to being 'on the margins on poverty' for another (while at the same time both may be thinking about the same material standard of living in terms of goods and services).

The overall conclusion must be that applications so far of the consensual income approach have not clearly shown that a social consensus on a minimum income level does exist, and that even if such a consensus would exist the results of these studies can at best give only a rather vague impression of its location.

Appendix 2.1 A re-analysis of consensual income amounts time series

The American get-along question

The data were constructed in the following way. Average get-along amounts were taken from Vaughan (1993, table 1), because he presents the most complete series. Source for most of his amounts is Rainwater (1974, 1990), but for some years it is the Gallup organization itself. Because the latter has apparently calculated these amounts in a different way (medians for persons in non-farm households, instead of arithmetic means for all persons), a dummy variable (D_{source}) has been introduced in the regression equation to correct for possible differences. (D_{source} takes a value of 1 if the source is Gallup, and 0 otherwise.) As indicator of average income, I use *after tax* median four-person family income, also provided by Vaughan (1991, table 1). While median or average income of *all* households would have been preferable, no consistent time series of data covering all years 1950-1989 could be reconstructed from the only source readily available to me, the Statistical Abstract of the U.S.. Moreover, the median family or household money incomes shown in that source are all *before* tax, while Vaughan's median four-person family income amounts are *after* tax. (Anyway, a regression of median household money income on median four-person family income for the years where this was possible produced an estimate for the elasticity of the former with respect to the latter of 1.003, with an R^2 of 0.998.) As index of price level, I have used the index of the purchasing power of the dollar (yearly averages), according to consumer prices (U.S. Bureau of the Census, 1991, table 737).

Table 2.A1
Gallup "Get - along" average responses related to household income, USA, 1950-1986

Model: $\log(\text{Av. Response}) = \beta_0 + \beta_1 \log(Y/P) + \beta_2 \log(P) + \beta_3 D_{source} + e$

	Undifferenced equation		Differenced equation	
	Estimate	Standard Error	Estimate	Standard Error
β_0	+1.807	0.678	-	-
β_1	+0.785	0.067	+0.763	0.308
β_2	+0.985	0.023	+1.143	0.284
β_3	-0.052	0.025	-0.053	0.014
R^2 (adj.)	0.995		0.426	
DW	1.043		2.425	
N	33		31	

Notes: P represents the price index, Y stands for the indicator of income (median four-person family income), D_{source} is a dummy variable that takes the value of 1 if the get-along amount for the year is the median for persons in nonfarm households and 0 otherwise, e is the error term.

All estimates are significantly different from zero at the 5% level, unless their standard errors are labeled n.s. (not significant).

All R-square estimates (R^2 (adj.)) are adjusted for the degrees of freedom; the R-squares for the change equations have been recalculated to make them comparable to the undifferenced equations. DW is the Durbin Watson coefficient for autocorrelation, which is equal to two when there is no autocorrelation.

The data were used in two ways: undifferenced and differenced. In the differenced equation, the values of the variables in the previous observation are subtracted from the values for the current observation. (This implies that there is no constant term in differenced equations.) The differenced values of the household income and price level indicators were adjusted to take account of the fact that the month of data collection varied across years. (The raw difference was multiplied by the number of months between two get-along observations, divided by twelve.) This adjustment did not affect the results much, though.

In the model, the average responses to the get-along question in *current* prices were regressed on household income in *constant* prices and the price level (Table 2.A1). The estimate of the elasticity of the get-along amounts with respect to price changes is 0.99, while the elasticity with respect to real changes in household real income is still 0.79. These results are confirmed by the estimates from the differenced equation, though the standard errors are much larger there. Formal tests not reported here have shown that the hypothesis that the elasticity with respect to price changes is equal to one, is clearly acceptable. But a similar hypothesis for the elasticity with respect to real income changes must be rejected. The same is true for the hypothesis that the two elasticities are equal to each other.

The Australian health-and-decency question

The original data used by Bradbury and Saunders (1991) were kindly sent to me by David Saunders. In a first step, the model of Saunders and Bradbury (i.e. all variables deflated by the consumer price index) was applied. The results were close to those of Saunders and Bradbury (1991: 62).

In the second step, the model was changed. The dependent variable is now the log of the nominal average response in current prices. On the right side, the consumer price index, and an interaction term between the dummy variable for the period after 1970 and the price index, are added to the equation used by Saunders and Bradbury. The results are shown in table 2.A2. The signs of the estimates of some parameters are reversed, compared those reported by Saunders and Bradbury. This is probably due to high multicollinearity between the two interaction terms and the dummy variable. The same effect is also to blame for the large standard errors. The elasticity with respect to price level changes seems to be close to one, being lower after 1970 than before. In the model with differenced data the effects of the interaction terms were not significant (t-values of 1.2 at most; a formal test of the removal of these variables resulted in Chi-square statistics with 2 degrees of freedom of 1.02, 1.53 and 0.023 for the HHDIPC, PFCEPC and MAWE equations, respectively.) The estimates for the elasticity with respect to price changes is very close to one, while the estimates of elasticity with respect to real income changes are much lower than in the undifferenced equations.

Formal tests, carried out with the SAS procedure CALIS, show that the hypothesis that the price level elasticity is equal to one during the whole period 1950-1988 is rejected by the undifferenced data, except for MAWE. But the alternative hypothesis, that the price level elasticity is equal to the real income elasticity is rejected even more strongly. In the differenced equations, on the other hand, the hypothesis that the price level elasticity is equal to one is not rejected. Again, the alternative hypothesis, that the price level elasticity is equal to the real income elasticity, or that both elasticities are equal to one, are strongly rejected.

Table 2.A2
"Health and decency" average response related to indicators of real income, Australia, 1950-1988

Model: log (Av. Response)= $\beta_0 + \beta_1 \log(Y/P) + \beta_2 D_{1970} + \beta_3 [D_{1970} * \log(Y/P)] + \beta_4 \log(P) + \beta_5 [D_{1970} * \log(P)] + e$

	HHDIPC		PFCEPC		MAWE	
	Estimate	St. Error	Estimate	St. Error	Estimate	St. Error
β_0	-5.62	0.16	-5.46	0.16	-5.35	0.18
β_1	0.60	0.05	0.72	0.07	0.66	0.08
β_2	0.90	0.63 n.s.	-0.47	0.89 n.s.	1.73	0.75
β_3	0.09	0.16 n.s.	0.42	0.26 n.s.	-0.32	0.17 n.s.
β_4	1.18	0.04	1.07	0.05	1.00	0.06
β_5	-0.20	0.04	-0.20	0.06	0.03	0.07 n.s.
R^2 (adj.)	0.999		0.999		0.999	
DW	1.334		1.459		1.681	
N	58		58		58	

(difference model)

	HHDIPC		PFCEPC		MAWE	
	Estimate	St. Error	Estimate	St. Error	Estimate	St. Error
β_1	0.474	0.092	0.640	0.160	0.156	0.096 n.s.
β_2	0.096	0.028	0.105	0.030	0.084	0.034
β_4	1.070	0.073	1.042	0.081	1.103	0.088
R^2 (adj.)	0.60		0.54		0.45	
DW	2.419		2.531		2.170	
N	57		57		57	

Notes: P represents the price index, Y stands for the indicator of income (PFCEPC: Private Final Consumption Expenditure Per Capita; HHDIPC: Household Disposable Income Per Capita; MAWE: Male Average Weekly Earnings), D_{1970} is a dummy variable that takes the value of 1 after 1970 and 0 before and in 1970, and D_{1971} is a dummy variable that takes the value of 1 for 1971 only, and 0 in all other years. represents the first difference operator; e is the error term.

All estimates are significantly different from zero at the 5% level, unless their standard errors are labeled n.s. (not significant).

All R-square estimates (R^2 (adj.)) are adjusted for the degrees of freedom; the R-squares for the change equations have been recalculated to make them comparable to the undifferenced equations. DW is the Durbin Watson coefficient for autocorrelation, which is equal to two when there is no autocorrelation.

Notes

1 Cf. Aguilar and Gustafsson (1988), who emphasize that it is important to distinguish between attitudes about income thresholds in social welfare, and opinions about total welfare expenditures. They argue that a respondent may well hold the view that thresholds should go up, while expenditures should go down, for instance by reducing the number of applicants.

2 The geometric means for a couple with two children in 1971 - Boston are: poverty: $4,508; get along: $7,586; comfortable: $11,402 (Rainwater, 1974: 96-97).

3 "Poor" is the modal response in the income range $4,200 to $9,450, while "Just getting along" is the modal response from $12,600 to $21,000, and "Living reasonably comfortably" is so between $24,150 and $32,500. The income levels estimated on the basis of a regression analysis, confirm this: for a family of four they are poor: $6,400; Near poor: $11,700; Just getting along: $21,300; Living reasonably comfortably: $38,900. The survey was held in Boston in 1983.

4 It is not regarded as inconsistent if a respondent puts the subsistence minimum at a higher level than e.g., the minimum employment benefit. In fact, there were several hundred respondents who did exactly this. They may have been motivated by a number of considerations. Unemployment benefits are not means-tested, while welfare payments are. Also, respondents may have felt that unemployment benefits are generally received during shorter periods than the subsistence minimum.

5 Though the probability of meeting the consistency conditions purely by chance is difficult to calculate, it is certainly quite small.

6 The value of 0.0322 can also be interpreted as the average, across respondents, of the variance of the equivalence scales of each respondent separately.

7 The formula of the intraclass correlation is as follows:
$(V_b - V_w) / (V_b + (n-1)V_w)$,
where V_b and V_w are the between classes and within classes estimates of variance respectively, and n is the number of cases in each class.

3 The Consensual Standard of Living Approach

1 Introduction and a cross-country comparison

It is partly because of the uncertainties surrounding the interpretation of the results of the consensual income approach, that Mack and Lansley (1985) have devised a method to try to identify in a direct way a minimum standard of living. They wanted "to discover whether there is a public consensus on what is an unacceptable standard of living for Britain in 1983" (p. 50). Being skeptical about people's ability to translate a certain standard of living into an income level, they tried to discover a minimum standard of living, by directly asking to a sample of people to indicate which items, of a list of goods and activities, were "necessities" for living in Britain in the 1980's, and which ones were merely "desirables" (pp. 43-44). The word "necessity" was further clarified for the respondents as something that all adults should be able to afford, and that they should not have to do without. This question is clearly consensual, because it refers to all adults in general, and not to the respondent in particular. It is also noteworthy that the question is expressed in terms of ability, and not in terms of what people should have, no matter how. "It was important that some people would manage without these 'necessities', some even from choice" (Mack and Lansley, 1985: 52). In this chapter we will focus our attention on the possibility of deriving a minimum standard of living, according to the answers given to the "necessities" question, and supposedly reflecting a social consensus on this matter.

Mack and Lansley's method was applied for the first time in 1983 in a British survey, which was conducted by MORI and commissioned by London Weekend Television. The same survey was repeated in Britain in 1990 (Gordon et al. 1994). Following in Mack and Lansley's footsteps, the "necessities" question, with a similar list of items, was used in surveys carried out in Denmark, Ireland and Belgium. Table 3.1 gives the main results, showing the percentages of respondents who classed an item as a necessity, as well as the percentage of people that actually had the item.

Table 3.1
Proportions of respondents regarding item as necessity (columns N) and proportions actually having it (columns P)

Item (as far as possible in rank order of proportion classing item as necessity)	Britain, 1983		Britain, 1990	
	N	P	N	P
- Heating to warm living areas of the home if it's cold	97	*92*	97	*96*
- Indoor toilet (not shared with another household)	96	*98*	97	*98*
- Damp-free home	96	*85*	98	*94*
- Bath (not shared with another household) ([1])	94	*97*	95	*97*
- Beds for everyone in the household	94	*97*	95	*97*
- A decent state of decoration in the home	-	-	92	*81*
- Public transport for one's needs	88	*87*	-	-
- A warm water-proof coat	87	*88*	91	*91*
- Two pairs of all-weather shoes ([2])	78	*84*	74	*90*
- A meal with meat, chicken or fish every second day ([3])	63	*81*	77	*90*
- Insurance of contents of dwelling	-	-	88	*83*
- Daily fresh fruit and vegetables	-	-	88	*88*
- Three meals a day for children*	82	*90*	90	*74*
- Self-contained accommodation	79	*93*	-	-
- To be able to save ([6])	-	-	*68*	60
- Enough bedrooms for children *	77	*76*	82	*65*
- Refrigerator	77	*96*	92	*98*
- Toys for children*	71	*92*	84	*75*
- Carpets in living rooms and bedrooms	70	*97*	78	*96*
- Celebrations on special occasions such as Christmas	69	*93*	74	*91*
- A roast meat joint or its equivalent once a week ([4])	67	*87*	64	*84*
- A washing machine	67	*89*	73	*88*
- A vacuum cleaner	-	-	-	-
- New, not second hand clothes	64	*85*	65	*89*
- A hobby or leisure activity	64	*77*	67	*76*

Notes: *: Items for families with children only.

(1): Ireland and Belgium: 'Bath *or Shower*'.

(2): Ireland: 'Two pairs of *strong* shoes'.

Denmark, 1983		Ireland, 1987		Belgium, 1985		Belgium, 1988	
N	P	N	P	N	P	N	P
97	*98*	99	*97*	95	*95*	97	*97*
94	*96*	98	*93*	97	*97*	97	*95*
90	*88*	99	*90*	97	*94*	98	*92*
89	*93*	98	*91*	93	*90*	94	*90*
-	-	-	-	-	-	-	-
-	-	-	-	-	-	-	-
-	-	-	-	-	-	-	-
89	*93*	93	*87*	97	*97*	98	*96*
64	*82*	88	*84*	92	*94*	90	*91*
69	*90*	84	*87*	94	*97*	94	*95*
-	-	-	-	-	-	-	-
-	-	-	-	-	-	-	-
91	-	-	-	98	*99*	97	*97*
-	-	-	-	-	-	-	-
	-	88	*43*	83	*58*	85	*60*
66	-	-	-	94	*93*	91	*86*
94	*98*	92	*95*	93	*98*	96	*97*
-	-	-	-	-	-	-	-
-	-	-	-	-	-	-	-
-	-	-	-	-	-	-	-
50	*75*	64	*76*	-	-	-	-
-	-	82	*80*	86	*88*	92	*89*
-	-	-	-	-	-	80	*90*
-	-	77	*90*	-	-	-	-
-	-	73	*67*	-	-	-	-

(3): Britain 1983 and Ireland: 'Meat or fish every other day'; Britain 1990: 'Meat or fish or its *vegetarian equivalent* every other day'.

Table 3.1 (continuation)

Item (as far as possible in rank order of proportion classing item as necessity)	Britain, 1983		Britain, 1990	
	N	P	N	P
- Two meals a day (for adults) (⁷)	64	*81*	90	*94*
- Child's participation in out-of-school activities*	-	-	69	*50*
- Presents for friends or family once a year	63	*90*	69	*90*
- A holiday away from home for one week a year	63	*68*	54	*65*
- Leisure equipment for children*	57	*79*	61	*67*
- A garden	55	*88*	-	-
- A television (⁵)	51	*98*	58	*97*
- Central heating in the house	-	-	-	-
- A 'best outfit' for special occasions	48	*78*	54	*85*
- A telephone	43	*82*	56	*87*
- An outing for children once a week*	40	*58*	53	*58*
- A dressing gown	38	*84*	42	*83*
- Child's music/dance/sport lessons*	-	-	39	*38*
- Fares to visit friends living far away 4 times a year	-	-	39	*48*
- A daily newspaper	-	-	-	-
- Children's friends around 'for' a snack once a fortnight*	37	*60*	52	*55*
- A night out once a fortnight (adults)	36	*57*	42	*62*
- Friends/family round for a meal once a month	32	*64*	37	*67*
- A car	22	*61*	26	*63*
- Holidays abroad annually	-	-	17	*38*
- Restaurant meal monthly	-	-	17	*44*
- A packet of cigarettes every other day	14	*39*	18	*37*
- A video-recorder	-	-	13	*66*
- A home computer	-	-	5	*26*
- A dishwasher	-	-	4	*17*

(4): Ireland: 'A roast meat joint once a week'; Britain 1990: 'A roast joint or its *vegetarian equivalent* once a week.'

(5): Ireland and Belgium: 'Colour television'.

(6): Britain 1990: 'Regular saving of £10 a month for rainy days or retirement'.

(7): Britain 1983: 'Two *hot* meals a day'.

Denmark, 1983		Ireland, 1987		Belgium, 1985		Belgium, 1988	
N	P	N	P	N	P	N	P
-	-	-	-	-	-	-	-
-	-	-	-	-	-	-	-
-	-	60	*76*	-	-	-	-
47	*58*	50	*32*	56	*50*	57	*50*
67	-	-	-	91	*95*	84	*91*
-	-	-	-	-	-	-	-
55	*93*	37	*80*	39	*83*	55	*87*
-	-	49	*55*	40	*62*	45	*64*
-	-	-	-	-	-	-	-
71	*92*	45	*52*	51	*74*	64	*83*
-	-	-	-	-	-	-	-
-	-	-	-	-	-	-	-
-	-	-	-	-	--	-	-
-	-	-	-	-	-	-	-
-	-	39	*55*	34	*51*	31	*46*
-	-	-	-	-	-	-	-
-	-	-	-	-	-	-	-
26	*48*	-	-	-	-	-	-
35	*69*	59	*62*	46	*72*	58	*76*
-	-	-	-	-	-	-	-
-	-	-	-	-	-		
-	-	-	-	-	-	-	-
-	-	-	-	-	-	8	*24*
-	-	-	-	-	-	-	-
-	-	-	-	-	-	-	-

Sources: Britain, 1983: Mack and Lansley (1985), p. 54, p. 66.
Britain, 1990: Gordon et al. (1994), p. 195.
Denmark: AIM, Copenhagen, quoted in Mack and Lansley (1985), p. 84.
Ireland: Callan, Nolan, et. al. (1989), p. 112.
Belgium: Deleeck, Cantillon, et. al. (1991), p. 720, a.

The most important result is that a wide range of items are regarded as necessities by a large majority of respondents in all countries where the "necessities" question was asked in a survey. There is virtual unanimity about the necessity of heating, an indoor toilet, a damp-free home and a bath. But also, a large majority – more than two-thirds in Britain, more than 80% in Ireland and Belgium – regard labor-saving household goods (such as a washing machine and a refrigerator) as "necessities". As Mack and Lansley (1985: 55-56) remark, this partly reflects "shifting standards and expectations; but it also reflects the fact that, in a practical sense, items that become customary also become necessary because other aspects of life are planned and built on the very fact that these items are customary." But there are also items which can be seen as necessities only because of their symbolic significance, or because of prevailing social norms and standards. Examples of these are 'Celebrations on special occasions', 'A roast meat joint on Sunday' and 'separate bedrooms for children'.

In all countries, we also find that for the items regarded by the majority as necessities, possession is widespread. Conversely, in general, the fewer people have an item, the less often it is seen as a necessity. This, as Mack and Lansley remark, comes as no surprise; most poverty studies are based on the assumption "that those styles of living that are widespread are equivalent to those that are socially approved, encouraged or expected" (p. 67). But there are some interesting exceptions, which show that other factors come into play. In all countries, a holiday is classed as a necessity by relatively many respondents, given the proportion who say they actually go on holiday. The discrepancy is even more glaring for the item 'being able to save': while more than 80% of all respondents in the Irish and Belgian surveys indicated that saving is a necessity, the number of respondents that actually do save is much smaller (43% in Ireland, 58-60% in Belgium). Conversely, a (colour) television is present in a large majority of households, but only slightly more than half, or even fewer, of all respondents regard it as a necessity. To a certain extent, these exceptions may be explained by price differences. A holiday is rather expensive, while a television is fairly cheap (when the purchasing cost is properly discounted; cf. Gordon et al. 1994: 19-21). For a poor family, it makes sense to buy a cheap 'luxury', if the price of a necessity is so prohibitively high, that it would not be able to afford the latter, even if it would forego the luxury. (Indeed, in all countries for which these data are available, 'holiday' is the item which the largest proportion of the respondents say they do not have it, because they cannot afford it, except saving; Mack and Lansley, 1985: 89; Callan, Nolan et al., 1989: 112; Deleeck, Cantillon et al., 1991: 720.) But, especially regarding the items 'saving' and 'a television', it seems that moral considerations are also of importance. In any case, it is clear that people's judgements about necessities are not just a reflection of what is customary.

These findings raise the question whether the lack of items like 'saving' or 'a holiday' should be regarded as ipso-facto, an indicator of poverty or deprivation. Even though a large majority may think those items are necessities, a person not saving or not going on holiday can hardly be said to be 'excluded from activities which are customary', if the majority, or at least a large minority, of households in the community are in the same situation. The question is, it must be granted, more of theoretical than of practical interest: in any empirical study, the safer option would be to drop these items from the list of necessities, provided enough items are left. This is the procedure followed by Callan, Nolan et al. (1989). But is it true, as these authors claim, (p. 114) that, "While Mack and Lansley do not explicitly state that a necessity must be possessed by a majority of the population, this may be regarded as implicit in their approach"?

Mack and Lansley (1985) define poverty in terms of "an enforced lack of *socially perceived* necessities. This means that the 'necessities' of life are identified by public opinion and not by [...] the norms of behavior *per se.*" (p. 45, italics in original) There is no intrinsic reason why it would be impossible that a majority of people does not have all those things that are regarded as necessities. Indeed, in the Third World this may be a common situation. But, as Mack and Lansley remark, in an affluent society like Britain, this is not to be expected (p. 67). The implicit assumption seems to be that in affluent western societies, most households will have sufficient resources to be able to afford the necessities of life. Thus, if they 'do not put their money where their mouth is', the suspicion may seem warranted that people are sometimes mistaken about the things they say are necessities. But this ignores the fact that some important things may be difficult to obtain on the market. For instance, the hypothetical item 'safe areas for children to play near the home' might well be seen by many as a necessity, while being available only to a minority. A less extreme but real example is 'a damp-free home'. There is almost total consensus that this is a necessity (except in Denmark), yet a substantial minority does not have it (see table 3.1). A deprivation does not stop being a deprivation just because it is expensive to remove it, nor does it become much less of a deprivation because it is shared with many other people.

There are some differences between the various countries. These appear sometimes to be related to the proportion of households actually possessing the item, but this is by no means always the case: in 1983 British households regarded a refrigerator, a washing machine, a telephone and a car less often as necessities than their Danish, Irish or Belgian counterparts did, even though possession rates did not differ much. (Part of the reason for this may be that in Britain respondents were asked which items they classed as necessities, and which as desirable, while in the Irish and Belgian surveys, people were asked just whether they regarded an item as a necessity or not.) Some differences are perhaps of a cultural nature, e.g. 'a meal with meat, chicken or fish every other day' is regarded as more important in Belgium and Ireland than in Britain and Denmark. (This illustrates nicely that even the ways in which basic needs such as that for food are satisfied are culturally and socially specific.) But the overall impression one gains from table 3.1 is one of very considerable agreement across countries about the necessities of present-day living.

It may be asked whether the similarity across countries of the pattern of proportions of respondents classing the various items as necessities is the result only of the similarity in possession patterns, or goes beyond that. This can be tested by calculating the correlations between those two patterns, i.e. by treating each item as a case, and each proportion as an observation on a variable. (In this way table 3.1 is treated as a data-matrix.) The results (as you can see in panel "Correlation N/N" of table 3.2) show that the correlation between the necessities patterns across countries is 0.80 or higher, except for Belgium-Denmark. (Since these correlations are based on different sets of items, cross-comparisons between pairs of countries are not very meaningful.) Without considering correlations between surveys within the same country (Britain 1983 - 1990 and Belgium 1985 - 1988), the average correlation is 0.86. This value is in fact higher than the average correlation between possession patterns (correlations P/P in table 3.2), which is 0.80, and also higher than the average of the correlations between the necessities pattern and the possession pattern within each country (correlations N/P in table 3.2), which is 0.79. This shows that there is cross-country agreement on the necessities of modern living beyond any expectation based only on the similarities in actual consumption patterns. (Calculations show that if the latter factor were to be the only reason to explain the similarity in necessities patterns, the average correlation would be only 0.50, instead of 0.86[1].)

The replication of the surveys in Britain and Belgium allows us to observe how perceptions of necessity evolve over time. The respondents in both countries show a clear tendency to consider more, rather than less items as necessary. In 1990, British respondents considered only three items as less important in comparison with what the respondents did in 1983; the largest decrease was measured for the item 'annual holiday' (-9%-points; Gordon et al., 1994: 67). As for Belgium, there were five items which were regarded as a necessity by fewer respondents in 1988 compared to 1985, but the changes were small (less than 5%-points) except for the item 'leisure equipment for children' (-7%-points). Few items in both countries registered a large *increase* (at least 12 %-points) in the proportion of people who regarded them as necessities. In Britain those items were: 'two hot meals a day', 'children's' friends round for a snack or tea', 'a refrigerator', 'meat or fish every other day', 'a telephone', 'toys for children' and 'an outing for children'. In Belgium, they were 'a colour television', 'a telephone' and 'a car'.

These changes are difficult to interpret. A general increase in the number of respondents considering any item to be necessary was to be expected, as in both countries average real income of households increased during the period of time passed between the two surveys. As Gordon et al. (1994: 67) state: "The relative theory of poverty predicts that, if a society gets richer, the number of people who perceive common possessions and activities as necessary will increase." But this theory cannot explain why there is so much variation in the changes in perceptions of necessity. Where the average perception of the necessity of an item has considerably changed, there had in most cases been no comparable change in the number of people actually having the item. In some cases (in particular the items related to food in Britain) modifications in the formulation of the item may have played a role. In others, perceptions of necessity may have been in the process of catching up with increases in possession rates that occurred before the year of the first survey. This may be true for the items 'refrigerator', 'colour television', 'telephone' and 'a car'. Some of the findings may be data quirks with no real significance. Nevertheless, the results for Belgium in particular show that some perceptions of necessity can change considerably in a fairly short span of time.

Table 3.2
Correlation of proportions of respondents regarding items as necessity, and possession rates, within and across countries

	Britain, 1983	Britain, 1990	Denmark	Ireland	Belgium, 1985	Belgium, 1988
Correlation N/P within countries	0.77 (35)	0.80 (44)	0.87 (14)	0.66 (20)	0.79 (19)	0.85 (21)
Correlation N/N across countries:						
Britain, 1983	-	0.95 (32)	0.85 (17)	0.83 (16)	0.82 (15)	0.81 (15)
Britain, 1990	0.95 (32)	-	0.93 (17)	0.84 (17)	0.87 (16)	0.92 (17)
Denmark	0.85 (17)	0.93 (17)	-	0.80 (12)	0.75 (14)	0.83 (14)
Ireland	0.83 (16)	0.84 (17)	0.80 (12)	-	0.97 (16)	0.94 (16)
Belgium, 1985	0.82 (15)	0.87 (16)	0.75 (14)	0.97 (16)	-	0.97 (19)
Belgium, 1988	0.81 (15)	0.92 (17)	0.83 (14)	0.94 (16)	0.97 (19)	-
Correlation P/P across countries:						
Britain, 1983	-	0.90 (32)	0.86 (14)	0.75 (16)	0.67 (15)	0.71 (15)
Britain, 1990	0.90 (32)	-	0.91 (14)	0.87 (17)	0.61 (16)	0.65 (17)
Denmark	0.86 (14)	0.91 (14)	-	0.79 (12)	0.85 (11)	0.91 (11)
Ireland	0.75 (16)	0.87 (17)	0.79 (12)	-	0.94 (16)	0.94 (16)
Belgium, 1985	0.67 (15)	0.61 (16)	0.85 (11)	0.94 (16)	-	0.97 (19)
Belgium, 1988	0.71 (15)	0.65 (17)	0.91 (11)	0.94 (16)	0.97 (19)	-

2 Factors influencing people's perception of necessities in Britain and Belgium

Individual possessions and perceptions of necessity

Which factors influence people's perceptions of necessities? This can be an interesting question in itself, but it becomes also important in order to interpret the minimum standard resulting from these perceptions. If disaggregated results were to show great differences of opinion across different social groups and categories in society classing items as necessities, it would be difficult to maintain that such a minimum standard reflects a social consensus. Unfortunately, to my knowledge, more detailed results for Denmark and Ireland have not been published. Here below, I will discuss those results for Britain and Belgium, in that order.

We have seen that at the aggregate level the extent of ownership is fairly closely related to the number of people classing an item as a necessity. It seems reasonable to expect, therefore, that a similar relation applies to the individual level. Mack and Lansley (1985: 69-73) have investigated this matter. They looked not only at differences between those who had an item, and those who did not, but also subdivided the 'haves' into those who said they could not do without the items and those who said they could, while the 'have nots' were subdivided into those that did not want the item, and those that could not afford it. It turned out that people who have an item and say they could not do without it, are the most likely to class it as a necessity for everyone. The next group most likely to classify an item as a necessity are those who don't have it, because they can't afford it. Those who do not have an item and do not want it are the least likely to regard it as a necessity. Finally, those who have an item but feel they can manage without it are in between the last two groups. Very similar results were obtained in the survey in 1990[2]. It should be noted that for each item these groups are composed of different persons. In spite of these differences between groups, all groups have a similar structure of priorities, that is to say, all groups display the same ranking of the items.

Very similar results are here reported for Belgium (table 3.3). Owing to the fact that the relevant question (about whether people could manage without the item or not) was not asked the "haves" could not be split up. Still, for all items except one (Colour television in 1985; Video Recorder in 1988), the majority of those who had it classed it as a necessity. Among respondents who did not have an item because they could not afford it, there were majorities classing items as necessities for 12 out of 19 items in

1985 and 12 out of 21 items in 1988. Within the group who did not have an item and did not want it, 3 items in 1985, and 6 items in 1988 were regarded by the majority as a necessity. Again, there was roughly the same ranking in all groups: all items classed as a necessity by at least 50% of the 'don't haves' were on the top of the 'necessities' list, and were regarded by at least 93% of the 'haves' as a necessity.

Two important conclusions can be drawn from these results. In the first place, a person's own situation, and her own personal desires are important for her judgments about the necessities of modern living. Nevertheless, they do not determine these judgments. This works in two directions. On the one hand, many of those who 'could not do without' a car or a telephone, do not regard these items as necessities, in the sense that no one should have to do without them. On the other hand, for a range of items, a majority, or at least a large minority, of those who do not have it and do not want it, do class it as a necessity. This, as Mack and Lansley (p. 72) remark, may indicate a degree of selfishness on behalf of the first group, but it is not inconsistent. It shows that people distinguish between what they want for themselves, and what they think are needs from a general, public, perspective. As argued above, only if respondents make such a distinction, and answer the 'necessities' question from the public perspective, is it appropriate to say that a minimum standard derived from these answers reflects a social consensus on these matters.

A second conclusion seems to be that a person's subjective attitude towards an item (i.e. how much he wants it for himself) is at least as important for his judgment about its necessity, than the objective circumstance whether he possesses it or not. This is important because it seems less likely that what people perceive as necessity is directly related to their actual living standard. If a person with a high standard of living regarded many more items as necessities than someone with a low living standard, it would be more difficult to speak of a consensus about the needs of present-day living.

Table 3.3
Percentage regarding items as necessity, by personal possession of items, in Belgium

	1985			*1988*		
Item	*A*	*B*	*C*	*A*	*B*	*C*
Waterproof coat	99	(89)	[45]	99	[69]	(54)
Damp-free home	99	94	[80]	99	85	89
Indoor toilet	99	75	(58)	99	[51]	(69)
Heating in living quarters	97	(70)	46	98	[69]	(65)
Refrigerator	95	[60]	(38)	98	[57]	(44)
Meal with meat, etc.	97	(72)	(23)	97	[58]	(20)
Bath or shower	97	79	51	98	(71)	58
Washing machine	92	60	40	98	(67)	44
Waterproof shoes	96	69	29	95	54	31
Regular saving	93	78	48	93	75	64
Telephone	63	31	13	72	29	22
Car	59	21	9	71	25	15
Holiday	78	43	24	78	43	28
Colour television	45	16	8	60	21	11
Central heating	55	30	10	62	21	14
Newspaper	58	23	7	58	12	5
Vacuum cleaner				85	34	15
Video-recorder				21	5	3

Notes: *: Items for families with children only.
A: Have; *B*: Don't have, can't afford; *C*: Don't have, don't want.
( ) Figures based on less than 100 cases; [ ] Figures based on less than 50 cases;
- Less than 20 cases in cell.

Source: Belgian Socio-Economic Panel, waves 1985 (N = 6471) and 1988 (N = 3779).

Background characteristics and perceptions of necessity

A further interesting question is whether different social groups and categories have different views about necessities. Mack and Lansley (1985: 59-83) have looked at social class, age, household type and party identification of British respondents in the 1983 survey. In Gordon et al. (1994: 184-193), who report on the British 1990 survey, results are disaggregated by the same variables, and in addition by deprivation status, self-assessed present level of poverty, self-assessed history of poverty, sex, and education.

Mack and Lansley report that, across *classes* (i.e. occupational groups), "the survey's findings show a remarkable degree of agreement about the necessities for living." Indeed, few items classed as necessities by an overall majority are not also classed as a necessity by a majority in every social class. Moreover, in 1983, the difference between the highest and lowest proportion regarding an item as a necessity, across classes, exceeds 20% for only four items: new clothes, hot meals, a garden, and a television. If the class of social security recipients, which is likely to be somewhat heterogeneous, is ignored, the greatest differences of opinion are found between the professional and managerial occupations on the one hand, and semi-skilled and unskilled manual workers on the other hand, with other non-manual workers and skilled manual workers in between. But the differences are not systematic, in the sense that the proportion of respondents classing an item as a necessity are always larger in one particular class. Moreover, many differences that are found in 1983 disappear in 1990, while others newly emerge. Looking only at items where the difference is at least 10%-points in both years, it is found that persons in professional and managerial occupations give relatively greater priority to a hobby and children's friends round once a fortnight. Semi-skilled and unskilled manual workers, on the other hand, regard carpets, a washing machine, new clothes, a television and a night out relatively more often as a necessity. This is an evidence of a tendency - confirmed by results not shown here - that persons from higher social classes attach relatively more importance to non-material items, while those from lower social classes give priority mainly to material items.

The pattern is somewhat different for the variation in judgments of necessity when related to people's level of education (results available only for 1990). For most of the items, especially the thirteen or so highest in the list of necessities, there is virtually no disagreement, but for some other items a clear tendency emerges to the effect that the higher the level of education, the less likely a respondent is to class an item as a necessity. The opposite pattern hardly occurs. Those items where the difference between people with university degrees and people without educational qualifications exceeds 15%-points are: carpets, washing machine, new clothes, roast joint, television, dressing gown and a night out. As Gordon et al. (1994: 71) remark, "this may reflect differences in lifestyle, age, household structure and financial resources between these groups".

Perhaps surprisingly, perceptions of necessity do not differ much by self-assessed poverty status (Gordon et al., 1994: 70-71). Those who say they are poor "all the time" are more likely to consider four items to be necessities, compared with those who are "never" poor, viz. cigarettes, a night out, carpets and a television. Gordon et al. suggest that these differences of opinion may be due to less awareness on the behalf of the non-poor of the need for some form of escape from the boredom and stress of living on a low income. If we differentiate the poor from the non-poor on the basis of objective circumstances (whether they suffer from multiple deprivation or not) instead of subjective self-assessments, there are only two items for which the difference in opinion between these two groups exceeds 12%-points: cigarettes, which the multiply deprived find more important, and a hobby, which is more often classed as a necessity by the less-deprived.

Differences in opinion between different age groups are more frequent. The differences seem larger and more systematic in 1990 than in 1983. In 1983 there are only three items which show at least 20%-points difference between any pair of age groups: shoes, telephone and dressing gown. In general, the youngest age groups (16-24 in 1983; 16-34 in 1990) class the fewest items as necessities. In 1990 the elderly (65+) are the ones most likely on average to class an item as a necessity; this was not so in 1983. Items to which older people, compared with younger people, in both years attach more importance include a television, a telephone and a dressing gown. In 1983 there were a number of items which were given relatively high priority by young people; in 1990 there was only one: a night out fortnightly.

Different family circumstances also have an effect on judgments about necessities, but the pattern changes considerably across the years. In 1983, single parents were the most likely, for most of the items, to class them as a necessity, while single people without children were the least likely to do so. In 1990, on the other hand, pensioners class the largest number of items as necessities, and households with children the smallest number. In 1983, there was a range of items to which single people attached less importance than persons in other household types; in 1990 there was only one of such items: a washing machine. On the other hand, single people are relatively more likely to regard a night out as a necessity. In 1990, the largest differences are found between pensioners and non-pensioners, in particular for the items telephone, dressing gown and fares to visit friends. In 1983, there was no systematic pattern in the reported differences among different non-pensioner household types, except for the ones above mentioned; in 1990 such differences have largely disappeared.

There are virtually no differences between men and women in the perception of necessities, except for one item: a dressing gown, which women find more important than men do.

It may surprise that "the influence of people's political outlook on their perception of necessities was found to be small" (Mack and Lansley, 1985: 80; Gordon et al. 1994: 71). Nevertheless, respondents identifying with the Labour Party tend to regard as necessities a larger number of items than the Conservatives. The difference is relatively large (and consistent across years) for carpets, a washing machine, a television, a best outfit, an outing for children and a night out. These differences of opinion, however, may be due to differences in age among people identifying with various parties, rather than being the result of political outlooks in itself.

A similar analysis has been carried out for Belgium. The results are shown in table 3.4. For the items waterproof coat, damp-free home, indoor-toilet, heating in living quarters, refrigerator, meal with meat etc., waterproof shoes and video-recorder and for those items specific for families with children, the differences were so small that it did not seem worthwhile to report them (almost everyone in every social group regards the items above indicated as necessities, except for the video-recorder, which almost no-one classes as a necessity).

Overall, *family composition and age* seem to have the greatest impact on judgments about necessities. Single elderly people relatively less often regard a bath or shower, a car and a holiday as necessities. Single people - elderly or not - attach less importance to a washing machine. Conversely, elderly persons - either couples or single - more often than younger persons say that a telephone, a colour TV and a newspaper are necessities. On the other hand a car is classed as a necessity by couples with children more often than by persons in other family types.

Judgments about necessity vary according to *education* for only three items: the higher a person's education, the more inclined one is to class a holiday and a car as necessities, and the less often a colour TV is regarded as a necessity. It seems that there is no direct bivariate relationship between education and the perception of a newspaper as a necessity.

Variations in perceptions of necessity by *household income* seem to fall into two distinct patterns. Where an item is classed as a necessity by a large majority - bath, washing machine, saving, vacuum cleaner - it is only the lowest income bracket which differs from the rest. For other items - holiday, car and central heating - the proportion of respondents judging it to be a necessity increases with household income up until a much higher level of income, or there is no clear pattern whatsoever - telephone, colour TV and a newspaper.

People in the *region* of Wallonia are less likely than those living in Flanders to consider a range of items as necessities; the only exception is a washing machine.

The patterns of differences in judgments about necessities described in the preceding paragraphs remain more or less the same from 1985 to 1988 for most items. The interesting exceptions are a telephone and a colour TV For both items, the overall proportion of respondents classing these items as necessities has increased considerably. But what is remarkable is that such increase is much stronger among the elderly than among the middle-aged, even though the elderly in 1985 were already more inclined to perceive a telephone and a colour TV as necessities. It contrasts with the increasing number of people who say that a car is a necessity, where the similarly strong increase seems to have been fairly uniform across social categories.

Of course, the bivariate relationships shown in table 3.4 may be misleading, in the sense that an apparent relationship between perceptions of necessity and, e.g., education may in fact be due to a relationship between these perceptions and age and the fact that people in older age brackets tend to have had less formal education. For this reason multivariate analyses, viz. logistic regressions have been carried out. This model also enabled us to examine whether differences in views about necessities across social categories only reflect differences in patterns of personal possession and personal wants (which, as we saw above, have an important effect on perceptions of necessity), or are independent from the latter.

Table 3.4
Differences in perceptions of necessities *

	Bath or shower		Washing machine		Regular saving		Holiday		Telephone	
	'85	'88	'85	'88	'85	'88	'85	'88	'85	'88
Household type										
Single elderly	-15	-17	-18	-20	-8	-9	-18	-18	+8	+19
Single non-elderly	-3	-7	-28	-23	-7	-5	+5	-3		
Couple elderly	-5	-6	-6	-5			-7	-8	+15	+20
Couple non-elderly			-6	-6						
Couple with children	*97*	*97*	*92*	*97*	*87*	*86*	*59*	*60*	*49*	*59*
One-parent					-9	-9			+1	+6
Other							-8	-3	+4	+11
Age head										
16-29			-10	-9	-5	-1	-2	-11	-11	-14
30-49	*97*	*97*	*90*	*94*	*87*	*85*	*61*	*62*	*49*	*59*
50-64									+6	+10
65-74	-6	-5	-5	-2			-9	-7	+9	+18
75+	-15	-18	-14	-18	-7	-8	-22	-25	+12	+19
Education head										
Only primary	*90*	*88*	*89*	*89*	*86*	*82*	*47*	*44*	*51*	*70*
Lower secondary	+5	+7	-1	+5			+6	+13	-4	-10
Higher secondary	+7	+9			0	+5	+15	+18	+1	-9
Higher	+7	+10	-6	+1			+22	+22	+8	-4
Household income										
25,000 BF or less	-13	-19	-16	-15	-10	-9	-13	-17	+5	+4
25,000-40,000 BF			-5	-5			-3	-9		
40,000-60,000 BF	*97*	*96*	*90*	*94*	*87*	*85*	*55*	*58*	*48*	*62*
60,000-80,000 BF							+6	+3	+6	-1
80,000 BF or more							+12	+5	+11	+5
Region										
Flanders	*96*	*94*	*87*	*91*	*90*	*87*	*57*	*58*	*51*	*64*
Wallonia			+6	+3	-9	-6	-9	-9		
Brussels			-22	-11	-16	-10	+21	+21	+10	+6

Notes: * Figures in italic refer to reference category of respective variable. Other figures show the deviation (in percentage points) in the particular category, relative to the reference category. Deviation is not shown, when it is smaller than 5%-points both in 1985 and 1988. The reference category is always the modal category (i.e. the one with the largest number of cases).

Car		Colour TV		Central Heating		Newspaper		Vacuum-cleaner	Number of cases in category (1)	
'85	'88	'85	'88	'85	'88	'85	'88	'88	'85	'88
-42	-45	+8	+16	-14	-2	-0	+8	-6	605	322
-18	-16			-5	-8			-7	453	164
-23	-18	+16	+26			+18	+27	+7	604	431
-6	-5					+5	+9		1207	655
57	*68*	*36*	*48*	*43*	*46*	*32*	*24*	*79*	*2696*	*1631*
-22	-8			+0	-8	-8	-1	-6	204	102
-8	-6	+10	+13	-5	+4	+8	+14		512	344
		-9	-8	-4	-8	-3	-7	-9	811	304
56	*67*	*36*	*46*	*42*	*44*	*31*	*24*	*79*	*2497*	*1494*
-7	-9	+10	+15	+1	+5	+7	+14		1680	1003
-24	-19	+12	+25	-5	+5	+11	+21	+6	793	522
-37	-39	+11	+17	-8	-2	+8	+17	-7	484	326
39	*50*	*46*	*66*	*34*	*43*	*35*	*36*	*75*	*2059*	*1069*
+8	+8	-6	-8	+6	0	-1	-7	+6	1517	947
+15	+15	-10	-18	+12	+6	-0	-7	+9	1491	778
+17	+15	-17	-31	+9	+4	+3	-6	+3	1116	663
-29	-38			-11	-7			-12	784	352
-15	-17	+2	+9						1492	701
52	*65*	*39*	*55*	*39*	*43*	*34*	*32*	*80*	*1750*	*966*
+5	+3	+0	-5	+7	+5				1251	825
+7	0	-1	-8	+8	+12				1004	805
49	*59*	*43*	*57*	*41*	*48*	*37*	*34*	*85*	*3632*	*2290*
-6	-2	-10	-4	-8	-10	-6	-4	-18	2068	1199
		-4	-11	+15	+1	-2	-12		581	160

Source: Belgian Socio-Economic Panel, waves 1985 and 1988.

The models without possession status generally confirmed the bivariate results shown above. Possession status (i.e. whether or not the household possesses the given item, and if not, whether it desires it or not) has a very large effect on perceptions of necessity, which generally surpasses that of all other variables combined. After the inclusion of possession status, the effects of the other variables are generally much smaller, and in many cases they are no longer significant. This suggests that possession status works as an intervening variable: views about necessities are much influenced by the personal possessions and personal desires of respondents, which in turn are affected by the social conditions of the latter. But there are a few instances where background variables exert an effect which is independent from possession status. Household type has an independent effect on views about a telephone, a colour TV and a newspaper, education on those about a colour TV, socio-professional category on those about a telephone, and region on those about a washing machine and a holiday. (Full results are reported in Van den Bosch, 1999.)

3 Perceptions of necessity of different items: are they related?

Until this point the perceptions of necessity have been examined item by item. The question can be asked whether and how these perceptions are related across items. Such relationships could be interesting both for what they reveal about respondents and about items. Some people might be systematically more ready than other people to regard any items as a necessity. Conversely, a subset of items could be related in the sense that people who perceive one item as a necessity are relatively more likely to regard the other items in the subset as necessities as well.

For the items about which there is almost consensus about their necessity - from damp-free home to regular saving - the answers appear hardly or not related. This is most easily checked by counting the number of items each respondent regards as necessities and comparing the resulting distribution with the binomial distribution. The binomial distribution is the distribution which would result when to the answers to the various items would be independent of each other. This has been done for those respondents who answered all these items (table 3.5). The binomial distribution shown is the expected distribution when each respondent would answer each item with a probability of 0.943 of a positive answer (i.e., the item is a necessity), and the answers were completely independent of each other. 0.943 is the average overall probability of a positive answer on these items, both in 1985 and 1988.

Table 3.5
Number of items regarded as necessity, of those highest on the list of necessities*, compared with a binomial distribution with number of trials = 10, and probability = 0.943

Number of items regarded as necessity	1985 (% of sample)	1988 (% of sample)	Binomial distribution (N = 10, p = 0.943)
10	63.6	64.2	55.6
9	23.5	22.8	33.6
8	8.1	8.8	9.1
7	2.9	2.7	1.5
6 or less	1.9	1.5	0.2
Number of cases	6112	3557	100

Note: * These items are: Damp-free home, Coat, Indoor toilet, Heating in living rooms, Meal with meat or fish, Bath or shower, All weather shoes, Refrigerator, Washing Machine and Regular Saving. Only records of respondents who answered all of these items (94% of total) were taken up in the analysis.

The number of respondents regarding all ten items as necessities, as well as the size of the small minority perceiving three or more of these items as non-necessities, is slightly larger than expected under the hypothesis that all answers would be independent of each other. But the distributions in both years are quite close to the binomial one, indicating that the answers are generally almost independent of each other. More detailed cross-tabulations show that two pairs of items are consistently somewhat related to each other: 'coat' and 'all weather shoes' on the one hand, and 'indoor toilet' and 'bath or shower' on the other; both relationships seem to make sense. In any case, table 3.5 shows that most of the most of the judgments of non-necessity for these items do not come from a small minority that thinks that none, or almost none, of these items are necessities, but rather from people who think that just one or two of these items are not necessities, while the rest of them are.

The situation is quite different for the six items lower down on the list of necessities - 'holiday' to 'newspaper' - which are regarded as necessities by between one-third and two-thirds of all respondents. Here we find that there is a sizable minority that regards all of these items as necessities, and also another one that says that none of them are (table 3.6). The comparison with the corresponding binomial distributions shows that these proportions are much larger than would be expected when the answers to different items would be independent of one another. The answers thus seem related, though not very strongly.

Table 3.6

Number of items regarded as necessity, of those lower down on the list of necessities*, compared with the binomial distribution with number of trials = 6, and probability = 0.446 (for 1985) or 0.516 (for 1988)

Number of items regarded as necessity	1985	1988	Binomial distribution (N = 6)	
			p = 0.446 (1985)	p = 0.516 (1988)
6	9.5	10.0	0.8	1.9
5	10.3	14.3	5.9	10.6
4	14.1	17.2	18.2	24.9
3	16.3	20.0	30.2	31.2
2	18.4	18.0	28.1	21.9
1	16.9	13.4	14.0	8.2
0	14.5	7.1	2.9	1.3
Total	100 (N = 6162)	100 (N = 3467)	100	100

Note: * These items are: Holiday, Telephone, Car, Colour TV, Central heating and Newspaper. Only records of respondents who answered all six items taken up in analysis (95% of all in 1985; 92% of all in 1988).

Further analysis shows that there are correlations of about 0.3 between almost any pair of these six items. The fact that correlations do not vary much across different pairs of items suggests that these correlations are the result of a general tendency of respondents either to perceive many things as necessities, or few things. The alternative would be that some items are especially related, in the sense that a person who finds central heating important is also likely to regard good heat insulation as a necessity, but may be indifferent as regards other items. To test this hypothesis a factor analysis has been carried out, trying to extract common factors. A common factor is a latent unobservable variable that is assumed to explain the *correlations* among a set of variables. Factor analysis is not really suited to binary data, such as the one at hand, and therefore the results can only be regarded as indicative. But, as far as they go, they are quite clear: in both years there is only one common factor for these six items, with which all items are more or less correlated[3].

Some readers, particularly those with a sociological or psychological background, might feel that the next step in the analysis obviously would be to investigate the relationships among the perceptions of necessity for different items in more detail and with more appropriate methods, and to construct one or more scales from these items. Techniques more suited to the dichotomous data at hand are for example the Mokken and Rasch models, which can be described as stochastic versions of the better known Guttman model (Niemöller and Van Schuur, 1983). Both models assume that the answers to a set of items can be explained in terms of an underlying single dimension, on which both respondents and items can be placed. The probability of a positive response (i.e. that a particular item is a necessity) is a function of the distance between the position of the respondent and that of the item.

While the application of these techniques might yield interesting results, this has not been done. A first reason for this decision is of a somewhat technical nature. As we have seen above, different groups have different perceptions regarding the necessity of a number of items. This implies that these items may well have different positions on the underlying dimension for different groups, which would make the comparability across groups of any scale constructed from these items less than straightforward. But this difficulty could be overcome, if necessary. The main reason for not pursuing the scale approach is that it is not clear to me what useful purpose would be served by it in the present context. Commonly, scale analysis is used for two purposes. The first is to establish whether the items are indeed indicators of a single underlying trait or dimension. The second is to estimate the position of respondents on this dimension. But I think that the validity of the consensual method and its results does not turn on whether perceptions of necessity can be reduced to a single dimension. If it would be found that there are several dimensions, or that there is no structure at all, this finding would have no direct bearing, as far as I can see, on the question whether or not the answers reflect a social consensus on the minimum standard of living.

4 Factors influencing the total number of necessities

Above we have seen that, in most cases, social characteristics of respondents have only limited effects on perceptions of necessity of individual items. However, the item-by-item analysis might fail to reveal a substantial effect on the aggregate level. That is, small effects on individual items that are all in the same direction, might add up to a substantial effect when we look at the total number of items that respondents class as necessities. To investigate this issue, the total number of items which each respondent has classed as necessities (only the sixteen items which are applicable to all respondents) was calculated, and this sum was regressed on the same variables as were used in the logistic regressions for individual items[4].

The results (fully shown in Van den Bosch, 1999) indicate that the influence of the background variables on the number of items classed as necessities is fairly small. The maximum difference between any pair of social categories is 1.29 item. Looking only at effects that are consistent across years, it was found that middle-aged and elderly couples tend to class a slightly higher number of items as necessities than people in other household types do. The same is true for one-parent families, when the effect of their low income and low standard of living is taken account of. People with higher levels of education on average regard more items as necessities than those with lower levels of education, and the same is true for differences by socio-professional category. But these effects seem to be due to differences in age, income or number of possessions between people with different levels of education or socio-professional status, rather than to the latter variables themselves. Respondents in Wallonia class slightly fewer items as necessities than those in Flanders do. Of all background variables (apart from the number of possessions) household income has the strongest influence on the number of items classed as necessities. However, the parameter estimate implies that a trebling of income corresponds to only one additional item being classed as a necessity. In any case, the effect of income wholly disappears after controlling for the number of possessions.

The number of items that a respondent actually possesses exerts a substantial effect on the number of items classed as necessities. For every 2.5 additional items possessed, one more item is classed as a necessity. The interpretation of this result is not straightforward, however. At first sight, it may seem to suggest that the higher a person's standard of living, the more extended the range of goods and services she will regard as necessities. But this interpretation may be slightly misleading. Above we saw that the circumstance of whether or not the respondent has an item to a great extent determines her perception of its necessity. Presumably people who are used to having a certain good or service come to regard it as indispensable, while, conversely, persons who find a certain amenity important will tend to buy or obtain it. The correlation between the number of possessions and the number of items classed as necessities may be solely or largely the result of this item-on-item effect. That is, people with a higher standard of living may not be more likely to regard any item as a necessity, but only those they themselves actually possess.

Now, at the aggregate level across items, it is, as far as I can see, not possible to distinguish between these two interpretations. But a test can be performed at the level of individual items, by estimating the following linear regression equations:

$$N_{ij} = b_{0i} + b_{1i}P_{ij} + b_{2i}TP_{ij} + b_{xi}X_j + e_{ij}, \; i = 1..16 \qquad (3.1)$$

where N_{ij} represents the perception of necessity about item i of respondent j, P_{ij} represents whether or not respondent j possesses item i, TP_{ij} the total number of items that respondent j possesses, *without* counting item i, X_j a vector of background characteristics of respondent j, as shown in table 3.4, b_{0i}, b_{1i} and b_{2i} parameters and b_{xi} a vector of parameters (which are allowed to vary across equations for different items), and e_{ij} a disturbance term. In equation (3.1), b_{1i} represents the item-on-item effect of possessing a particular item, and b_{2i} the general effect of the standard of living on perceptions of necessity. The results of running these sixteen regression equations on the 1985 data show that all b_{1i} estimates are highly significant, and have an average value of 0.34, varying between 0.266 and 0.475 (except for the item damp-free home). On the other hand, the b_{2i} estimates are statistically significant (at the 5% level) for only 5 of the 16 items, and even then are equal to 0.022 at maximum. Moreover, it can be shown[5] that the regression coefficient of the number of possessions in the regression for the total number of necessities is approximately equal to the average of the b_{1i} coefficients plus the sum of the b_{2i} coefficients. The latter is equal to 0.061, while the former is equal to 0.340. Thus, it appears that more than 80% of the influence of the number of items possessed on the number of items classed as necessities is due to the item-on-item effect, while less than 20% reflects a greater probability on the part of those with a higher standard of living to class any item, whether possessed or not, as a necessity.

This finding is of some importance, since it indicates that the views on necessities of the better-off and the worse-off are less different than at first sight might appear to be the case, or at least that the difference is not situated at a very 'deep' level. People with a high standard of living are not, because of that circumstance alone, more inclined than persons with a lower standard of living to regard any good or service as a necessity. It is, rather, that persons who have a particular good or service tend to regard it as a necessity. And, of course, well-off persons are more likely to possess any item than less well-off persons.

5 Stability in time of perceptions of necessity in Belgium

Above we have seen that the proportions of people perceiving the various items as necessities remain generally rather stable over time. The panel data of the Belgian Socio-Economic Panel make it possible to investigate whether perceptions of necessity are also stable at the individual level. What do we hope to find? At first sight, it might seem that it would enhance the validity and credibility of the approach if people would stick to the same opinions about necessities three years later. After all, one might say, if people change their minds very much about what they regard as necessities, these opinions are apparently not deeply held, and there is less reason to take them seriously. But there is another side to this matter, which has to do with the consensual nature of the approach. As we have seen above, in Belgium, as in other countries, there is a range of items about which opinions whether they are necessities or not are divided about fifty-fifty. This does not look much like a consensus, even if the differences in views do not follow political party lines, or class or other social divisions. After all, we would not speak of a 'consensus' if, say, 50% of the population in a country would favor joining the EU, while the other half is against it, even if the controversy would cross-cut social and political boundaries. But the interpretation would be different, if it could be shown that the apparent difference of opinion at the aggregate level corresponds to uncertainty at the individual level. In other words, if it would be the case that those who class, say, a car as a necessity are much less sure of this than about the necessity of an indoor toilet, while those who do *not* class a car as a necessity are also less confident about this than about the same judgment as regards a video-recorder, then the difference of opinion is much smaller than it appears to be. An indicator of such uncertainty is that respondents give different answers to the same question after some time has elapsed. (It is unfortunate, in this context, that respondents have to choose from only two possible answers to the necessities question, and cannot indicate the degree of their conviction.)

Taking the two considerations mentioned into account, what we hope to find, therefore, is that there is stability at the individual level for the items at both ends of the necessities scale - those which almost everybody regards as necessities and those which almost nobody regards as necessities, and, at the same time, more change for the items in the middle of the scale, where opinions are more evenly balanced. In fact, the results reported in table 3.7 confirm these expectations almost perfectly. The items have been ordered according to the proportions classing them as a necessity in 1985, from high to low. For the first ten items, up to regular saving, which at least 85% of the sample regards as necessities, we observe that a very large majority of those who did so in 1985 stick to their judgment in 1985. On the other hand, an almost equally large majority of those who did not class these items as necessities in 1985, have changed their minds in 1988. In fact, for several of the items the difference between the two groups is so small that it is not statistically significant, and, also in view of the nature of these items, one may wonder whether most of the recorded answers classing these items as non-necessities are not in fact due to mistakes, either by the respondent or by the interviewer, or at the data-entry stage. (For the item, 'two pairs of all weather shoes', the clause, 'two pairs' may be a source of confusion, some people thinking that one pair is sufficient, others overlooking it.) It seems, therefore, that as far as these ten items are concerned, people classing them as necessities are rather sure of their opinion, while people who do not are very uncertain about it[6].

Table 3.7
Stability of perceptions of necessities across time at the individual level, Belgium, 1985-1988

Item (K): Items for families with children	Nec. '85	Necessity '88				N
			Necessity '85			(6)
		All	Yes	No	Diff.	
	(1)	(2)	(3)	(4)	(5)	
Damp-free home	99	98	98	100		3553
Coat	98	98	98	97		3569
Indoor toilet	98	97	98	88	10	3580
Heating in living rooms	97	97	97	97		3534
Meal with meat or fish	95	95	95	85	11	3553
Bath or shower	95	94	95	73	22	3567
All-weather shoes	95	90	90	88		3542
Refrigerator	94	96	97	89	8	3578
Washing machine	90	93	95	77	18	3564
Regular saving	87	85	87	75	12	3513
Holiday	56	57	67	44	23	3508
Telephone	51	65	77	53	24	3524
Car	49	59	72	47	26	3498
Colour TV	39	56	68	48	19	3488
Central heating	38	46	58	38	20	3479
Newspaper	35	33	48	25	24	3490
Three meals a day (K)	99	98	98	96		1828
Separate bedrooms (K)	93	92	93	83	10	1773
Leisure equipment (K)	91	86	87	76	11	1767

Notes: (1) Percentage saying item is necessity in *1985*, of those answering the question both in '85 and '88.
(2) Percentage saying item is necessity in *1988*, of those answering the question both in '85 and '88.
(3) Percentage saying item is necessity in 1988, of those saying item is necessity in '85.
(4) Percentage saying item is necessity in 1988, of those saying item is not a necessity in '85.
(5) Difference between columns (3) and (4); it is only reported when it is statistically significant at the 1%-level.
(6) Number of cases for columns (1) to (5).

Source: Belgian Socio-Economic Panel, Waves 1985 and 1988.

As regards the other six items, both those who in 1985 had classed it as a necessity, and those who had not, are fairly likely to change their opinion. In fact, across items, the proportions in both groups saying that an item is a necessity move in tandem, the percentage point difference being between 19% and 26%. The more often an item is regarded as a necessity overall, the less often people classing it as a necessity in 1985 changed their mind, and the more often people who had the opposite opinion did. The results show that, as far as these items are concerned, there is only a fair degree of correlation over time in the perceptions of necessity. Looking at the percentage differences it seems, though, that there is more correlation across time for the items which are less often classed as a necessity than for the items which almost everyone regards as a necessity. But if one uses log-linear estimates of correlation (not shown here), the situation is less clear: where the correlation is statistically significant for items high up on the list of necessities, it is stronger than for items further down the list. The choice between a percentage difference as an estimate of correlation and a log-linear estimate is in fact a choice between an additive model and a multiplicative one, and no clear criteria for making this choice seem to exist.

The log-linear model has the advantage, in any case, that it enables us to investigate to what extent the correlations across time in perceptions of necessity are mediated by the possession of these items. That is, a correlation across time might be solely or mainly the result of the fact that at both points in time people who possess the item are more likely to regard it as a necessity (assuming, of course, that possession is strongly correlated across time). Results reported in Van den Bosch (1999) show, however, that after the effects of possession status (i.e., whether the item is possessed or not, in 1985 and in 1988) have been factored out, the correlation generally drops, but in most cases by less than half (except for washing machine). The correlation for a colour TV does not drop at all, which again suggests that normative considerations are important when respondents make judgments about the necessity of this item. These results show that the judgments about necessities have some stability independent of that induced by the inertia of possession patterns.

Until now we have looked at the results across time for individual items. I have suggested that the instability of the judgments about the necessity of some of these items reflects uncertainty in respondents' minds about these judgments. This interpretation would be difficult to maintain if it could be shown that in fact some people change their judgments a great deal, while others do not alter them at all. But this does not seem to be the case.

Looking only at the people who at both points in time answered at least 14 of the 16 items applicable for everyone (95% of all those whose records could be linked), it turns out that less than 6% of these respondents do not change their judgment about any item, while 90% make between one and six changes. If attention is restricted to the items lower down on the list of necessities, holiday to newspaper, where the bulk of the changes occur, it is found that 13% make no changes in their judgments and 68% make one, two or three changes. These figures indicate that the changes in judgments for different items are not completely independent of each other[7], but it is certainly not the case that there is a large number of people who do not change their mind at all.

6 Summary and conclusions

In this section I will first summarize the findings reported in the second part of this chapter, and then try to answer the main question posed in the introduction: is there a consensus about a minimum standard of living?

When respondents in national sample surveys are asked which items, out of a list of activities and amenities, they thought were necessary, a range of items are classed as necessities by a very large majority (more than 80%). These items do not only include amenities that are needed to maintain health and decency (such as a damp-free home), but also households goods that save time and effort (such as a washing machine). There is also a wide range of items about which opinions are divided, in the sense that the proportion of respondents regarding them as necessities lies between 30% and 70%.

Across countries, there is a remarkable degree of convergence in perceptions of necessity. It is greater than could have been expected on the basis of the similarity of possession rates. This is an important result for comparative studies of deprivation, as it often maintained (e.g. Whelan, 1993: 33) that cultural differences between countries make it difficult to develop deprivation indicators that are valid in several countries. This may in fact be less of a problem than one might think it to be. Apparently, the requirements and conditions of modern living are fairly similar across Western European countries. The number of items where cultural differences are important (such as 'a roast meat joint on Sunday') is limited, and these items seem easy to spot.

In general, we find that items for which possession rates are high, are also very often classed as necessities, and vice versa. This seems natural:

people will tend to regard things as necessities which are customary in society, and, conversely, they will tend to acquire the items that are socially approved, encouraged or expected. But there are some exceptions to this rule, a colour TV being the most notable example, where normative considerations apparently predominate.

The correlation between possession and perceptions of necessity is also found at the individual level. Whether or not the respondent possesses the item is by far the most important determinant of his or her perception of its necessity. Furthermore, among those who do not possess an item, there are large differences between those who say they do not have it because they cannot afford it, and those who say they do not want it. In fact, people in the former category are often more likely to class an item as a necessity than respondents who have an item, but say they could do without it. This finding shows that not only objective circumstances, but also subjective wants strongly influence perceptions of necessity.

Correlations of perceptions of necessity with other characteristics of respondents are generally not large. For the items which are on the top of the list of necessities there are virtually no differences between various social categories, and for the other items they are mostly fairly limited. The largest differences occur between different age brackets, in particular between the elderly and the non-elderly. Whether the respondent lives single or as a couple, and whether he or she has children also exerts an influence. At least in Belgium, most of these differences between social categories are due to differing item possession rates.

In Britain, in particular in 1990, there are fairly large differences in perceptions of necessity for some items by level of education and by social class. Moreover, and in contrast to the situation in 1985, if there is a difference, it is always in the same direction: persons with more education and from higher social classes are less likely to consider the item as a necessity. In Belgium, it is the reverse that is true. In Britain, no differences in perceptions of necessity are found between the deprived and the non-deprived. Also, persons identifying with different political parties do not have divergent views on necessities.

Analysis of the Belgian data showed that perceptions of necessity of different items are not strongly correlated, i.e. people who class one item as a necessity are not much more likely than the average person to class any other item as a necessity. Partly as a consequence of this, differences in the total number of items classed as necessities across social categories are quite small. The only variable with an important effect is the total number of items possessed. However, this reflects a tendency of people who have a particular item to consider it a necessity, rather than a correlation between the standard of living in general and perceptions of necessity.

Across time, perceptions of necessity do not much change in the aggregate. That is, the overall proportion of respondents who class an item as a necessity generally remains fairly stable or it rises only a bit. There are a few items where the increase is quite substantial, and a few others where a decrease was found. The Belgian panel data allow us to look at changes in perceptions of necessity at the individual level. There is a range of items which virtually everyone classed as a necessity in both years. For the other items lower down on the list of necessities, however, it is found that although there is a fair amount of correlation across time, many respondents have changed their perceptions of necessity after a few years.

Conclusion: Is there a consensus about the minimum standard of living?

Having reviewed the empirical findings, we must now address the question: is there a social consensus about the minimum standard of living? In the introduction to chapter 2 I have argued that two conditions must be met before we can say that such a social consensus exists. In the first place, respondents should be able to take a 'publicly-oriented' point of view when considering this matter, and to distinguish between what they want for themselves, and what should be included in a community minimum standard of living. Secondly, the views on this matter in society should not be too divergent.

It seems to me that the first condition is reasonably well met. As reported above, many people who have an item but could do without it, as well as many of those who do not have it and do not want it for themselves, still say that it is a necessity in the sense that everyone should be able to afford it. Conversely, it also happens quite often that respondents who say they themselves could not do without a particular item, still do *not* class it as a necessity. This shows that respondents do make the distinction between their own private wishes and a more public point of view. Of course, their publicly-oriented judgments are colored, if not largely shaped, by their personal circumstances and experiences, but that is an unavoidable fact of life, and does not detract from the validity of the distinction.

The second condition is perhaps more of a problem. We have seen that in all countries for which we have data, there is near unanimity about the necessity of a number of items. But there is also a range of items where opinions are more or less evenly divided. We have also seen that, in general, these divisions of opinion do not coincide with social or political boundaries. Mack and Lansley (1985: 86) conclude on the basis of the latter finding that:

> "The survey found widespread agreement between all groups in society about the items that are classified as necessities. The homogeneity of views is striking. People from all walks of life [...] share the same view of the kind of society Britain should be in terms of the minimum standards of living to which all citizens should be entitled. Their views are based, it seems, on a general cultural ethos of what is decent and proper."

But this interpretation is not wholly convincing. If, for instance, about half of all respondents class a holiday as a necessity, while the other half does not, it seems somewhat forced to talk about a consensus, even if the same balance of opinion is found to exist across all social and political groups. To use an analogy with a different domain: a country where half of all inhabitants want to join the European Union, while the other half does not, would not be described by most observers as showing a great deal of consensus, even if the controversy would cross-cut all social and political divisions.

One might try to circumvent this problem or objection by saying that there is at least virtual consensus about the items which at least 80% of respondents class as necessities. But if a minimum standard of living were to be defined using only these items, it would be difficult to maintain that it reflects a social consensus, as it would not include items that a large majority regards as necessities.

Mack and Lansley (1985) use a cut-off point of 50% to select the items which go into the minimum standard of living. As suggested in the introduction, the 50% cut-off point could be defended by analogy with a voting procedure (although Mack and Lansley do not do this). If a vote were to be taken on each item whether or not it should be included in the minimum standard of living, then presumably those items would go through which a majority class as necessities (assuming voting outcomes for one item would not influence those for another). However, as Halleröd et al. (1994: 4) remark, "majority is not the same as consensus".

Thus the results do not warrant the conclusion that there is consensus about a minimum standard of living. But there seems to be no dissensus either. There are a number of items where the answers to the question whether it is a necessity are about equally divided. But all available empirical evidence (in particular the Belgian panel results) suggests that in general respondents do *not* have strong feelings about these items. Above I compared differences in perceptions of necessity with a hypothetical controversy in a country about joining the European Union. This comparison was in so far misleading, that there is likely to be a real social and political controversy about joining the EU, which there is not about the necessity of, say, an annual holiday. In fact, where opinions are evenly balanced at the aggregate level, this seems to correspond to uncertainty at the individual level. Few people appear to have settled views on these issues. Walker (1987: 219) may well be justified in his suspicion that many people might modify their perceptions of necessity after receiving additional information or discussing the matter with other people. There is a range of goods and services which almost everyone classes as necessities. There is also another range of items which everyone agrees are not necessities. But in between there is a large gray area, where there is not so much disagreement as uncertainty about the necessity of goods, amenities and activities.

In this context, the finding that differences between 'vertical' strata, i.e. between people with varying levels of education, from different social classes and with different incomes are generally small, is very important. Some critics of the consensual method have argued that "the opinions of the poor, of the rich, of the middle income bands, of the tax payers will almost certainly clash and differ" (Stitt, 1994: 73). These critics seem to expect that people in more favorable social positions will have a more stringent view on the minimum standard of living. In that case, it would be clearly inappropriate to talk about a consensus. However, the results show clearly that this is simply not the case. Views on necessities do not differ much between different social strata, whether these are distinguished according to income, education or professional class. In Belgium, at least, we have seen that people who are richer or better educated or who have more prestigious jobs are, if anything, more, not less generous than the average person.

As shown above, the largest differences in perceptions of necessity are often found between different social or demographic groups, such as age brackets and household types. In contrast to the 'vertical' stratification according to education, income or social class, we might call these kinds of classifications 'horizontal'. These 'horizontal' differences do not seem to be the result of divergent views about how stringent or generous the minimum standard of living should be, but, rather, reflect the fact that some items are more important for some kinds of people than for others. Older people, for instance, have more need for a telephone and a television, and less need for a car, while the reverse is true for younger people. Mack and Lansley (1985) implicitly recognized that what counts as a necessity may vary according to the circumstances of individuals when they introduced special items for families with children. But otherwise their method implies that an item is either a necessity for everyone or for no-one. Both the British and Belgian results show that this is not a realistic assumption (cf. Halleröd et al., 1994: 5).

People in different circumstances need different items to reach a minimum standard of living. This raises a problem, however. In what sense is it still possible to say that the minimum standard living is at the same level for different people, when it is composed of different goods and services? The theoretically most satisfying strategy to answer this question would be to establish a correspondence between a list of items and a number of capabilities. The same set of capabilities might correspond to different lists of items for people with different characteristics or living in different circumstances. But I doubt whether a useful list of capabilities can be made up. If they are to apply to everyone equally, they are likely to be so general (e.g. maintaining social contacts) that a translation into specific items would not be feasible. However, the lack of a solution to this problem does not mean that we should fall back on a definition of the minimum standard of living in terms of the same set of goods and services for everyone. This would be evidence of a rather strong form of commodity fetishism. A typical 85 year old person with a car but without a telephone does not have the same standard of living as a 25 year old person in the same circumstances. Account must be taken of 'horizontal' differences in perceptions of necessity.

The main conclusions of this review can now be stated as follows. First, there is not a well-defined public consensus on the minimum standard of living. The reason is not so much that there are strong disagreements about this matter, but rather that individuals are apparently uncertain about the necessity of a range of items for modern living. Secondly, depending on a person's circumstances and characteristics, perceptions of necessities differ, indicating that the minimum standard of living is composed of different items for different groups in society.

If this summing up of the results is correct, how can we proceed in this situation? Walker (1987: 220-224) proposes to have intensive group discussions between people representing a wide cross-section of the public, to elucidate the public conception of poverty, and to derive a consensual monetary poverty line from this. This is an interesting suggestion, but, to my knowledge, it has not been followed up. (The consultation processes used by Stitt and Grant, 1992, and Bradshaw, 1993, while developing budget standards go someway towards it.) In the meantime, can we use the results of the consensual approach to determine a poverty threshold for use in empirical work into poverty and the standard of living?

In view of the conclusions reached, it seems inappropriate to follow Mack and Lansley's method, which divided all items sharply into necessities and non-necessities. It is much more defensible to follow the method proposed by Halleröd et al. (1994: 9), who give each item a weight based on the proportion of the population that regards it as a necessity. This weight can be interpreted as the likelihood that the average person will regard the item in question as a necessity. Given the conclusion that differences in responses probably reflect uncertainty rather than disagreement, the weight can also be regarded as an indicator of how certain the average person is about the necessity of the item. An advantage of this method is that we do not need a more or less arbitrary cut-off point to classify items into necessities and non-necessities. Furthermore, the method provides a simple way to take account of differences in perceptions of necessity between different demographic groups. Instead of having the same set of weights for all persons, the weights for each item are allowed to vary from one group to another. A disadvantage of the weighting method, compared with Mack and Lansley's index of deprivation, is that the former may have less appeal for a lay audience. Mack and Lansley were able to present a list of necessities, and consequently, when they identified a household as living in deprivation, it was very clear what this meant. With the weighting method, some of this clarity is lost.

Notes

1 To see how this is derived, consider the following model:

$$N_{ij} = b_0 + b_1 P_{ij} + e_{ij} ,$$

where N_{ij} is the proportion of respondents in country j classing item i as a necessity, P_{ij} is the proportion of respondents in country j having item i, and e_{ij} is an error term with the usual properties; b_0 and b_1 are parameters. Now suppose that b_1 after standardization is equal to 0.79 (average correlation N/P), and that the correlation between the possession patterns of country j and country k is 0.80 (average correlation P/P). Then the correlation between the necessities patterns of countries j and k would be 0.50 *if* the error-terms would be uncorrelated across countries. The latter condition is perhaps unrealistic. One would expect that the differences between possession rates and proportions of people classing them as necessities would to a certain extent be parallel across countries, if only because of similar price structures. In the extreme, the differences would be the same, viz. $e_{ij} = e_{ik}$ for all items. Now, simple calculations show that in the latter case (and using the same values for b_1 and

the correlation P_j/P_k), the correlation between the necessities patterns of countries j and k would be equal to 0.86, which is the same as the average observed correlation between necessities patterns.
Thus, the observed correlations are consistent with a model according to which respondents take actual possession patterns in their respective countries as their starting point, and then use exactly the same normative considerations to form their judgments about necessity. Unfortunately, a formal test of this model was not possible, because of the low number of common items across all countries. Of course, quite different models may also be consistent with these correlations.

2 The number of items classed by at least 50% of respondents as a necessity in the different groups was in 1983: 'have and could not do without': 34 out of 35; 'have and could do without': 14 out of 35; 'don't have and can't afford': 21 out of 34; 'don't have and don't want': 5 out of 32. In 1990 the numbers were: 'have and could not do without': 40 out of 44; 'have and could do without': 19 out of 44; 'don't have and can't afford': 16 out of 36; 'don't have and don't want': 8 out of 37. The total number of items varies across groups, as no results were reported if the number in a group for a particular item was too low. The relatively low number of items classed as necessities by the 'don't have / don't want' group in 1990 is due to no results being reported for this group for seven items high on the list of necessities.

3 More technically: the first factor had an eigenvalue of 1.61 in 1985 and 1.25 in 1988; subsequent factors had eigenvalues smaller than 0.03 in both years; no residual correlation after extracting the first factor was higher than 0.07. Estimated correlations of items with this factor (factor-loadings) ranged from 0.39 to 0.57 in 1985 and from 0.33 to 0.52 in 1988.

4 Some readers might question whether adding up respondents' scores on individual items into a sum-score is appropriate, given that in the previous section I have reported that the answers to the various items do not correlate very much with each other. I think that this is not inappropriate, as long as it is recognized that the sum-score has no meaning beyond the total number of items that respondents class as necessities, and does not, for instance, measure an underlying tendency on the part of the respondent to be more or less generous in her perceptions of necessities.

5 This goes as follows. Equation (3.1) can be rewritten as (assuming that P_{ij} has been coded 1 for possessing and 0 for not possessing):

$$N_{ij} = b_{0i} + (b_1^* + b'_{1i})P_{ij} + (b_2^* + b'_{2i})(TP_{ij} - P_{ij}) + b_{xi}X_j + e_{ij}\ , \ i = 1..16$$

where TP is the total number of possessions (also counting item i), b_1^* and b_2^* are the average values across items of the b_{1i} and b_{2i}, respectively, and b'_{1i} and b'_{2i} the deviations from the average value ($b'_{ki} = b_{ki} - b_k^*$). Summing these equations over the 16 items, we obtain, using the facts that $\varepsilon p_i = tp$ and $\varepsilon b'_{1i} = \varepsilon b'_{2i} = 0$:

$TN_j = \varepsilon b_{0i} + (b_1^* + 15b_2^*)TP_j + \varepsilon[P_{ij}(b'_{2i} - b'_{2i})] + \varepsilon b_{xi}X_j + \varepsilon e_{ij}$, ε over i, i = 1..16

where TN_j is the total number of items classed as necessities. The third term on the right hand side of this equation is likely to be small, unless the size of the coefficients b_{1i} and b_{2i} would be strongly related to the possession rates of items. Therefore $(b_1^* + 15b_2^*)$ will be close to the regression coefficient of the total number of items possessed in the equation for the total number of items classed as necessities.

6 One might object to the first part of this statement by pointing out that it could hardly be otherwise, given that in both years there is virtual unanimity about the necessity of these items. That is, if both in 1985 and 1988 95% of respondents regard an item as a necessity, then, even at the maximum rate of change, at least 90% of those who did so in 1985 must continue to do so in 1988. Mathematically this argument is of course quite correct, but in the real world it was, equally obviously, not a pre-ordained fact that the overall proportion classing the item as a necessity remained unchanged. Rather, the 1988 situation is a result of the changes that occurred between 1985 and 1988.

7 For each of the six items from holiday to newspaper about 61% of respondents gave the same answer in both years. Thus, if these changes were statistically independent of each other, 0.61**6 = 5% would give the same answer to all six items, instead of 13%.

4 Income Evaluation Methods: A Review

1 Introduction

In chapter 2, I have argued that the important variation found in the answers to consensual income questions undercuts the validity of the resulting income thresholds. Two reasons for the variation were that respondents had to make estimates for household situations that were not very well defined and with which they were unfamiliar in most cases. An obvious alternative, which avoids these problems, is to ask questions about the respondent's own situation, instead of a hypothetical household type. For example, the Gallup question might be reformulated to: "How much income would you need under your conditions for your household to get along?"

Of course, a large number of income evaluation questions of this kind could be conceived. In practice, two questions have been most popular, at least in poverty related research. These are the Minimum Income Question (MIQ), and the Income Evaluation Question (IEQ, details are given below) (Goedhart et al., 1977; Van Praag, Hagenaars and Van Weeren, 1982). The corresponding poverty lines derived from the answers to the MIQ and the IEQ have been labeled SPL (Subjective Poverty Line) and LPL (Leyden Poverty Line)[1].

The change in formulation implies, however, that the MIQ and the IEQ cannot be interpreted as consensual questions. In terms of the concepts introduced by Barry (1990), referred to in the introduction of chapter 2, the income evaluation questions do not ask for public-regarding evaluations, but for self-regarding ones. In fact, the income evaluation method is perhaps best seen as a way to estimate a respondent's subjective welfare, or more precisely, a respondent's evaluation of his own income. Through a comparison of the answers to the MIQ and IEQ with the respondent's actual household income, the researcher can infer how the respondent would evaluate his or her own income. This interpretation of the income evaluation method links it to the income satisfaction measures, which will be discussed in chapter 7. More about the interpretation of the answers to the MIQ and the IEQ will be said in chapter 6.

The chapter is organized as follows. After a description of the standard methodology of the SPL and LPL in section 2, the main part of the chapter is devoted to a review of empirical results regarding subjective income evaluations. Section 3 looks at the reported effects of household income and household size (the main determinants) on the answers to the MIQ and the IEQ, and at the resulting equivalence scales and poverty lines. In section 4 reported effects of a range of other variables are reviewed. Section 5 is about the influence of reference groups. Section 6 discusses possible bias due to the income concept in the mind of the respondent not being equal to the income concept measured in the survey. A summary and conclusions are given at the end of each section. Overall conclusions are drawn in chapter 6.

2 The SPL and LPL methods

The Subjective Poverty Line (SPL)

The SPL is derived from answers to the Minimum Income Question (MIQ), which reads:

> "We would like to know which net family income would, in *your* circumstances, be the absolute minimum for *you*. That is to say, that you would not be able to make both ends meet if you earned less. In my circumstances, I consider the following net family income the absolute minimum."

Different versions of these questions have been used in empirical research. A respondent's answer to the minimum income question is called the respondent's minimum income, or Ymin. Now, it appears that Ymin correlates with a number of variables, in particular household income itself. Although there are no theoretical reasons to choose a particular functional form, it turns out that a double log-linear equation fits the data generally quite well (i.e. the log of Ymin is linearly related to the log of household income). The relationship is shown in figure 4.1.

Figure 4.1
The relationship between log-minimum income and log-income for a given family size

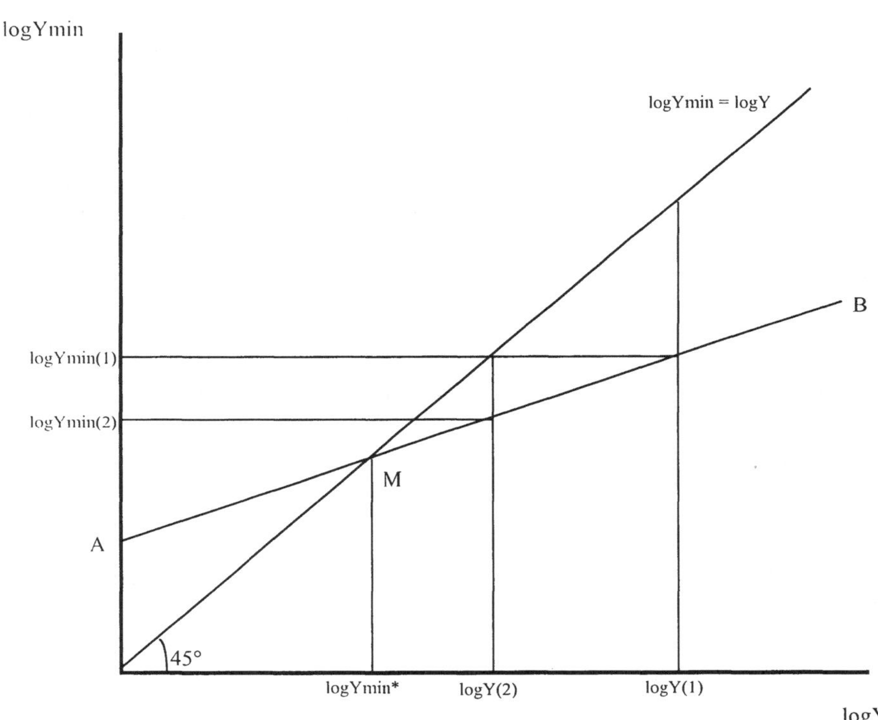

Source: Wansbeek and Kapteyn (1983).

Given this variation in the answers, how can we obtain a single poverty line? The following reasoning is applied (Goedhart et al., 1977: 514; cf. Wansbeek and Kapteyn, 1983: 262-263). Consider an individual with income $Y^{(1)}$. His minimum income will be $Y^{(1)}$min, below $Y^{(1)}$. Now let his income fall from $Y^{(1)}$ to $Y^{(2)}$, $Y^{(2)}$ being equal to $Y^{(1)}$min. Immediately after the change, his new income will be considered minimal. However, as time passes he will become accustomed to the new situation and he will realize that $Y^{(2)}$ is a tolerable income, and that $Y^{(2)}$min is the minimum income. If his income would fall further, a similar adaptation process would start. The process stops when Y = Y*min at point M. Apparently, a respondent's perception of the poverty line is distorted by the fact that his actual income is not equal to his minimum income level. There is only one income level, Y*min, where there is no misperception. Therefore, Y*min appears to be the natural candidate for the poverty line (Goedhart et al., 1977: 514).

An alternative motivation is given by Van Praag, Goedhart and Kapteyn (1980). This one does not depend on hypothetically putting an individual in different situations (dynamic interpretation) but is based on a static comparison across households. Ignoring variation around the regression line A-B, everyone with an income above Y*min has an income higher than his or her stated minimum income, and is therefore able to make ends meet. Conversely, people below Y*min apparently feel that they cannot make ends meet. Therefore, if we identify the poverty line with the income level below which people do not feel able to make ends meet, Y*min is the poverty line SPL.

The line A-B applies to one particular family type. For other family types, the line A-B is shifted upwards or downwards, as perceived needs are greater or smaller. If there is no interaction between the effects of household type and household income on Ymin, all lines are parallel.

In practice, the position of the lines is estimated with a regression equation like the following one:

$$\log Ymin = \alpha_o + \alpha_1 \log Y + \alpha_2 \log FS + \varepsilon, \qquad (4.1)$$

where Y represents household income, FS household size, ε a disturbance term with the usual properties, and α_o, α_1 and α_2 are parameters to be estimated. By setting Ymin equal to Y, and ignoring ε, the poverty line Y*min for a given family size FS_o is found as follows:

$$\log Y^*min = \alpha_o/(1-\alpha_1) + [\alpha_2/(1-\alpha_1) \,.\, \log FS_o \qquad (4.2)$$

The approach immediately yields equivalence factors. If we divide the poverty line for a certain household type FS_n with the poverty line for reference household type FS_o, we obtain:

$$Y^*min(FS_n) \,/\, Y^*min(FS_o) = (FSn/FS_o)^{(\alpha_2/1-\alpha_1)} \qquad (4.3)$$

Therefore, the factor $\alpha_2/(1-\alpha_1)$ is the elasticity of the equivalence factors implicit in the SPL with respect to household size (cf. Wansbeek and Kapteyn, 193; Bradbury, 1989).

It may not be intuitively clear why the factor $(1-\alpha_1)$ appears in the denominator of the equivalence scale elasticity. After all, if family size increases by k percent, minimum income (Ymin) rises by α_2k percent, keeping household income constant, according to (4.1). So why does the term $1/(1-\alpha_1)$ come in? The problem is that when household income is held at a constant level, welfare is not. What happens is shown in figure 4.2.

Figure 4.2
The effect of a change in family size on log-minimum income and the log-poverty line

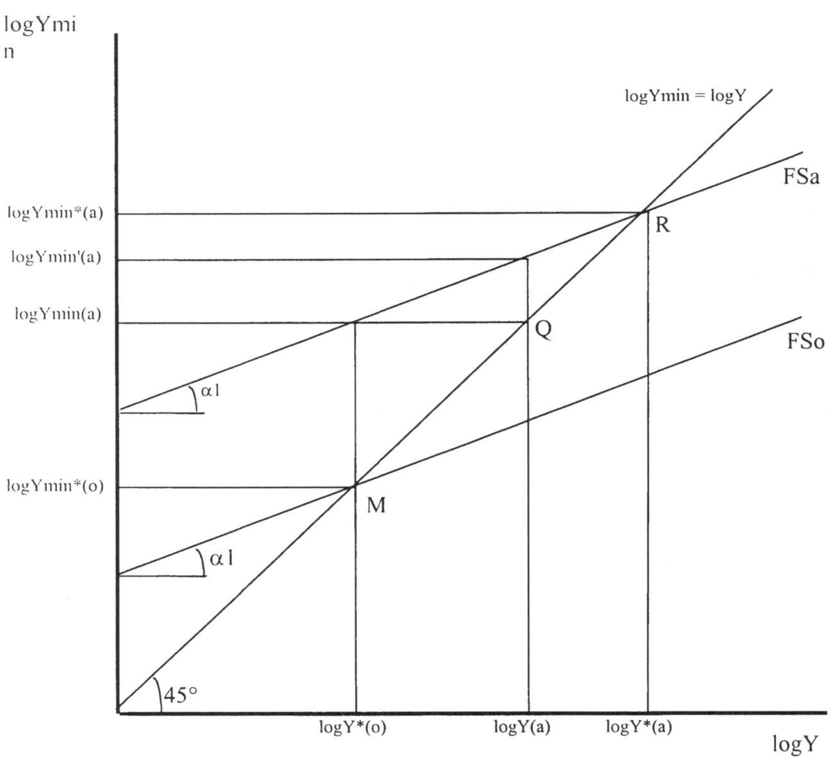

Source: Adapted from Wansbeek and Kapteyn (1983).

Consider an individual who is at point M with family size FS_o, and actual household income and minimum income both equal to the poverty line for that family size, Y*min(o). Now, suppose that family size increases to FS_a, with household income unchanged. Minimum income will immediately increase to Ymin(a). The difference logYmin(a) - logY*min(o) is equal to $\alpha_2(\log FS_a - \log FS_o)$. In that situation she clearly cannot make ends meet. Suppose that actual household income is increased to logYmin(a). At first, the individual will feel satisfied, but after a while she will find that she has misperceived the minimum income level, and that it is in fact equal to Y'min(a). This process will continue until she reaches point R, where both actual household income and minimum income are equal to the poverty line for family size FS_a, Y*min(a). The steeper the slope of the regression lines, i.e. the larger α_1, the greater the effect of this adaptation process.

Another formulation may clarify matters further. Suppose that subjective welfare, W, is equal to the log of the ratio of actual household income to minimum income, i.e.:

$$W = \log(Y/Y\min) = \log Y - \log Y\min \tag{4.4}$$

Substituting the right-hand side of (4.1) for logYmin, we obtain:

$$W = -\alpha_0 + (1 - \alpha_1)\log Y - \alpha_2 \log FS + \varepsilon \tag{4.5}$$

To obtain the equivalence factor for family size FS_a, relative to reference family size FS_o, we must determine the income ratio Y_a/Y_o, where families of both sizes attain the same subjective welfare level W*. Thus there must hold (dropping ε):

$$-\alpha_0 + (1-\alpha_1) \log Y_a - \alpha_2 \log FS_a = W^* = -\alpha_0 + (1-\alpha_1)\log Y_o - \alpha_2 \log FS_o$$

The solution to this equation is:

$$Y_a/Y_o = (FS_a/FS_o)^{\alpha_2/(1-\alpha_1)} \tag{4.6}$$

This is of course equal to result (4.3) obtained earlier.

The Leyden Poverty Line (LPL)

The Leyden Poverty Line is derived from the answers to the Income Evaluation Question (IEQ), which reads as follows (Hagenaars, 1985: 44):

> "Please try to indicate what you consider to be an appropriate amount of money for each of the following cases. Under my (our) conditions I would call an after-tax income per week/month/year (please encircle the appropriate period) of:
>
> about ... very bad
> about ... bad
> about ... insufficient
> about ... sufficient
> about ... good
> about ... very good."

There has been experimentation with different versions of the IEQ, especially with the labels used to describe the amounts, but the formulation quoted here seems the one that is most widely used.

Now, the amounts stated in response to each of these labels could be used to calculate income thresholds in the same way as is done with the answers to the Minimum Income Question (e.g. Van Praag and Van der Sar, 1988). But in the "Leyden" approach, the answers are used to estimate individual Welfare Functions of Income (WFIs), which, it is claimed, are cardinal and interpersonally comparable measures of welfare (Van Praag, 1993).

A WFI is a function that describes the relationship between welfare or utility and income for a particular individual. Figure 4.3 shows how they are estimated. In the first place, it is assumed that the six verbal qualifications "very bad" to "very good" correspond to the midpoints of six equal intervals, into which the finite welfare scale is divided. If welfare is assumed to run from zero to one, the boundaries of the intervals are 1/6, 2/6, ...5/6, and the midpoints 1/12, 3/12, and so on, as shown in figure 4.3. This is called the equal quantile assumption, and it can be shown that it is reasonable when it is assumed that respondents try to maximize the information value of their answers (Van Praag, 1971: 342-344). In chapter 6 we will look more closely at the validity of the equal quantile assumption.

Figure 4.3
Welfare functions of income (WFIs) of three individuals

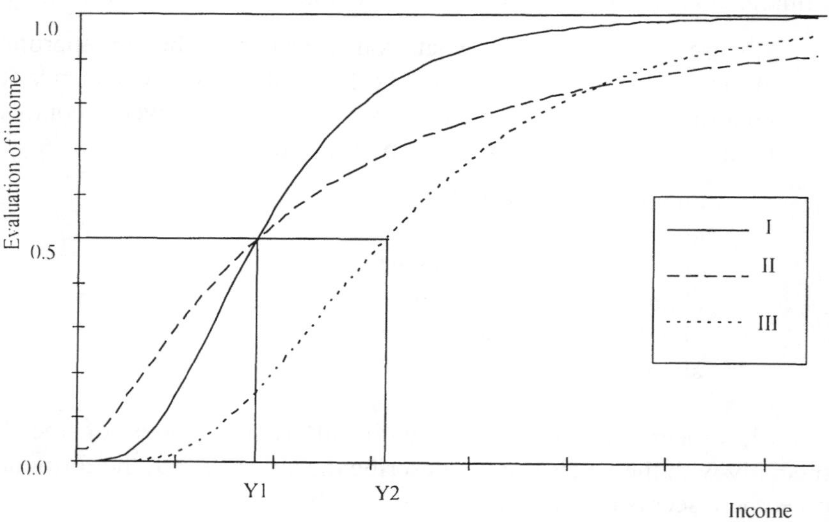

Source: Wansbeek and Kapteyn (1983).

We can now plot the answers of a respondent in figure 4.3, as has been done for respondents I, II and III. If we choose a certain functional form for the relation between income and welfare, we can draw a smooth curve through the six points, which would represent the WFI. According to theories developed by Van Praag (1968) and Kapteyn (1977), the WFI should follow the lognormal cumulative distribution function. Empirically, it has been found that this function fits the data quite well (Van Herwaarden and Kapteyn, 1981). The lognormal cumulative distribution function is completely described by two parameters: μ, a location parameter, and σ, a dispersion parameter. These parameters may differ across households. The higher μ, the more the WFI is shifted to the right. The quantity exp(μ) is the income that is evaluated by 0.5, i.e. exactly in the middle of the welfare scale. Thus, individuals I and II evaluate income Y, by 0.5; individual III needs almost two times as much income to reach the same welfare level. Parameter μ can therefore be interpreted as an indicator of the (subjective) needs of a household in terms of monetary income (Hagenaars, 1985: 49).

Parameter σ affects the slope of the WFI. For instance, the WFI of individual II has the same μ as I's WFI, but a higher value for σ. If σ is higher, income has to change more to go from one welfare level to another, for a given μ. The quantity σ is called the welfare sensitivity of income (Hagenaars, 1985: 49). The slope is also influenced by μ, however. For instance, the WFI of individual III appears to be more flat than that of I, but it has approximately the same value for σ. However, if log-income had been put onto the horizontal axis, so that the WFI would follow cumulative normal distribution curves, the WFI's of I and III would run more or less parallel to each other.

The parameters μ and σ can be estimated if at least three amounts have been given in response to the Income Evaluation Question. The equal quantile assumption and the assumption that the WFI follows a lognormal distribution curve imply together that the logs of the income amounts, corresponding to the descriptions "very bad" to "very good", are a linear function of the 1/12, 3/12, 5/12, 7/12, 9/12 and 11/12 quantiles of the standard normal distribution (which has mean 0 and variance 1). These quantiles are approximately: -1.38, -0.67, -0.21, 0.21, 0.67 and 1.38, respectively. (The pth quantile is the value, below which a proportion p of the total distribution lies.) Therefore, calling these quantiles q_n and the stated income amounts A_n (n running from 1 to 6), we can obtain estimates of μ and σ for each respondent by estimating the following regression equation for each respondent separately:

$$\log(A_n) = \mu + \sigma q_n + \varepsilon_n, \tag{4.7}$$

where ε_n is a disturbance term with the usual properties. (For a more formal description of the procedure, see Hagenaars, 1985: 48.) An alternative method to estimate μ (if all six amounts have been given) is to calculate simply the average of the logs of the six income amounts. This estimate is equal to the one obtained by applying (4.7). Similarly, the standard deviation of the log-amounts is an estimate of σ. It is identical to the estimate derived from (4.7) only if the log-normality assumption is exactly true (Van Praag, 1991).

It may be useful to note that, although the concepts of the log-normal distribution function, and the parameters μ and σ have been borrowed from statistical theory, only their mathematical properties are used in the context of the WFI, and they have no statistical interpretation.

The values of μ and σ vary across households. A simple equation explaining differences in μ is the following one:

$$\mu = \beta_0 + \beta_1 \log(Y) + \beta_2 \log(FS) + \varepsilon \tag{4.8}$$

where Y and FS represent household income and household size, respectively. Parameter β_1 is often called the 'preference drift', as it reflects the tendency that subjectively felt needs or preferences, drift upward with increasing income (Hagenaars, 1985: 50). Equation (4.8) is clearly analogous to (4.1), and income thresholds by family size are determined in a similar way:

$$\log Y^{*}_{0\,5} = \beta_0 / (1-\beta_1) + [\beta_2 / (1-\beta_1)] \log FS_0 \tag{4.9}$$

where Y^{*}_{05} is the income threshold corresponding to welfare level 0.5 for family size FS_0. Similarly, the equivalence scale elasticity with respect to family size is $\beta_2/(1-\beta_1)$. The interpretation of the income threshold log $Y^{*}_{0\,5}$ is also similar. Figure 4.1 applies here also, with μ replacing logYmin. The line A-B now represents the relation between log-income and μ. The positive slope of this line (proportional to β_1) implies that μ will change after a change in income. This means that an individual's WFI will shift up or down when his or her income increases or decreases. One may therefore distinguish between the *ex-ante* or *virtual* WFI (which is the WFI that is described by the answers to the IEQ), and the *ex-post* or *true* WFI, where the "preference drift" has been taken into account (Van Praag, 1991). The latter describes the welfare evaluation of an individual for his or her own current income, when he or she has had sufficient time to adapt to the new income situation. The income threshold $Y^{*}_{0\,5}$ lies where respondents evaluate their own income by 0.5.

In contrast to the SPL method, the LPL-methodology makes it possible to estimate income thresholds corresponding to any welfare level. This is done in the following way (Hagenaars, 1985: 51). First, choose a welfare level, say δ. Now, we have to find an income level Y_δ for which it is true that the welfare evaluation is equal to δ. As it is assumed that the WFI of a particular individual i is characterized mathematically as a log-normal cumulative distribution function with parameters μ_i and σ_i, this income level is the solution to:

$$\delta = CLD(Y_{\delta,i}, \mu_i, \sigma_i) = CND(\log Y_{\delta,i}, \mu_i, \sigma_i)$$

where CLD is the cumulative log-normal distribution function, and CND the cumulative normal distribution function. This is equivalent to:

$$(\log Y_{\delta,i} - \mu_i) / \sigma_i = CND^{-1}(\delta; 0,1) = q_\delta$$

where q_δ is defined as the δth quantile of the standard normal distribution. Substituting (4.8) for μ_i, and rearranging, we obtain:

$$\log Y_{\delta,i} = \beta_0 + \beta_1 \log Y_i + \beta_2 \log FS_i + \bar{\sigma}\, q_\delta. \tag{4.10}$$

Parameter σ_i has been replaced by a constant $\bar{\sigma}$, because σ_i (the welfare sensitivity parameter) appears not to be correlated with background characteristics, though its average value does vary considerably across countries (Van Praag, 1991: 83; Hagenaars, 1985: 228). Now, analogously to the SPL-procedure, the income threshold is defined as the income level where respondents evaluate their own income with δ, which means that $\log Y_{\delta,i} = \log Y_i$. Imposing this condition on (4.10), the income threshold is found by solving for $Y_{\delta,i}$:

$$\log Y^*_\delta = (\beta_0 + \beta_2 \log F_\delta + \bar{\sigma}\, q_\delta) / (1 - \beta_1) \tag{4.11}$$

Equation (4.10) describes lines that run parallel to line A-B in figure (4.1), when μ has been substituted for log Ymin. The distances between the lines are determined by parameter σ. The income thresholds Y^*_δ are located at the intersection of these lines with the 45°-degree line.

Whether the income thresholds corresponding to certain welfare levels can be regarded as poverty lines is a matter of judgment. The developers of the LPL have usually assigned this task to politicians (e.g. Van Praag, Goedhart, Kapteyn, 1980). To my knowledge, no politician has yet given an opinion regarding which minimum welfare level he or she finds acceptable, in terms of a point on a zero-one continuum. In practice, income thresholds corresponding to welfare levels 0.4, 0.45, or 0.5 have been used as poverty lines (Van Praag, Hagenaars, Van Weeren, 1982, among others).

How does the SPL relate to the LPL? An obvious possibility is that the description "absolute minimum income to make ends meet" corresponds to a particular point on the zero-one scale of welfare. If that point would be the same for all respondents, Ymin occupies a fixed position on all WFIs.

A somewhat less restrictive assumption is that the welfare value (the position on the WFI) of Ymin varies from respondent to respondent, but that this variation is not systematically correlated with background characteristics such as household income and household size. This would imply that $\alpha_1 = ß_1$ and $\alpha_2 = ß_2$ (Van Praag, Goedhart, Kapteyn, 1980). The SPL would in that case be equal to the LPL income threshold corresponding to the average welfare evaluation of Ymin. If $\alpha_1 <> ß_1$ or $\alpha_2 <> ß_2$, than the SPL poverty lines would not represent a constant welfare level across households of different sizes. Which of these possibilities is closest to the truth is an empirical matter, which will be looked at below.

This concludes the discussion of the basic LPL-methodology. The method and its assumptions will be critically reviewed in chapter 6. First, I will review the empirical results obtained, as well as a number of extensions and methodological refinements to the basic methodology of both the SPL and the LPL.

3 Main results: a review

Results on household size and household income

In table 4.A1 I have summarized the main results of a large number of studies using the income evaluation method. I focus here on the regression coefficients for household income and household size; in the next subsection the resulting equivalence scales or factors will be discussed. The effects of other variables will be reviewed in section 4.4. The list of studies is not exhaustive. Where several studies have used the same data and identical or virtually identical models, I have presented results only for what I believe to be the best study. The unlisted studies are mentioned in the footnotes, where applicable. Secondly, results from some studies where the focus is almost exclusively on a methodological or theoretical issue are not shown. Examples are Tummers (1991, 1994) and Van der Sar et al. (1988). Thirdly, I may have overlooked some studies. On the other hand, I considered it useful to present results of applications of several model specifications to the same data (e.g., Muffels et al., 1990; Van Praag and Flik, 1992). This enables the reader to gauge the impact of various alternative specifications of the relevant equations on the estimates of regression coefficients and equivalence factors. (Below, I will refer to the results reported in table 4.A1 by the number and letter shown in the first column.)

Let us first look at the regression coefficient of log-income, which is an estimate of the so-called preference effect. Excluding a few studies which for various reasons are not quite comparable to the other ones (20k, 20l, 23), the estimates range from a low of 0.25 (17d) to a high of 0.71 (22a). The average value is 0.45, the median value is 0.43. Since this coefficient can be interpreted as elasticities, an estimate of 0.45 means that if income increases by 10 percent, the answers to the MIQ and the IEQ will rise by 4.5 percent, on average. Although there is a certain plateau in the range 0.35 to 0.48, the estimates are fairly evenly distributed over the entire range; the interquartile range is 0.36-0.53. Perhaps surprisingly, no patterns readily emerge from this variation. In studies where answers to the IEQ and the MIQ have both been used, the log-income coefficients in the μ and the logYmin equations are very close together (8a-b, 12a-b, 20a-c, 20b-d, 20e-g, 20f-h, 20i-j, 20k-l; the only exception is 22a-b). Within the only country for which there are a number of independent estimates, which is The Netherlands, the estimates vary from 0.35 to 0.71. Some consistency can also be discerned: in (24) the Italian estimate is lower than that for France and Belgium; the same result is reported in (7) and (10) using independent samples.

Whether or not a lot of other variables are included in the equation, does not seem to make much difference for the estimates of the preference effect; compare, for instance, the estimates in (10) with the estimates in (7), which are based on the same data; or (25) and (26). From the results of (20), who give estimates for a number of different specifications, it appears that taking account of the ages of children, reference groups and selectivity bias has the effect of reducing the coefficient estimate for log-income by at most 0.10. More detailed results in Muffels, Kapteyn et al. (1990: 145-157), which are not reported in table 4.A1, show that most of this effect is due to the correction for selectivity bias. The inclusion of reference groups has almost no impact. (The results from the dynamic equations are not comparable to those from the static ones, see section 4.5.)

There appears to be less variation across studies in the coefficient for log-household size. Excluding equations where there is a significant and substantial interaction effect (15a, 20f, 20h), the estimates range from 0.05 in The Netherlands (20c) to 0.32 in Ireland (18). The average value is 0.17, the median 0.16. Two-thirds of all estimates are in the range 0.10-0.20. Where the ages of children are taken into account by using a cubic spline, the estimates are relatively large: compare (20a) and (20b), or (20c) and (20d). This is to be expected, as in these equations the number of household members is replaced by the number of equivalent adults, i.e., children count for only a proportion of adults. In studies where both the IEQ and the MIQ have been used, the estimate for the logYmin equation generally appears to be slightly larger than that for the μ equation, but the difference is quite small.

Across studies, there is a clear tendency that where the coefficient for household size is relatively large, the coefficient for household income is relatively small and vice versa. The correlation between the two series (where there is an estimate for both, N = 52), is in fact equal to -0.63. The reason for this is at least in part of a technical nature: because household income and household size are strongly correlated in most countries, the estimates of their coefficients in the μ and logYmin equations will be inversely correlated. That is, across samples from the same population, one will be relatively high, where the other is relatively low, and vice versa.

The R-square coefficient is an index of the success of the regression equation in explaining the variation in μ or logYmin across respondents. It varies between 0.25 (26a) and 0.83 (7b); however, about two-thirds of all R-square estimates are in the range 0.50 to 0.70. The average value is 0.55. In general R-square estimates seem to be high where the coefficient for household income is also high, and vice versa. The correlation between these two series of figures is 0.56. Studies where a number of additional variables are entered in the equations do not seem particularly more successful than others in terms of R-square: compare (10) and (7), which have used the same database, and also (16), (21) and (25). In statistical terms, household income is clearly the most important determinant of the answers to income evaluation questions.

Equivalence scale estimates

As explained in section 4.2, the estimates of the effects of household income and household size can be used to calculate equivalence scales. I use three statistics to describe the equivalence scales that result from the reported estimates. The first is the elasticity of the equivalence factors with respect to household size. When the specification has used log (household size) to represent household type, the equivalence factors can be exactly reproduced from the reported equivalence scale elasticity. Otherwise, in particular when household type dummies were used, the elasticity is an approximate indicator of the steepness of the equivalence scale. Where the ages of children have been taken into account, the elasticity has been calculated with respect to the number of (equivalent) adults; this is likely to result in a higher value than the elasticity with respect to the number of household members. The household size elasticities range from 0.09 (20c) to 0.48 (17b); however, almost 90 percent is contained in the range 0.15 to 0.40, within which they are fairly evenly distributed. The mean, as well as the median value is 0.29. This median is higher, and also the range is wider than those reported by Buhmann et al. (1988).

The equivalence factor of single persons with respect to two-adult households (=100) is a second characteristic of the equivalence scale. In studies where the age of the head of household is taken into account, both households are assumed to be within the same age bracket (where relevant: age 40) for the calculation of the equivalence factor. Those equivalence factors seem relatively higher, compared with specifications where no account is taken of the age of the head of household. (Compare 24a and 24b, 24d and 24e, 24g and 24h.) This is as expected, because a large proportion of single persons are elderly people, whose subjective income needs appear to be smaller than those of non-elderly persons (see below). The single person factors range from 72 (17) to 94 (20c). Within this range, the distribution is almost rectangular; the mean value is 82, the median value is 81.

The equivalence factor of a couple with three children with respect to a two-adult household is a third characteristic of the equivalence scale, that is reported in table 4.A1. Where no account is taken of the ages of children, the figure reported is simply the equivalence factor of five-member households with respect to two-member households. However, because in most countries the large majority of five-person households will in fact be couples with three children, this is unlikely to make much difference. The equivalence factors range from 103 (10c) to 155 (17b); but 80 percent of all factors are contained within the range 110 to 140; the mean value as well as the median value is 128. Particularly low equivalence factors are found in (10), where a dummy household type specification is used. Examination of the more detailed results in the source (Hagenaars, 1985: 241: 246) reveals that the equivalence factors for two adult households with zero to five children follow rather peculiar patterns in a number of countries. In some countries, children seem to carry virtually no cost (The Netherlands, UK) in others only fifth and higher ranking children appear to have an important effect on household costs (Belgium, Denmark, France). These patterns are not necessarily the result of a dummy specification for household type; other studies using it (21, 24) obtain much more plausible results. An advantage (or, perhaps, disadvantage) of the log(household size) specification is, of course, that such jumps in the equivalence scale are smoothed away.

Otherwise, it is hard to discern any patterns in the equivalence scale elasticities and factors. It is sometimes suggested (e.g. Van Praag and Flik, 1992: 72) that equivalence scales tend to be steeper in 'poorer' countries. And indeed, children appear to be relatively expensive in Ireland (7f, 10f, 18), which is probably the poorest country among those listed in table 4.A1. Another interpretation, suggested by Van Praag and Flik (1992: 37), has to do with the contraceptive behavior of couples. If couples can freely choose whether or not to have children, there is no reason why a couple with two children would feel worse off than a childless couple, providing they have the same income. Application of the income evaluation method can be expected to yield flat equivalence scales in that situation. On the other hand, if the number of children is not completely a matter of free choice, they are more likely to be perceived as a burden. Thus, in countries where contraceptives are not widely available, the subjective equivalence scales are likely to be steeper.

However, a problem for both interpretations is that the largest equivalence factors for couples with three children are found in Denmark (17b) and Sweden (26b). Both countries are not notably poor or sexually repressive. The Danish result might be dismissed as being due to bad data (see below footnote 2); also, using the same database, much lower equivalence factors for Denmark are found in other studies (7b, 10b). These qualifications do not apply to the Swedish result, though.

LPL thresholds

In table 4.A2 an overview is given of the Leyden Poverty Lines and the Subjective Poverty Lines, where these have been calculated in the studies shown in table 4.A1. As indicator of the level of the poverty lines, I use the amount for a two-adult household. Where poverty lines are differentiated according to age, it is assumed that both adults are non-elderly. The equivalence factors shown in table 4.A1 enable one to calculate poverty thresholds for other household types; the household size elasticity of the poverty lines has been included as a rough indicator of how the income thresholds vary across family types. In order to make it possible to compare the amounts across studies and across countries, I have also expressed the amounts as a percentage of median household income in the sample, whenever the latter figure could be found in the study, or, in some cases, elsewhere. Alternatively, mean household income has sometimes been used when no data about median income were available. (When comparing these percentages across studies, I have assumed that the mean is 15 percent above the median. This is clearly arbitrary, but the assumption does not affect the conclusions drawn.)

As explained in section 4.2, the LPL-methodology enables the researcher to define income thresholds for any chosen welfare level. In practice, only two levels appear to have been used: 0.5, the level corresponding to μ, and 0.4. Starting with the LPL-0.5, it is clear that its level varies considerably across countries, and also across studies within a single country. As a percentage of median income, the two-adult income thresholds range from 42 percent to 94 percent. The lowest value is an estimate for Wisconsin by Colasanto et al. (1984) (8b in table), who remark that it is below the official American poverty line. Both extreme values are outliers; 17 out of 22 estimates are in the range of 56 percent to 81 percent of median income. Average and median values are 68 percent and 69.5 percent, respectively. Looking across the table, it is difficult to discern any pattern in this variation. Relatively high LPL-0.5 thresholds are found both in poor (5f) and in rich countries (7b, 7c). The same is true for relatively low thresholds (7g, 19a vs. 7d, 8b).

Apparently mainly as a result of the variation in the level of the LPL-0.5, the proportion of households with incomes below this threshold also varies enormously. It ranges from 6 percent (10d) to 43 percent (7c); the average is 24 percent; the median percentage is 48.5 percent. If we exclude outliers, we find that about two-thirds of the proportions in poverty are in the range 16 percent to 38 percent, which is still rather wide. Of course, this is in itself not particularly worrying, but, again, it is hard to make sense of this variation. Very high proportions of households below the LPL-0.5 thresholds are registered in Ireland, (7f, 10f), but also in France (7c, 10c), Denmark (7b, 10b) and The Netherlands (20j). On the other hand, fairly low proportions are found in Germany (7d, 10d). These results are rather out of line of the results obtained in comparative poverty research using relative poverty lines for the same period and the same countries (e.g., O'Higgins and Jenkins, 1990), and also in themselves do not seem very plausible. Van Praag, Hagenaars and Van Weeren (1982: 357) remark in this context: "The resulting poverty ratios hence do not merely reflect income differences but differences in aspiration levels between countries as well."

Strange things are also discovered when we look at the evolution of poverty over time in some countries, as implied by the figures reported. For instance, in The Netherlands the following trend is found for the percentage of households below the LPL-0.5: 16 percent in 1979 (7h, 10h); 29 percent in 1985 (20j) and 36 percent in 1986 (20j) (disregarding the estimate of 10 percent for 1983 from (22a), which is not based on microdata). This would seem to indicate an ongoing and accelerating social disaster in The Netherlands, or a very strong rise in aspiration levels. The opposite evolution appears to have occurred in France: 42 percent in poverty in 1979 (10c), dropping to 19 percent in 1989 (24f).

Several of the LPL-0.5 results are clearly implausible, and do not give a realistic picture of the level and evolution of poverty in a country. However, one must be careful not to write off the LPL methodology too quickly. In many cases, small and/or experimental surveys were used. In particular, the data used by Van Praag, Hagenaars and Van Weeren (1980; 1982) and Hagenaars (1985) in a European Community - wide study are of doubtful quality for the purpose of poverty research[2]. This can affect not only the estimated proportions of households below the LPL-thresholds, but also those thresholds themselves.

Among the best data are probably those used by Muffels, Kapteyn, Berghman (1990), which come from a high quality special household income panel (the Socio-Economic Panel, conducted by the Dutch Central Bureau of Statistics). However, even in this case we find that the LPL-0.5 thresholds rise strongly from one year to the next, resulting in a 7-percent-point rise in measured poverty (from 29 percent to 36 percent). There is no apparent explanation for this drastic change; the Dutch economy was quite stable (though stagnating) in the years 1985-86. This result is a rather alarming one for the LPL methodology. Not only were high quality data used, but the fact that they came from a panel study implies that many, if not most of the respondents in the two years were in fact the same individuals. Secondly, the model from which the poverty thresholds were derived is a state-of-the-art one, taking account of a number of factors, including sample selectivity and the actual reference group of respondents (cf. table 4.A1, line 20j). Moreover, parameter stability across the two years was imposed in the estimation of the models (Muffels, Kapteyn, Berghman, 1990: 161-170). A similar finding is reported by Aalbers et al. (1990). Using four years of the SEP, they report, somewhat perversely, that the stability of the LPL (as well as the SPL) is more satisfactory *without* than with a correction for selectivity bias.

Perhaps partly because of the high level of the LPL-0.5 income thresholds, LPL-0.4 lines have also been used fairly often. Unless an interaction term between household income and household size is included in the μ-equation, the LPL-0.4 line has the same equivalence scale as the corresponding LPL-0.5 line, and is always below it. How much the former is below the latter, depends on the average value of the σ parameter in the sample. Among the studies where both thresholds are reported, the level of the LPL-0.4 as a proportion of the LPL-0.5 varies between 76 percent and 86 percent, with mean and median values of 81 percent. Because of this fairly narrow range, the LPL-0.4 moves more or less in tandem with the LPL-0.5 across countries and studies. As a proportion of median household income, the LPL-0.4 thresholds for two adult households varies between 34 percent and 72 percent, with an mean and median value of 53 percent. The proportion of households below the LPL-0.4 also varies greatly: from 3 percent to 27 percent, with an mean value of 12 percent and a median one of 10 percent. The pattern of these proportions across countries replicates that of the LPL-0.5. Some of these results appear rather implausible, but, as suggested above, this may have to do more with the quality of the data than with the validity of the LPL.

SPL thresholds

The SPL has been applied in a larger number of studies than the LPL. We find even more variation in the level of the SPL than in that of the LPL: as a percentage of median income, the range runs from 32 percent (7d) to 88 percent (13l). Although these extreme values are outliers, only two-thirds of all estimates shown are in the range of 42 percent to 77 percent, which is still quite wide. The mean and median value is 59 percent.

The variation in the number of households below the SPL is also quite large: the range is 2 percent (5d) tot 42 percent (Bl); the mean and median proportion is 20 percent. The number of SPL-poor households is highest where one would expect this, given the results of other studies, using relative income thresholds: in countries more or less on the periphery of the EC such as Ireland (18, Bi, j), Catalonia (Bk) and Greece (Bl), and also in Italy and the USA. The lowest proportions are found in W. Germany (5d, Belgium (5a) and The Netherlands (5h, 9, Bc). However, above-average proportions in poverty are also registered in countries where one would not have expected this: Belgium (Ba), Luxembourg (Be) and Sweden (27). Perhaps even more problematically, the evolution implied by the figures is sometimes quite implausible: comparing (5g) and (19b), poverty has increased in Italy between 1979 and 1987 from 9 percent to 33 percent; in Belgium it has risen from 4 percent in 1979 (10a) to 25 percent in 1985 (Ba). Even for the same year and the same country the estimates can vary by as much as 12 percent-points: compare (A) and (20i), both for The Netherlands in 1986. As explained above, poor quality of the data used in some studies, in particular (5), may be to blame for some of these peculiar results. The data used in (A) are from the official household budget survey; the rather low SPL in this study may be the result of selective non-repines: perhaps only households who manage their budgets well, and therefore have smaller income needs, participate in budget surveys. However, even where data from household income panels of high quality are used, the level of the poverty line, and the number of households below it, can vary quite strongly from one year to the next: (Ba-b), (Bc-d), (Be-f). Finally, even the specification that is applied can make a considerable difference: (Bc-d) and (20i) are based on the same data, but the model in (20i) is a much more sophisticated one, resulting (for 1985) in a SPL that is about 20 percent higher, and an estimate of the number in poverty that is 8 percent-points higher. Similarly, SPL-poverty in Sweden appears to be much higher according to (27) than to (26b), even though both studies use the same data-set. The main differences are that the regression specification used to derive poverty lines in (27) is linear, instead of log-linear, and takes account of age and region.

How does the level of the SPL compare with that of the LPL? We have seen that as a percentage of median income, the average SPL for a two adult household is equal to 59 percent, while the corresponding figures for the LPL-0.4 and LPL-0.5 are 53 percent and 68 percent, respectively. But, these are averages across different sets of studies, and therefore not quite comparable. In figure 4.4 the level of the SPL and that of the LPL-0.4 and/or the LPL-0.5 is shown graphically for those studies where both are reported[3]. It is immediately clear that in most cases, the SPL is below or at about the same level as the LPL-0.4. There are two exceptions: (19) and (22). In the latter, the SPL lies on the same level as the LPL-0.5; in the former, the SPL considerably exceeds the LPL-0.5. The reasons for these exceptions are obscure. The wording of the MIQ in (19) was fairly restrictive; it contained the words "absolute minimum" (Moriani, 1990:

140). Another study did not find the same result for the country involved, viz. Italy (7g).

Van Praag, Hagenaars and Van Weeren (1982: 358) conclude, on the basis of the results in (7), that the welfare evaluations of the poverty lines based on the MIQ differ considerably over countries. That is, from the LPL-results one can deduce that the average respondent within different countries would give different evaluations, in terms of the IEQ, of the income level corresponding to the SPL. This appears to be an empirical fact. However, Van Praag and Flik (1992: 24) go further and draw a conclusion regarding the comparability of the SPL across countries. After noting that the basic assumption of the SPL is that the verbal label 'making ends meet' is always similarly understood in different populations, they state, referring to the finding just mentioned, that "there are indications that this assumption is not justified so the SPL is not a proper measure to use when populations are compared".

Figure 4.4
LPL0.4, LPL0.5 and SPL income thresholds, as a percent of median income in sample, according to a number of studies (cf. table 4.A2)

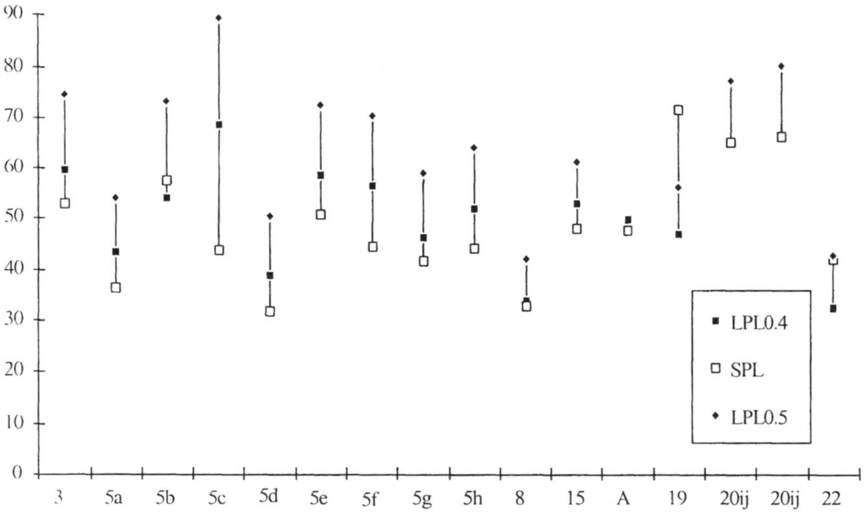

The assumption implicit in Van Praag and Flik's (1992) argument is, of course, that the labels 'bad', 'sufficient', 'good' and so on, do have the same meaning in all countries. The same assumption also lies behind Van Praag, Hagenaars and Van Weeren's (1980: 5.5) assertion that the LPL thresholds constitute international equivalent poverty lines, in contrast to the thresholds derived from answers to the MIQ. They formulate one qualification, though: "We remind explicitly that international equivalent poverty lines cannot be interpreted as *materially* equivalent but only as *welfare* equivalent where welfare is meant to be the subjective welfare concept." (Van Praag, Hagenaars and Van Weeren, 1980: 5.5; emphasis in original). In the Leyden approach the subjective welfare concept is more or less defined by the IEQ method, so this statement almost amounts to a declaration that the LPL-thresholds are comparable or equivalent by definition. The issue of cross-national comparability is, of course, strongly linked to the question whether the answers to the IEQ provide a cardinal interpersonally comparable measure of welfare. This question will be considered in chapter 6.

In the meantime, let me note another finding of Van Praag, Hagenaars and Van Weeren (1980: 5.5), that is relevant here. In the surveys used in this study, the following question was asked (right after the IEQ and MIQ): "And what would your net household income have to become before you would consider yourself to be *really poor*"? (Van Praag, Hagenaars and Van Weeren, 1980, Appendix A: 10; emphasis in original). It turns out that, just as for the MIQ, the expression 'really poor' is associated with different welfare levels in different countries; across countries, the average implicit welfare evaluation of the income below which one would feel 'really poor' varies from 0.12 to 0.24.

Summary of findings

In this section I have reviewed a large number of studies which report estimates of the effects of household income and household size on subjective income evaluations. The resulting equivalence scales and income thresholds were also discussed. Most of these studies have been conducted in Western European countries, in particular in the Netherlands. There are also some results for Australia, Canada and the USA.

The most important determinant of subjective income evaluations is clearly household income. The median estimate of the elasticity of μ and Ymin with respect to household income is 0.43[4]. However, different studies produce different estimates; the total range is 0.25 to 0.71. Little pattern can be discerned in this variation, except that within the same sample, the income elasticities of μ and Ymin are always quite close.

The influence of household size is much smaller; the median elasticity is 0.16, the highest estimate is 0.32. As a result of these low values, the *equivalence scales* derived from subjective evaluations tend to be rather flat. The median elasticity of subjective equivalence scales with respect to household size is 0.24; the median equivalence factor of single persons relative to two-person families is 0.81, that of couples with three children is 1.28. Although some estimates for the latter factor are as high as 1.55, others are as low as 1.03. It is unclear what determines the differences in equivalence scale estimates across studies. Rather flat equivalence scales are measured in the Netherlands; fairly steep ones are found in Southern European countries and in Ireland, but also in Denmark and Sweden.

Using the estimate parameters in a μ equation, LPL (Leyden Poverty Line) *income thresholds* can be calculated for any welfare level. In practice, only two levels haven been used, 0.5 and 0.4 (on a scale which runs from 0 to 1). Generally, the LPL0.5 threshold for a two-adult household is somewhat above half of median household income in the sample. Most LPL0.5 thresholds are in the range of 56 to 81 percent of the sample median income. The LPL0.4 thresholds are mostly about 20 percent lower than the LPL0.5.

Mainly as a result of the variation in the level of the thresholds relative to the median, *the proportion of households with an income below the LPL0.5 and LPL0.4* varies enormously. The mean proportion of households below the LPL0.5 across the studies reviewed here is 24 percent, but the range goes from 6 to 43 percent. High percentages (over 30 percent) are found for countries where average income is relatively low and/or inequality is high, but also for some countries characterized by relatively high income levels and low inequality. Percentages of households below the LPL0.4 threshold are less elevated (the mean is 12 percent), but display the same kind of variation. Van Praag et al. (1982) remark in this context that these percentages do not merely reflect income differences, but also differences in aspiration levels. What lies behind these differences in aspiration levels remains unclear, however.

The SPL (Subjective Poverty Line) can be calculated on the basis of results for the logYmin equation. Across the studies reviewed, the average SPL threshold for two adults is situated at 59 percent of median income. Where a comparison is possible, it is found that, with a few exceptions, the

SPL is about equal to or somewhat below the LPL0.4. The proportion of households below the SPL ranges from 2 percent to 42 percent, with an average value of 20 percent. As is true regarding the LPL, relatively high proportions of households below the SPL are found in countries for which other studies, using non-subjective poverty measures, come up with low poverty rates.

Strong variation is also found in the proportions of households below the SPL and the LPL for different years *within the same country*. The trends that are discovered are often quite implausible, and do not agree with the results of studies using non-subjective poverty measures. Some of these peculiar findings may be due to bad data. However, even when high quality panel data, and state-of-the-art models are used, the proportion of households below the LPL thresholds can shift by as much as 7 percent-points in the course of a single year, without there being an explanation for such a large change.

4 The effects of other variables: a review

Incorporation of additional variables

A number of studies have extended the basic models (4.1) and (4.8) by adding further explanatory variables. In particular Hagenaars (1985) and De Vos and Garner (1991) have included a large number of variables in their models, including age, sex, education, professional status and disability status of the head of household, the number of earners, fluctuations in income and region. The purpose of this section is to review the findings of these studies. Before embarking on the detailed review, some general remarks about the incorporation of additional variables are made.

It is not very difficult to estimate the effects of various variables on μ and logYmin. However the interpretation of these effects is not always straightforward. Variables can influence the command over resources, or they can have reference effects (Hagenaars, 1985: 86). The first kind of variables reflect cost differences between households; the prime example is family size. Reference variables affect the aspiration level of persons; e.g. the standard of living of relatives and friends probably exerts an important reference effect. In many cases, however, a variable can have both cost effects and reference effects. For instance, differences in μ or logYmin between regions (controlling for other factors) can be the result of differences in price levels, or of the fact that some regions have a higher average standard of living than other regions. Attempts to model and estimate the effects of the social reference group on the evaluation of income, will be discussed below.

A difficult question is whether and how the effects of these additional variables should be incorporated into the poverty lines. In the first place one must decide whether the poverty lines should reflect the reference effects. This will depend on the underlying concept of poverty. If poverty is defined as a situation of low welfare, and welfare is regarded as a subjective state of mind, there is no reason why the poverty lines should not incorporate reference effects, i.e. they could be higher for (groups of) persons with higher aspiration levels. In this case, poverty lines should be differentiated by every characteristic that is found to have an effect on μ or logYmin. This approach has been adopted in Van Praag, Hagenaars and Van Weeren (1982). In the extreme, and assuming that there is no measurement error, each household would have its own poverty line, derived from its own WFI or from its own answer to the minimum income question.

On the other hand, if a concept of poverty is adopted that refers to the material standard of living of households, and not to subjective feelings of well-being, poverty lines for various household types should only reflect differences in the costs of reaching a certain minimum standard of living. This requirement is not easy to satisfy, because the social reference group is difficult to observe. Below we will look at a specific attempt to operationalize the "reference process". But if the operationalization is not perfect, there is the risk that variables that in themselves represent only costs differences are collinear with unobserved reference variables. In that case, the estimates of the differences in costs between different household types are of course distorted.

In this context, it may be interesting to consider in what way estimated poverty lines are distorted if we would omit relevant variables from the logYmin or μ equations. Suppose that the true model is:

$$\log Y\min = \alpha_0 + \alpha_1 \log Y + \alpha_2 \log FS + \alpha_3 Z + \varepsilon_2.$$

Moreover, suppose that an auxiliary regression of Z on logY and log FS yields:

$$Z = d_0 + d_1 \log Y + d_2 \log FS + e_3.$$

If Z would be unobserved and we would estimate the following regression equation:

$$\log Ymin = a_0 + a_1 \log Y + a_2 \log FS + e_2,$$

then the expected values of the estimates a_0, a_1 and a_2 are:

$$E(a_0) = \alpha_0 + d_0\alpha_3$$
$$E(a_1) = \alpha_1 + d_1\alpha_3$$
$$E(a_2) = \alpha_2 + d_2\alpha_3$$

(cf. Fomby et al., 1988: 404). If the sample size is large, this means that estimated poverty lines based on a_0, a_1 and a_2 are approximately equal to:

$$\log Y^*min = [\alpha_0 + \alpha_2 \log FS + \alpha_3 (d_0 + d_2 \log FS)] / (1 - \alpha_1 - d_1\alpha_3). \quad (4.12)$$

In case $d_1 = 0$, i.e. Z is related only with family size, it is easily shown that for each family size, the estimated poverty line is equal to the average (geometric mean) of the 'true' poverty lines. This would also have resulted if Z would have been taken into account (since in that case the term (d_0 + $d_2$logFS) is equal to the mean of Z across households with family size FS). Thus, if Z can be regarded as a cost-variable, *average* poverty lines by family size are not biased when $d_1 = 0$. In all other cases, where d_1 or d_2 are not equal to zero, the poverty lines are biased.

Age of head of household

A number of studies have looked at the effect of the age of adults on the answers to the MIQ and the IEQ; the results are shown in table 4.A3. With the exception of (2), only the age of the head of household, or the main breadwinner, is taken into account. Two kinds of specifications appear to be popular: one is a series of dummy variables, representing consecutive age brackets; the number of brackets that are distinguished varies between two and seven. The other specification uses the log and the square of the log of the age of the head or the main breadwinner of the household.

The first study to consider the effects of the age of adults (2), found, after controlling for household income and size, that subjective needs rise strongly between the ages of 25 and 50, and after that remain constant.

This rather peculiar result has not been replicated in later studies. In most studies, the estimated coefficients indicate that subjective needs first rise with increasing age, and then decline. The top of the curve varies considerably across countries, however: sometimes it is located around the age of 55 (6a, 6h, 21a, 21b), sometimes around 40 (6b, 10b, 10c, 16, 24f). Not too much should be made of these differences, as standard errors are in all cases relatively large. Also, the results may be influenced by the specification used; compare (6e) and (10i), which are based on the same data. In a few countries, the curves are virtually flat, notably in Ireland (6f, 10f) and in Italy (6g, 10g, 24c). In most cases, the elderly (65+) are the age category with the smallest subjective needs (after controlling for income and household size). The effect is very pronounced in the USA (7) and Canada (16). Exceptions are found, as noted, in Ireland and Italy, as well as in the USA (8a) and Slovenia (23a) and, according to one study (21b), in The Netherlands.

The regression results obtained make it possible to calculate elderly equivalence factors, as shown in the last column of table 4.A3. These indicate how much income a household where the head is elderly needs in order to be as well of as an otherwise similar household where the head is non-elderly. In the present context, being 'as well off' means of course expressing the same evaluation of its income. Where the specification used implies that needs vary across all age categories, the equivalence factor shown refers to households headed by persons aged 70, relative to households headed by persons aged 40. The variation in the elderly equivalence factors appears to be quite large: they range from 57 to 130. Both extreme values are outliers, however; in fact about three-fifths of all estimates are contained in the range from 78 to 98. Average and median values are about 85. Almost all estimates (28 out of 32) indicate that the elderly need less income than non-elderly people living in similar circumstances, to be as well off. A few studies (2, 21b, 23a) indicate that the elderly need more income than the non-elderly. By contrast, two other studies (7, 16) obtain results that indicate that the needs of the elderly are only 60% of the needs of non-elderly.

It must be stressed that the elderly equivalence factors are not estimated with a great deal of precision. Although their standard errors are difficult to determine exactly, they cannot be small, given that the standard errors of the underlying age effects are always rather large. Within the same country and within a period of a few years, the estimates vary considerably: compare 7, 8a, 21a. Even the specification used can have an important effect: compare 6h and 10h. Nevertheless, for most countries the general conclusion appears to be warranted that, when living in similar circumstances as regards household income and household size, elderly people give lower answers to the IEQ and the MIQ, indicating that they need less income to feel as well off.

It is not entirely clear how one should interpret this effect. The important question is whether the age effect reflects cost differences between different age groups, or reference group effects. There may be a number of reasons why the elderly need less income to achieve a particular material standard of living. They have less work-related expenses, and they often possess a mortgage-free home. Also, they may supplement their income by dissaving. On the other hand, they may be burdened by health related expenses. Note that where home tenure and labor market status are included in the equations, the age effects are not eliminated (16, 25).

As a number of authors have noted (e.g. Halleröd, 1995), the curve describing the effect of age on the answers to the IEQ and MIQ is roughly similar to the curve of the level of household income by age. Furthermore, it is noteworthy that according to the results of Hagenaars (1985: 214), measured age-income curves are rather flat precisely in those countries where there is no significant age effect on the answers to the IEQ and the MIQ, viz. Ireland and Italy. This suggests (but it certainly does no more than suggest) that the age effect is partly or wholly a reference effect. That is, when evaluating income amounts, respondents are not only influenced by their own income and household circumstances, but also by the incomes of other people in their age group with whom they associate or with whom they compare themselves. These people are likely to be in the same age bracket as the respondent. Thus, for example, a single elderly person may say that her income of £1200 is 'good', because most persons she knows, who are in the same situation, have smaller incomes. At the same time a single 30-year old person may regard it as only 'sufficient', because many of his former fellow students now earn more. Unfortunately, none of the studies reviewed have explicitly taken account of reference group effects.

Ages of children

The specification of family size that has been used up to this point is, of course, rather primitive. The needs of a household are not only influenced by the number of household members, but also by the characteristics of those members. In particular, we would expect differences in needs between children and adults, and also between younger and older children. Furthermore, the 'economies of scale' (i.e., the phenomenon that the cost per person is smaller, the larger the family, ceteris paribus) may not follow the smooth exponential pattern implied by the term $\beta_2\log(FS)$.

In one of the earliest applications of the subjective method, Kapteyn and Van Praag (1976) took account of both considerations by introducing a rank function and an age function for each individual into the definition of family size. Both the rank function and the age function were specified by lognormal distribution functions. This had the advantage that the model was very flexible, but the disadvantage that the model was nonlinear in the parameters and variables. Surprisingly, the results indicated that the level of (subjective) needs are not influenced by the ages of the children, but only by the ages of the parents. Between the ages of 24 and 48, adults' needs appeared to grow considerably. It is not clear whether this result can be generalized, as the family size specification of Kapteyn and Van Praag (1976) does not seem to have been applied in any other study.

In Kapteyn, Kooreman and Willemse (1988) a more simple specification for family size is introduced. $\text{Log}(FS_n)$ is defined as follows:

$$\log(FS_n) = \Sigma_j \quad w_j\, f(age_{jn}), j = 1..J_n \qquad (4.13)$$

where J_n is the number of household members in family n, w_j is the rank weight of family member j and f( ) is an age function. While the rank weights w_j could be unrestricted, in all applications they have been specified as follows:

$$w_j = \log(j/(j=1))\ j = 2..J,\ w_1 = 1 \qquad (4.14)$$

(The family members are ordered from old to young.) This specification of the rank weights implies that if $f(age_j) = 1$ for all household members, the log of family size, defined according to (4.13), reduces to the log of the number of household members plus one (i.e. $\log(FS_n) = \log(J) + 1$).

The age function is defined as follows:

$$f(age_j) = 1 \text{ if } age_j > 18$$
$$f(age_j) = 1 + \beta_{21}(18\text{-}age_j)^2 + \beta_{22}(18\text{-}age_j)^2(36+age_j) \text{ if } age_j <=18. \qquad (4.15)$$

The age function is a third degree polynomial for children aged 18 or less, with two parameters, β_{21} and $\beta 2_{2}$, that are to be estimated. This form of the age function (a so-called cubic spline) is flexible, and also ensures that it describes a smooth curve at all ages. (As the reader can check, f(18)=1, while the value of its first derivative at 18 is equal to zero.) After the age of 18, needs are assumed not to be influenced by age.

This specification of the age function has been used in several studies, as shown in table 4.A4. The estimates of $\beta_{21}$and β_{22} in themselves do not convey much information, as they are difficult to interpret, and also because they are usually estimated with great imprecision. This is due to the very high multicollinearity between the squared and the cubic term in the age function (4.15). However, the age function itself can usually be estimated with a reasonable degree of precision. (Kapteyn, Kooreman, Muffels et al., 1985: 131). (Because of the high negative covariance between β_{21} and β_{22}, a positive fluctuation in β_{21} is generally compensated by a negative fluctuation in β_{22}, making the age function more stable across samples than β_{21} and β_{22} themselves.) For this reason, I have calculated estimates of the costs of children of various ages, relative to the cost of an adult with the same rank number in the household, using the reported estimates of β_{21} and β_{22}. These are shown in table 4.A4.

The results seem to vary quite considerably depending on the data and the particular specification used. This is unsurprising, given the fact that the confidence interval around the age function is generally rather wide. Even the age function which seems to have been estimated with the greatest precision has a confidence interval varying from about 0.35 at the age of one to about 0.18 at the age of ten (Muffels, Kapteyn et al., 1990: 158, fig. 3.5; results for this age function shown in line 20b-d in table 4.A4.) Keeping this in mind, and disregarding some outlying results, the estimates seem to indicate that the requirements of young children are about half of those of an adult, or perhaps slightly less. Costs seem to rise steadily with the age of children. Some results suggest, however, that babies are more expensive than toddlers.

Interaction of family size and income

The models presented up to this point have the implication that the elasticity of the equivalence scale with respect to household size ($\beta_2/(1-\beta_1)$) is the same for all households regardless of income. This implies that the cost of an additional child as a proportion of income is the same at all income levels. But it is plausible that the cost of an additional child as a fraction of income drops as income increases (although it may rise as an absolute amount). To take this possibility into account, parameter $ß_2$ is replaced by ($ß_{20}$ + β_{23}logY). This creates in effect an interaction term between household size and income. If a static model is used, and the reference group variables are set at a constant C for all households, the expression for the income threshold associated with welfare level δ, $Y^*\delta$ becomes (cf. 4.11):

$$\log(Y^*\delta) = [ß_0 + ß_{20}(1-ß_1)\log(FS) + \sigma q\delta] / [(1-ß_1)(1-\beta_{23}\log(FS))] \qquad (4.16)$$

As can be gathered from examining (4.16), the elasticity of the poverty line, and, thus, the equivalence scale, with respect to household size is no longer a simple expression. Of course, the log(Ymin) equation can be adapted in a similar way (cf. Kapteyn, Kooreman, Willemse, 1988).

Only a limited number of studies, which are exclusively Dutch, have entered such an interaction term in the equations (see table 4.A1: rows 15, 20). In most of these the estimate turns out to be not statistically significant, or very small. In all other cases, the estimates are negative, indicating that at higher income levels the effect of household size is smaller than at lower income levels. One should not be misled by the apparent smallness of the estimates: a value of -0.06 (in 15) implies that when income increases five-fold, the coefficient for household size is more than halved (at realistic income levels). However, in all cases, the standard error of the interaction term estimate is relatively large.

Gender

A few studies have included the gender of the head of household in the equations (7, 8, 16, 21). All of these use the answer to the MIQ as the dependent variable. The results are listed in table 4.1.

The effect of the head of household being female is most often negative. A small positive effect is found only in The Netherlands (21b). The effect of gender can be quite large: according to (7), female headed households need 31% less income than similar male headed households. Unfortunately, the effect of gender is often rather difficult to interpret, because different studies may use different procedures to establish which one of the adults in a household is the head. In (8), and presumably also in

(7), the head of household can only be female, if there are no adult males in the household. In other studies, the respondent in the survey may indicate who is to be regarded as the head of household. If the first rule is used, virtually all female-headed household consist of single adults, and most of them will be elderly widows. In that case, the regression coefficient of gender may reflect age-related effects.

Table 4.1
Reported effect of gender on answers to minimum income questions

	Study	Effect when head of household is female	Remarks
7	Danziger et al. (1984)	-0.25	
8	Colasanto et al. (1984)	not significant	
16	Poulin (1988)	-0.10	
21a	De Vos and Garner (1991)	USA: -.08 USA: not significant	(never married females) (other females)
21b		Netherlands: +0.03	

Home tenure and housing cost

The possible influence of home tenure or housing costs on the answers to the IEQ and the MIQ is considered in four studies (13, 16, 25 and 27). Saunders and Matheson (1993: 11) (25) find that, compared to persons who own their home outright, both mortgagees and private renters say that they need more income to make ends meet. They interpret the fact that the coefficient for mortgagees (0.11) exceeds that for private renters (0.08) as reflecting the high level of interest rates in existence at the time of the survey. Poulin (1988: 45) (16) reports that owners with a mortgage give answers to the MIQ that are, on average, about 6% higher than those of non-mortgaged owners. Surprisingly, she also finds that the average answer of renters is about 2% *lower* than that of outright owners. No explanation is given for this finding. Halleröd (1995: 9) (27) has included housing costs as an amount in the equation for Ymin, using a linear specification. The estimated coefficient is 0.86, implying that for every 100 Swedish Krona added to housing costs, the answer to the MIQ rises by 86 Krona.

In Homan, Hagenaars and Van Praag (1986: 27-28, 91, 103-105) (13), a more complex specification is used. They estimate the relation between outlays for housing, water, gas, electricity and other utilities on the one hand and a number of demographic and socioeconomic characteristics of households on the other. This enables the researchers to calculate for each household the deviation between individual expenses and average expenses for the particular kind of household. This deviation (in log form) is brought into the equation for the income level deemed 'just sufficient' (i.e. the average of the third and fourth level of the IEQ). The assumption is therefore, that these expenses only have an effect on the subjective evaluation of income when they differ from what other people in similar circumstances on average pay for housing and utilities. The results indicate that after correcting for the effect of household income, the elasticity of the income level needed to attain the welfare level 'just sufficient' with respect to the deviation in housing and utilities expenses is 0.23 or 0.29 for tenants and 0.32 or 0.34 for home-owners (where in each case the first figure refers to one-earner households, and the second figure to two-earner households). When converting these percentages into absolute amounts, it turns out that every guilder added to housing and utilities costs results in slightly more than one guilder being added to the income needed to reach the welfare level 'just sufficient'.

At first sight, the interpretation of the effects of home tenure and housing costs is straightforward. According to Saunders and Matheson (1993: 11), they

> "can be understood directly in terms of the costs associated with particular housing arrangements. Because housing costs - mortgage repayments or rent - tend to have a first claim on family budgets, where these costs are high they have a positive impact on the income required to allow families to meet their other needs."

However, although this is a reasonable interpretation, some additional points can be made. In the first place, from a life-time perspective, people who have fully paid off their mortgage and people who are still paying for their mortgage are equally well off, other things equal. Assuming that most non-mortgaged owners did have a mortgage in a previous stage of their life, the positive effect of being mortgaged for homeowners therefore suggests that respondents do *not* take a life-time perspective when answering the MIQ.

More importantly, a distinction needs to be made between the effects of home tenure and those of the amounts paid. There can be no doubt that at a particular point in time, people who own their home outright are better off than persons in otherwise similar circumstances, who rent their home or pay for a mortgage. The effects of home tenure can therefore be regarded safely as reflecting cost differences between households. The issue is more complicated regarding the amount of rent or mortgage payments. As Halleröd (1995: 12) remarks, everything depends on the question whether or not housing costs are an outcome of free choice. If yes, differences in housing costs reflect different tastes for housing, and given a certain level of income and family composition, there is no reason why persons who have chosen expensive housing should be regarded as worse off than families with more modest housing. On the other hand, housing market conditions may be such that families have essentially no free choice regarding housing, and that there is little relationship between the quality of the dwelling and the amount paid in rent or for the mortgage. This may be the case if the housing market is highly regulated, but also if demand greatly exceeds supply. In such a situation, families with high housing costs are likely to be effectively worse off than people in otherwise similar circumstances, but with lower rents or mortgage payments. People may well perceive these payments as just a deduction from their income, not as a price paid for equivalent housing services.

The results of Halleröd (1995), reported above, showing a strong relation between rent or mortgage payments and the answer to the MIQ, would therefore seem to suggest that in Sweden the latter situation prevails. Other interpretations are also possible, however. As several writers have remarked, when respondents answer the MIQ they must make a number of assumptions regarding which aspects of their living situation they take as given, and which aspects could be adjusted. As far as housing is concerned, it is likely that most respondents state the amount of income they consider they need to make ends meet, assuming that they would continue to live in their present dwelling and consequently, would continue to have to pay the same rent or mortgage payment. Thus, even when quality and cost of housing are a matter of free choice, persons with high housing costs may well give higher answers to the MIQ than people in otherwise similar circumstances who spend less on housing. In fact, this effect can be regarded as a special kind of preference drift: when people have got used to a certain standard of living, they will adjust their standards of what they regard as a minimum. Another possible explanation for a measured effect of housing costs and housing tenure on the answer to the MIQ, even in circumstances when housing is a matter of free choice, is that both variables are a proxy for unobserved variables. For instance, whether people are renters or homeowners, and how much they are willing or able to pay for housing, is likely to depend to a large extent on the incomes they enjoyed in the past, as well as on income expectations for the future. Both a person's income history, and his income prospects, may well influence his answers to the MIQ. This hypothesis might explain why Poulin (1988) finds that, ceteris paribus, renters say they need *less* income than outright owners.

Region and urbanization

A number of studies (10,16,21,24,27) have looked at the influence of the place where the respondent lives on his or her answers to the MIQ or IEQ, i.e. the region and the degree of urbanization. As regards *urbanization*, Hagenaars (1985: 217) (10) finds that in most countries the inhabitants of large towns, and in some countries those living in small towns as well, give up to 8% higher answers to the IEQ than people living in rural areas. Differences of a similar direction and magnitude between rural and urban areas are reported by Poulin (1988: 45) (16) for Canada. De Vos and Garner (1991: 276) (21) on the other hand, find no significant difference between rural areas and cities in the USA. Halleröd (1995: 7) (27) reports that people in the two largest cities say they need about 11% more income to make ends meet - other things equal - than people in the rest of Sweden.

De Vos and Garner's (1991) (21) results indicate that significant differences exist between various *regions* of the USA; the maximum difference in average response (after controlling for other factors) between any two regions exceeds 10%. Fairly large regional differences are also reported by Van Praag and Flik (1992: 75-77) (24). Maximum differences between any two regions amount to 14% in Italy, 13% in France and 17% in Belgium. In both studies, no more than three or four regions were distinguished in each country, implying that they are relatively large. It appears that, roughly, answers are higher in the more urbanized regions.

Both cost differences and reference group influences are probably involved in the effects of urbanization and region on the answers to the MIQ and IEQ. Halleröd (1995: 7) suggests that it is more expensive to live in large cities, as housing costs are higher there, and the possibilities to take advantage of non-monetary resources are lower. On the other hand, people in rural areas probably need to spend more on transport. Reference group effects may play a role when incomes are higher in large cities than in rural areas (Hagenaars, 1985: 95).

Working status

Whether or not people are in paid employment may have a positive effect on income needs. Because of child care costs, transportation costs and other work-related expenses, persons in paid employment may have higher money needs than non-working persons in otherwise similar circumstances. Moreover, working people have less time left for home production, and may substitute market goods for time, leading again to a greater income requirement to reach a particular level of welfare.

Table 4.A5 summarizes the results of income evaluations studies where the working status (i.e. whether or not employed, or number of hours in paid employment) of household members was taken up in some way in the regression equation. In Hagenaars (1985) (10) and Van Praag and Flik (1992) (24), where the focus of the study was not on the effect of working status, two, three or four dummy variables were used to represent the number of earners. In most cases, the effect of these variables appears to be limited, when it is not statistically insignificant. The equivalence factor of two-earner couples with respect to one-earner couples in otherwise similar circumstances exceeds 110 only in two instances: Denmark 1979 (line 10b) and Belgium 1987/88 (line 24i).

A more complex specification is used by De Vos and Garner (1991) (21). They have separate dummies for several combinations of household size and number of earners. However, few of the number of earners-effects are statistically significant. According to the authors, "the distinction of this many variables probably makes too many demands on the data" (p. 274-275). In The Netherlands, the effect of a two-person, two-earner household relative to a two-person, one-earner household (not shown in table 4.1) is significantly positive, but "this coefficient is very sensitive to our choice of the method to correct for neglected income components" (p. 275). In the USA, households composed of more than two persons, but without any earners, give answers to the MIQ that are considerably lower than those of similar households with one earner. The differences among households with one, two or more earners are small and not significant, however.

The sensitivity of the estimates of the effects of the number of earners with respect to the specification used is illustrated by the results of De Vos, Hagenaars and Van Praag (1987) (14). Using the same Dutch dataset, and the same dummy variables to represent household size - number of earners combinations as De Vos and Garner (1991) (21), but with otherwise different independent variables in the equation, they find small, but statistically significant, *negative* effects for two-earner households relative to one-earner households. Other things equal, the answer to the MIQ *de*creases consistently with the number of earners. Having one earner instead of no earners in a two-person household has a small but significant positive effect on the income regarded as 'just sufficient'[5]; but two earners instead of one has again a negative effect. Both in (14, 36) and in (21: 275) the sensitivity of the number of earners effects to the choice of the method to correct for neglected income components is stressed. Yet, both studies use the same method for this purpose, the only difference apparently being that in (14) the weights used in the correction procedure are estimated simultaneously with the other regression parameters, while in (21) these weights are calculated in a separate step.

Some Dutch researchers from the Universities of Leyden and Rotterdam have used the income evaluation method specifically to estimate differences in income needs between one-earner and two-earner families. The results have been published in Hagenaars, Homan and Van Praag (1984) (9) and Homan, Hagenaars and Van Praag (1986) (13); see also Homan (1988). Both studies rely on the newspaper survey data that were also used by (14) and (21). The authors of (9) specify an equation for μ which includes time spent in household work by the husband and by the wife, as well as the number of hours of leisure of husband and wife, and a dummy variable indicating whether or not the wife is in paid employment. The coefficient of the number of hours of household work by the wife is specified as: $a_1 + a_2P$, where P is an index of the extent of labor market participation of the wife which is equal to one if she works full-time and zero if she does not work. The estimates of a_1 and a_2 turn out to be -0.03 and +0.06, respectively. The estimate of the preference effect (coefficient of household income) being 0.80, the authors calculate (p.557) that a two-earner couple where the wife works full-time needs about 30% more income than a one-earner couple in otherwise similar conditions, in order to feel as well off.

Unfortunately, this study (9) suffers from obscurities and apparent inconsistencies at several levels. In the first place, it is not clear how the 30% estimate is derived from the coefficient estimates. Using the standard procedure to calculate equivalence scales from the results of income evaluation regression equations, I obtain an equivalence factor that exceeds 2.0. Secondly, the authors provide no justification for neglecting the coefficient for the one-earner vs. two earner dummy variable, when computing the equivalence factor. When this factor, as well as the effect of leisure time is taken into account, the regression results imply that two-earner couples actually need *less* income than one-earner couples to feel as well off (Van Schaaijk, 1984). Thirdly, the estimates of a_1 and a_2 are themselves difficult to interpret. They imply that for two-earners couples, an increase in the number of hours of household work lead to a rise in μ, while for one-earner couples the reverse is true. This can only make sense if income and time spent on household work are complements, not substitutes for two-earner families. This implication clashes with the household production theory, as well as with common sense[6].

In Homan, Hagenaars and Van Praag (1986) (13) a very different approach is used. They estimate separate equations for one-earner and two-earner household. Both equations include a correction term in order to prevent bias due to the endogeneity of the choice of one-earner or two-earner status. The two-earner equation also contains a variable measuring the number of hours in paid employment of the wife. The results indicate that two-earner households have higher income needs than one-earner household, although the difference becomes smaller as income rises. In order to reach the welfare level that is described as "just sufficient", two-earner households need about 23% more income than one-earner households (calculated from table 7.5 in (13) p.93). Peculiarly, this proportion drops with increasing household size, from 26% for two-person households. Another peculiarity is that income needs rise much more when a wife starts to work half-time, than when she goes from half-time to full-time. Intuitively, one would expect the opposite pattern to emerge, because the pressure on the time available for household work becomes increasingly acute the closer both partners are to working full-time.

As mentioned earlier, in (14), where the same data were used, it was found that two-earner households need *less* income than one-earner households to feel as well off. As an explanation of this discrepancy, the authors point to the sensitivity of the results for the method used to correct for misperception of income by the respondent. The pattern of differences in income needs between one-earner and two-earner households, is indeed consistent with the hypothesis that these differences reflect statistical artifacts due to the fact that respondents tend to forget the wife's income, rather than the value of the household production of the wife.

In summary, most studies using the income evaluation method to estimate cost differences between families with varying numbers of earners find that these differences are non-existent or small. Two Dutch studies report that the income needs of families where the wife works full-time are 20 to 30 percent higher than those of similar families where the wife has no paid employment. However, other studies using the same data-base found much smaller differences, or even that two-earner families need *less* income than one-earner families to feel as well off.

Education and occupation

A few studies (10, 21, 25) have looked at the effects of *education* on the answers to the MIQ or the IEQ. Hagenaars (1985: 84) (10) found that, ceteris paribus, people with high education state higher amounts, compared with those with low levels of education. Because of the complex normalization of the education variable in this study, the coefficients are difficult to interpret. It appears that education has a relatively large effect in the UK Belgium and France, and a relatively small effect in Italy and Denmark (Hagenaars, 1985: 217). Whether the respondent has had a general or technical education seems to have no significant effect in any country. De Vos and Garner (1991: 275) (21) found no significant differences between different education groups for The Netherlands. In the USA, however, the difference between the highest and lowest education groups amounts to some 22 per cent. Saunders and Matheson (1993: 10-11) (25) estimate that each successive year of post-secondary education adds about 2 per cent (income etc. remaining the same) to the average answer to the MIQ.

De Vos and Garner (1991: 275) offer two kinds of explanation for the education effect (cf. Hagenaars, 1985: 99). The first is that more highly educated people will have invested more in their education, both in the form of direct outlays, and in the form of foregone earnings. Therefore, in order to reach a given level of welfare, they need higher amounts of income, if only to allow them to repay debts incurred while undergoing education. This factor may explain why the effect of education is so much stronger in the USA than in The Netherlands, where the private financial costs of obtaining higher education were small. The second explanation is that there is a reference group effect. More highly educated people tend to mix with and compare themselves to other highly educated persons, who tend to have higher incomes. Consequently, they may feel they need higher incomes in order to live up to the standards of their reference group. Saunders and Matheson (1993: 12) consider the reference group explanation of much greater relevance than the first one for Australia, where higher education was very largely publicly funded. In addition to, and more or less independently from the cost and reference group effects, people may have come to expect high incomes in virtue of their higher education. It is even possible that the relationship is the other way around: young people who aspire to a high standard of living later in life may for that reason choose to obtain higher levels of education.

The only study to look at the effects of *occupation* on the answers to the IEQ (or the MIQ) is Hagenaars (1985: 217) (10). For presently non-working people, occupation refers to their former occupation (Hagenaars, 1985: 85). The results show that in a number of countries, employees and civil servants state higher amounts in response to the IEQ than do manual workers. The difference is not large though, 9 per cent at most. On the other hands, farmers generally give significantly lower (down to -11%) answers to the IEQ compared to manual workers. For self-employed persons, there is no significant difference in most countries. As Hagenaars (1985: 98) writes, the employees and civil servants effect is probably due to the high-income reference groups of persons with those occupations. For farmers, cost effects may also play a role, as farmers may enjoy substantial income in kind, enabling them to reach a given standard of living with less money compared to non-farmers.

Fluctuations and changes in income

Hagenaars (1985) (10) has also looked at the effects of fluctuations and changes in income on the answers to the IEQ. She reports that in three out of eight countries, people who say they experience large fluctuations in income give significantly higher (up to + 12%) answers to the IEQ. Hagenaars (1985: 96) interprets this as a cost effect, since "people with large fluctuations in income will have to build up savings during prosperous times in order to provide for their needs when the income flow becomes smaller". Hagenaars also finds that changes in financial situation over the last two years have an important, but asymmetric effect on answers to the IEQ. When the situation has improved, the answers are up to 4% lower than if the situation is unchanged; this effect is significant in three out of eight countries. When income has decreased, however, answers are between 3% and 10% higher, depending on the country, and the effect is statistically significant in all countries except one. Hagenaars (1985: 96) attributes the effect of changes in the financial situation to the memory of past incomes. Due to the preference drift effect, people who recently had higher incomes than they have now, will give higher answers to the IEQ than people whose incomes have not changed for some time. The reverse is true for people whose income has increased recently. She does not comment on the asymmetry in the parameter estimates, however.

Why should people react in a different way to improvement and deterioration in income? The most plausible explanation is that it takes longer to adjust to a worsening in the financial situation, than to an improvement. Many households may have pre-committed expenditures, such as rent or mortgage payments, which are difficult to cut back on in the short term. Getting used to a higher standard of living may be more quickly accomplished. Thus, the effect of an income increase may get absorbed into the answer to the IEQ in a smaller period of time than the effect of an income decrease. Provided respondents remember income increases and decreases equally well, the difference in the time needed for adjustment could explain the asymmetry in the estimated coefficients. Note that this explanation focuses on the *time* needed for adjustment, the assumption being that after sufficient time has elapsed, an income increase or decrease, when they are of equal magnitude, should have an equally large effect on the answers tot the IEQ. If the eventual impact of a decrease in income would be smaller than that of an income increase, the average answer to the IEQ would be constantly on the rise, due to a kind of ratchet effect, even if there is no long-term change in the income distribution.

Another possible reason for the finding that people adjust faster when their financial situation gets better than when it gets worse, is that the former event is more often foreseen than the latter one. Many improvements in income may have been expected, for instance because they are part of a normal professional career, and may have already been discounted for in people's minds. Conversely, a deterioration in the financial situation may often be unpredictable, because they result from unemployment, sickness or unexpected expenditures. Another possibility is that people do not respond differently to positive and negative changes in income, but that the perception, or at least the reporting of those changes, differs. Respondents may be more inclined to say that the financial situation has worsened when it was already bad, while the same may not be true for improvements. In this case, reported changes in income serve in fact as a proxy for unobserved differences in subjective needs between respondents.

Subjective income evaluations and consumption expenditure

A few studies have looked at the relationship between subjective income evaluations and expenditure on various categories of goods and services. Garner and De Vos (1995) have used Dutch and American data (also utilized by De Vos and Garner, 1991) to study the relationship between responses to the MIQ and an (incomplete) set of expenditure components. In order to avoid multicollinearity with income and demographic variables, the authors have estimated expenditure equations with the latter variables as explanatory variables, and used the resulting residuals as additional explanatory variables in the logYmin equation.

In both countries expenditure on housing and utilities have an important effect on minimally necessary income, while the impact of food expenditure is moderate. In the USA, relatively high expenditures on transport and leisure are also associated with relatively high answers to the MIQ. In the Netherlands, the corresponding coefficients are not significant, or even negative. It appears "that in answering the MIQ in the Netherlands, respondents more clearly distinguished between (fixed) expenditures which they would want to continue and luxury or variable expenditures which could be reduced" (pp. 128-129). The authors suggest that one of the reasons for the different results is that circumstances differ between the USA and the Netherlands. American respondents may consider transportation expenditure to be fixed to a greater extent than Dutch ones would, because in the USA there are fewer substitutes for private transport.

However, the authors seem to favor an alternative explanation, which is that respondents in the two countries interpreted the MIQ somewhat differently. Given that in the American questionnaire the MIQ was preceded by questions about household expenditures:

> "it may be that the question was understood in the United States as asking for the minimum income needed 'to continue your present living pattern'."

In the Netherlands, on the other hand, the context may have made respondents

> "more predisposed to provide a necessities-based minimum income for their households" (p. 129).

This would mean, according to the authors, that for the USA, the SPL thresholds cannot be regarded as a type of poverty line. The assumption that everyone adheres the same welfare connotation to their answer to the MIQ would not be valid across the two survey, and not even within populations.

Kapteyn (1994) uses the income evaluation approach to address the problem that household demand data are insufficient to identify a household cost function. This implies that equivalence scales are also not identified; in fact, Blundell and Lewbell (1991) show that within a given price regime any equivalence scale is consistent with observed demand. One way out of this problem is to invoke additional information, e.g. answers to direct questions on household cost functions. Kapteyn shows that the IEQ can be interpreted as a direct measure of a cost function of a particular form. The availability of direct (IEQ) and indirect (i.e. preferences revealed through demand behavior) measures means that there are two ways to estimate the cost function, and this makes it possible to test whether both approaches measure the same thing. (Actual testing involved a number of difficulties. Since there must be variation in prices, panel observations of expenditures and answers to the IEQ are required. In fact, two datasets referring to the same period had to be used.)

Unfortunately, the results are ambiguous. Formally, the hypothesis that both approaches measure the same cost function is rejected. Yet, the results also suggest that this hypothesis is reasonably close to the truth. There are a number of reasons to suspect that the model chosen is misspecified, and this may be the cause of the rejection of the hypothesis that the direct and indirect measures are equivalent.

Other variables

De Vos and Garner (1991: 274) (21) find that whether or not the respondent is *disabled* has no statistically significant effect on the answers to the MIQ in The Netherlands and the USA. Surprisingly, the sign of the coefficient for the USA is negative, which would indicate that, ceteris paribus, disabled people say they need less income to make ends meet.

Their results also show that whether or not the respondent is *black* makes no difference whatsoever - controlling for income, household composition and other variables - for the answers to the MIQ in the USA. Saunders and Matheson (1993: 11) (25) report that in Australia "Liberal or National Party voters think they require higher incomes to make ends meet than Labor voters". The difference is about 8%. The authors mention three possible explanations for this intriguing finding. First, "the lower income requirements of the Labor voter [might] reflect a willingness to depend upon state-provided services, whereas the political conservative in similar circumstances would prefer 'cash in hand' in order to allocate expenditure according to their own preferences". An alternative explanation revolves around the relationship between political allegiance and long-term economic aspirations. A more expensive lifestyle may be both an end and a means to 'getting on'. Finally, it seems likely that reference group effects are at work: Liberal or National party voters may well associate with richer persons than Labor party voters do.

Conclusion

In this section I have reviewed published estimates of the effects of variables other than household income and household size on the answers to income evaluation questions. The findings are summarized in table 4.2. One needs to keep in mind that even where significant effects are found, the contribution of these variables to the explained variance of μ and logYmin is almost always quite small. There are some recurring patterns, e.g. as regards the effect of the age of the head of household. There are also some intriguing findings that need to be confirmed, e.g. the almost complete discounting of housing costs. Most effects are in the expected direction. The interpretation of measured effects in terms of reference or cost effects is often rather uncertain, though.

Table 4.2
Summary of review of estimated effects of various variables on subjective income evaluations (i.e. μ and logYmin)

Variable	Countries for which estimates have been found	Description of effect	Most probable interpretation
Age head	Many European countries, USA, Canada, Australia	'Inverted U': negative for young households, and in particular for the elderly, positive for the middle-aged	Reference effect
Age of children	Netherlands	Increases with age; effect for pre-school children about half of that of adults	Cost effect
Gender head	USA, Canada, Netherlands	Not significant, or negative for women	May be artefact
Home tenure	Australia, Canada	Positive for mortgaged owners relative to outright owners, mixed for tenants	Cost effect
Housing costs	Sweden, Netherlands	Positive, almost complete discounting of housing costs	Cost and refer. effects
Working status	Many European countries (in particular the Netherlands), USA, Australia	No effect or limited positive effect of one-earner vs. no-earner, and two-earner vs. one-earner families	Unclear
Education	Many European countries, USA, Australia	Positive but generally limited effect, relatively strong effect in the USA	Reference effect
Occupation	Several European countries	Positive for white-collar workers and civil servants, negative for farmers	Reference effect
Fluctuations in income	Several European countries	Positive for fluctuating vs. stable incomes	Cost effect
Recent change in income	Several European countries	Positive for drop in income, negative (but smaller) for rise in income	Reference effect
Urbanization	Several European countries, USA, Canada	Positive for urban vs. rural areas	Cost and reference effects
Region	USA, Italy, France, Belgium	Moderate differences between regions	Cost and refer. effects

5 Reference group effects

Introduction

It seems reasonable to assume that a person's evaluation of his or her income is influenced not only by his or her own situation, but also by the circumstances of others. An evaluation is often, if not always, a comparative evaluation: an income is good or bad only in comparison with other persons' incomes, as well as one's own income in the past. This basic idea has been extensively developed and formalized in the literature on the income evaluation approach. Most of this work has been done within the framework of a particular theory about the welfare evaluation of income, viz. the theory of preference formation (Kapteyn, 1977). Essentially, this theory states that an individual's Welfare Function of Income is identical to his perceived income distribution, which implies that a person's welfare is determined by his position within the perceived income distribution. (Kapteyn and Wansbeek, 1985; Alessie and Kapteyn, 1988.) For the estimation of poverty lines and equivalence scales, this theory is not directly relevant. In this section, I will concentrate on measurement issues and empirical results, which can be discussed independently from this specific theory of preference formation.

This section is organized as follows. In the first subsection, the theoretical model is described. The second subsection considers measurement issues. The third subsection reviews empirical findings regarding the effect of the incomes of others on subjective income evaluations.

The theoretical model

The comparative process is modeled in the following way. The answer of individual n to the income evaluation question represented by μ_n, depends on the average income in her reference group (or, more exactly, in her perceived income distribution). The reference group is made up of all people to whose incomes individual n attaches any importance. The notion of a reference group is formalized through the use of reference weights. Average income in the reference group is the weighted sum of all incomes in the reference group. These weights vary across individuals. The weights have an objective component, reflecting the number of times individuals come into contact with one another, as well as a subjective one, reflecting the importance, or weight, that an individual attaches to contacts with another particular individual (Kapteyn, 1977: 176). If an individual does not belong to the reference group, the weight is zero. In addition to reference weights, memory weights are introduced, which capture the influence of past incomes of herself and of others. Thus, the 'reference income' of individual n, called M_n can be expressed as follows:

$$M_n = \sum_{t=\infty}^{0} a_{nt} \sum_{k=1,\, k\neq n}^{N} w_{nk,t} \cdot \log(Y_{kt}), \tag{4.17}$$

where a_{nt} is the memory weight of individual n for time t, $w_{nk,t}$ the reference weight of individual n for individual k at time t, and $Y_{k,t}$ the income of individual k at time t. The memory weights and the reference weights are normalized so that they sum to one[7]. Before we can add a term with M_n to the μ_n equation, we have to deal with a complication: what is relevant is not income as such, but income per equivalent adult. As explained above, within the WFI framework, income per equivalent adult is equal to $Y/FS^{\beta'_2}$, where $\beta'_2 = \beta_2/(1-\beta_1)$. Thus, in (4.17), $\log(Y_{kt})$ is replaced by $[\log(Y_{kt}) - \beta'_2\log(FS_{kt})]$, and, consequently, M_n by $[M_n - \beta'_2 HS_n]$, where M_n retains its original meaning, and HS_n is the weighted average of the family sizes in individual n's reference group, now and in the past.

In addition to the reference effect, we also want to model the preference effect of the individual's own income, now and in the past. Again, what is relevant is income per equivalent adult, which reflects consumption possibilities. Therefore, we define a term $(Y_n - \beta'_2 FS_n)$, where Y_n and FS_n represent the weighted averages of log-income and log household size now and in the past, i.e., $Y_n = \Sigma_t\, a_{nt} \cdot \log(Y_{nt})$ and $FS_n = \Sigma_t\, a_{nt} \cdot \log(FS_{nt})$, where in both cases the summation is from $t = -\infty$ to $t = 0$. However, in addition to the preference effect through the income per equivalent adult, household size also has a direct cost effect on μ. That is, the larger the household, the more income one needs to attain a particular standard of living. A term $\beta'_2\log(FS)$ is therefore also included in the model. (In fact, the parameter β_2 in the most simple μ-model encompasses both the cost effect, β'_2, and the preference effect $\beta'_2\beta'_1$, of household size. In a way, the simple model $\mu = \beta_0 + \beta_1\log(Y) + \beta_2\log(FS)$ can be better interpreted when it is rewritten in terms of β'_2 and the preference effect β'_1: $\mathrm{EXP}(\mu/FS^{\beta'_2}) = \beta_0.(Y/FS^{\beta'_2})^{\beta'_1}$. The latter expression in effect says: the standard of living (income per equivalent adult) that is evaluated by 0.5 (on a scale from one to zero) is a function of the actual standard of living. Altogether, the μ_n equation is now as follows:

$$\mu_n = \text{ß}_0 + \text{ß}'_2 \log(FS_n) + \text{ß}'_1(Y_n - \text{ß}'_2 FS_n) + \text{ß}_3(M_n - \text{ß}'_2 HS_n) + \varepsilon_n \tag{4.18}$$

The parameters in (4.18) each have a clear theoretical meaning: $\text{ß}'_2$ reflects the cost effect of household size, $\text{ß}'_1$ represents the preference effect, and ß_3 represents the reference effect.

Measuring reference group variables

The problem with equation (4.18) is, of course, that there are far too many reference weights and memory weights in (4.17). For estimation to be possible, both sets of weights must be parametrized, i.e. expressed as a function of a limited number of parameters. As regards the memory weights, it is assumed in all empirical applications (e.g. Van de Stadt, Kapteyn, Van de Geer, 1985; Kapteyn, Van de Geer, Van de Stadt, 1985) first, that they are the same for all individuals, and secondly that they follow a decreasing geometric pattern, i.e. $a_{nt} = (1\text{-}a)a^{-t}$. Thus, the memory function is governed by only one parameter, viz, a.

Constructed social group model – More attention has been devoted to the specification of the reference weights. Kapteyn (1977) has developed a complicated model, where the reference weight given by an individual of type A to an individual of type B depends on the relative frequencies of types A and B in the population and the social distance between them. (These two factors determine the probability of contacts between individuals of types A and B, as well as the importance attached by individuals of type A to contacts with B-type people.) By further imposing a number of restrictions, m_n (average income in the reference group of individual n) could be expressed as a function of a limited number of parameters. Individuals were characterized by a number of social characteristics (education, type of job, degree of urbanization, age, region and employment status). The estimates of the parameters involved were sometimes suggestive, but rather unstable. The resulting estimate for ß_3

was 0.29 (the main results are also reported in Kapteyn, Van Praag, Van Herwaarden, 1978).

In later work the complicated model of Kapteyn (1977) seems to have been abandoned in favor of a more simple one (see, among others, Van de Stadt, Kapteyn, Van de Geer, 1985; Kapteyn, Van de Geer, Van de Stadt, 1985; Alessie and Kapteyn, 1988). Only two kinds of people are distinguished (other than the referring individual him- or herself): those within the social group of the individual and those outside it. Because direct information on the reference process is generally lacking, the social group is assumed to consist of those individuals who have a number of characteristics in common with the referring individual; say, same age bracket, same level of education and same employment status.

Given a few assumptions, this model of the reference process implies that the reference income M_n of individual n can be approximated by (Van de Stadt, Kapteyn, Van de Geer, 1985):

$$M_n = \sum_{t=\infty}^{0} a_{nt} \left[k_t M_t + (1-k_t).M_{nt} + u_{nt}\right], \tag{4.19}$$

where M_t represents average log-income in the society as a whole (a proxy for average log-income of individuals not in the social group of n), M_{nt} average log-income of individuals within the social group of n, k_t a parameter that can be interpreted as the total reference weight of individuals *outside* the social group of individual n, and u_{nt} a disturbance term. A similar equation is specified for the reference household size:

$$HS_n = \sum_{t=\infty}^{0} a_{nt} \left[k_t HS_t + (1-k_t).HS_{nt} + v_{nt}\right], \tag{4.20}$$

where HS_t and HS_{nt} represent average log-household size in the society as a whole, and in the social group of n, respectively, and v_{nt} is a disturbance term.

After substituting (4.19) and (4.20) into (4.18) and applying the Koyck transformation[8], we obtain the following equation:

$$\begin{aligned} \mu_n = \; & ß'_0 + ß'_2\log(FS_n) - a.ß'_2\log(FS_{n,-1}) + (1-a)\, ß_1(\log(Y_n) \\ & - ß'_2\log(FS_n)) + (1-a)\, ß_3\, (1-k)\, (M_n - ß'_2 HS_n) - a\, \mu_{n,-1} + e'_n, \end{aligned} \tag{4.21}$$

where $\beta'_0 = \beta_0 + (1\text{-}a)\ \beta_3\ k\ (M - \beta'_2 HS)$, as average income and household size are constant across all individuals of course.

Equation (4.21) can be estimated, as all variables in it are observable, if panel data for at least two periods are available. There is one difficulty, however. Parameters β_3 and (1-k) occur together in (4.21), and cannot both be estimated at the same time. Either one can only be estimated if restrictions are imposed on the other. Restrictions that have been used are $k = 0$, which implies that individuals only refer to people within their own social group, and $\beta_1 + \beta_3 = 1$, which implies that welfare is completely relative. Models very similar to (4.21) have also been estimated with cross-sectional data. In that case, one necessarily has to assume that $a = 0$, which, if (4.21) is the true model, produces a specification error. Finally, a similar model can be specified for log(Ymin), the answer to the minimum income question, but, of course, with different parameters. By convention, it seems, the parameters in the log(Ymin) equation are called α_i, so α_3 takes the role of β_3.

Direct information model – A clear disadvantage of the reference group models presented so far is that they are based on unconfirmed hypotheses about the reference process. Lacking direct information on reference groups, there was no alternative to this procedure, of course. In De Vos, Hagenaars and Van Praag (1987: 16-18), the reference weights were derived from data from another survey, where people were asked to indicate the distribution of the people they came into contact with across age brackets, education levels and employment statutes. Using these weights, average income in the reference group could be estimated for each household in the sample.

This 'direct-questioning' approach has been further developed in the October 1985 and 1986 waves of the Dutch Socio-Economic Panel (run by the Central Bureau of Statistics). There questions were asked about the "social environment" of people, "that is people whom you meet frequently, like friends, neighbors, acquaintances or possible people you meet at work." People were asked about the age class to which people in their social environment primarily belonged, about the typical householdsize in their environment, about the average after tax household income and about the education level of people in their environment (Muffels, Kapteyn et al., 1990: 161-163). (Incidentally, in the question quoted 'relatives' are not mentioned among the kinds of people constituting a person's social environment. It is not clear whether this was intentional or an oversight.)

The answers to these questions are used as indicators of the 'true' family size and household income in the reference group of each respondent. By applying a confirmatory factor analysis model, proxies of the true variables can be constructed on the basis of these indicators (Muffels, Kapteyn et al., 1990: 161-167; see also Melenberg, 1992: 183-208). The three indicators for average income in the reference group are defined as follows. The first indicator is the answer to the direct question about average income in one's social environment (with interpolation of the brackets). The second indicator is the mean income of all individuals in the sample who have the same education level, age bracket and sex as the respondent, i.e. mean income M_n in the social group as defined above. The third indicator is the mean income of all people in the sample who have the education level and age which the respondent has indicated as typical for people in his or her social environment. For average household size in the reference group there are also three indicators, analogously defined.

The relationship between the 'true' mean income in the reference group, represented by Mn and its indicators is assumed to be as follows:

$$X_{in} = \lambda_i M_n + \delta_{in}, i = 1, 2, 3, \tag{4.22}$$

where X_{in} is the value of the i- th indicator for respondent n, measured as deviations from the mean, λ_i parameters to be estimated and δ_{in} disturbance terms which are mutually independent. (A subscript t for time has been omitted; the models are estimated for each year independently.) A similar relationship is postulated between 'true' family size in the reference groups, HS_n and its indicators:

$$X_{in} = \lambda_i HS_n + \delta_{in}, i = 4, 5, 6. \tag{4.23}$$

This model is a confirmatory factor analysis model, and estimation of the parameters λ_i is straightforward, after λ_1 and λ_4 have been arbitrarily set to one to fix the scale of the "true" or latent variables M_n and HS_n.

Muffels, Kapteyn et al. (1990) nor Melenberg (1992) explain how this confirmatory factor analysis model is to be interpreted in terms of the reference group model, summarized in (4.17). As explained, the indicators are assumed to be equal to 'true' reference income plus an error term. Three sources of error in the indicators can be identified. In the first place, respondents may misperceive the incomes in their reference group, introducing error into the first indicator. (As the reference weights are subjective by nature, misperception of these weights can be ruled out.) Secondly, the reference group of a respondent may not coincide with a particular social category constructed according to age brackets and education levels; in general it will contain non-random samples of people from several categories. This is a source of error in the second and third indicator. In the third place, the second and third indicators are based on present income only, and do not take into account past incomes. Whether such an error structure can be represented adequately by a factor model with mutually independent error terms is at least doubtful. In particular, the disturbances of the second and third indicator may well be correlated, as these indicators are both based on the same sample estimates of average income in age and education cells.

Nevertheless, the results of the factor analyses are interesting. For reference they are given in table 4.3. Muffels, Kapteyn et al. (1990) limit themselves to the observation that these results are "satisfactory from a statistical viewpoint" (p.165). But the clear patterns in these estimates also suggest a number of substantive interpretations.

In the first place, the high R^2s for the third indicator (mean income in the age-and-education brackets that the respondent says are typical for his social environment) suggest that it almost perfectly coincides with the true, latent variable - mean income in the reference group. The finding that in both years λ_1 is virtually equal to λ_3 implies that respondents make no systematic errors in their perception of incomes in their social environment. But the low R^2s for the first indicator mean either that respondents have only a rather vague idea of the incomes of people in their social environment or that age-and-education categories do not catch the greater part of the actual variation in mean incomes of people's reference groups. Finally, the results indicate that mean income of the group of individuals with the same characteristics as the respondent (the second indicator) is not a very good indicator of mean income in the reference group. The R^2s of around 0.4 imply that the correlation with the third indicator can only be moderate, suggesting that most of the time the age bracket and education level respondents say are typical for their social environment are different from their own age and education. The finding that the estimates of λ_2 are below 1.0 could reflect a tendency of respondents in lower income groups to attribute to their social environment more favorable age and education characteristics than their own. The second indicator is, in fact, the reference group income variable that is most often used in studies where direct indicators of the reference group were lacking. The factor analysis results suggest, therefore, that this constructed variable is not very adequate in this respect.

Table 4.3
Results of factor analysis of indicators of group mean income and mean household size in individual's reference groups, The Netherlands, 1985 and 1986

	1985		1986	
Parameter	Estimate	R^2	Estimate	R^2
λ_1	1.00	0.33	1.00	0.30
λ_2	0.65	0.40	0.73	0.43
λ_3	0.97	0.81	1.08	0.84
λ_4	1.00	0.39	1.00	0.41
λ_5	0.68	0.58	0.72	0.61
λ_6	0.82	0.69	0.86	0.78

Notes: - λ_1 - λ_3 refer to reference group mean income, λ_4 - λ_6 to reference group mean household size.

* - λ_1 and λ_4 are fixed equal at one.

- All standard errors of estimated parameters are 0.04 or smaller.

Source: Muffels, Kapteyn et al., 1990: 165.

These patterns are repeated, though less clearly, in the results for the indicators of mean household size in the reference group. The higher R^2s for the fifth indicator, compared with those for the corresponding second indicator, suggests that the ages of people in a respondent's social environment are close to his own, but that this is less true for education. (Household size varies strongly by age, but hardly by education level; household income correlates with both variables.)

Estimates of the effect of reference groups

What estimates of the reference group effect β_3 and α_3 do these models produce? As table 4.A6 shows, a number of studies present estimates of β_3

and α_3. All of these studies use Dutch data, and most of them employ the 'constructed social group' measurement model, most fully worked out in Van de Stadt et al. (1985). Let us review the latter studies first. Some of these impose the constraint $ß'_1 + ß_3 = 1$ without a test statistic being reported whether this constraint fits the data. The resulting estimates of $ß_3$ or α_3 do not seem trustworthy as estimates of the reference group effect. Four studies have attempted to estimate $ß_3$ or α_3 in a *static model*. Those using the "NPAO" labor market survey (Kapteyn, Kooreman, Muffels et al., 1985; Kapteyn, Kooreman, Willemse, 1988) come up with estimates varying from 0.13 to 0.20. Those using the Socio-Economic Panel produce estimates varying between 0.25 and 0.38. Recall that if equation (4.21) with a>o (i.e., there is influence from the past) is the true model, using a static model introduces specification error. Depending on the serial correlation of reference group income and reference household size across time, static estimates of $ß_3$ will most likely be biased downwards. Taking this into consideration, a value of around 0.3 seems fairly high.

In principle, *dynamic models* should produce better estimates of $ß_3$. There are three studies using panel data (the "CBS household panel") and employing the 'constructed social group' model. As explained above, the parameters in model (4.21) can only be estimated if one assumes either $ß_1 + ß_3 =1$, or $k = 0$. The validity of these assumptions can only be tested if they are imposed in conjunction with other constraints. Kapteyn, Van de Geer, Van de Stadt (1985) and Alessie and Kapteyn (1988) only report estimates of equations where $ß_1 + ß_3 = 1$ has been imposed. The estimates of $ß_3$ and α_3 vary between 0.30 and 0.40, but unfortunately the estimates for k are around 0.8, and are not significantly different from one. Given this high value of k , $ß_3$ can take on almost any value, regardless of the actual effect of incomes in the respondent's own social group. This means that the estimate of $ß_3$ is in fact determined by $1-ß_1$, and is of little value as an indicator of the actual reference group effect. In any case, the estimates imply that the effect of average income in the respondent's social group on μ and log (Ymin), measured by $ß_3$ (1-k), is rather small. This interpretation of the results is confirmed in the study by Van de Stadt et al. (1985), who have estimated several specifications. If $ß_1 + ß_3 = 1$ is imposed, the results are the same as in the studies just mentioned. If, instead, k is restricted to zero, the estimate of $ß_3$ is not significantly different from zero. If one is unwilling to give up the reference group theory, one must conclude (as both Van de Stadt et al., 1985: 184 and Alessie and Kapteyn, 1988: 84, do) that the social groups as constructed in these studies are a poor proxy of people's actual reference groups. This conclusion confirms, of course, my interpretation of the results of the factor analyses reported in Muffels, Kapteyn et al. (1990).

The question can be asked, if the age-bracket-by-education-level cells are such poor approximations of people's actual reference groups, how is it possible that this variable seems to produce satisfactory results in the static models of Muffels, Kapteyn et al. (1990) and Aalbers et al. (1990)? Without further analysis of the data this question is difficult to answer, but one reason may be the following one. It seems likely that compared to the income concept that the respondent has in mind when answering the IEQ or MIQ, household income-as-measured contains random errors, both because of reporting mistakes, and because of random fluctuations in income from one year or month to another. To the extent that age and education (the variables used in the construction of the social groups) are good predictors of income, average income by age bracket and education level can play the role of an instrumental variable for household income. In other words, some of the apparent effect of income in the social group may in fact be due to the respondent's own household income.

It is no surprise now that the 'factor-analytic' model, which incorporates direct information on respondents' social environment, performs much better than the 'constructed social group' model. According to the estimates of the dynamic equation by Muffels, Kapteyn et al. (1990), the reference group effect is around 0.57, which is larger than the preference effect of the respondent's own household income. The static specifications come up with even higher estimates, but for reasons given above, these are perhaps less credible.

At this point it is also useful to look briefly at the estimates of a, the 'memory' or 'inertia' parameter. A most striking result is that three studies which use the same 'CBS household panel' data set produce widely divergent estimates of a: Van de Stadt et al. (1985): 0.81-0.90; Kapteyn, Van de Geer, Van de Stadt (1985): 0.37; and Alessie and Kapteyn (1988): 0.64. Of these, the second one is perhaps the most valid one, as it is based on all three waves of the panel. A value of 0.37 for a would imply a very short time horizon. There are some reasons to have more trust in the data from the Socio-Economic Panel: the sample is larger, and data collection procedures may have worked better. (The 'CBS household panel' apparently served as a pilot panel for the SEP.) Those data produce an estimate for a of about 0.5. This would imply that the present year gets a weight of 0.5, the previous year a weight of 0.25, the year before that a weight of 0.125, and so on. The time horizon would thus be rather limited: All past years together are only as important as the present year; events that happened more than three years ago have almost no influence.

Conclusion

Two conclusions emerge from the above review. In the first place, reference group variables constructed on the basis of the assumption that people's reference groups are composed of persons of the same age and with the same kind of education, are apparently poor proxies of the incomes and household sizes in the true reference group. Secondly, the results of measures based on direct questions about the social environment show that the incomes in the reference groups of respondents have very important effects on subjective income evaluations.

6 The income concept in the mind of the respondent

The problem and some correction procedures

It seems reasonable to assume that in answering the MIQ and the IEQ, the respondent will use his own estimate of his actual income as a point of reference (Kapteyn, Kooreman and Willemse, 1988; De Vos and Garner, 1991). However, researchers have recognized that respondents may have only a vague idea of what their actual household income is. Respondents may easily forget income components that are received with longer intervals (e.g. interests from savings) or irregularly (e.g. overtime payments) or that are received by other persons in the household (e.g. earnings of children). Misperception of income might therefore easily distort the results of the income evaluation method.

The best solution for this problem would be to make sure that the respondent has an accurate conception of his or her own household income. To a certain extent this goal could be achieved through the design of the questionnaire. For instance, the MIQ and the IEQ could be preceded by a short introduction, in which all relevant income components are mentioned. (This is done in the BSEP surveys.) It might also help if the income evaluation questions are placed just after the questions about actual income, but this is often not practical. In any case, none of these procedures guarantees that the respondent has an accurate conception of his household income. In many cases, especially for large households, it seems unrealistic to expect respondents to make the complicated mental calculations that would be required. (The calculation could be made explicitly by the interviewer, who could then present the resulting estimate of total household income to the respondent, but this does not seem to be feasible in actual interview settings.)

An alternative procedure is to ask the respondent to give an estimate of his or her household income. The answer can then be used to correct the answers to the subjective income questions. The most obvious adjustment is to multiply the given amounts by the ratio of actual household income to the respondent's perception of it. This is the approach pursued by Kapteyn, Kooreman and Willemse (1988). Their procedure is as follows. The relation between the income concept Yp, the income as perceived by the respondent, and the various income components Yi, which together make up total household income, is modeled as follows:

$$Yp = [\Sigma_i \theta_i Y_i] EXP(u) \tag{4.24}$$

where the θ_i's are unknown parameters, which are expected to lie between zero and one, and u is an error term. The lower parameter θ_i is, the more the respondent 'forgets' the corresponding income component. The measured values of exp(μ) and Ymin of each respondent are multiplied by the ratio of actual household income (the sum of the income components) and the estimate of the respondent's income perception Yp.

Kapteyn et al. (1988) use data from a Dutch survey in which the respondent was asked (just before the income evaluation questions) to indicate in which of seven income brackets his net household income falls. Assuming that the respondent will choose a certain bracket if Yp lies between the lower and upper bound of that bracket, they estimate the parameters in equation 4.24. The results indicate that only the respondent's own regular earned income is fully taken into account when the respondent tries to estimate his or her total household income. Income of the spouse and fringe benefits are less often present in her or his mind. Incomes of other household members, family allowances and rent subsidies are forgotten more often than not. In the case of the data used by Kapteyn et al. (1988), the correction of μ and Ymin has very important consequences for the estimated poverty lines and equivalence scales. Without the correction, the SPL and the LPL-0.4 lines are considerably below the statutory minimum income in The Netherlands. More seriously, the equivalence scales are very flat, or even have negative slopes: families with four children would need less income then childless families to reach the same welfare level. After correction for misperception, the SPL lies at about the same level as the statutory minimum income, while the LPL-0.4 and LPL-0.5 thresholds exceed the latter. The equivalence scale is still flat, but less implausibly so.

The same procedure has been applied by Melenberg (1992), using data from the Dutch Socio-Economic Panel (SEP), waves 1985 and 1986. His results (p. 203) are qualitatively the same as those of Kapteyn et al. (1988), though most income components seem to have been taken into account to a greater extent than was the case in the survey used by the latter. Melenberg (1992) does not present results for the uncorrected μ and Ymin equations, so that it is unclear what has been the effect of the correction. (The same author also proposes an alternative procedure to estimate 4.24, which, he argues, is in some respects superior to the maximum likelihood method used by Kapteyn et al. (1988). However, it seems he does not apply this alternative method for actual estimation.)

In Homan, Hagenaars and Van Praag (1986), De Vos, Hagenaars and Van Praag (1987) and De Vos and Garner (1991), another method is used to correct for respondents' misperception of their actual income. Lacking an estimate by the respondent of his or her actual income, these studies make the additional assumption that the income of the main breadwinner is fully taken into account. This makes it possible to estimate the other weights θ_i in 4.24 in the μ and Ymin equations themselves[9]. Unfortunately, the resulting estimates of the weights are very sensitive to the inclusion of household composition in the equation (De Vos and Garner, 1991: 281). The results of De Vos and Garner (1991) indicate that in The Netherlands the income of the spouse only partially counts in Yp; if the spouse's income is seen as temporary, it counts only for one half. In the USA, on the other hand, the spouse's income gets a weight of one. Other incomes generally get smaller weights, though they tend to be larger in the USA than in The Netherlands.

Interpretation of the notion 'frame of reference'

Kapteyn et al. (1988) have shown that misperception of actual household income by respondents is a serious problem for the income evaluation method, and can affect the results significantly. But it is not entirely clear why the correction factor should be exactly equal to ratio of actual to perceived income. The authors do not provide arguments for the choice of this particular factor, except the assumption that the respondent takes his or her estimate as a 'frame of reference' when answering the subjective income questions. Below, I will develop two plausible interpretations of the notion of 'frame of reference'.

A first possible interpretation of the notion of 'frame of reference' is that a respondent who misperceives his income answers the IEQ and the MIQ *as if* perceived income was his actual income. In other words, if John erroneously thinks that his income is z, while Jack, who lives in otherwise similar circumstances, correctly perceives his income as z, then John and Jack will give the same answers to the MIQ and the IEQ. If the relation between these answers and household income is correctly described by an equation like (4.1), than it follows directly that the answers to the MIQ are underestimated by the factor $EXP(\alpha_1(\log(Y) - \log(Yp)))$, which implies, if $\alpha_1 < 1$, that the adjustment should be less than proportional. (Similarly, of course, answers to the IEQ would be underestimated by the factor $EXP(\beta_1(\log(Y) - \log(Yp)))$.)

In another interpretation, the basic assumption is that respondents do *not* misperceive their own consumption level (in the sense of concrete goods and services consumed) and the welfare they derive from it. But because of misperception of their income, they underestimate the money expenditure that is needed to achieve their own consumption level, as well as other ones. In other words, the respondent applies equation (4.4) as it were in the reverse direction: given the welfare level she experiences, and her estimate of her household income, she derives the answer to the MIQ, such that equation (4.4) holds. A similar argument can of course be applied to the IEQ. More formally, suppose that A_{qi} is the answer of respondent i to the q-th level of the IEQ, or to the MIQ, and that $\log(A_{qi}) = \mu_i + k_q$, where k_q is a different constant for each level, then these answers are assumed to be generated by the following equation:

$$\log(A_{qi}) = \log(Yp_i) - W_i^{-1}(U_i(Y_i)) + k_q \tag{4.25}$$

where $U(Y_i)$ is the actual welfare experienced by the respondent, and W_i the function which translates income into welfare (and which has the parameters μ_i and σ_i). It is immediately apparent that according to this interpretation of the notion 'frame of reference', misperception of income by x percent leads to answers to the IEQ and the MIQ that are also x percent lower than would be the case if there had been no misperception.

Thus, proportional adjustment of the IEQ and MIQ responses would be appropriate.

The first, *as if*, interpretation may at first sight seem much more obvious and straightforward than the second one. There are two implications of the *as if* interpretation, which might give reason for pause, however. In the first place, the *as if* interpretation implies, which the second one does not, that a respondent's real income, and thus his real consumption level has no effect on the answers to the IEQ and the MIQ, when his perception of his income has been taken into account. Secondly, when the adjustment of the IEQ and the MIQ responses is less than proportional, the welfare level that follows from the respondent's answers before adjustment, which might be described as his 'perceived welfare level', is smaller than the implied welfare level after correction. That is, $W(\log(Yp); \mu p_i, \sigma_i) < W(\log(Y); \mu_i, \sigma_i)$, where μp is the value of μ without adjustment.

Is the last implication a problem? The answer to this question depends on one's view of the concept of individual welfare. Three possible views can be distinguished. If welfare is regarded as a construct by the researcher, i.e. a concept used by the researcher to describe or explain the situation or behavior of an economic actor, which does not necessarily correspond to anything present in the consciousness of that actor, then there does not seem to problem. On the other hand, if welfare is seen as a mental feeling, then the *as if* interpretation appears to lead to an inconsistency. A feeling that is based on misperceptions may be inappropriate, but it is still there, so there is no ground for correcting it. Thirdly, welfare can be regarded as the respondent's evaluation of his or her economic situation. In this case, the situation is somewhat ambiguous. On the one hand, it seems that, explicitly or implicitly, the respondent evaluates his welfare by $W(\log(Yp); \mu p_i, \sigma_i)$. On the other hand, evaluations can be mistaken in a way that feelings cannot. The important issue of the welfare concept underlying the WFI-approach will be discussed at length in chapter 6.

Estimation

Fortunately, as Tummers (1994) has shown, it is possible to estimate to what extent the answers to the IEQ and the MIQ are affected by misperception of income, and therefore which interpretation is the correct one. This is done through the introduction of a term $-\alpha_{12}\log(Y_n/Y_{pn})$ into equation (4.1)[10]. If $\alpha_{12} = 1$ the adjustment should be proportional, if $\alpha_{12} < 1$, the adjustment should be less than proportional. The amended logYmin-equation is then:

$$\begin{aligned} \text{LogYmin} &= \alpha_0 + \alpha_1 \log(Y) + \alpha_2 \log(FS) - \alpha_{12} \log(Y/Y_P) + e \\ &= \alpha_0 + (\alpha_1 - \alpha_{12}) \log(Y) + \alpha_{12} \log(Y_P) + \alpha_2 \log(FS) + e, \end{aligned} \quad (4.26)$$

where subscripts indicating individual households have been dropped. An alternative, equivalent, specification now suggests itself (cf. Tummers, 1994: 269):

$$\log\text{Ymin} = \alpha_0 + \alpha_1[(1 - \eta_1) \log(Y) + \eta_1 \log(Y_P)] + \alpha_2 \log(FS) + e. \quad (4.27)$$

This specification makes more explicit that the needed adjustment is a matter of which income serves as the frame of reference. If $\eta_1 = 1$ (equivalent to $\alpha_{12} = \alpha_1$), perceived income is the frame of reference, while actual income is the frame of reference when $\eta_1 = 0$. If η_1 is between zero and one, a combination of actual and perceived income is the frame of reference. Proportional adjustment ($\alpha_{12} = 1$) would correspond to $\eta_1 = 1/\alpha_1$, which would imply that η_1 is greater than one. Similar specifications can of course be worked out for the μ equation.

Tummers (1994) has estimated η_1 and α_{12} in a logYmin equation, using data from the 1986 wave of the Dutch Socio-Economic Panel survey (N=4091). The estimate for η_1 turns out to be 1.11, which corresponds to a value for α_{12} of about 0.41 (in Tummers' specification, the value of the latter varies by family size). However, a model in which η_1 is fixed at one (corresponding to a value for α_{12} of about 0.38) performs only slightly worse.

It appears therefore, that respondents answer the MIQ *as if* the income they perceive is their actual income. As noted, this means that implicitly respondents misperceive the welfare derived from their income.

Summary and conclusion

Respondents often do not have a correct perception of their household income, and this may affect their answers to the income evaluation quests, resulting in biased parameter estimates, as well as distorted poverty lines and equivalence scales. Earlier correction procedures were proportional, i.e. assumed that if a respondent underestimated her income by say 8 percent, the answers to the MIQ and IEQ should be adjusted upwards by 8 percent. Empirical analyses have shown, however, that people respond to the MIQ and the IEQ *as if* the income they perceive is their actual income. This finding implies that the adjustment should be less than proportional, depending on the values of α_1 and β_1. It also means that, implicitly, respondents misperceive the welfare they derive from their income.

Notes

1 There seems to have been some confusion about these labels. Van Praag, Hagenaars and Van Weeren (1980: 21) have called the poverty line derived from the minimum income question the "Leyden Poverty line definition". Here the abbreviations as introduced by Kapteyn, Van de Geer and Van de Stadt (1985) have been adopted. These seem to have been generally accepted now (cf. Van Praag and Flik, 1992).

2 The survey was in the form of a mail-back questionnaire (i.e. it was left behind by an interviewer, to be completed and sent back by the respondent) in all countries except Ireland and Italy, where an oral survey was conducted. The original samples were quota samples in four of the eight countries: Belgium, France, the UK and Italy; in other countries respondents were randomly selected. While the response rates were generally reasonable (56 to 93%), less than two-thirds of the questionnaires received appear to have been used in the actual analysis (compare the figures in table 4.A1 to those in table 5.1 in Van Praag, Hagenaars, Van Weeren, 1980). The samples have been reweighted, in order to make the sample distributions agree with independent national statistics regarding occupation, family size, urbanization, region etc. This procedure provides no guarantee, however, that the reweighted sample is representative for all income groups.

A further problem with the data is that even for the households that were included in the analysis, household income may not have been measured very accurately. The questionnaire included two questions about income amounts. One asked for the net-incomes of the main wage-earner and of his or her partner, where the explanation could have suggested to some respondents that the question referred to earnings only. The other question was about holiday allowances and contribution to household income from other members of the family. No explicit questions have been asked about social benefits and rents or interests. Measuring household income through such a small number of general questions may produce severe underestimation of household income.

3 As noted above, where only average income was available, I have assumed that the average is 15 percent above the median. In order to be able to include thresholds from (A) in the figure, I have used a median income estimate from (20j), which uses another survey for the same country and the same year. Similarly, an average income estimate from (21) has been used for (22), as both studies share the same database. This procedure implies that one must be cautious when comparing the level of income thresholds across studies. However, the main purpose of figure 4.4 is to show the relative position of the SPL vis-à-vis the LPL-0.4 and LPL-0.5 in each study, and these are unaffected. For (5), LPL-0.4 and LPL-0.5 thresholds have been taken from (5), instead of (6). The sets of estimates from (5) and (6) are quite close to each other.

4 Since in empirical work double-log regression equations are mostly used, the resulting parameter estimates can be interpreted as elasticities. An elasticity of 0.43 means that if household income rises by 1 percent, the answers to the IEQ and the MIQ will increase on average with 0.43 percent.

5 From the text of De Vos, Hagenaars and Van Praag (1987), it is not entirely clear how the income deemed 'just sufficient' is measured. Presumably, the same definition as in Homan et al. (1986) applies, which is, the average of the third and fourth level of the IEQ.

6 In their interpretation of this result, Hagenaars et al. (1984) refer to their theoretical introduction, in which they raise the possibility of 'backward-bending' indifference curves in the income-time space. According to the authors, many two-full-time-earner families would like to work less, but due to market imperfections are unable to do so. However, 'backward-bending' indifference curves are not needed to understand this phenomenon, and are difficult to make sense of in any case. (They imply that people are indifferent between a particular combination of income and leisure, and a situation where they have less of both.) Moreover, neither 'backward-bending' indifference curves, nor two-earner households being unable to reduce their market work can explain, as far as I can see, why income needs would go up with the number of hours spent on household work.

7 Because I have simplified the exposition compared with those of Kapteyn and his co-authors (e.g. Kapteyn and Wansbeek, 1985; Van de Stadt, Kapteyn and Van de Geer, 1985; Alessie and Kapteyn, 1988), the symbols as used here do not always mean the same thing here as in those papers. For

instance, the $w_{nk,t}$ as defined here are equivalent to the $q_{nk}(t)$, as used in Van de Stadt, Kapteyn and Van de Geer (1985).

8 The Koyck transformation, roughly speaking, amounts to replacing all lagged right-hand-side variables with the left-hand-side variable lagged one period, see Gujarati (1988: 513-515).

9 This is done as follows (De Vos and Garner, 1991: 280-282). Supposing that Ymin is underestimated by the same percentage as Yp underestimates actual income Y (i.e. $\log Ymin - \log Ymin^c = \log Yp - \log Y$, where $\log Ymin^c$ is the 'correct' or unbiased answer), that the following equation holds for $\log Ymin^c$:

$$\log Ymin^c = \alpha_0 + \alpha_1 \log Y + \alpha_2 \log FS + e$$

and that

$$Yp = Yh + \Sigma_i\ \theta_i Y_i,\ i = 2..\ I,$$

where Yh is the income of the main breadwinner, the following estimable equation is obtained by substitution and rearranging:

$$\log Ymin = \alpha_0 + (\alpha_1 - 1)\log Y + Yh + \Sigma_i\ \theta_i Y_{i\,+}\ \alpha_2 \log FS + e.$$

10 Tummers' specification is actually much more complicated than this, because in the survey which is the source of his data, respondents were only asked to indicate in which of seven income brackets they thought their household income was situated. Furthermore, he includes an interaction term between household size and household income. I have simplified the equations.

Tables to Chapter 4

Table 4.A1
Overview of main results of studies using subjective income evaluations

	Study	Country	Year	N	Income Evaluation	Ages	logFS	Coefficients for household composition dummies 1A+1C	2A	2A+1C	2A+2C	2A+3C	2A+4C	logY	Interaction	R2	HH-size elast.	Single factor	Couple + 3 childn factor	Other variables in equation: details of specification
1	Van Praag (1971)	Belgium	1969	2789	mu	-	0.30							0.19	-	0.20	0.37	78	140	
2	Kapteyn, Van Praag (1976)	Netherlands	1971	2573	mu	A,C	n							0.64	-	0.65	0.30	-	135	
3a	Goedhart et al. (1977)	Netherlands	1975	1748	mu	-	0.13							0.53	-	0.60	0.28	83	128	
b		Netherlands	1975	1748	Ymin	-	0.12							0.60	-	0.57	0.30	81	132	
4a	Van Herwaarden, Kapteyn and Van Praag (1977)	Belgium	1969	2522	mu	-	0.14							0.68	-	0.61	0.44	74	150	
b		Belgium	1970	2268	mu	-	0.13							0.66	-	0.59	0.39	76	143	
c		Belgium	1973	2179	mu	-	0.14							0.61	-	0.51	0.35	78	138	
d		Netherlands	1971	2952	mu	-	0.14							0.60	-	0.63	0.35	78	138	
e		Netherlands	1974	919	mu	-	0.11							0.66	-	0.66	0.32	80	134	
5a	Van Praag, Hagenaars and Van Weeren (1980)	Belgium	1979	1193	Ymin	-	0.13							0.53	-	0.58	0.28	83	129	
b		Denmark	1979	2145	Ymin	-	0.10							0.74	-	0.78	0.38	77	142	
c		France	1979	2456	Ymin	-	0.08							0.68	-	0.71	0.25	84	126	
d		W.Germany	1979	1870	Ymin	-	0.14							0.63	-	0.65	0.38	77	141	
e		Great Britain	1979	1561	Ymin	-	0.14							0.54	-	0.57	0.30	81	132	
f		Ireland	1979	1864	Ymin	-	0.18							0.53	-	0.57	0.38	77	142	
g		Italy	1979	2076	Ymin	-	0.16							0.56	-	0.54	0.36	78	140	
h		Netherlands	1979	2047	Ymin	-	0.15							0.54	-	0.58	0.33	80	135	
6a	Van Praag, Hagenaars and Van Weeren (1982)	Belgium	1979	1272	mu	A	0.10							0.43	-	0.70	0.17	89	117	Sex, Work, Educ, Prof, Urb
b		Denmark	1979	1972	mu	A	0.08							0.63	-	0.83	0.20	86	120	Sex, Work, Educ, Prof, Urb
c		France	1979	2052	mu	A	0.06							0.51	-	0.68	0.12	92	112	Sex, Work, Educ, Prof, Urb
d		W.Germany	1979	1574	mu	A	0.11							0.58	-	0.69	0.27	83	128	Sex, Work, Educ, Prof, Urb
e		Great Britain	1979	1183	mu	A	0.12							0.36	-	0.58	0.18	89	118	Sex, Work, Educ, Prof, Urb
f		Ireland	1979	1733	mu	A	0.17							0.46	-	0.64	0.31	81	133	Sex, Work, Educ, Prof, Urb
g		Italy	1979	1911	mu	A	0.16							0.38	-	0.51	0.25	83	126	Sex, Work, Educ, Prof, Urb
h		Netherlands	1979	1933	mu	A	0.10							0.54	-	0.66	0.22	86	122	Sex, Work, Educ, Prof, Urb
7	Danziger et al. (1984)	USA	1979	2464	Ymin	A	0.21							0.33	-	0.48	0.31	81	133	Sex
8a	Colasanto et al. (1984)	Wisconsin	1981	1372	Ymin	A	0.26							0.45	-	0.45	0.47	72	154	Sex
b		Wisconsin	1981	1372	mu	-	0.20							0.45	-	0.42	0.37	78	140	Sex
9	Hagenaars et al. (1984)	Netherlands	1983	4901	mu	-	0.003							0.80	-	0.66	0.02	99	101	Work
10a	Hagenaars (1985)	Belgium	1979	1269	mu	A	-	-	.06	.06	.08	.09	.14	0.46		0.59	0.21	80	106	CY, Work, Educ, Prof, Urb
b		Denmark	1979	1981	mu	A	-	-	.09	.12	.13	.12	.13	0.64	-	0.82	0.27	75	108	CY, Work, Educ, Prof, Urb
c		France	1979	2334	mu	A	-	-	.06	.08	.09	.07	.09	0.48	-	0.64	0.22	83	103	CY, Work, Educ, Prof, Urb
d		W.Germany	1979	1572	mu	A	-	-	.02	.07	.09	.13	.16	0.57	-	0.65	0.28	93	128	CY, Work, Educ, Prof, Urb
f		Ireland	1979	1734	mu	A	-	-	.08	.16	.19	.20	.30	0.47	-	0.63	0.24	87	129	CY, Work, Educ, Prof, Urb
g		Italy	1979	1924	mu	A	-	-	.10	.15	.19	.20	.30	0.41	-	0.53	0.25	81	117	CY, Work, Educ, Prof, Urb
h		Netherlands	1979	1890	mu	A	-	-	.12	.16	.15	.18	.14	0.47	-	0.64	0.17	79	113	CY, Work, Educ, Prof, Urb
i		Great Britain	1979	1383	mu	A	-	-	.14	.19	.16	.22	.18	0.42	-	0.51	0.16	75	114	CY, Work, Educ, Prof, Urb
11a	Janssens et al. (1985)	Flanders	1976	4829	Ymin	-	0.18							0.44	-	0.55	0.33	80	135	
b		Flanders	1982	3619	Ymin	-	0.23							0.31	-	0.35	0.34	79	136	
12a	Kapteyn, Van de Geer and Van de Stadt (1985)	Netherlands	1980-82	616	mu	-	0.10							0.42	-	n.r.	0.17	89	117	Ref.G, Dyn
b		Netherlands	1980-82	616	Ymin	-	0.12							0.45	-	n.r.	0.21	86	121	Ref.G, Dyn
13	Homan et al. (1986)	Netherlands	1983	3607	n	-	0.12							n		n.r.	0.42	-	147	CY,Work,HomeT;Und.Y
14a	De Vos et al. (1987)	Netherlands	1983	?	Ysuf	A		-	.08	.14	.18	.24	.30	n	-	0.72	0.46	78	153	CY,Work,Ref.G;Und.Y
b		Netherlands	1983	?	Ymin	A		-	.14	.19	.24	.30	.36	0.56	-	0.33	0.34	84	138	CY,Work,Ref.G;Und.Y
15a	Kapteyn, Kooreman and Willemse (1988)	Netherlands	1982	773	mu	C	0.76							0.55	-0.06	0.59	0.33	78	126	Ref.G; Und.Y, Select
b		Netherlands	1982	773	Ymin	C	0.22							0.43	n.s.	0.56	0.39	76	134	Ref.G; Und.Y, Select

Table 4.A1 (continuation)

	Study	Country	Year	N	Income Evalu-ation	Ages	logFS	Coefficients for household composition dummies						logY	Inter-action	R2	HH-size elast.	Single factor	Couple + 3 childn factor	Other variables in equation: details of specification
16	Poulin (1988)	Canada	1983	37602	Ymin	A	0.10							0.36	-	0.36	0.16	90	117	Sex. HomeT. Urb
17a	Van Praag and Van der Sar	Belgium	1979	1600	Yinsuf	-	0.25							0.31	-	0.40	0.36	78	139	
b	(1988)	Denmark	1979	2300	Yinsuf	-	0.20							0.58	-	0.65	0.48	72	155	
c		France	1979	2700	Yinsuf	-	0.15							0.41	-	0.42	0.25	84	126	
d		W.Germany	1979	2200	Yinsuf	-	0.28							0.25	-	0.32	0.37	77	141	
e		Ireland	1979	2300	Yinsuf	-	0.13							0.41	-	0.38	0.22	86	122	
f		Italy	1979	2520	Yinsuf	-	0.20							0.30	-	0.31	0.29	82	130	
g		Netherlands	1979	2160	Yinsuf	-	0.15							0.48	-	0.54	0.29	82	130	
h		UK	1979	1950	Yinsuf	-	0.21							0.29	-	0.26	0.30	81	131	
i		Boston (USA)	1983	480	Yinsuf	-	0.14							0.65	-	0.76	0.40	76	144	
18	Callan. Nolan et al. (1989)	Ireland	1987	3294	Ymin	-	0.32							0.27	-	0.49	0.44	74	149	
19a	Moriani (1990)	Italy	1987	15712	mu	-	0.23							0.32	-	0.66	0.34	79	136	
b		Italy	1987	15712	Ymin	-	0.29							0.31	-	0.66	0.41	75	146	
20a	Muffels. Kapteyn. Berghman	Netherlands	1985	2948	Ymin	-	0.06							0.44	n.s.	n.r.	0.11	93	110	Und.Y
b	(1990)	Netherlands	1985	2948	Ymin	C	0.23							0.35	-0.00	n.r.	0.36	78	114	Ref.G; Und.Y. Select
c		Netherlands	1985	2948	mu	-	0.05							0.45	n.s.	n.r.	0.09	94	108	Und.Y
d		Netherlands	1985	2948	mu	C	0.17							0.35	0.00	n.r.	0.29	82	111	Ref.G; Und.Y. Select
e		Netherlands	1986	3796	Ymin	-	0.16							0.40	n.s.	n.r.	0.27	83	128	Und.Y
f		Netherlands	1986	3796	Ymin	C	0.59							0.40	-0.04	n.r.	0.29	80	126	Ref.G; Und.Y. Select
g		Netherlands	1986	3796	mu	-	0.16							0.39	n.s.	n.r.	0.26	82	130	Und.Y
h		Netherlands	1986	3796	mu	C	0.55							0.37	-0.04	n.r.	0.29	81	123	Ref.G; Und.Y. Select
i		Netherlands	1985&6	4558	Ymin	C	0.20							0.35	-	n.r.	0.31	81	121	Ref.G; Und.Y. Select
j		Netherlands	1985&6	4558	mu	C	0.17							0.38	-	n.r.	0.27	83	116	Ref.G; Und.Y. Select
k		Netherlands	1985-6	n.r.	Ymin	C	0.15							0.20	-	n.r.	0.15	90	111	Ref.G; Und.Y. Select. Dyn
l		Netherlands	1985-6	n.r.	mu	C	0.20							0.23	-	n.r.	0.20	87	115	Ref.G; Und.Y. Select. Dyn
21a	De Vos and Garner (1991)	Netherlands	1983	10389	Ymin	A.C	n	.09	.09	.13	.19	.23	.29	0.55	-	0.34	0.35	78	132	Sex.Work.Educ.Disab; Und.Y.Select
b		USA	1982	4830	Ymin	A.C	n	.16	.14	.21	.28	.33	.28	0.43	-	0.49	0.38	72	145	USA only: Race. Region. Urb
22a	Flik and Van Praag (1991)	Netherlands	1983	6313	mu	-	0.08							0.71	-	0.63	0.29	81	131	
b		Netherlands	1983	6313	Ymin	-	0.11							0.59	-	0.31	0.26	83	127	
23a	Stanovnik (1992)	Slovenia	1983	1369	'Ymin'	A	n							0.71	-	0.71	<0.52	-	-	
b		Slovenia	1988	1738	'Ymin'	A	n							0.52	-	0.62	<0.59	-	-	
24a	Van Praag and Flik (1992)	Italy	1987	15230	mu	-	0.25							0.32	-	0.51	0.37	77	141	
b		Italy	1987	15230	mu	A	-	.19	.11	.25	.28	.33	.41	0.32	-	0.51	0.33	85	139	
c		Italy	1987	15230	mu	A	0.27							0.27	-	0.54	0.37	76	140	Work. Region
d		France	1989	7800	mu	-	0.16							0.45	-	0.62	0.30	81	132	
e		France	1989	7800	mu	A	-	.09	.07	.14	.19	.20	.21	0.46	-	0.62	0.23	88	127	
f		France	1989	7800	mu	A	0.12							0.42	-	0.64	0.21	87	121	Work. Region
g		Belgium	1987/8	1917	mu	-	0.18							0.42	-	0.57	0.31	81	132	
h		Belgium	1987/8	1917	mu	A	-	.15	.11	.19	.24	.26	.41	0.43	-	0.57	0.36	82	130	
i		Belgium	1987/8	1917	mu	A	0.17							0.37	-	0.60	0.26	83	127	Work. Region
25	Saunders et al. (1993)	Australia	1988	950	Ymin	A	n	.03	.12	.15	.18	.20	.23	0.26	-	0.32	0.17	85	112	Work. Educ. HomeT. Party
26a	Saunders. Halleröd and	Australia	1988	1029	Ymin	n	n	.04	.09	.13	.17	.21	.25	0.30	-	0.25	0.19	88	119	
b	Matheson (1994)	Sweden	1992	717	Ymin	n	n	.10	.15	.25	.35	.45	.55	0.32	-	0.39	0.44	80	155	
27	Halleröd (1995)	Sweden	1992	705	Ymin	A	n	.10	.20	.30	.40	.50	.60	0.25	-	0.43	0.77	77	149	Region

Notes: n = see note by row; n.r. = not reported; n.s. = not statistically significant;

Notes for column headings:

N:	Number of observations used in regression analysis; this may be (much) lower than the number of cases in the sample.
Income evaluation:	Income evaluation variable used; mu = μ, Ymin = logYmin, Yinsuf = amount evaluated as 'insufficient' (3rd level of IEQ), Ysuf = amount evaluated as 'sufficient' (4th level of IEQ).
Ages:	Whether ages of adults and/or children are taken account of in model; A: Age of adults (mostly head of household); C: Ages of children; n: see Notes by row.
logFS:	Regression estimate of log(Family size) parameter; n = see Notes by row.
Coefficients for household composition dummies:	Reference household is a single adult; where necessary and possible, these are calculated from coefficients actually reported. 1A, 2A: Number of adults; 1C .. 4C: number of children.
logY:	Regression estimate of log(Household income) parameter.
Interaction:	Regression estimate of parameter for interaction of log(Household size) and log(Household income).
R2:	R-square for regression equation.
HH-size elast.:	Elasticity of the equivalence scale with respect to household size. If household size is represented by dummies, the elasticity has been estimated by calculating the equivalence factors, taking logarithms, and regressing these on log(household size).
Single factor:	Equivalence factor of single persons, two adult household = 100.
Couple + 3 childn factor:	Equivalence factor of households composed of two adults + 3 children, two adult household = 100; when ages of children are taken into account, these are assumed to be 12, 6 and 1.
Other variables in ...:	The following abbreviations are used: *Sex*: Sex head of household. *CY*: Changes or fluctuations in income. *Work*: Number of persons at work, or number of earners in household. *Educ*: Level or kind of education. *Prof*: Professional status. *Disab*: Whether or not respondent is disabled. *Ref.G*: Reference Group (constructed or measured). *Party*: Identification with political party. *HomeT*: Home Tenure (Renter, Owner with mortgage or Owner outright). *Urb*: Degree of urbanization. *Region*: Region. *Und.Y*: Correction for Underestimation of own income (cf. section 4.6). *Select*: Correction for non-response selectivity bias. *Dyn*: Dynamic model used, i.e. one requiring panel data.

Notes by row:

1	According to Van Herwaarden et al. (1977), data used in this study suffered from a number of punching errors; corrected results are shown in line 4a.
2	Authors use complex specification where age and rank functions are lognormal distribution functions.
3a	Results also presented in Van Herwaarden, Kapteyn and Van Praag (1977).
4	Some results are also shown in Van Praag and Kapteyn (1973).
12	A similar model using data from the same household panel is estimated in Van de Stadt, Kapteyn and Van de Geer (1985) and in Alessie and Kapteyn (1988), but in these studies data from only two waves, instead of three, are utilized.
13	Results for single-earner couples only; authors use specification with log-income (est.: -0.87) and square of log-income (est.: +0.08).
14	Authors use specification with log-income (est.: -1.03) and square of log-income (est.: +0.08).
15	A similar model (but without correction for selectivity bias) using data from the same survey is estimated in Kapteyn, Kooreman, Muffels et al. (1985), with very similar results.
15a	Equivalence factors are computed at the average income level in the sample.
17	In this study separate equations are estimated for each level of the IEQ. Only results for the 'insufficient' amount are shown here, as this level appeared to be the one most relevant for poverty studies. Results for other levels were mostly quite similar.
19	In addition to reference shown, I have used data from an unpublished paper by Moriani.
20f	Equivalence factors are computed at the level of the poverty line for a two adult household.
20h	Equivalence factors are computed at the level of the poverty line for a two adult household.
20j	Results for similar model using the same data are reported in Kapteyn and Melenberg (1993).
21	Coefficients for household composion dummies recalculated from reported coefficients for families with one earner.
23	A rather different version of the MIQ was used in this study.
23	Instead of log(Household size), log(Equivalent household size) was entered in equations.
24	Distinction between elderly and non-elderly is only made for single people, not for other household types.
25, 26, 27	Number of adults and number of children were entered in equations. Coefficients for household composion dummies shown here are calculated from reported coefficients for those variables.
27	Equivalence scale parameters are not those reported by Halleröd which are based on a linear regression specification, but are calculated from regression results reported by Halleröd (1995: 7, table 2, equation 9i), as the latter are more comparable to those from other studies.

Table 4.A2
Overview of LPL and SPL poverty lines

	Study	Country	Year	N	Type of PL	Absolute level	Poverty line for 2 adult family as % of median Y	Poverty line for 2 adult family as % of average Y	HH-size elasticity	% in poverty
3a	Goedhart et al. (1977)	Netherlands	1975	1748	LPL0.4	10910 Fl/yr	-	52	0.28	-
5a	Van Praag, Hagenaars and Van Weeren	Belgium	1979	1272	LPL0.4	7155 $/yr	49	-	0.17	12
b	(1982)	Denmark	1979	1972	LPL0.4	6892 $/yr	64	-	0.20	23
c		France	1979	2052	LPL0.4	8314 $/yr	72	-	0.12	27
d		W.Germany	1979	1574	LPL0.4	5089 $/yr	39	-	0.27	3
e		Great Britain	1979	1183	LPL0.4	5946 $/yr	58	-	0.18	14
f		Ireland	1979	1733	LPL0.4	4938 $/yr	61	-	0.31	26
g		Italy	1979	1911	LPL0.4	5593 $/yr	47	-	0.25	10
h		Netherlands	1979	1933	LPL0.4	6903 $/yr	52	-	0.22	6
8b	Colasanto et al. (1984)	Wisconsin	1981	1372	LPL0.4	6011 $/yr	34	-	0.37	-
15a	Kapteyn et al. (1988)	Netherlands	1982	773	LPL0.4	17100 Fl/yr	53	-	0.33	-
Aa	Ghiatis (1990)	Netherlands	1986	2936	LPL0.4	16994 Fl/yr	N.A.			7
19a	Moriani (1990)	Italy	1987	15712	LPL0.4	841000 l/mth	-	41	0.34	10
22a	Flik and Van Praag (1991)	Netherlands	1983	6313	LPL0.4	9835 Fl/yr	-	-	0.29	4
24c	Van Praag and Flik (1992) Van Praag and	Italy	1987	15230	LPL0.4	N.A.	-	-	0.37	9
i	Flik (1992)	Belgium	1987/8	1917	LPL0.4	N.A.	-	-	0.26	4
3a	Goedhart et al. (1977)	Netherlands	1975	1748	LPL0.5	13570 Fl/yr	-	65	0.28	-
6a	Van Praag, Hagenaars and Van Weeren	Belgium	1979	1272	LPL0.5	8566 $/yr	59	-	0.17	18
b	(1982)	Denmark	1979	1972	LPL0.5	8566 $/yr	81	-	0.20	35
c		France	1979	2052	LPL0.5	10430 $/yr	90	-	0.12	43
d		W.Germany	1979	1574	LPL0.5	6550 $/yr	50	-	0.27	8
e		Great Britain	1979	1183	LPL0.5	7105 $/yr	70	-	0.18	22
f		Ireland	1979	1733	LPL0.5	5996 $/yr	74	-	0.31	38
g		Italy	1979	1911	LPL0.5	7004 $/yr	59	-	0.25	18
h		Netherlands	1979	1933	LPL0.5	8364 $/yr	63	-	0.22	16
8b	Colasanto et al. (1984)	Wisconsin	1981	1372	LPL0.5	7515 $/yr	42	-	0.37	-
10a	Hagenaars (1985)	Belgium	1979	1269	LPL0.5	17347 Fl/yr	61	-	0.21	14
b		Denmark	1979	1981	LPL0.5	16694 Fl/yr	78	-	0.27	29
c		France	1979	2334	LPL0.5	21509 Fl/yr	94	-	0.22	42
d		W.Germany	1979	1572	LPL0.5	13217 Fl/yr	58	-	0.28	6
f		Ireland	1979	1734	LPL0.5	12448 Fl/yr	73	-	0.24	37
g		Italy	1979	1924	LPL0.5	15013 Fl/yr	64	-	0.25	17
h		Netherlands	1979	1890	LPL0.5	18338 Fl/yr	71	-	0.17	16
i		Great Britain	1979	1383	LPL0.5	13997 Fl/yr	69	-	0.16	28
15a	Kapteyn et al. (1988)	Netherlands	1982	773	LPL0.5	19800 Fl/yr	61	-	0.33	-
19a	Moriani (1990)	Italy	1987	15712	LPL0.5	999000 l/mth	-	49	0.34	17
20j	Muffels, Kapteyn, Berghman (1990)	Netherlands	1985	4558	LPL0.5	2058 Fl/mth	77	-	0.27	29
j		Netherlands	1986	4558	LPL0.5	2281 Fl/mth	80	-	0.27	36
22a	Flik and Van Praag (1991)	Netherlands	1983	6313	LPL0.5	12949 Fl/yr	-	-	0.29	10
24f	Van Praag and Flik (1992)	France	1989	7800	LPL0.5	N.A.	-	-	0.21	19

Table 4.A2 (continuation)

	Study	Country	Year	N	Type of PL	Absolute level	Poverty line for 2 adult family as % of median Y	as % of average Y	HH-size elasticity	% in poverty
3b	Goedhart et al. (1977)	Netherlands	1975	1748	SPL	9510 Fl/yr	-	46	0.30	-
5a	Van Praag, Hagenaars and Van Weeren	Belgium	1979	1193	SPL	3639 EAU/yr	36		0.28	4
b	(1980)	Denmark	1979	2145	SPL	4383 EAU/yr	58		0.38	19
c		France	1979	2456	SPL	3572 EAU/yr	44		0.25	10
d		W.Germany	1979	1870	SPL	2856 EAU/yr	32		0.38	2
e		Great Britain	1979	1561	SPL	3218 EAU/yr	51		0.30	15
f		Ireland	1979	1864	SPL	2957 EAU/yr	45		0.38	14
g		Italy	1979	2076	SPL	3412 EAU/yr	42		0.36	9
h		Netherlands	1979	2047	SPL	4004 EAU/yr	44		0.33	3
7	Danziger et al. (1984)	USA	1979	2464	SPL	1016 $/mth	-	67	0.31	-
8a	Colasanto et al. (1984)	Wisconsin	1981	1372	SPL	5831 $/yr	33	-	0.47	-
11a	Janssens et al. (1985)	Flanders	1976	4829	SPL	26900 BF/mth	N.A.	-	0.33	-
b		Flanders	1982	3619	SPL	26900 BF/mth	-	58	0.34	-
15b	Kapteyn et al. (1988)	Netherlands	1982	773	SPL	15400 Fl/yr	48	-	0.39	-
16	Poulin (1988)	Canada	1983	37602	SPL	18678 C$/yr	-	67	0.16	-
18	Callan, Nolan et al. (1989)	Ireland	1987	3294	SPL	92.3 Ir£/wk	-	47	0.44	32
Ab	Ghiatis (1990)	Netherlands	1986	2936	SPL	16216 Fl/yr	N.A.			5
19b	Moriani (1990)	Italy	1987	15712	SPL	1264000 l/mth	-	62	0.41	33
20i	Muffels, Kapteyn, Berghman (1990)	Netherlands	1985	3693	SPL	1734 Fl/mth	65	-	0.31	17
i		Netherlands	1986	4472	SPL	1870 Fl/mth	66	-	0.31	21
21a	De Vos and Garner (1991)	USA	1982	3520	SPL	16753 $/yr	-	73	0.38	42
b		Netherlands	1983	10389	SPL	22025 Fl/yr	-	63	0.35	17
22b	Flik and Van Praag (1991); Van den Bosch	Netherlands	1983	6313	SPL	12807 Fl/yr	-	-		12
Ba	et al. (1993), also Deleeck et al. (1992)	Belgium	1985	6471	SPL	797 ECU/mth	67	-	0.27	25
b		Belgium	1988	3379	SPL	757 ECU/mth	59	-	0.42	21
c		Netherlands	1985	3405	SPL	632 ECU/mth	54	-	0.28	9
d		Netherlands	1986	4480	SPL	743 ECU/mth	60	-	0.27	16
e		Luxembourg	1985	2013	SPL	1016 ECU/mth	62	-	0.40	23
f		Luxembourg	1986	1793	SPL	902 ECU/mth	53	-	0.28	13
g		Lorraine	1985	715	SPL	821 ECU/mth	69	-	0.25	29
h		Lorraine	1986	2092	SPL	816 ECU/mth	66	-	0.30	27
i		Ireland	1987	3294	SPL	544 ECU/mth	58	-	0.44	32
j		Ireland	1989	947	SPL	576 ECU/mth	69	-	0.44	40
k		Catalonia	1988	2976	SPL	925 ECU/mth	69	-	0.36	37
l		Greece	1988	2958	SPL	707 ECU/mth	88	-	0.44	42
26a	Saunders, Halleröd and Matheson (1994)	Australia	1988	1029	SPL	248 $/wk	-	51	0.19	22
b		Sweden	1992	717	SPL	214 $/wk	N.A.	-	0.44	13
27	Halleröd (1995)	Sweden	1992	705	SPL	11355 SK/mth	N.A.	-	0.45	21

Numbers in first column refer back to table 4.A1 and other review tables; A and B indicate studies that are not listed in other tables.

Notes: n = see note for row; n.r. = not reported; n.s. = not statistically significant;

N:	Number of observations used in regression analysis; this can be lower than the number of cases in the sample.
Type of PL	Kind of poverty line: LPL0.4, LPL0.5 or SPL.
Absolute level:	Amount of poverty line for a two-adult household as given in source;
	Fl: Dutch guilders; $: US dollars; l: Italian lire; BF: Belgian Franc; C$: Canadian dollar; EAU: European Accounting Unit; ECU: European Currency Unit; SK: Swedish Krona; yr: year; mth: month; wk: week.
as % of median Y:	Poverty line for two adult household as a percentage of median household income in the sample.
as % of average Y:	Poverty line for two adult household as a percentage of average household income in the sample.
HH-size elasticity:	Elasticity of poverty lines with respect to household size.
% in poverty	Percentage of households with incomes below poverty line.

Notes by row:

19 In addition to reference shown, I have used data from an unpublished paper by Moriani.

22 Percentages in poverty are not based on sample data, but on interpolation of estimated poverty lines in income distribution figures published by the Dutch Central Bureau of Statistics.

Table 4.A3
Overview of results of studies using subjective income evaluations, regarding age of head of household

	Study	Specification	Country	Year	N	Income Evaluation	Estimated effects for five ages, age 25 = 0 (see note)					Significance	Elderly equivalence factor
							35	45	55	65	75		
2	Kapteyn, Van Praag (1976)	See note	Netherlands	1971	2573	mu	.21	.38	.42	.43	.43		130
6a	Van Praag, Hagenaars and Van Weeren (1982)	Dummy (5)	Belgium	1979	1272	mu	.04	.05	.09	-.06	-.05		84
b		"	Denmark	1979	1972	mu	.02	.03	.00	.00	-.11		68
c		"	France	1979	2052	mu	.05	.05	.05	-.01	-.10		74
d		"	W.Germany	1979	1574	mu	.00	.02	.02	-.09	-.10		77
e		"	Great Britain	1979	1183	mu	.08	.10	.11	.04	-.11		72
f		"	Ireland	1979	1733	mu	.00	-.03	-.01	.00	-.05	n.s.	95
g		"	Italy	1979	1911	mu	-.00	.00	-.00	-.04	-.03	n.s.	94
h		"	Netherlands	1979	1933	mu	.05	.06	.08	.03	-.03		80
7	Danziger et al. (1984)	Dummy (2)	USA	1979	2464	Ymin				-.29			61
8a	Colasanto et al. (1984)	Dummy (2)	Wisconsin	1981	1372	Ymin				.04		n.s.	107
10a	Hagenaars (1985)	Log + Log2	Belgium	1979	1269	mu	.06	.07	.05	.02	-.02		88
b		"	Denmark	1979	1981	mu	.03	.01	-.02	-.07	-.12		73
c		"	France	1979	2334	mu	.05	.04	.02	-.02	-.06		84
d		"	W.Germany	1979	1572	mu	.03	.03	.02	.00	-.02		91
f		"	Ireland	1979	1734	mu	-.01	-.03	-.05	-.07	-.09	n.s.	89
g		"	Italy	1979	1924	mu	.01	-.01	-.03	-.06	-.09	n.s.	89
h		"	Netherlands	1979	1890	mu	.07	.08	.07	.04	.00		90
i		"	Great Britain	1979	1383	mu	.12	.12	.07	-.01	-.10		73
14a	De Vos et al. (1987)	See note	Netherlands	1983	n.r.	Ysuf				+.03			113
b		See note	Netherlands	1983	n.r.	Ymin				+.05			118
16	Poulin (1988)	Dummy (7)	Canada	1983	37602	Ymin	.02	-.02	-.09	-.34			57
21a	De Vos and Garner (1991)	See note	USA	1982	4830	Ymin	.09	.14	.15	.11	.03		87
b		"	Netherlands	1983	3520	Ymin	.06	.10	.12	.12	.09		113
23a	Stanovnik (1992)	Dummy (2)	Slovenia	1983	1369	'Ymin'				.04			116
b		"	Slovenia	1988	1738	'Ymin'				-.08			85
24b	Van Praag and Flik (1992)	Dummy (2)	Italy	1987	15230	mu				-.11			86
c		Log + log2	Italy	1987	15230	mu	.04	.05	.04	.03	.02		98
e		Dummy (2)	France	1989	7800	mu				-.14			78
f		Log + log2	France	1989	7800	mu	.07	.07	.04	-.01	-.06		83
h		Dummy (2)	Belgium	1987/8	1917	mu				-.05			91
i		Log + log2	Belgium	1987/8	1917	mu	.06	.06	.05	.03	-.01		92
25	Saunders et al. (1993)	Dummy (2)	Australia	1988	950	Ymin				-.12			85
27	Halleröd (1994)	See note	Sweden	1992	705	Ymin	.07	.17	.10	.01	-.09		70

Numbers in first column refer to table 4.A1 and other review tables.

Notes for column headings:

Specification:	Specification used for age head; if dummy variables are used, the number of age brackets distinguished is reported between brackets; log+log2 = log(age head) + square of log(age head).
N:	Number of observations used in regression analysis; this may be (much) lower than the number of cases in the sample.
mu or logYmin:	Income evaluation variable used; mu = μ, Ymin = logYmin, Ysuf = log of amount regarded as sufficient (3rd level of IEQ).
Estimated effects:	Effects on mu or logYmin for various ages, effect at age 25 is set at zero; if dummy variables specification is used, figure shown is effect of age bracket in which age is located; in other cases, figures are calculated from reported results.
Significance:	Statistical significance of age effect; n.s. means that none of the age of head effects were significantly different from zero.
Elderly factor:	Equivalence factor of households where head is elderly (65+) with respect to similar households with a non-aged head. If several age brackets or a log(age) specification is used, factor shown is the equivalence factor for households with heads aged 70 with respect to households with heads aged 40.

Notes by row:

2	Authors use complex specification where age functions for all household members are lognormal distribution functions.
14	Authors use separate dummies for single elderly people and elderly couples, results shown are for single elderly people relative to non-working non-elderly single people.
21	Authors use specification which includes age head, and square of age head, as well as dummy variables for "single, 65+" and "2 persons, 65+". 'Regression coefficients' shown here are based only on reported coefficients for age and square of age, as the effects of the dummy variables were not significant, and of opposite sign; elderly equivalence factor is mean of equivalence factors for singles and couples, calculated from poverty lines reported in source.
24	Distinction between elderly and non-elderly is only made for single people, not for other household types.
27	Specification used is: ABS(44-age), where ABS stands for absolute value.

Table 4.A4
Estimates of costs of children, relative to those of adults, using the income evaluation method

Ref. Nr.	Study (6)	Sample used (1)	Income Eval. (2)	Static Or Dynamic	Other features of model (3)	Estimates of b21*100 (and standard errors)	Estimates of b22*1000 (and standard errors)	Estimates of the cost of children, relative to those of an adult of the same rank, by age: 0	3	6	9	12	15	18
	Kapteyn, Kooreman, Muffels et al., 1985	'NPAO labor market survey' (non-elderly only), 1982, N=774	Comb.	Static	R2, UY	+0.297 (1.17)	-0.134 (0.303)	0.40	0.49	0.62	0.75	0.88	0.97	1.00
15	Kapteyn, Kooreman, Willemse, 1988	'NPAO labor market survey' (non-elderly only), 1982, N=774	Comb.	Static	R2, UY, SB	+0.185 (1.2)	-0.080 (0.3)	0.67	0.71	0.78	0.86	0.93	0.98	1.00
20b, d	Muffels, Kapteyn et al., 1990	'Socio-Economic Panel' of the CBS, 1985, N=2948	Comb.	Static	R2, UY, SB	+2.47 (0.070)	-0.73 (0.18)	0.49	0.15	0.14	0.34	0.63	0.89	1.00
20f, h		'Socio-Economic Panel' of the CBS, 1986, N=3796	Comb.	Static	R2, UY, SB	+1.25 (0.84)	-0.34 (0.22)	1.08	0.83	0.74	0.77	0.86	0.96	1.00
20j		'Socio-Economic Panel' of the CBS, 1985+86,	mu	Static (4)	R3, UY, SB	+0.998 (1.132)	-0.328 (0.297)	0.41	0.37	0.45	0.61	0.79	0.94	1.00
20i		N=4558	Ymin	Static (4)	R3, UY, SB	+0.878 (0.845)	-0.284 (0.222)	0.53	0.48	0.55	0.68	0.83	0.95	1.00
20l		'Socio-Economic Panel' of the CBS, 1984-86 (5)	mu	Dynamic	R3, UY, SB	-0.716) (1.979)	+0.133 (0.530)	0.23	0.56	0.77	0.90	0.97	1.00	1.00
20k		'Socio-Economic Panel' of the CBS, 1985-86 (5)	Ymin	Dynamic	R3, UY, SB	+0.382 (3.238)	-0.138 (0.876)	0.63	0.65	0.72	0.81	0.90	0.97	1.00
	Aalbers et al. 1990	'Socio-Economic Panel', 1984+85+86+87, N=670	mu	Static (4)	R2, UY, SB	1.634 (0.896)	-0.507 (0.237)	0.38	0.23	0.29	0.48	0.71	0.91	1.00
		'Socio-Economic Panel', 1985+86+87+88, N=598	Ymin	Static (4)	R2, UY, SB	+1.168) (1.052)	-0.374 (0.279)	0.42	0.35	0.42	0.58	0.77	0.93	1.00

Numbers in first column refer to table 4.A1 and other review tables.

Notes:

(1) All samples are Dutch; sample size reported is the number of cases effectively used in regressions.

(2) Comb.: Combined mu and logYmin equations, i.e. age parameters were constrained to be equal in mu and logYmin equations.

(3) R2: Reference group effect, 'constructed social group' model, see section 4.5; R3: Reference group effect, 'factor' model; UY: Correction for underestimation by respondent of own income, see section 4.6; SB: Correction for sample selectivity bias.

(4) Parameter stability across years imposed.

(5) Number of cases not reported.

(6) Tummers (1992: 30) also reports estimates of the age parameters. Calculations of the corresponding age function did not agree with the curves drawn by Tummers (figure 3), possibly because the estimates as reported by Tummers contain only one significant digit. For this reason, his results are not included in the table.

Table 4.A5
Overview of results of studies of subjective income evaluations, regarding working status of household members

	Study	Specification	Country	Year	N	Income evaluation variable	Single. working	Couple. one earner	Couple. two earners	Signifi-cance	Eq.factor 1 vs. 0 earners	Eq.factor 2 vs. 1 earners
9	Hagenaars et al. (1984)	See text	Netherlands	1983	4901	mu	-	-	.06	sig.	-	130
10a	Hagenaars (1985)	2 dummies	Belgium	1979	1269	mu	-	.06	.07	sig.	112	102
b		"	Denmark	1979	1981	mu	-	.01	.07	sig.	103	118
c		"	France	1979	2334	mu	-	.04	.06	sig.	108	103
d		"	W.Germany	1979	1572	mu	-	.01	-.01	n.s.	103	95
f		"	Ireland	1979	1734	mu	-	-.00	.01	n.s.	99	102
g		"	Italy	1979	1924	mu	-	.02	-.01	n.s.	103	95
h		"	Netherlands	1979	1890	mu	-	.01	-.01	n.s.	101	97
i		"	Great Britain	1979	1383	mu	-	.03	.02	n.s.	104	98
13	Homan (1988)	2 equations	Netherlands	1983	6178	mu	-	n.a.	n.a.		-	123
14a	De Vos et al. (1987)	See note	Netherlands	1983	?	Yjsuf	.02	-.00	-.04	sig	106	88
b		See note	Netherlands	1983	?	Ymin	-.08	-0.5	-0.8	sig	89	93
21a	De Vos and Garner (1991)	See note	USA	1982	3520	Ymin	.03	.23	.25	sig	141	103
b		"	Netherlands	1983	10389	Ymin	-.05	-.06	-.05	sig	94	101
24c	Van Praag and Flik (1992)	4 dummies	Italy	1987	15230	mu	.12	.03	.11	sig.	104	103
f		2 dummies	France	1989	7800	mu	-	.03	.08	sig.	105	108
i		3 dummies	Belgium	1987/8	1917	mu	-	.03	.13	sig.	105	115
25	Saunders et al. (1993)	See note	Australia	1988	950	Ymin	-	-	-	n.s.	-	-

Numbers in first column refer to table 4.A1 and other review tables.

Notes for column headings:

Specification:	Specification used for working status household members.
N:	Number of observations used in regression analysis; this may be (much) lower than the number of cases in the sample.
mu or logYmin:	Income evaluation variable used; mu = μ, Ymin = logYmin, Yjsuf = Average of 3rd and 4th level of IEQ ('just sufficient').
Single, working	Effect of household head being single and working, non-working single person is reference category (regression coefficient).
Couple, one earner	Effect when only one partner in a couple is working, non-working couple is reference category (regression coefficient).
Couple, two earner	Effect when both partners of a couple are working, non-working couple is reference category (regression coefficient).
Significance:	Statistical significance of age effect; n.s. means that none of the work effects are significantly different from zero; sig. means that at least one of the work effects is significantly different from zero.
Eq. factor 1 vs. 0 earners	Equivalence factor of couples with one partner working with respect to non-working couples.
Eq. factor 2 vs. 1 earners	Equivalence factor of couples where both partners work with respect to couples where one partner works.

Notes by row:

9	Effect for two-earner couple shown is relative to one-earner couple.
14	Authors use specification with separate dummies for several household size - working status combinations; couple effects shown are those for households composed of more than 2 persons.
14a	Equivalence factors shown are geometric means across a range of household sizes.
14b	Couple effects and equivalence factors shown are those for households composed of two persons or more.
13	Author estimated separate equations for one-earner and two-earner families; equivalence factor shown is unweighted median across a range of family types; see text for more details.
21	Authors use specification with separate dummies for several household size - working status combinations; couple effects shown are those for households composed of more than 2 persons.
24	Specification used for c and i include separate dummy for couples where at least one of the partners is working part-time.
25	Specification includes labor force status of respondent (seven categories), none of the labor force status effects were significant.

Table 4.A6
Overview of studies of reference group effect on subjective income evaluations

Ref. nr.	Study	Sample used (1)	Construction Reference Group Variables		Static or Dynamic	Incom Eval. variable	Restrictions imposed (3)	Estimates and (standard errors)		
			Model (2)	Variables used				α3, β3	κ	α
	Kapteyn, 1977, see also Kapteyn, Van Praag, Van Herwaarden, 1978	'Dutch Consumer Union', 1974, N = 2774	Dist.	education type of job urbanization age region employment (4)	Static	mu	a = 0 (i)	0.29 (.03)		
	Van de Stadt, Kapteyn and Van de Geer, 1985 (5)	'CBS-household panel', 1980-81, N=775	Group	education age employment (4)	Dynamic	mu	β1+β3=1 (13)	0.34 (.14)	0.42 (.50)	0.83 (.15)
							β1+β3=1, k=1 (13)	0.27 (.08)		0.81 (.04)
							k=0 (13)	0.20 (.20)		0.83 (0.15)
							β1+β3=1, k=0 (13)	0.30 (.24)		0.90 (.08)
12	Kapteyn, Van de Geer, Van de Stadt, 1985	'CBS-household panel', 1980-82, N=616	Group	education age employment (4)	Dynamic	mu	β1+β3=1	0.33 (.10)	0.79 (.15)	0.36 (.05)
						Ymin	α1+α3=1	0.30 (.12)	0.89 (.18)	0.36 (.06)
						mu + Ymin	β1+β3=1, αι=βι (6)	0.33 (.10)	0.81 (.15)	0.37 (.05)
	Kapteyn, Kooreman, Muffels et al., 1985	'NPAO labor market survey' (non-elderly only), 1982, N=774	Group	education age	Static	mu	a=0, k=0 (i)	0.13 (.04)		
						Ymin	a=0, k=0 (i)	0.20 (.05)		
14	De Vos, Hagenaars, Van Praag, 1987	'GPD-newspaper survey', 1983, (12)	Weighted Group	education age employment	Static	Yjsuf (13)	a=0, k=0 (i)	0.28 n.r.		
						Ymin	a=0, k=0 (i)	0.23 n.r.		
15	Kapteyn, Kooreman, Willemse, 1988	'NPAO labor market survey' (non-elderly only), 1982, N=773	Group	education age	Static (7)	mu	a=0, k=0 (i)	0.14 (.04)		
						Ymin	a=0, k=0 (i)	0.20 (.05)		

Table 4.A6 (continuation)

Ref. nr.	Study	Sample used (1)	Construction Reference Group Variables		Static or Dynamic	Incom Eval variable	Restrictions imposed (3)	Estimates and (standard errors)		
			Model (2)	Variables used				$\alpha3, \beta3$	κ	α
	Alessie, Kapteyn, 1988	'CBS-household panel', 1981-82, N=629	Group	Education Age Employment (4)	Dynamic	mu (11)	$\beta1+\beta3=1$	0.40 (.04)	0.83 (.52)	0.64 (.02)
	Tummers, 1992	Socio-Economic Panel' of the CBS, 1986, N=4091	Group	Education Age	Static (7)	Ymin	$\alpha1+\alpha3=1$ a=0, k=0 (i)	0.66 (.03)		
20	Muffels, Kapteyn et al., 1990 (9)	Socio-Economic Panel' of the CBS, 1985, N=2948	Group	Education Age	Static (7)	mu Ymin	a=0, k=0 (i) a=0, k=0 (i)	0.25 (.02) 0.26 (.03)		
		Socio-Economic Panel' of the CBS, 1986, N=3796	Group	Education Age	Static (7)	mu Ymin	a=0, k=0 (i) a=0, k=0 (i)	0.38 (.04) 0.32 (.03)		
		Socio-Economic Panel' of the CBS, 1985 + 86, N=2948	Factor	Education Age	Static (7) (11)	mu Ymin	$\beta1+\beta3=1$, (10) a=0, k=0 (i) $\alpha1+\alpha3=1$, (10) a=0, k=0 (i)	0.62 (.02) 0.65 (.03)		
		Socio-Economic Panel', 1984-86 (12)	Factor	Education Age	Dynamic (7)	mu	$\beta1+\beta3=1$, (10) k=0 (i)	0.56 (.04)		0.47 (.08)
		Socio-Economic Panel', 1985-86 (12)	Factor	Education Age	Dynamic (7)	Ymin	$\alpha1+\alpha3=1$, (10) k=0 (i)	0.58 (.05)		0.52 (.08)
	Aalbers et al. 1990	Socio-Economic Panel' of the CBS, 1984+85+86+87, N=670	Group	Education Age	Static (7) (11)	mu	a=0, k=0 (i)	0.29 (.04)		
		Socio-Economic Panel' of the CBS, 1985+86+87+88, N=598	Group	Education Age	Static (7) (11)	Ymin	a=0, k=0 (i)	0.31 (.04)		

Number in first column refers to table 4.A1 and other review tables.

Notes:

(1) All samples are Dutch; sample size reported is the number of cases effectively used in regressions.

(2) Dist: 'Social distance' model as developed by Kapteyn, 1977.

Group: Reference group is assumed to consist of persons with same characteristics, as in Van de Stadt et al., 1985; see text for details.

Weighted Group: Reference group income derived from direct questions about reference group; see text for details.

Factor: Reference group variables derived from direct questions about reference group, using factor analysis; see text for details.

(3) See text for explanation; (i) signifies restriction is imposed implicitly, i.e. parameter is not in model.

(4) Employment: i.e. Wage-earner, Self-employed or Not employed.

(5) Only results of models where measurement error in Mn and HSn is assumed are given.

(6) An interaction term Mn*HSn was also included in the model, and turned out to have a statistically significant effect.

(7) Model used takes account of effects of response bias, ages of children and non-response selectivity bias; see text for details.

(8) mu-equation estimated jointly with mu2 + sigma2 equation.

(9) Some of the results presented here have also been reported in Kapteyn and Melenberg, 1993 and in Melenberg, 1992.

(10) Restriction imposed after a test showed that it was not rejected by the data.

(11) Parameter stability across years imposed.

(12) Number of cases not reported.

(13) Average of 'sufficient' and 'insufficient' amounts in IEQ.

5 Income Evaluation Methods: Empirical Results for Belgium

1 Introduction

In the previous chapter I have reviewed the literature on the factors influencing the answers to the Income Evaluation Question (IEQ) and the Minimum Income Question (MIQ), as well as on the resulting equivalence scales and income thresholds. In this chapter I will present extensive new results based on the Belgian Socio-Economic Panel (SEP). The SEP is a panel household income survey, using a probability sample from the population of private households in Belgium. It is conducted by the Center for Social Policy at the University of Antwerp. Data from three waves (1985, 1988 and 1992) were available at the time the analyses were carried out. For further details about the SEP see appendix A.

In the next section of this chapter I look at the internal structure among the answers to the IEQ and the MIQ, i.e. at their correlations. This section also presents estimates of the reliability and 'construct validity' of μ and logYmin[1]. In the third section, the empirical determinants of μ and logYmin are examined in detail. In the fourth section, the resulting equivalence scales and LPL (Leyden Poverty Line) and SPL (Subjective Poverty Line) income thresholds are considered, as well as the number of households and individuals below those thresholds. Summaries of the findings are provided at the end of each section. Final conclusions about the income evaluation methods will be drawn at the end of the next chapter, after we have looked in depth at possible interpretations of the answers to the IEQ and the MIQ.

2 Quality, reliability and construct validity of the answers to the IEQ and the MIQ

Introduction

The aim of this section is to assess the quality, reliability and 'construct validity' of the variables μ and logYmin. In the next subsection, I will discuss an earlier study on this matter by Antonides et al. (1980). In the following subsections, I will look briefly at the quality of the answers to the IEQ and MIQ in the SEP in terms of non-response, consistency and extent of rounding off of the amounts. The main part of this section is devoted to an analysis of the internal structure of these answers, i.e. how they correlated among each other. The question to be answered is whether particular patterns can be discovered in these correlations, and whether these are stable over time. The analysis of the correlations will proceed as follows. In subsection four, results of a factor-analysis of the answers to the IEQ are presented. In the fifth subsection, I compare a number of explicit models of answers to the IEQ, which link those answers to the latent traits (μ and σ) they are supposed to measure. In subsection six, the retained model is extended with the answer to the MIQ, as well as household income and household size. Section seven presents some panel results on the subject. The results of this analysis make it possible to give estimates of the reliability of μ, σ and logYmin in subsection eight. In section nine I summarize and discuss the findings and draw some conclusions about the 'construct validity' of these variables.

How are the terms 'reliability' and 'construct validity' to be understood? Reliability is the consistency of measurement (Bollen, 1989: 206). It can be understood as the extent to which repeated applications of the same instrument produce the same result. Independent repeated measurements with the same instrument on the same object would be expected to fluctuate more or less because of random errors. Therefore, reliability is that part of a measure that is free of purely random error (Bollen, 1989: 207). The reliability of a measure can be estimated by comparing two or more administrations of the same measure. If one is certain that two measures refer to exactly the same concept, the correlation between those two measures can also be regarded as an estimate of their reliability.

Reliability must be distinguished from the wider concept of validity. "Validity is concerned with whether a variable measures what it is supposed to measure" i.e., whether a measure corresponds to a theoretical concept (Bollen, 1989: 184-185). Therefore, a valid measure cannot be totally unreliable (because random disturbances are generally not what one wants to measure), but a reliable measure can be perfectly invalid. 'Construct validity' is a particular way to evaluate the validity of a measure. "Construct validity assesses whether a measure relates to other observed variables in a way that is consistent with theoretically derived predictions" (Bollen, 1989: 188). Since the MIQ and the IEQ both ask for income evaluations, we would expect the answers to be highly correlated. Also, as we have seen in section 4.2, the expectation is that μ and logYmin will be positively related to household income (because of the preference effect) and to household size (because of cost effects). If in fact we would find such correlations, confidence in the validity of μ and logYmin is strengthened. Conversely, a finding of small, zero or negative correlations would cast serious doubt on the validity of these measures.

Antonides et al. (1980) on the reliability and validity of the IEQ

The reliability and validity of the answers to the IEQ, and of the WFI parameters μ and σ derived from these answers, has not received much attention in the literature. In fact, I am aware of only one study on this subject, viz. that of Antonides et al. (1980). This study uses data from an experimental survey of about 400 households, randomly drawn from the Dutch population. Ten different methods for the measurement of the parameters (μ and σ) of individual WFI's are compared, using the Multitrait-Multimethod (MTMM) approach. However, several of these methods are based on the same empirical material, and are therefore not wholly independent from each other. Apart from the IEQ itself, respondents had to answer the following six questions: (1) a version of the IEQ where the usual labels were replaced by letters A, B, ... to F; (2) an evaluation of the IEQ-labels on a 0 to 10 scale; (3) giving points from 0 to 100 to six particular income levels; (4) evaluating six income levels on a six-point scale, where only the ends were labeled 'bad' and 'good', respectively; (5) the same question with labels 'dissatisfied' and 'satisfied'; (6) and again the same question with labels 'high' and 'low'.

The results of the MTMM model indicate that the methods where respondents score income levels on a labeled six-point scale (items 4, 5 and 6) are the most reliable, followed by the regular IEQ, while the other methods are less reliable. Another finding is that μ is always measured more reliably than $\log(\sigma)$. The published results indicate, in fact, that the reliability coefficient (1 - error variance / total variance) of μ, as measured by the IEQ, is at least 0.70, while for $\log(\sigma)$, the error variance far exceeds both trait and method variances. Regarding validity (sum of error and method variances), the methods with a labeled six-point scale again seem to be the best ones, while those based on giving points to income levels are the worst. Also, substitution of individual evaluations of the IEQ labels on a numerical scale for fixed values derived from the equal interval assumption (cf. section 5.2.2) appears to produce larger amounts of error variance in the estimates of μ and $\log(\sigma)$. Remarkably, the IEQ with letters A-F instead of the usual labels 'very bad' - 'very good' seems more valid than the usual phrasing of the IEQ.

Another way to assess the validity of measures is to inspect the correlations of these measures with variables, which one would expect to be related to those measures (i.e. to look at the 'construct validity'). Antonides et al. use family income and family size for this purpose. It turns out that when the various measures of μ are regressed on these variables, the R-squares are highest for the regular IEQ (0.66), and much lower for the other measures. This is surprising, since the results of the MTMM model indicated that the methods using a labeled six-point scale had the highest validity, and therefore one would expect high R-squares for these measures. Antonides et al. (1980: 28-31) think this is due to the limited response options the six-point scale offers. This places restrictions on the way in which the respondents can express information. Therefore, these methods tend to give similar outcomes across individuals, even though the 'true' values of μ might be quite different. As Antonides et al. (1980: 34) recognize, this hypothesis implies that the MTMM model used is inappropriate for these measures; and the model is indeed rejected by a Chi-square test.

Finally, an interesting finding of Antonides et al. (1980: 29) is that when the individual welfare evaluations of the labels are substituted for the equal interval values in the calculation of μ, the variance of μ increases, but the R-square in the regression on family size and family income remains the same. This suggests that this substitution adds some error variance, but also some true variance in μ, which is suppressed when fixed welfare values are used.

Non-response, consistency and the extent of rounding

In this section and the next one, I will provide some indicators about the quality of the answers to the Income Evaluation Question (IEQ) and the Minimum Income Question (MIQ) in the Belgian SEP. In this section I consider the question whether all respondents answers these questions fully and consistently. In the next one, I look at the extent of rounding off of the amounts, as an indicator of the subjective precision of those answers.

Not all respondents provide answers to the income evaluation questions, and some of those who do, give amounts that are inconsistent or clearly implausible. Before any further analysis was done, some simple consistency and out-of-range checks were carried out. The results are reported in tables 5.1 and 5.2.

Overall, the *IEQ* has been answered adequately by a proportion of all respondents varying between 92 per cent in 1992 and 83.5 per cent in 1988. The immediate reason for the bad result in 1988 is that almost 13 per cent of respondents did not answer the IEQ at all, or gave amounts for only one or two levels, while only 2.3 per cent did so in 1992, and 5.2 per cent in 1985. In 1988 data for more than half of the sample households were gathered through a mail questionnaire, and about 20 per cent of those who sent in a mail questionnaire gave less than three IEQ amounts. Interestingly, 57 per cent of those filled in exactly one level. By contrast, oral interviews in 1988 yielded a corresponding non-response rate for the IEQ of only 4.5 per cent. Clearly, it is impossible to estimate μ where only one level of the IEQ has been answered, and while μ can mathematically be derived from two amounts, the resulting estimates were judged to be too unreliable to be usable in analysis.

Table 5.1
Quality of answers to the Income Evaluation Question in the SEP

	1985 Percent	1988 Percent	1992 Percent
Unusable answers:			
- No amounts given	2.8	4.4	1.8
- Less than three amounts	2.4	8.3	0.5
- Decreasing amounts	2.5	2.2	2.7
- Outside of range (1)	0.2	0.1	0.2
- Inconsistent with Ymin (2)	2.2	1.5	2.8
Total of unusable answers	10.2	16.5	7.9
Valid answers:			
- three amounts	0.9	1.0	0.5
- four amounts	1.5	1.4	0.8
- five amounts	2.1	2.4	0.7
- six amounts	85.3	78.6	90.1
Total of valid answers	89.8	83.5	92.1
All	100 (n = 6471)	100 (n = 3779)	100 (n = 3821)

Notes: (1) Range is 2000 - 500,000 BF for all amounts.
(2) Ymin outside of range defined by incomes regarded as 'very bad' and 'very good' by respondent.
All figures are unweighted, weighted results were virtually the same.
For unusable answers, figures reported refer to reason why answers were excluded in a cumulative selection process, i.e. those with 'decreasing amounts' may also have been inconsistent with the MIQ, but not vice versa.

Source: Belgian SEP, waves 1985, 1988, 1992.

Where at least amounts for three levels of the IEQ had been given, three checks of consistency and minimum plausibility were carried out. In the first place, when going across the levels, from 'very bad' to 'very good', the amounts should not decrease. This consistency requirement excluded about 2.5 per cent of all cases in each year. Secondly, none of the amounts should be outside the range 2.000 to 500.000 BF (about £40 to £10,000) per month. These boundaries are arbitrary, and are mainly imposed to ensure that extreme values do not affect the analysis too much. In any case, only a very small proportion of cases was dropped because amounts were out of range. Thirdly, the answer to the MIQ should lie within the range bordered by the 'very bad' and 'very good' amounts (boundaries included).

While it is strictly speaking not necessarily inconsistent to give an answer to the MIQ that is outside this range, such a pattern is strongly suggestive of a respondent being careless in his responses. The imposition of this consistency requirement excluded about 2 per cent of all cases.

The *MIQ* has been adequately answered by about 93-94 per cent of respondents in all waves (see table 5.2). Survey by mail has apparently had a smaller effect on MIQ response rates than on IEQ response rates. Two checks were carried out on the answers given. In the first place, the amounts should lie inside a certain reasonable range. The lower boundary of this range was set at 5,000 BF (about £100), the upper one at 100,000 BF in 1985, 110,000 BF in 1988 and 130,000 BF in 1992; boundaries not included. (These amounts are equivalent to £20,00, £22,00 and £26,00, respectively.) Again, the main purpose of this range check was to ensure that extreme values would not bias the results of analysis. Secondly, the cases that failed the third consistency check for the IEQ (cross-consistency with the MIQ) were also dropped from the MIQ analysis.

Table 5.2
Quality of answers to the Minimum Income Question in the SEP

	1985 Percent	1988 Percent	1992 Percent
Unusable answers:			
- No amount given	2.5	5.2	2.1
- Outside of range (1)	1.5	0.6	0.7
- Inconsistent with IEQ (2)	2.6	1.7	2.9
Total of unusable answers	6.7	7.5	5.6
Valid answers:	93.3	92.5	94.4
Valid answers to IEQ and MIQ, used in section 5.3	87.4	80.9	90.7
Complete and valid answers to IEQ and MIQ, used in section 5.2	82.7	76.2	88.6
All	100 (n = 6471)	100 (n = 3779)	100 (n = 3821)

Notes: (1) Lower bound of range is 2000 BF, higher bound is 100,000 BF in 1985, 110,000 BF in 1988 and 130,000 in 1992.

(2) Amount outside of range bounded by incomes regarded as 'very bad' and 'very good'.

For other notes see table 5.1.

Source: Belgian SEP, waves 1985, 1988, 1992.

In section 5.3, where the empirical determinants of μ and logYmin are studied, only cases with valid answers to the IEQ and MIQ are used. For the analysis of the correlations below in this section, the subsample was limited further. Observations with incomplete answers to the IEQ were excluded, as well as a small number of cases where the 'very bad' income was below 5,000 BF, or where the ratio between two subsequent IEQ-amounts exceeded 4.5.

Most respondents give answers that are not very precise. Half or more of all amounts are multiples of 10.000 BF (about £ 200), with the exception of the 'bad' income; for the 'very good' amount, three out of four respondents give an answer that ends in four zeros. The large majority of the remaining amounts end in -5.000, only a fairly small minority is apparently more precise. Answers to the bottom three levels of the IEQ end less often in -0.000 or 5.000, compared with answers to the upper three levels and the MIQ. The main reason for this is probably that the former amounts are smaller than the latter ones. Assuming that people answer the Income Evaluation Questions in such a way that on average the error induced by rounding is roughly proportional to the 'true' amount, smaller amounts should be less often rounded to multiples of 10,000 or 5,000 than larger amounts.

Results of a factor-analysis

In the next sections I will study the correlations among the answers to the IEQ and the MIQ, and the parameters derived from those answers, i.e. μ, σ and logYmin. As a first step in the analysis of the correlations, I want to present some results of a common factor-analysis of the answers to the IEQ. The use of such an exploratory technique may seem inappropriate for variables for which an explicit model exists (see below). The reason I show them is that they are rather suggestive in a number of respects.

A common factor is a latent, unobserved variable that is assumed to explain the correlation between at least two observed variables. The model of the common factor model is as follows:

$$X_{ij} = b_{1j} F_{1i} + b_{2j} F_{2i} + ... + b_{Kj} F_{Ki} + l_{ij} , \qquad (5.1)$$

where X_{ij} is the value of the i-th case on the j-th observed variable, F_{1i}... F_{Ki} are the K common factors, b_{1j} ... b_{Kj} are K regression coefficients of the j-th observed variable on the K common factors; and l_{ij} is a "unique factor", i.e. an error term that contributes to the variance of X_{ij} only. A crucial assumption is that the common factors and the unique factors are uncorrelated with each other, i.e. all factors are orthogonal to each other. Even under this assumption, there is, for any measured set of variables, an infinite number of solutions satisfying (5.1). The usual procedure to get a particular solution is to choose the first factor in such a way that it explains as much as possible of the correlations between the measured variables (in technical terms; it corresponds to the largest eigenvalue of the correlation matrix). In most cases, the number of common factors is equal to the number of observed variables, but generally only a subset of these factors are considered to be meaningful and are retained for further analysis. (For an introduction to factor analysis, see Harman, 1976).

Table 5.3 shows the results of the factor analysis for 1985. Only three common factors are retained from the six originally extracted; the remaining three factors had very small (and negative) eigenvalues. The figures shown under 'factor pattern' are estimates of the b_{kj} regression coefficients of the observed variables on the factors. The 'communality estimates' can be interpreted as the proportion of the total variance of the measured variables accounted for by the factors that are retained. The eigenvalues of the factors are proportional to the amount of common variance of the measured variables accounted for by each factor.

The results for 1988 and 1992 were strikingly similar. Most estimates differ by only 0.01 or 0.02. This shows that the structure in the answers to the IEQ is extremely robust across time[2]. The first factor is clearly the most important; it alone accounts for 91 per cent of the common variance. All observed variables are strongly related to this factor, though the coefficients of the extreme IEQ-levels ('very bad' and 'very good') are somewhat smaller than the others. The obvious interpretation of this factor is that it corresponds to WFI-parameter μ. The second and third factors have small to very small eigenvalues, and would not have been retained, if the symmetry in the factor pattern and the stability over time had not suggested that these factors are meaningful. The pattern of the second factor is monotonously rising, and, moreover symmetric about zero. A high value on this factor corresponds to IEQ-amounts that are widely dispersed. The obvious interpretation of this factor is that it refers to σ.

The third factor has a pattern that first falls and then rises in a symmetric way, while the falling and rising parts are each symmetric about zero. There is no WFI-parameter that corresponds to this factor; it appears to be a new discovery. Compared with the average observation, observations with high values on this factor have 'very bad' and 'very good' amounts that are shifted upwards, while the middle IEQ-income amounts are shifted downwards. In terms of a statistical distribution, where μ is equivalent to the average, and σ to the standard deviation of the (logs of) the answers to the IEQ, the third factor refers to the skewness of those amounts. Below, the interpretation of this factor is discussed further.

Table 5.3
Results of factor-analysis of answers to the IEQ, Belgium, 1985

	Factor pattern			Commun. estimates
	Factor 1	Factor 2	Factor 3	
Very bad income	0.88	-0.39	0.12	0.94
Bad income	0.96	-0.27	0.03	0.99
Insufficient income	0.98	-0.12	-0.11	0.98
Sufficient income	0.96	0.09	-0.14	0.96
Good income	0.94	0.30	0.02	0.97
Very good income	0.83	0.41	0.11	0.88
Eigenvalues factors	5.14	0.51	0.06	
Proportion of total	0.91	0.09	0.01	

Notes: All variables entered as log(amount).
Only cases with valid answers to both the IEQ (see table 5.1).
A small number of cases were excluded where the ratio between two subsequent amounts exceeded 4.5.
Factors with eigenvalues > 0 were retained; no rotation was executed.
Source: Belgian SEP, waves 1985.

A formal test of IEQ-models

In this section, I report on formal tests of various models of the 'internal structure' of the answers to the IEQ. The "Structural Equations with Latent Variables" approach has been used (Bollen, 1989). In this approach, the sample covariance matrix is compared with a covariance matrix derived from a model, including a set of estimated or fixed parameters. If the model is correct, both covariance matrices should be equal. A number of indices are available to evaluate how well, or how badly, the model covariance matrix fits the measured one, i.e. how large the differences between the matrices are. A bad fit is an indication that the model is incorrect. Three measures to test the fit are used. The Chi-square is a test-statistic for the null-hypothesis that the estimated or model covariance matrix is the population covariance matrix, or, in other words, that the differences between the estimated and the sample covariance matrix are due to sample fluctuations. The Root Mean Square Residual (RMR) is exactly what its name says it is: the square root of the average of the differences between the model and measured covariance matrices. The Adjusted Goodness of Fit Index (AGFI) measures the relative amount of the variances and covariances in the measured covariance matrix that are predicted by the estimated covariance matrix with an adjustment for the degrees of freedom of the model. A value of 1 indicates perfect fit, values below 0.90 are a sign of fairly bad fit. (See Bollen, 1989: 256-289 for details.)

In the first step, a range of models were tested on the SEP 1985 data; the selected model was then also applied to the 1988 and 1992 data. In table 5.4 results for six models are summarized; the model equations are also shown in that table. Model (5.2) is the standard WFI model used to estimate μ and σ, including the equal interval assumption (EIA; see section 5.2 for a description of this assumption). It is clear that this model does not fit the data at all. In model (5.3), the EIA has been dropped, but this modification does not produce a well-fitting model[3]. (In order to achieve identification, the constraint has been imposed that the quantiles add up to zero, while the variance of σ' has been arbitrarily set to 1[4].) In model (5.4), a third latent variable has been added to the model, corresponding to the third factor identified in the factor analysis. This latent variable will be called ξ (pronounced 'ksi'). Again, in order to achieve identification, various restrictions had to be imposed, including the one that ξ does not correlate with μ' and σ'. This model fits very well; the chi-square statistic is not significant at the 1 per cent-level; the AGFI-statistic is virtually equal to one; while the average residual is very small.

Model (5.5) is similar to model (5.4), except that a condition of symmetry has been imposed on the σ-quantiles, i.e. $q_1 = -q_6$, $q_2 = -q_5$ and $q_3 = -q_4$. Substantively this means that (when $\xi = 0$) the distances of the 'very bad', 'bad' and 'insufficient' amounts from the midpoint of the scale (i.e. μ) are equal (though of opposite sign) to those of the 'very good', 'good' and 'insufficient' amounts, respectively. (Also, the restriction that σ' and ξ are uncorrelated has been dropped.) The symmetry condition leads to an increase in Chi-square that is clearly significant, but, given the number of cases, not very large. The other goodness-of-fit indices change only marginally.

Model (5.6) is the same as model (5.5), except for the addition of a symmetry constraint on the ξ–regression coefficients, i.e. $v_1 = v_6$, $v_2 = v_5$ and $v_3 = v_4$, inspired by the results of the factor analysis. This constraint produces a clear worsening of fit. Model (5.7) is another variant of model (5.5), with the imposition of the equal interval hypothesis. The results show clearly that the equal interval hypothesis must be rejected, even when a third factor ξ is included in the model. (However, the qualification of footnote 3 also applies here.)

Model (5.5) is retained as the favored model. Although it cannot reproduce the measured variances and covariances exactly, it is a reasonable compromise between theoretical considerations and empirical fit. Table 5.4a presents the parameter estimates for this model. (Recall that the coefficients for μ' were fixed at 1, and that the symmetric pattern of the σ'-coefficients has been imposed.) The estimated σ'-coefficients for the "bad" and "good" amounts are relatively close to those for the "very bad" and "very good" amounts, respectively, while those for the "insufficient" and "sufficient" amounts are at some distance from each other. These results are the opposite of those predicted by the WFI measurement model, i.e. the equal interval assumption and the lognormal distribution function. They seem to be in better agreement with a hypothesis according to which the answers are determined by the everyday meaning of the IEQ-labels, where the biggest gap is between "insufficient" and "sufficient", and where "very bad" is only a qualification of "bad".

Table 5.4
Tests of various models for the answers to the IEQ, Belgium, 1985

Model			
Model 5.2:	Specification:	$\log A_{i,j} = \mu_i + q_j{*}\sigma_i + e_{i,j}$	
	Restrictions:	$N(q_j) = (2{*}j-1)/12$, (N represents the cumulative normal distribution function)	
	Chi-square:	4236.6	df = 12
	AGFI:	0.640	
	RMR:	0.0055	
Model 5.3:	Specification:	$\log A_{i,j} = \mu_i + q_j{*}\sigma_i + e_{i,j}$	
	Restrictions:	$SUM(q_j) = 0$, $VAR(\sigma) = 1$	
	Chi-square:	2342.7	df = 8
	AGFI:	0.682	
	RMR:	0.0030	
Model 5.4:	Specification:	$\log A_{i,j} = \mu_i + q_j{*}\sigma_i + v_j{*}\xi_i + e_{i,j}$	
	Restrictions:	$SUM(q_j) = 0$, $SUM(v_j) = 0$, $VAR(\sigma) = 1$, $VAR(\xi) = 1$, $COV(\mu,\xi) = 0$, $COV(\sigma,\xi) = 0$	
	Chi-square:	8.9	df = 3
	AGFI:	0.996	
	RMR:	0.0008	
Model 5.5:	Specification:	$\log A_{i,j} = \mu_i + q_j{*}\sigma_i + v_j{*}\xi_i + e_{i,j}$	
	Restrictions:	$q_j = -q_{7-j}$, $SUM(v_j)=0$, $v_2=v_5$, $VAR(\sigma)=1$, $VAR(\xi)=1$	
	Chi-square:	36.7	df = 4
	AGFI:	0.988	
	RMR:	0.0012	
Model 5.6:	Specification:	$\log A_{i,j} = \mu_i + q_j{*}\sigma_i + v_j{*}\xi_i + e_{i,j}$	
	Restrictions:	$q_j = -q_{7-j}$, $v_j=v_{7-j}$, $VAR(\sigma)=1$, $VAR(\xi)=1$, $COV(\mu,\xi)=0$	
	Chi-square:	147.0	df = 6
	AGFI:	0.969	
Model 5.7:	Specification:	$\log A_{i,j} = \mu_i + q_j{*}\sigma_i + v_j{*}\xi_i + e_{i,j}$	
	Restrictions:	$N(q_j) = (2{*}j-1)/12$, $SUM(v_j) = 0$, $VAR(\xi) = 1$, $COV(\mu,\xi) = 0$	
	Chi-square:	1520.3	df = 6
	AGFI:	0.709	
	RMR:	0.0075	

Notes: AGFI: Adjusted Goodness of Fit Index; RMR: Root Mean Square Residual. Selection of cases: see table 5.1; Number of observations: 5334.

Source: Belgian SEP, wave 1985.

Table 5.4a
Parameter estimates for IEQ-model 5.5, Belgium, 1985

IEQ-level	Coefficients for σ		Coefficients for ξ		R-
	Value	St. error	Value	St. error	square
Very bad	-0.157	0.002	-0.016	0.002	0.90
Bad	-0.113	0.001	-0.012	0.001	1.02
Insufficient	-0.041	0.001	0.035	0.002	0.96
Sufficient	0.041	0.001	0.072	0.002	0.99
Good	0.113	0.001	-0.012	0.001	0.98
Very good	0.157	0.002	-0.067	0.003	0.90

Covariance matrix of latent variables (starred figures are fixed):

	μ	σ	ξ
μ	0.119		
σ	-0.035	1.000*	
ξ	-0.007	-0.012	1.000*

Notes: For model, constraints, goodness-of-fit statistics and selection of cases see table 5.4, model 5.5.

Source: Belgian SEP, wave 1985.

The coefficients for ξ display the same increasing, then decreasing pattern as was found in the factor analysis, but without the nice symmetry. The R-squares are extremely high for the four middle IEQ-levels, and somewhat lower for the extreme ones, indicating that the latter are a little more affected by random errors. The 1.02 figure for the 'bad' level implies a negative error-variance, and is another sign that the model does not fit perfectly. However, all models listed in table 5.4 suffered from this problem. The covariances of the latent variables indicate that μ' and σ' correlate very weakly, while there is a moderate correlation between μ' and ξ.

The formal tests confirm the results of the factor-analysis, in that a third factor or parameter ξ is necessary to explain the measured covariances between the IEQ-amounts. As said in the previous section, in terms of a statistical distribution, where μ is a measure of central location, and σ one of dispersion, ξ can be interpreted as the degree of skewness of the amounts. What this means becomes perhaps more clear by looking at figure 5.1, where three hypothetical response patterns are plotted. Pattern I are the answers of the average respondent. The answers of II have been generated using the same values for μ and σ as those of I, but with an extremely low value for ξ. (Given the signs of the estimated parameters in table 5.4a, a low value of ξ corresponds to a high degree of skewness.) Compared with respondent I, this causes respondent II to have somewhat higher answers to the 'very bad' and 'bad' levels, lower answers to the 'insufficient' and 'sufficient' levels, while his 'very good' income is considerably higher. The pattern is clearly different from that of a respondent with a higher value of σ, viz. III. The answers of III are characterized by the same values of μ and ξ as those of I, but his σ is higher than that of I and II.

Figure 5.1
Interpretation of IEQ-parameter ξ: answers to IEQ of three hypothetical respondents

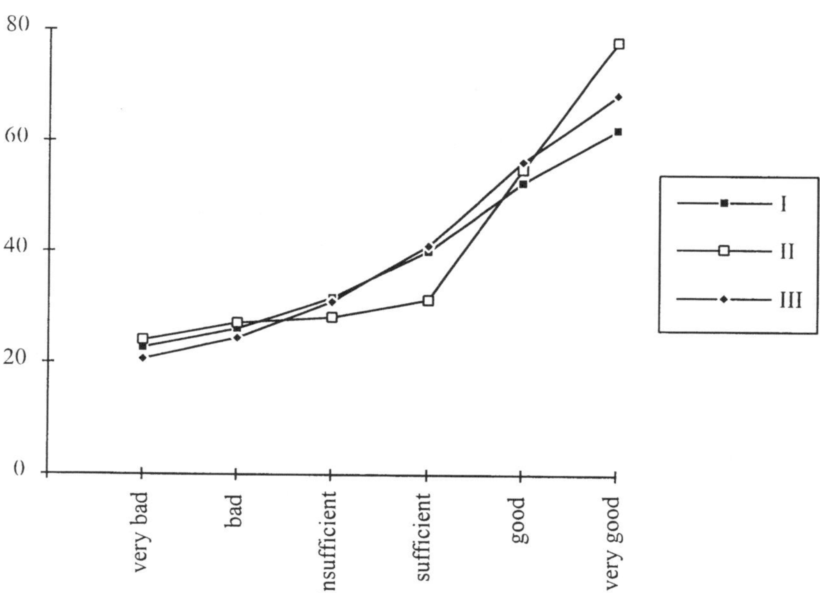

Note: Respondent I has the answers of the average respondent in the SEP (1985). Respondent II has the same μ and σ values, but a much lower value for ξ. Respondent III has the same μ and ξ values as respondent I, but a higher value for σ, such that the calculated standard deviation of the amounts is the same for respondents II and III. The hypothetical response patterns have been calculated using the parameter estimates presented in table 5.5, based on model 5.5. A low value for ξ corresponds to high degree of skewness.

In chapter 6 I will discuss the implications of the finding that the answers to the IEQ are characterized by three instead of two parameters for the WFI-measurement model, in particular regarding the claim that the latter provides a cardinal en interpersonally comparable measure of welfare.

Although the finding of a third WFI-parameter may be interesting from a theoretical point of view, one must keep in mind that the total variation induced by ξ is rather limited. A change of one standard deviation (relative to the total sample) in ξ produces, ceteris paribus, changes of 7 percent in the incomes deemed 'sufficient' and 'very good'. In fact, ξ explains about 4 percent of the total variance of the 'sufficient income' and about 3 percent of the variance of the 'very good' income; the corresponding figures for the other IEQ-levels do not exceed 1 percent. These limited effects might even lead one to question the significance of ξ. One hypothesis could be that it is an artifact of the tendency by respondents to round the amounts to multiples of 5000 BF. However, when the analysis was repeated on the rather small subsample of respondents who have not rounded at least three amounts, the results were virtually the same. Again model (5.3), without a third factor, was clearly rejected by the data.

Having developed it using the SEP 1985 data, model (5.5) has been tested on the 1988 and 1992 data. The results confirm that this model is a reasonable description of the relationships between the variables. In 1992 the fit is slightly worse than in 1985 and 1988. The parameter estimates are virtually equal across the years. The R-square figures for 1992 are somewhat lower than those for 1985 and 1988, confirming an impression gained earlier on the basis of the extent to which IEQ amounts are rounded, that in 1992 respondents have been a bit less careful in their answers to the IEQ.

The question can now be asked to what extent the latent variables μ' and σ' coincide with the measured variables μ and σ, respectively. In other words, what is the correlation between μ and μ' and between σ and σ' ? The question is easy to answer for μ[5]. Calculations using the results of model 5.5 produce the following estimates for this correlation: 1985: 0.995; 1988: 0.996; 1992: 0.994. In other words, for all practical purposes, μ is equal to μ'.

The expression for the measured variable σ in terms of the parameters of model 5.5 is rather complicated, and involves cubic and quadratic terms in σ' and ξ, for which the CALIS-program does not provide estimates. Therefore, the correlation between σ and σ' has been estimated by including σ in model 5.5, as a function of σ' and ξ, while leaving the covariances of the error term of the σ-equation with those of the IEQ-amounts unconstrained. (This ensures that the estimates of the rest of the model are not affected by the inclusion of σ.) The resulting correlations, which must be regarded as approximations, are: 1985: 0.895; 1988: 0.905; 1992: 0.957. This shows that the measured variable σ is a good indicator of the latent variable σ'.

Formal tests of the relations between answers to the IEQ and the answer to the MIQ, household income and household size

In this section, model (5.5) is augmented to include logYmin, household income and household size. This will enable us to investigate whether μ and logYmin are measures of the same concept or of different ones, and to assess the reliability and construct validity of these variables, and of σ. For this purpose, the following model was specified:

$$
\begin{aligned}
\log A_{ij} &= \mu'_i + q_j\sigma'_i + v_j\xi_i + e_{ij}\,,\ i = 1 \,..\, N,\ j = 1 \,..6, \\
&\quad q_j = -q_{7-j}\ j = 1 \,..\, 3\,, \\
&\quad \Sigma\, v_j = 0,\ v_2 = v_5,\ j = 1 \,..\, 6, \\
\mu'_i &= \mu''_i + e'_{\mu i}\,, \\
\log Ymin_i &= \mu''_i + q_7\sigma'_i + v_7\xi_i + e_{mi}\,, \\
\mu''_i &= b_1\log Y_i + b_2\log FS_i + b_3\log C_i + e''_{\mu i}\,, \\
\sigma'_i &= b_4\log Y_i + b_5\log FS_i + b_6\log C_i + e'_{\sigma i}\,, \\
\xi_i &= b_7\log Y_i + b_8\log FS_i + e_{\xi i}
\end{aligned}
\qquad (5.8)
$$

where A_{ij} is the answer of the i-th respondent to the j-th level of the IEQ, $Ymin_i$ is the answer to the MIQ, μ'_i, μ''_i, σ'_i and ξ_i are latent (unmeasured) variables, supposedly determining the answers to the IEQ and MIQ, q_j, v_j, q_7, v_7, and b_1 to b_8 are parameters to be estimated, and e_{ij} $e'_{\mu i}$, em_i, $e''_{\mu i}$, $e'_{\sigma i}$ and $e_{\xi i}$ are error terms with the usual properties; $e''_{\mu i}$, $e'_{\sigma i}$ and $e_{\xi i}$ are allowed to be mutually correlated. Y_i and FS_i represent household income and household size, respectively; C_i is a correction factor, which picks up the possible effect of the underestimation by the respondent of his own income (see section 4.6 for details).

Model (5.8) incorporates the notion that the answers to the MIQ are a function of the IEQ-parameters μ', σ' and ξ. If $e'_{\mu i}$ would be zero for all cases (implying that $\mu'_i = \mu''_i$), the MIQ could be regarded as no more than an additional level of the IEQ. If $e'_{\mu i}$ does not have zero variance, the answers to the IEQ are influenced by a common factor, which does not affect logYmin. Another question is whether e_{mi} is correlated with logY and logFS. Such a correlation, pointing to an effect of household income and household size on Ymin independent of the IEQ-parameters, would suggest that the MIQ and the IEQ are measures of related, but different concepts. The IEQ-parameters μ'', σ' and ξ are assumed to be functions of household income and household size. Compared with model (5.5), identification has here been achieved in a different way. In order to give σ' and ξ somewhat meaningful scales, q_6 and v_6 were fixed at 1. This implies that the variances of σ' and ξ are measured in terms of the (proportional) variation in the answers to the 'very good' level of the IEQ[6].

Table 5.5 shows the main results of model 5.8, for the 1985 wave of the Belgian SEP. (Since the estimates of the $\log A_j$ equations differ very little from those shown in table 5.4a, except as a result from the changes in the scales of σ' and ξ, these are not shown.) The fit of model 5.8 appears to be quite reasonable. The Chi-square values are much higher than those for model 5.5, but given the much larger number of degrees of freedom of the present model, they do not seem excessive. The values of the other goodness-of-fit indices AGFI and RMR are quite acceptable. Perhaps more importantly, none of the residual variances and covariances were statistically significant, and their pattern seemed fairly random.

The estimates in the logYmin equation show that the answers to the MIQ are related to all three IEQ-parameters, including σ' and ξ. The R-square figures for the μ'-equation show that the variance of e'_μ is not zero, or, in other words, μ' is not equal to μ''. Imposing the restriction that $\mu' = \mu''$ on the model leads to a large increase in Chi-square (459 for df=1) and a drastic worsening of the fit. This implies that the average level of the answers to the IEQ is influenced by a common factor, which does not affect the answers to the MIQ. In a second variant of model 5.8, the assumption that the error-term of the logYmin equation is uncorrelated with the background variables logY, logFS and logC was relaxed. (Alternatively, one could also relax the assumption that e'_μ is uncorrelated with those household characteristics. Statistically, both changes to model 5.8 are exactly equivalent. Thus, a test of the one is also a test of the other). The resulting decrease in Chi-square (20.3 for df=3) is statistically significant, but not very large. The other goodness-of-fit indices change only marginally. The small correlations between the error-terms and the background variables may be due to the order of the questions in the questionnaire. The MIQ just precedes a question about total household income, while the IEQ follows it. For the sake of model parsimoniousness, these correlations are ignored. Model 5.8 is thus retained as an adequate description of the relations between the variables in the model.

Table 5.5
Results for model 5.8 of answers to income evaluation questions, Belgium, 1985

Parameter estimates (standard errors between parentheses):				R-square
logYmin	1 μ'	- 0.211 σ'	- 0.638 ξ	0.786
		(.022)	(.046)	
μ'	1 μ'			0.856
μ'=	+ 0.410 logY	+ 0.160 logFS	+ 0.539 logC	0.655
	(.008)	(.008)	(.028)	
σ'=	+ 0.049 logY	- 0.023 logFS	- 0.039 logC	0.017
	(.006)	(.005)	(.020)	
ξ=	+ 0.020 logY	- 0.009 logFS		0.011
	(.003)	(.003)		

Covariance matrix of the error-terms of the IEQ parameters:

	μ'	σ'	ξ
μ'	.0169		
σ	-.009	.0253	
ξ	-.001	-.0002	.0060

Goodness of fit indices:

Chi-square:	168.3 (df = 20)
AGFI:	0.982
RMR:	0.0012

Notes: Only cases meeting the criteria mentioned in tables 5.1 and 5.2, and without imputation of household income.

Source: Belgian SEP, waves 1985.

The results for the μ" equation are very similar to those obtained in other studies of μ and logYmin (cf. section 4.3). The relations of μ and logYmin with background variables are further discussed in section 5.3. The parameter estimates for the σ' and ξ equations are generally statistically significant, but quite low. It seems that both the dispersion and the skewness of the answers to the IEQ increase with rising welfare, but as the R-square figures indicate, the associations are very small.

What can we now say about the position of Ymin relative to the IEQ-scale? The (geometric) average of Ymin is situated between the midpoint of the IEQ-scale (or μ') and the 'sufficient' level. This is not true for every respondent, though. In about 40 percent of all cases are responses to the MIQ equal to the 'sufficient' level of the IEQ; 70 percent of all respondents give answers to the MIQ that are in the range bordered by the incomes they deem 'insufficient' and 'sufficient'. The other answers are distributed fairly evenly across the IEQ-scale. (Recall that observations where Ymin is smaller than the 'very bad' income or higher than the 'very good' income were excluded.) Does this mean that different respondents assign different meanings to the phrase 'minimum income to make ends meet', at least in terms of the IEQ? Possibly, but the varying positions of Ymin may also be due to random error. Certainly, when these positions as implied by the answers of the same respondents in different waves of the SEP are compared, it is found that the correlations are very low. (Gamma coefficients are below 0.05 and not statistically significant.)

Interestingly, the results for the logYmin equation of model (5.8), as reported in table 5.5, suggest that the position of Ymin on the IEQ-scale is somewhere *below* the midpoint between the 'insufficient' and 'sufficient' amounts. In particular, the coefficient for σ' has a negative sign and is quite close to that for the 'insufficient' level of the IEQ. Apparently, although the average answer to the MIQ is equal to or slightly above μ, when looking at differences across respondents, Ymin behaves as if it is on a point on the IEQ-scale below μ' and above the 'insufficient' level. It is not quite clear how to interpret this finding. It is quite clear, however, that for many respondents the MIQ is associated quite closely with the 'sufficient' level of the IEQ, and to a lesser extent with the 'insufficient' amount. Ymin is more strongly correlated with 'insufficient' income than with any of the other IEQ-amounts, or even μ itself. Also, when logYmin is regressed on all six IEQ (log) amounts, in two of three waves only the 'insufficient' and 'sufficient' amounts are found to have a substantial and significant effect[7].

Reliability of μ, logYmin and σ

The findings reported in the previous section suggest that both logYmin and μ are indicators of the same underlying concept. (As shown above, the measured variable μ and the latent variable μ' are practically interchangeable.) The R-square statistics reported in table 5.5 can therefore be seen as reliability estimates. However, given the similarities in the phrasing of the MIQ and the IEQ, and their proximity in the questionnaire, the possibility that their error-terms are correlated cannot be excluded. For this reason, the estimates should be seen as upper bounds of the true reliabilities. Even so, the R-squares for logYmin, varying between 0.79 and 0.83 are quite high for a single question. Those for μ', which range from 0.85 to 0.90, are not that much higher, even though μ' is an average across six amounts.

Since we have only a single measure of σ, the reliability of σ cannot be estimated in the same way as that of μ and logYmin. However, as mentioned in section 4.2, we need only three levels of the IEQ to determine σ. Therefore, it is possible for each respondent with a complete answer to the IEQ to calculate two estimates of σ, one based on the three lower levels ('very bad', 'bad' and 'insufficient'), the other on the three higher levels ('sufficient', 'good' and 'very good'). The correlation between these two estimates is a measure of the reliability of σ, as calculated in the usual way. The correlations are as follows: 1985: 0.164; 1988: 0.227; 1992: 0.123[8].

These correlations are surprisingly low. By contrast, the correlation between two estimates of μ, obtained in the same way, is 0.82. They indicate that σ is measured with little reliability. This finding confirms results reported by Antonides et al. (1980), as discussed above. Although those authors do not explicitly point out this finding, the results of the MultiTrait-Multi-Method exercise they perform indicate that most of the variation in σ is measurement error. The conclusion must be that either respondents do not have a very precise idea of the slope of their WFI, or, alternatively, that the IEQ is not a very reliable instrument to measure this characteristic.

Some panel results

In this section, I present some results about the answers to the IEQ and the MIQ using the linked panel data for 1985, 1988 and 1992. Unfortunately, two circumstances limit the kinds of analyses that can be performed with these panel data. In the first place, the panel waves have not been conducted in consecutive years, while the income information, as well as the MIQ and the IEQ, refer to the current month. The gap of several years between successive waves means that dynamic models, such as those developed in Van de Stadt et al. (1985), cannot be applied. A second problem is that it is not known which person in the household answered the income evaluation questions in 1985 and 1988. For this reason, only cases were used where the head of household remained single throughout the three waves (with or without children), or where both the head of household and his partner were the same persons in all three waves. This selection ensures that either the same person has answered the IEQ and the MIQ in all three waves, or the respondents have lived for some time together within the same household. Unfortunately, this selection procedure, in combination with the consistency and completeness requirements explained above, leaves only 1,092 cases.

Table 5.6
Correlations across time of IEQ-parameters μ, σ and ξ and logYmin, Belgium, 1985-1988-1992

	1985-1988	1988-1992	1985-1992
Latent var.'s:			
μ''	0.659	0.731	0.597
μ'	0.637	0.680	0.550
σ'	0.143	0.127	0.049
ξ	0.097	0.048	0.066
Measured var.'s:			
μ	0.624	0.681	0.550
σ	0.143	0.188	0.135
logYmin	0.533	0.625	0.473

Notes: n= 1092.
See text for details about sample selection.
Source: Belgian SEP, waves 1985, 1988, 1992.

Because of these problems, I only look at the correlations across time of the IEQ parameters μ, σ and ξ, and logYmin. As table 5.6 shows, these correlations are quite high for μ and logYmin, and fairly low for σ, σ' and ξ. This is again an indication that most of the variation in σ is due to measurement error, or to rather short-lived influences[9]. Using a stripped-down version of model 5.8, it appeared that even when past incomes are taken into account, there remains a substantial amount of serial correlation in the error terms of μ''. These unexplained covariances amount to between 12 and 15 percent of the total variance of μ.

Summary and discussion

In this section I have looked at the quality of the answers to the IEQ and the MIQ, and at their correlations, with the aim to assess the reliability and 'construct validity' of these questions. What conclusions can be drawn from the results?

In the first place, almost all respondents in the Belgian Socio-Economic Panel (SEP) survey provide answers to the IEQ and MIQ, and relatively few of the recorded answers fail to meet minimum criteria of consistency and plausibility. However, when completing a mail questionnaire by themselves, i.e. when not prompted by interviewers, a substantial minority of all respondents do not answer the IEQ, or only answer it for one level. The same effect is not found for the MIQ, which suggests that respondents find the MIQ easier to answer than the IEQ.

Secondly, more than half of the stated amounts are multiples of 10,000 BF (£200), most of the rest are multiples of 5000 BF. This degree of rounding suggests that the average SEP respondent does not have a very precise idea of the income amounts corresponding to the descriptions used in the IEQ and the MIQ.

Thirdly, a factor analysis of the answers to the IEQ in the SEP showed that the correlations among the six levels of the IEQ can be explained by three factors. The first one, which explains more than 90 percent of the common variance, corresponds to the (geometric) average of the amounts, i.e. μ. The second factor can be interpreted as the degree of dispersion of the amounts around the average, i.e. σ. The third factor appears to indicate the skewness of the amounts. This characteristic of response patterns to the IEQ, which does not seem to have been previously recognized in the literature, has here been christened ξ. The factor patterns are remarkably stable over time. Tests of a number of formal models confirm that three factors, or parameters, are necessary to account for the covariances between the IEQ-amounts. The standard WFI measurement model is clearly rejected by the data. This means that either the equal interval assumption, or the assumption that the WFI has the form of a lognormal cumulative distribution must be dropped.

Fourthly, results of a model relating the MIQ and IEQ responses to household income and household size show that logYmin and μ appear to be measures of the same underlying concept, although Ymin cannot be regarded as just another level of the IEQ. Estimated reliability coefficients vary from 0.79 to 0.83 for logYmin and from 0.85 to 0.90 for μ[10]. These high reliability estimates are consistent with the results of panel analyses, which indicate that the correlation between the values of logYmin and μ in subsequent waves of the SEP varies from 0.5 to 0.7. The answer to the MIQ is found to be related to all three IEQ-parameters, μ, σ and ξ. For most respondents, Ymin appears to be closely related to the 'sufficient' income in the IEQ, and to a lesser extent also to the 'insufficient' income. As has been found in other studies, μ and logYmin are strongly related to household income and household size; the signs of the effects are positive. The results are highly stable over time. Panel data show that, apart from current income, past incomes also have a substantial impact on the answers to the MIQ and the IEQ. Past household size has no significant effect. A peculiar finding is that underestimation by the respondent of her income has a significant effect on her income evaluations in the next wave.

Finally, the results also reveal that σ and ξ, which measure the distribution of IEQ-amounts around μ, are hardly at all affected by the background variables. Other calculations, as well as results from a previous study by Antonides et al. (1980) suggest that the reliability of σ is quite low, i.e. the main source of variance are random errors, or very short-lived influences. This is consistent with the finding that the correlation between observations of σ for the same households in subsequent waves of the SEP is always below 0.2.

Since the findings regarding μ and logYmin unambiguously bear out the expectations stated in the introduction, we can conclude that μ and logYmin possess a high degree of construct validity. Results are consistent with the hypothesis that both are highly reliable measures of the same concept, i.e. an evaluation of income levels from the point of view of the standard of living it enables households to have.

On the other hand, it is not clear whether the distribution of IEQ-amounts around their average value μ points to anything very substantive. According to Van Praag (1971), the dispersion of the answers to the IEQ is an indicator of the slope of a person's WFI, i.e. the welfare gain associated with a certain proportional increase in income. However, since the correlations across years of σ, which measures the dispersion of the IEQ-amounts, is quite low, it must be the case that either σ has low reliability, or that the phenomenon it is supposed to measure is highly changeable over time. In fact, there are indications that the first possibility is closest to the truth. One might argue that the finding that the 'internal structure' of the IEQ response patterns is highly stable across years, disproves the suggestions just made. These response patterns do not necessarily reveal latent traits of respondents, though, but may just reflect constraints imposed by the format of the IEQ, in particular the fact that it asks for monotonously increasing amounts of income.

3 Empirical determinants of income evaluations

Introduction

In this section I will present empirical results concerning the determinants of subjective income evaluations, using data from the Belgian Socio-Economic Panel (SEP), waves 1985, 1988 and 1992. The analysis will build on the review of published research results in chapter 4, but I will also explore some issues that appear to have been neglected in the literature.

In order to avoid potential distortions, only a subsample of all households will be used in the analyses below. The sample used consists of single people and couples, with no children or with dependent children only, where neither the head of household nor his partner are or were self-employed. Thus, two categories of households are excluded: 'complex' households and the self-employed. (That is, in addition to those who have not answered the MIQ or the IEQ consistently, see the previous section.) 'Complex' households are households in which, apart from the core family, other relatives, non-relatives, or, in most cases, independent children are living. Independent children are children who are older than 25 and/or who have left school, and who, in most cases, have an income of their own. For 'complex' households it is ambiguous to what extent the presence and incomes of these other persons have been taken into account when the income evaluation questions were answered. Self-employed persons are excluded because their income situations are difficult to measure, unstable, and often even unclear for the persons concerned themselves. This is less true for the retired self-employed, but even for this category errors in the measurement of income may be large, because income from liquid assets is not measured well.

The sizes of the resulting subsamples in each year are shown in table 5.7. The cumulative exclusion of cases mean that only 51 to 59 percent of all sample households will be used for analysis. However, the remaining number of cases seem sufficient to estimate most parameters of interest with a reasonable degree of reliability, while the greater degree of homogeneity within the subsamples should enhance their validity. Depending on the purpose of the analysis, sometimes smaller subsamples will be selected from the 'general' subsamples just defined. This will be indicated in each sub-section.

Table 5.7
Sizes of subsamples used for analysis of empirical determinants of μ and logYmin in the Belgian Socio-Economic Panel (BSEP)

	1985 Percent	1988 Percent	1992 Percent
Complex household (1)	16.6	19.4	17.7
(Former) self-employed (1)	20.6	21.7	21.6
Not one of the above	66.8	63.0	64.4
Not one of the above, and adequate answers to the MIQ and IEQ (2)	59.5 (n = 3851)	51.4 (n = 1941)	58.6 (n = 2240)
Total	100.0 (n = 6471)	100.0 (n = 3779)	100.0 (n = 3821)

Notes: (1) Categories overlap.
(2) See section 5.2.3 for details about criteria used to assess adequacy of answers.
Complex household: household with independent children, other relatives, or non-relatives.
(Former) self-employed: household where either the head or the partner is or has been self-employed.

Source: Belgian SEP, waves 1985, 1988, 1992.

Household income and perception bias

First of all, I will take a closer look at the relationship between household income and the answers to the income evaluation questions. The effect of household income on subjective income evaluations can be interpreted as an estimate of the 'preference effect'. One should keep in mind, though, that because the income of the respondent is likely to be collinear with the level of income in the reference group and no measure of the latter is included in the models used here, the measured effect of household income may also partially reflect the 'reference effect' (see section 4.5). In this section two specific issues are explored. In the first place, the influence of income perception bias will be investigated. Secondly, the functional form of the relationship between respondent's income and the answers to the MIQ and the IEQ will be looked at.

As shown in the review in section 4.6, it has been recognized by researchers that respondents may have only a vague idea of what their actual household income is (Kapteyn et al., 1988). Respondents may easily forget income components that are received at longer intervals (e.g. interests from savings) or irregularly (e.g. overtime payments) or that are received by other persons in the household (e.g. earnings of children). It seems reasonable to assume that when answering the IEQ and the MIQ, the respondent will use his own estimate of his actual income as a frame of reference. Misperception of income might therefore easily distort the results of the subjective method.

As a solution to this problem, Kapteyn et al. (1988) suggested to ask the respondent to give an estimate of his or her household income and to use this estimate to adjust the answers to the subjective income questions. The most obvious adjustment is to multiply the given amounts by the ratio of actual household income and the respondent's perception of it, i.e. proportional adjustment. However, the appropriate adjustment depends on the degree to which the respondent's perception of income serves as his frame of reference when answering the MIQ and the IEQ. Empirical analysis by Tummers (1994) has shown that, at least in the Dutch Socio-Economic Panel, people respond to the MIQ *as if* the perceived income is their actual income, i.e. perceived income is the sole frame of reference. This implies that the adjustment should generally be less than proportional, depending on the value of the log-household income parameter in the logYmin regression equation (see section 4.6 for a fuller exposition of this issue).

In this section, I will analyze this matter using the SEP data. The SEP questionnaire includes a question asking for the total disposable income of the household[11]. In addition, a number of detailed questions are asked about the incomes from various sources of each household member. The sum of these income components is generally used as the correct measure of household income.

First, these data are used to see to what extent the respondent is aware of various income components when answering the question about total disposable income. The answers to the latter question have been regressed on the various income components. (No intercept was included in the regression equation.) The results (not tabulated) show that income of the head of household (who usually is the respondent) is taken into account almost completely, income of the partner and child allowances are somewhat less so. Incomes of children living with their parents, study grants and income from letting houses appears to have been forgotten quite often. Some of the parameter estimates fluctuate quite strongly across years. The reason for this is not clear; they cannot be readily explained by changes in the order of the relevant income questions in the SEP questionnaire. Anyway, the income components concerned constitute only a very small part of aggregate household income. The parameter estimates have been used to impute perceived income for those households where the respondent had not answered the question about total disposable household income. The imputation was also used when the ratio of perceived income to measured income was smaller than 0.5.

The number of cases involved is rather small as shown in the following table:

Perceived income imputed:		1985	1988	1992
- In total sample	N	650	357	291
	%	10.0	9.5	7.7
- In subsample used for analysis	N	201	76	72
	%	5.2	3.9	3.2

Secondly, following Tummers (1994), a number of different models are estimated in order to gauge the bias due to income misperception and to find out which income concept is adopted by Belgian SEP respondents as the frame of reference. Table 5.8 reports estimates for a model with both measured and perceived income. It is clear that perceived income is the main determinant of subjective income evaluations. The parameter estimates for measured income are small and statistically insignificant. (There is no apparent explanation for the finding that they are negative in 1985 and 1988 and positive in 1992.)

Alternatively, the model could be formulated in terms of a parameter η, which indicates which income variable respondents refer to when answering the MIQ and IEQ, or more exactly what weights those variables get in this process[12]. If $\eta = 0$, measured income is the frame of reference, if $\eta = 1$, perceived income is the frame of reference. Values for η between 0 and 1 indicate that both variables have some weight. Estimates for η are somewhat above 1 in 1985 and 1988 and somewhat below 1 in 1992; again the reason for this change is not clear. Differences between the μ and logYmin equation estimates of η are negligible. Further tests showed that the hypothesis that $\eta = 1$ is clearly consistent with the data. This suggests that perceived income is the exclusive frame of reference for respondents when answering the MIQ and the IEQ. In that case, the reported parameter estimates for logYp are unbiased estimates of the effect of log-household income on μ and logYmin.

Table 5.8
Household income perception bias: estimates of impact, Belgium, 1985, 1988 and 1992

		1985		1988		1992	
		mu	logymin	mu	logymin	mu	logymin
Measured income (Ym) and perceived income (Yp)							
Yp	Parameter est.	0.481	0.429	0.554	0.424	0.362	0.314
	(Standard error)	(.036)	(.041)	(.042)	(.050)	(.049)	(.055)
Ym	Parameter est.	-0.061	-0.058	-0.057	-0.024	0.059	0.065
	(Standard error)	(.036)	(.041)	(.042)	(.050)	(.048)	(.055)
η:	Parameter est.	1.157	1.156	1.116	1.061	0.861	0.829
	(Standard error)	(.086)	(.111)	(.086)	(.125)	(.115)	(.144)

Notes: Subsample used includes only non-complex households where head nor partner are or were self-employed, and who have answered the IEQ and MIQ adequately.

- Models includes variables representing the number of children in four age ranges, dummies for home tenure, whether elderly or not and region, and a sample selection bias correction term.
- Ym: Measured income.
- Yp: Perceived income.
- All parameter estimates are statistically significant at the 0.1 percent level, except those for Ym, which are not significant at the 5 percent level.

Source: Belgian Socio-Economic Panel, waves 1985, 1988, 1992.

Equivalently, one might use a model that includes measured income and a correction term for income perception bias. The latter is defined as log(Yp/Ym). Using this model the parameter estimates for measured income are virtually equal to those for perceived income in table 5.8. This shows that the inclusion of the correction term does indeed remove the bias due to income misperception. Including the correction term leads to parameter estimates for measured income that are 5 to 7 percent higher; these percentages give an indication of the size of the bias induced by income misperception. The estimates of the effect of the number of adults appear hardly affected by income perception bias. However, without a correction for the bias in the estimated effect of household income, the adult equivalence factor would be underestimated. This specification will be used for all subsequent analyses.

Functional form

Most researchers analyzing subjective income evaluations choose the double-log specification for the regression equations, which is:

$$\mu = \beta_0 + \beta_1 \log Y + \beta_{\mathbf{x}}\mathbf{X} + e,$$

where Y represents household income, **X** a vector of other characteristics of the household, β_0 and β_1 are parameters to be estimated, and $\beta_{\mathbf{x}}$ is a vector of parameters. Some, however, have used a linear specification (e.g. Poulin, 1988; Halleröd, 1995):

$$\exp(\mu) = \beta_0' + \beta_1' Y + \beta_{\mathbf{x}}' \mathbf{X} + e'. \tag{5.9}$$

Similar double-log and linear equations can of course be specified for (log)Ymin. Although the issue of the correct functional form of course potentially involves all independent variables, I concentrate here on household income, the most important determinant. The specification regarding the family size variables will be looked at below. The choice of functional form has important consequences for the estimates of the costs of children and adults. When a double-log specification is used (without interaction terms), costs of children will be proportional to income or expenditure. On the other hand, a linear form will produce estimates of the costs of children in terms of fixed money amounts, independent of the level of income.

Of course, other functional forms can be easily conceived, but the double-log and linear ones are the most obvious possibilities. Mixed forms, i.e. linear-log or log-linear ones seem intrinsically implausible. A linear-log specification (i.e. Ymin = $\beta_1' \log Y$) would mean that any given proportional increase in income would produce the same absolute increase in Ymin, irrespective of the level of income, and of Ymin. Conversely, a log-linear form (i.e. logYmin = $\beta_1^{o} Y$) would imply that any given absolute increase in income would produce the same proportional increase in Ymin, again irrespective of the level of income, and of Ymin.

In order to test whether a functional form is misspecified for certain data, several methods can be used (cf. Fomby et al., 1988: 409-436). Here, three have been considered. The first is the Durbin-Watson test for serial correlation. When there is misspecification regarding a certain variable, the regression residuals, ordered according to that variable, will be serially correlated. Durbin-Watson test statistics have been calculated for the double-log and linear specifications of the μ/exp(μ) and (log)Ymin equations, after ordering the observations according to the level of household income, using the 1985, 1988 and 1992 data. In each instance, the Durbin-Watson statistic was slightly lower for the linear equation than for the corresponding double-log one, implying that the first one had more serial correlation of the residuals. The differences were quite small, however. The highest degree of serial correlation was measured for the 1985 linear exp(μ) regression, but it still amounted to only 0.065[13]. Since the double-log and linear specifications cannot both be correct at the same time, we must conclude that, given the moderate R-squares (.50 - .65), the Durbin-Watson test is not powerful enough to detect misspecification. Apparently, the regression errors due to misspecification are swamped by random errors.

The second test consisted of the introduction into the regression equations of the squares and cubes of income or log-income. This test can be seen as a somewhat informal version of the RESET-test devised by Ramsey, 1969. If a linear equation is specified, while in fact the double-log form is correct, the sign pattern of the resulting specification errors (ordered according to income) should look something like this: ---+++++-------. One would then expect a regression term equal to the square of household income to be able to pick this up and come out significant (and with a negative sign). The same is true, mutatis mutandis, for the double-log specification. Other forms of misspecification might be detected through the introduction of cubic transformations of household income.

The results of this exercise revealed that the introduction of the square and cube of log-income into the double-log equations leads to only very small increases in R-square (0.00053 at most), which are statistically significant only in the case of the 1985 μ equation. In the latter case, the sign of the regression coefficient is negative, so this result does not indicate that a linear specification might be closer to the correct form. On the other hand, the R-square gain due to the introduction of the square of household income into the linear equations is always statistically significant, and for the 1985 equations even relatively large. The sign of the regression coefficient for the squared term was always negative. These results indicate that the pattern of the residuals in the linear specifications is consistent with the hypothesis that the double-log specification is the most correct one.

The third test for functional (mis)specification used here relies on the Box-Cox transformation (Box and Cox, 1964; I follow the exposition in Fomby et al., 1988: 423-431). The Box-Cox procedure allows a more formal comparison of models having different dependent variables, as is the case for the double-log and linear models which concern us here. The Box-Cox transformation is defined as:

$$Z^{(\lambda)} = (Z^{\lambda} - 1)/\lambda, \qquad \text{if } \lambda <> 0,$$
$$Z^{(\lambda)} = \log(Z), \qquad \text{if } \lambda = 0.$$

Depending on the parameter λ, this transformation makes it possible to define a range of functional forms for the μ-equation, as follows:

$$\exp(\mu)^{(\lambda)} = \beta^*_0 + \beta^*_{11} Y^{(\lambda)} + \beta^*_{12} C^{(\lambda)} + \beta^*_x \mathbf{X} + e^*, \qquad (5.10)$$

where Y represents household income, C the income perception bias correction term, **X** a vector of other characteristics of the household, β^*_0, β^*_{11} and β^*_{12} are parameters to be estimated, and $\beta^*_{\mathbf{x}}$ is a vector of parameters. A similar equation can of course be formulated with transformations of Ymin as the dependent variable. The transformation involves only μ and logYmin, household income and the perception bias correction term; the other independent variables remain untransformed. If $\lambda = 1$ a linear model results, if $\lambda = 0$, we have a double-log model, and if $\lambda = -1$, an inverse model[14]. The maximum likelihood estimate of λ is that value of λ which maximizes the likelihood function L:

$$L = (\lambda - 1)\Sigma\mu_i - (N/2)\log(VAR(e^{(\lambda)})),$$

where the summation is across all observations, N the total number of observations, and $VAR(e^{(\lambda)})$ is the estimated variance of the residuals in the regression equation resulting from the particular value of λ.

The log-likelihood function L was computed for 21 values of λ, ranging from -1 to 1 with steps of 0.1, using the amalgamated SEP data of 1985, 1988 and 1992 (N=8039). The coefficients β^*_0 and β^*_{11} were allowed to vary across years, through the introduction of dummies and interaction terms with household income for the years 1988 and 1992. A similar procedure was applied to Ymin. The resulting values of L are shown in figure 5.2. Both for the μ and logYmin equations the log-likelihood function reaches its maximum at $\lambda = 0$, indicating that the double-log functional form fits the data better than not just the linear or inverse models, but also than any 'intermediate' one.

The conclusion of this section is that the tests performed show that the double-log specification is the best among plausible models.

Figure 5.2
Box-Cox transformation test of functional form of μ and logYmin equations: Log-likelihood for a range of λ's (see text for details)

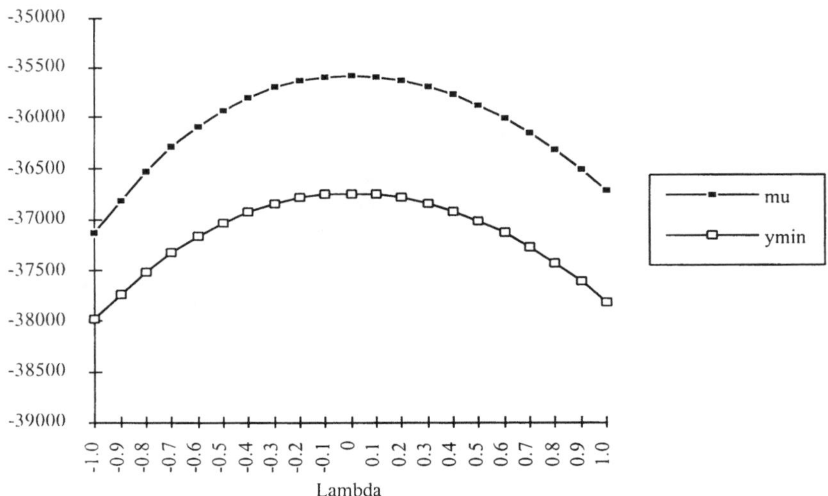

Source: BSEP, amalgamated data of waves 1985, 1988 and 1992.

A closer look at the relationship between minimum income and actual household income

Figure 5.3 provides a more detailed picture of the relationship between Ymin and household income (as perceived by the respondent, Yp), using the amalgamated data of the three SEP waves. The long axis of figure 5.3

represents the answer to the MIQ, expressed as a percentage of perceived household income (divided into brackets that are five percent wide). Each of the five graphs, or 'jagged walls' shows the percentage distribution of that variable within one of five income groups, where the bottom income category is in the back, and the highest one in front.

Figure 5.3
Distribution of answers to MIQ (Ymin), as a percentage of perceived household income (Yp), for five income groups (lowest income group in background), Belgium, 1985, 1988 and 1992

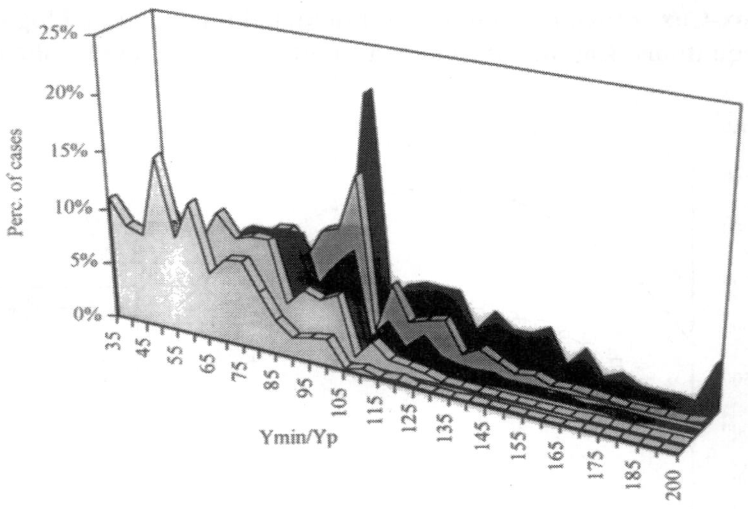

Note: Distributions shown are of 100*Ymin/Yp for five (perceived) income groups. Brackets of Ymin/Yp are five percent wide; labels in graph indicate upper boundary. Income groups are defined as follows, from back to front, in thousands of BF per month: 0-35 (N=2190), 35-55 (N=3363), 55-75 (N=2660), 75-95 (N=1715) and 95+ (N=1325). Incomes in 1985 and 1988 waves have been updated using the consumer price index. Subsample used includes only cases with adequate answers to the MIQ and the IEQ, and who have answered the question about total household income.

Source: Belgian Socio-Economic Panel, amalgamated data of waves 1985, 1988 and 1992.

The most striking aspect of the graph is the 'continental rift', bordered by high peaks at 100 percent and by a trough at 105 percent. For a large number of respondents, especially in the lower income groups, minimum income is equal to actual household income. The number of respondents whose income exceeds their actual income is limited, only 22 percent overall, though they form a (small) majority in the bottom income group (up to 35,000 BF/month). For some reason, almost no one gives an answer to the MIQ that is between 100 and 105 percent of his or her actual income. Another interesting feature is the bimodal (double-peaked) distribution in the three middle income groups. Apparently, for some respondents in these groups the minimum income they need to make ends meet is equal to or close to their actual income, while for others it is some distance below the latter amount. These patterns suggest that some respondents take their actual income as a point of departure when estimating their minimum income, while others arrive at it independently from their actual income (cf. Stinson, 1997: 34).

Costs of children

In this section, the specification of family size, in particular regarding the number and ages of dependent children will be considered. As the review in section 5.3 has shown, most studies of the determinants of μ and Ymin take account only of the number of household members. In Kapteyn, Kooreman and Willemse (1988) a more sophisticated specification is introduced, taking account of the ages of children (see section 4.4). It has the following form:

$$\log(FS_n) = \Sigma_i\, w_i\, f(age_{in}) \qquad (5.11)$$

where *i* is a subscript that runs across the members of household *n*, from the oldest to the youngest. The w_i are a set of weights that follow a decreasing logarithmic pattern: $w_1 = 1$, $w_2 = \log(2)$, $w_i = \log(i/i\text{-}1)$ if $i>2$. The age function of Kapteyn, Kooreman and Willemse (1988) is a cubic spline.

The purpose of this section is to examine two questions: first, whether the decreasing logarithmic pattern of the rank weights is in accordance with the data, and secondly, whether an age function is necessary, i.e. whether the effect of children on subjective income evaluations varies by their ages.

The age function that I will use for all specifications is different from that of Kapteyn, Kooreman and Willemse (1988). It consists of five dummy variables representing age brackets; formally:

$$f(age_i) = \delta_1 \text{ age0-3}_i + \delta_2 \text{ age4-10}_i + \delta_3 \text{ age12-17}_i + \delta_4 \text{ age18-25}_i + \text{adult}_i \qquad (5.12)$$

where $age0\text{-}3_i$ is a dummy variable that is equal to one if the i - th household member is aged between 0 and 3, and is zero otherwise. The other age variables correspond to the other age ranges; $adult_i$ is dummy variable indicating whether the household member is an adult. Parameters δ_1, δ_2, δ_3 and δ_4 are to be estimated. They are measures of the costs of a child in the particular age bracket, relative to those of an adult with the same rank number in the household. This specification has the advantage that the resulting parameter estimates are readily interpretable. A disadvantage is that the implied costs of a child do not develop smoothly as the child becomes older, but change abruptly at the bracket boundaries. Such abrupt changes may not be completely unrealistic, though, when a child enters secondary or higher education (which in Belgium usually happens at the ages of 12 and 18, respectively).

The decreasing logarithmic pattern of the weighs w_i imposes certain characteristics on the resulting equivalence scale. This is most easily seen by considering couples with children who are all in the same age bracket, say 4 to 11. In that case, (5.11) can be rewritten as:

$$\log(FS_n) = C + \delta_2 \log(K_n/2 + 1), \qquad (5.13)$$

where $C = 1+\log(2)$ and K_n is the number of children in family n. Substituting (5.13) into the standard μ equation (5-8), we obtain the following expression for the equivalence factor E_n, which indicates by what proportion the income of a family with K_n children should be larger than that of a childless couple, in order to have the same level of welfare:

$$E_n = (K_n/2 + 1)^{\beta'_2\delta_2}, \qquad (5.14)$$

where $\beta'_2 = \beta_2/(1\text{-}\beta_1)$. The first derivative of E_n with respect to K_n is $(1/2)\beta'_2\delta_2(K_n/2 + 1)^{\beta'_2\delta_2-1}$. It is immediately seen that as long as $\beta'_2\delta_2 < 1$, there are economies of scale in raising children, i.e. the second child costs less than the first one, and the third one less still. For instance, if $\beta'_2\delta_2 =$

0.25, costs for the second and third child amount to 77 percent and 64 percent of those of the first child. Only if $\beta'_2\delta_2 = 1$ is it true that children of all ranks are equally costly. But in that case $E_1 = 1.5$, $E_2 = 2.0$, $E_3 = 2.5$, and the equivalence scale boils down to the number of family members divided by two, i.e. a per capita scale.

Is this pattern of decreasing costs justified by empirical subjective income evaluations? In the ideal test the weights w_i would be replaced by parameters to be estimated. However, the resulting equation would be complicated and non-linear in the parameters. Therefore, I will compare four alternative specifications of the effect of children on μ and logYmin. The first specification is the *logarithmic* one, as proposed by Kapteyn, Kooreman and Willemse (1988). In the second, *linear* alternative, the weights are all set equal to 1. Given the age function (5.12), this specification amounts to entering the number of children in the various age brackets in the regression equation. Perhaps surprisingly, a linear specification does *not* mean that children of all ranks are all equally expensive, but implies that there are *dis*economies of scale in the costs of children. This becomes evident if we again assume that all children are aged 4 to 11. The linear specification can then be written as $2 + \delta_2 K_n$, and the equivalence factor E'_n is then defined as $EXP(K_n/2 + 1)^{\beta'_2\delta_2}$. The first derivative of E'_n with respect to K_n is $\beta'_2\delta_2 EXP(K_n)^{\beta'_2\delta_2}$. If $\beta'_2\delta_2 > 0$, this expression is increasing in K_n, which means that a child of rank i is more expensive that one of rank i-1.

In the third alternative, the effects of rank and age are assumed to be *additive*; in formula: $\log(FS_n) = \Sigma_i \rho_i r_{in} + f(age_{in})$, where r_{in} is a dummy variable which is equal to one if there is a child of rank i in family n and the ρ_i are parameters to be estimated[15]. This specification means that the rank weights can take any pattern, but also that the age effects are independent of the rank, which is perhaps implausible. More precisely, the effect on a family's equivalence factor of a child moving from one age bracket to another is independent of its rank. The fourth alternative specification has dummies for every possible combination of rank and age bracket. This is the most unrestricted or *full* specification, of which the other three are special cases.

In order to compare the alternative specifications and test the necessity of the age function within a homogeneous subsample, I use only observations on non-aged couples with zero, one, two or three dependent children, with no other household members, and who are not self-employed. The F-test can be used for comparisons between the 'full' model and the three other ones, since the latter result from (sometimes non-linear) restrictions on the former. In order to discriminate among the three more restricted models, I use the residual variance criterion, which is equivalent to the maximum adjusted R-squared criterion (Fomby et al., 1988: 416-18). In order to increase the power of the tests, I have amalgamated data across the three waves of the SEP. This means that in a large number of cases, observations on the same family at two or three different points in time are treated as if they are independent observations.

As the results in table 5.9 show, the data do not allow to discriminate between the four models. The 'full' model has higher adjusted R^2 statistics than the other models, but the differences are not significant at any conventional level, despite the large number of cases.

Table 5.9

Comparison of four model specifications of effects of children on subjective income evaluations, Belgium, 1985, 1988 and 1992

Equation		Full model	Additive model	Logarithmic model	Linear model
μ	R2	.45959	.45854	.45828	.45847
	Adj.R2	.45738	.45699	.45695	.45714
	F-test*		1.60	1.49	1.27
logYmin	R2	.36162	.36008	.35968	.35964
	Adj.R2	.35901	.35825	.35811	.35807
	F-test*		1.97	1.86	1.90
Degrees of freedom		20	14	12	12

Notes:
- Subsample used includes only non-complex families of non-aged couples with 0, 1, 2, or 3 children, where head nor partner are or were self-employed, and who have answered the IEQ and MIQ adequately (see section 5.3.4 for details) (N=4908).
- Models include log-household income, a income perception bias correction term, log-rent, log-mortgage payment, dummies for region, and a sample selection bias correction term. Number of degrees of freedom refer to complete model.

* F-test statistic for comparison of model with full model; none of these are significant at the 5 percent level.

Source: Belgian Socio-Economic Panel, amalgamated data of waves 1985, 1988, 1992.

The R^2's for the other three models are virtually identical (difference of 0.00019 at most) and do not consistently favor one particular model. Apparently, the data contain too much noise for a clear signal about the correct model to emerge. Adding the observations for the small number of families (178) with four or more dependent children did not change any of these results.

The parameter estimates shown in table 5.10 for the 'full' model are interesting in that they suggest that the second child is cheaper than the first one, but that the third is again at least as expensive as the first one. Intuitively, this result makes some sense, since important consumer durables like houses and cars are often adapted to the 'standard' family with two adults and two children. Thus, there may be important economies of scale for the second child, while the birth of a third child may necessitate a larger house and a bigger car. However, given the relatively large standard errors, and the indeterminateness of the R^2 comparisons, the finding needs to be confirmed by independent results before definitive conclusions can be drawn.

Table 5.10
Parameter estimates of effects of children on subjective income evaluations, Belgium, 1985, 1988 and 1992

Full model

Rank	Age	mu		logYmin	
		est.	st. error	est.	st. error
1	0-3	0.026	.012*	0.026	.014
1	4-11	0.052	.011**	0.067	.013**
1	12-17	0.063	.012**	0.082	.013**
1	18-25	0.074	.013**	0.117	0.015**
2	0-3	0.022	.013	0.018	.015
2	4-11	0.025	.012*	0.027	.013*
2	12-17	0.063	.014**	0.063	.016**
2	18-25	0.064	.026*	0.048	.029
3	0-3	0.064	.018**	0.065	.021*
3	4-11	0.044	.016*	0.081	.018**
3	12-17	0.015	.025	0.025	.028
3	18-25	0.106	.058	0.113	.066

Notes: See table 5.9.

* Estimate significant at the 5-percent level.

** Estimate significant at the 0.1-percent level.

Source: Belgian SEP, amalgamated data of waves 1985, 1988 and 1992.

The question can be asked what effect the choice of model has on the estimates of children's costs. As could be expected, the logarithmic model produces higher estimates of the cost of the first child, while for the second and third children, costs are higher according to the linear model. The differences are fairly small, however. Moreover, since a family with a third ranking child necessarily also has first and second ranking children, the differences partially cancel each other out. The additive model produces equivalence factors that are generally quite close to those derived from the linear model.

Fortunately, the findings are less ambiguous regarding the age function. Table 5.11 shows that the removal of the age function would result in significantly lower R^2 values for all models. The parameter estimates in table 5.10 indicate that children become considerably more expensive as they get older. Children aged 18 to 24 appear to cost two to three times as much as babies and toddlers. The estimates based on Ymin are generally somewhat higher than those based on μ, except for the youngest age bracket.

Table 5.11
Statistical significance of age function within four model specifications of effect of children on subjective income evaluations, Belgium, 1985, 1988 and 1992

		Full model	Additive model	Logarith-mic model	Linear model
mu	R2 with age function	.45959	.45854	.45828	.45847
	R2 without	.45577	.45577	.45514	.45563
	F-test for difference	3.85	8.37	9.48	8.58
	Significance of F	<.0001	<.0001	<.00001	<.0001
log-Ymin	R2 with age function	.36162	.36008	.35968	.35964
	R2 without	.35430	.35430	.35298	.35369
	F-test for difference	6.25	14.78	17.12	15.20
	Significance of F	<.00001	<.00001	<.00001	<.00001
Degrees of freedom of F-test		9	3	3	3

Notes: See table 5.9.

Source: Belgian SEP, amalgamated data of waves 1985, 1988 and 1992.

Variation in equivalence factors by income level (interaction between income and household size)

A final issue concerns the possible dependence of the costs of children on the level of household income. The models used so far in this subsection incorporate the assumption that the costs of children amount to the same percentage of income at all income levels. This constraint is not necessarily realistic. In order to test the hypothesis that the equivalence factors (= percentage costs) of children vary with income, a term $\log(FS_n)\log(Y_n)$ was added to the regression equations. This in effect creates four interaction terms of log-household income with the four variables representing the number of children in four age brackets. The results (not shown here) indicate that the inclusion of the interaction terms produces a small but statistically significant increase in R-square in both equations. Surprisingly, all coefficients for the interaction terms are *positive* (though not always significant). That is, the effect of the presence of children on the answers to the MIQ and IEQ increases with rising income. The effect is particularly pronounced for teenagers.

These results would mean that for rich parents the costs of children are greater, as a percentage of their income, than for poor parents. At the level of the income thresholds SPL and LPL0.5 the equivalence scale becomes much flatter than at average levels of income, especially for families with teenagers. Following the results based on the μ-equation with interaction, a family with three children aged 12 to 17 would need only 9 percent more income than a childless couple, in order to feel equally well off; the corresponding figure based on the logYmin equation is 15 percent. It is difficult to believe that at relatively low incomes, the costs of children as a percentage of total expenses would be this small. Also, the interaction terms had fairly large standard errors, and these were not retained for the final models.

Determinants of subjective income evaluations

In this subsection, I will present results for the full μ and logYmin equations. At the same time, I will compare those with estimates derived from two alternative models. The first alternative model is the most elementary or 'simple' model, which includes only log-household income and log-household size. The other alternative is an adaptation of the model developed by Muffels et al. (1990: 137-175), which is one of the most sophisticated in the literature. The (static) 'Kapteyn - Muffels' model takes account of income perception bias, ages of children, preference interdependence (i.e. reference groups), and item non-response. All these elements are retained in my adaptation of the Kapteyn-Muffels model, though the exact specification differs in more or less important ways, as indicated in the following table:

	Muffels et al.	My adaptation
Income perception bias	Perceived income estimated using question with 7 income brackets	Perceived income asked as amount
Ages of children 0-18 years	Third degree polynomial 'cubic spline' (cf. section 4.4)	Three age categories: 0-3, 4-11, 12-17
Preference interdependence	Based on direct questions about income in reference groups (cf. section 4.5)	Dummies for selected social categories
Item non-response	Joint estimation of selection equation	Heckman two-step procedure

The models also differ in that the simple model and the Kapteyn-Muffels model are estimated using all cases where the MIQ and the IEQ have been answered adequately, whereas the model developed here excludes households where the head or partner are or were self-employed, as well as complex households, i.e. households which include persons other than the head, spouse and dependent children (see above for details). Below, this model will be called the 'selective' model.

I will now discuss estimates of the three models, based on the amalgamated data of the Belgian SEP waves 1985, 1988 and 1992, as shown in table 5.12, while at the same time summarizing results more fully reported in Van den Bosch (1999)[16]. The estimated equations for the simple model are as follows (see table 5.12 for notes):

$$\mu = 0.365 \log Y + 0.164 \log FS - 0.257\, MailSurvey + 0.049\, MailSurvey{*}\log Y + 3.501$$

(R-square = 0.531, n = 12171)

$$\log Ymin = 0.320 \log Y + 0.194 \log FS - 0.188\, MailSurvey + 0.035\, MailSurvey{*}\log Y + 3.769$$

(R-square = 0.452, n = 12171)

Table 5.12
Summary models of μ and logYmin, Belgium, 1985, 1988 and 1992

	Kapteyn-Muffels model		Selective model	
	μ	logYmin	μ	logYmin
logY	0.390	0.339	0.424	0.375
	(.006)	(.007)	(.008)	(.009)
logC	0.501	0.407	0.491	0.397
	(.017)	(.019)	(.025)	(.029)
logFSA*	0.158	0.194	0.158	0.202
	(.007)	(.008)	(.011)	(.012)
logFSCh3	0.132	0.130	0.098	0.101
	(.017)	(.019)	(.018)	(.021)
logFSCh11	0.150	0.184	0.120	0.150
	(.010)	(.012)	(.012)	(.013)
logFSCh17	0.212	0.247	0.169	0.207
	(.012)	(.013)	(.013)	(.015)
logFSCh25			0.201	0.260
			(.016)	(.018)
Tenant			0.018	0.028
			(.006)	(.007)
Mortgagee			0.036	0.040
			(.007)	(.008)
Head below 25	-0.052	-0.069	-0.043	-0.068
	(.014)	(.016)	(.014)	(.016)
Head above 64	-0.054	-0.048	-0.039	-0.022
	(.006)	(.007)	(.007)	(.008)
University educ.	0.065	0.035	0.037	-0.011 ns.
	(.009)	(.010)	(.011)	(.012)
Flanders, 1988	-0.021	-0.035	-0.026	-0.040
	(.008)	(.009)	(.010)	(.011)
Flanders, 1992	0.077	0.018	0.067	0.004 ns.
	(.007)	(.008)	(.008)	(.009)
Wallonia, 1985	0.068	0.037	0.065	0.040
	(.007)	(.008)	(.008)	(.010)
Wallonia, 1988	0.072	0.065	0.058	0.049
	(0.009)	(.011)	(0.011)	(.012)
Wallonia, 1992	0.151	0.184	0.148	0.176
	(.009)	(.010)	(.010)	(.011)

Table 5.12 (continuation)

	Kapteyn-Muffels model		Selective model	
	μ	logYmin	μ	logYmin
Brussels, 1985	0.079	0.120	0.066	0.108
	(.011)	(.013)	(.013)	(.015)
Brussels, 1988	0.078	0.107	0.078	0.102
	(.024)	(.026)	(.029)	(.034)
Brussels, 1992	0.182	0.238	0.152	0.190
	(.019)	(.022)	(.022)	(.026)
Mail survey	-0.294	-0.344	-0.530	-0.573
	(.110)	(.123)	(.136)	(.157)
Mail survey *	0.057	0.059	0.089	0.088)
logY	(.017)	(.019)	(.021)	(.024)
Mills' ratio	0.153	-0.029 ns.	0.036 ns.	-0.137
	(.041)	(.046)	(.046)	(.053)
Constant	3.065	3.495	2.967	3.358
	(.054)	(.061)	(.062)	(.071)
R-square	0.582	0.500	0.642	0.551
N of cases	12171		8039	

Notes:
- Only cases with adequate answers to the MIQ and IEQ.
- Subsample used for 'Selective model' includes only non-complex households, where neither head nor partner are or were self-employed.
- logC: Income perception bias correction term.
- logFSA: log(Number of adults + 1).
* In 'Kapteyn-Muffels model' adults are defined as all persons aged 18 or older; in 'Selective model' only the head and partner can be adults.
- logFSCh3: Number of children aged 0-3, weighted by rank.
- logFSCh11: Number of children aged 4-11, weighted by rank.
- logFSCh17: Number of children aged 12-17, weighted by rank.
- logFSCh25: Number of children aged 18-25, weighted by rank.
- All parameters are significantly different from zero at the 1 percent level, except those marked 'ns.'.

Source: Belgian Socio-Economic Panel, amalgamated data of waves 1985, 1988 and 1992.

Household income is the most important determinant of answers to the income evaluations questions. As has been shown above, the functional form of the relationship is double logarithmic, which implies that a given percentage increase in income produces, on average, a constant percentage increase in the answers to the MIQ and the IEQ, regardless of the level of income. The estimates of the size of the resultant change differ by model and by dependent variable. The Kapteyn-Muffels model estimates are slightly higher than those of the simple model, while those of the selective model are slightly higher still. The reason for these differences is first of all that in the two latter models a term logC has been included, which corrects for income perception bias. Results presented above indicate that respondents tend to forget certain income components when answering questions about household income. The resulting misperception of household income, if not corrected for, leads to a downward bias in the regression coefficients of log-income.

A second reason for the differences is that the selective model excludes complex households and the self-employed. The effect of the incomes of non-core family members on answers to the MIQ and IEQ is often smaller than that of core family income (Van den Bosch, 1999). Also, results not reported here indicate that the estimated regression coefficient among the self-employed is smaller than the same among the non-self employed. The latter difference is probably due to errors in the measurement of the earnings of the self-employed. The best estimates of the impact of log-income on subjective income evaluations are therefore probably those produced by the selective model, which indicate that a 10 percent rise in household income results in an increase in MIQ and IEQ answers of about 4 percent. Another finding is that for each model, the logY coefficient in the μ equation exceeds that in the logYmin equation by about 0.05. However, as shown in section 5.2, the effect of household income on logYmin is not significantly different from that on μ when the IEQ-parameters σ and ξ are also included in the equation.

Family size is represented in the simple model by the log of the number of family members, while the other models distinguish between adults and children and in addition take account of the age of children. In the Kapteyn-Muffels model this is done by constructing four age groups, 0-3, 4-11, 12-17 and 18 and older. The last age group are regarded as adults. The selective model is similar, except that dependent children aged 18 to 25 (mainly students in higher education) are distinguished as a separate category. For all models, a logarithmic specification has been chosen, in order to retain comparability with most previous studies. Above I reported on a comparison of the 'logarithmic' specification used here with a linear one, where rank weights are all set to one, and with one where all rank weights were left unconstrained. None of these performed significantly better or worse than the other ones. There was a suggestion that second ranking children had a smaller impact than first ranking children, while that of third-ranking children was as important as that of first children.

Since complex households are excluded for the selective model, the specification used implies that the number of adults can only be either one (for singles) or two (for couples). The size of the estimates indicates that answers to the MIQ and the IEQ of couples are 15 and 12 percent higher, respectively, than those of single persons. The other models produce quite similar estimates of the effect of the number of adults. Results of both the Kapteyn-Muffels model and the selective model indicate clearly that the effects of the presence of children increase substantially with the age of those children. Teenagers (12-17) and in particular children aged 18 or older appear even to have a greater impact than adults. However, one has to keep in mind that all family members are weighted by weights which decrease logarithmically with increasing rank number, and which are thus in most cases smaller for children than for adults. Generally, the logYmin equation produces slightly larger estimates than the μ equation. The same is true for the Kapteyn-Muffels model compared to the selective model. Since in both cases the logY coefficient is somewhat smaller where the family size variable coefficients are larger, this finding may have to do with collinearity between the latter variables and household income. In fact, the significance of these differences is best appreciated by an inspection of the resulting equivalence factors, which will be done in the next subsection.

Home tenure status is taken account of in the selective model only, by including dummies for tenants and for owners having a mortgage. The impact of these variables on the answers to the MIQ and the IEQ is quite small. The relation between actual housing costs - rent or mortgage payments - and subjective income evaluations has been explored in detail in Van den Bosch (1999). It was found that different model specifications lead to very different results, some of which were rather implausible. Those unsatisfactory results, as well as the limited effect of the home tenure dummies, are probably at least partly due to the ambiguousness of housing costs with regard to the MIQ and the IEQ. Some respondents may take the phrase 'in your circumstances' which appears in both income evaluation questions as meaning 'assuming you stay in your present home'. Others may consider that living on a minimum income involves moving to cheaper accommodation (cf. Stinson, 1997: 29). Moreover, depending on market circumstances as well as individual choices made in the past, some respondents may perceive housing costs as something that is imposed on them, while others may see them as expenses that they have voluntarily incurred.

There were no direct questions about people's reference groups in the Belgian SEP. In Van den Bosch (1999) the relationship was examined between subjective income evaluations and a number of social characteristics which were presumed to be indicators of an individual's reference group, in particular age, education and profession of the head of household. (Also included was region; results for that variable are discussed below.) The overall impact of those variables was quite limited. The few significant or consistent effects are included in the Kapteyn-Muffels model and the selective model, and even these are rather small. It is seen that when the head is below 24 or over 64, answers to the MIQ and the IEQ are slightly below those of persons in households headed by middle-aged persons, but in otherwise similar circumstances. Conversely, when the head has had university education, answers are slightly more elevated, ceteris paribus. Another finding was that no effect of the working status of the head or spouse on the answers to the MIQ and the IEQ could be measured.

By contrast, the effect of region is quite important. In all years, respondents in Wallonia give higher answers to the MIQ and the IEQ than their Flemish counterparts do who live in otherwise similar circumstances. In 1985 the size of the effect is about 4 percent for logYmin and about 7 percent for μ. Remarkably, across years the difference between Wallonia and Flanders remains about the same for μ, but increases to more than 18 percent for logYmin in 1992. The responses in Brussels seem closer to those in Wallonia than to the Flemish answers[17].

The evolution across years of the answers to the MIQ and the IEQ within the three regions, as revealed by the region-year dummies, after controlling for the effects of income, household size and other variables, is remarkably different. In 1988, responses have declined in Flanders, while remaining at about the same level in Wallonia. In 1992, Flemish answers to the MIQ return to their 1985 level, while those of the Walloon population rise considerably. Responses to the IEQ increase by about the same percentage in both of the main regions of Belgium, which still leave the Walloon answers at an 8 percent higher level than the Flemish ones. One must keep in mind that the reported effects of region are controlled for (changes and differences in) income and other variables. Since incomes have increased substantially in both periods, and have always been larger in Flanders than in Wallonia, the simple averages of μ and logYmin have increased more, while the difference between Flanders and Wallonia is somewhat smaller than the dummy coefficients indicate.

All amounts (IEQ and MIQ answers as well as household incomes) have been entered in current prices in the regression equations. In order to keep up with inflation, the 1988 dummy coefficients should have been equal to 0.023 in the μ equation and to 0.025 in the logYmin equation. The corresponding values for 1992 are 0.092 and 0.100[18]. Comparing these figures with estimated parameters show that in Flanders answers to the IEQ have declined in real terms by about 2.5 percent in the period 1985 to 1992, while MIQ amounts have fallen by no less than 10 percent. At the same time, IEQ responses in Wallonia have remained more or less constant in real terms, and MIQ answers have risen by about 4 percent. Again, it must be stressed that the effects of rising incomes in both regions have been discounted for in these calculations. It is not clear what factors lie behind these different evolutions. Unfortunately, regional consumer price indices are not available. It is possible that slight changes in the wording and placement of the MIQ and the IEQ in the SEP questionnaire are responsible.

4 Equivalence scales, income thresholds and low-income rates

Introduction

In this section, I want to present the equivalence scales, income thresholds and low-income rates resulting from the three models of μ and logYmin discussed in the previous section. Since it is in my view an open question whether the subjective approach can be used to measure poverty, I prefer to employ the neutral terms 'income thresholds' and 'low income' instead of 'poverty lines' and 'poverty'. As before, data from the 1985, 1988 and 1992 waves of Belgian Socio-Economic Panel (BSEP) are used. In the next subsection, the equivalence scales are discussed. The third subsection looks at the level and evolution of the LPL (Leyden Poverty Line) and SPL (Subjective Poverty Line) income thresholds. (Given the specification of the models used, the resulting equivalence scales are the same for all waves of the BSEP, while the levels of the LPL and SPL income thresholds vary across years.) While most attention is given to 'national' income thresholds, I also calculate LPLs and the SPL for each region separately. The percentages of households and individuals below those thresholds are the subject of subsection four. Again, both 'national' and 'regional' low-income rates are presented. Also discussed in that subsection is the variation in the incidence of low income across various subgroups in the population, as well as the impact of using age-specific equivalence scales on low income rates among children. The statistical reliability of the results is the subject of a special subsection, since this issue appears to have received scant attention in the literature on the subjective approach to measuring poverty.

Subjective equivalence scales

Equivalence factors indicate how much larger the income of a particular type of family should be relative to the income of a reference household, so that the first family is equally well off as the reference family. In the present context, equally well off means having the same evaluation of their income. An equivalence scale is a set of such factors for a range of household types. (See section 4.2 for a more formal introduction.) The equivalence scales resulting from the estimates of the three μ and logYmin models are shown in table 5.13[19]. Since in all models the regression coefficients for household income and the household size variables were constrained to be at the same values in all years, the resulting equivalence scales do not vary across time.

The most important observation is that these subjective equivalence scales are rather flat, i.e. the equivalence factors of families with children are rather low relative to those of childless couples. They are roughly only half of those of the 'adjusted' OECD scale, introduced by Hagenaars et al. (1992, 1994), even though the latter was adopted by those authors precisely because it is more or less at the midpoint between 'flat' and 'steep' scales (see also Buhmann et al. 1988). Conversely, the subjective scales suggest that single persons need as much as 80 percent or more of the income of two-adult families in order to feel as well off.

Table 5.13
Equivalence factors (childless couple = 100) based on three models of subjective income evaluations

Family composition		Simple model		Kapteyn-Muffels model	
Adults:	Children:	mu	logYmin	mu	logYmin
1	0	83.6	82.1	83.6	81.6
		(0.7)	(0.7)	(0.9)	(0.8)
1	1, aged 0-3	100	100	97.1	93.5
		(0)	(0)	(2.3)	(2.3)
1	1, aged 4-11	100	100	99.1	99.0
		(0)	(0)	(1.3)	(1.4)
1	1, aged 11-17	100	100	106.4	105.7
		(0)	(0)	(1.5)	(1.4)
1	1, aged 18-24	100	100	100	100
		(0)	(0)	(0)	(0)
1	2, aged 0-3	111.0	112.2	106.0	101.3
		(0.5)	(0.5)	(3.7)	(3.9)
1	2, aged 4-11	111.0	112.2	109.5	110.8
		(0.5)	(0.5)	(2.1)	(2.4)
1	2, aged 11-17	111.0	112.2	122.5	122.9
		(0.5)	(0.5)	(2.4)	(2.4)
1	2, aged 18-24	111.0	112.2	111.1	112.6
		(0.5)	(0.5)	(0.7)	(0.6)
2	0	100	100	100	100
		(0)	(0)	0	0

(Standard errors between parentheses)

Table 5.13 (continuation)

Family composition		Selective model		Adjusted
Adults:	Children:	mu	logYmin	OECD (2)
1	0	82.7	79.9	66.7
		(1.1)	(1.2)	
1	1, aged 0-3	93.0	89.4	86.7
		(2.6)	(2.5)	
1	1, aged 4-11	95.6	94.4	86.7
		(1.9)	(2.1)	
1	1, aged 11-17	101.4	100.6	86.7
		(2.2)	(2.3)	
1	1, aged 18-24	105.3	106.6	100
		(2.6)	(2.9)	
1	2, aged 0-3	99.6	95.4	106.7
		(4.1)	(3.9)	
1	2, aged 4-11	104.0	104.1	106.7
		(2.8)	(3.2)	
1	2, aged 11-17	114.2	115.0	106.7
		(3.4)	(3.5)	
1	2, aged 18-24	121.3	126.2	120
		(4.2)	(4.8)	
2	0	100	100	100
		0	0	

Table 5.13 (continuation)

Family composition		Simple model		Kapteyn-Muffels model	
Adults:	Children:	mu	logYmin	mu	logYmin
2	0	100	100	100	100
		(0)	(0)	0	0
2	1, aged 0-3	111.0	112.2	109.2	108.3
		(0.5)	(0.5)	(1.4)	(1.6)
2	1, aged 4-11	111.0	112.2	110.5	112.0
		(0.5)	(0.5)	(0.8)	(0.9)
2	1, aged 11-17	111.0	112.2	115.2	116.3
		(0.5)	(0.5)	(0.9)	(0.9)
2	1, aged 18-24	111.0	112.2	111.1	112.6
		(0.5)	(0.5)	(0.7)	(0.6)
2	2, aged 0-3	119.6	121.8	116.2	114.6
		(1.0)	(1.0)	(2.6)	(2.9)
2	2, aged 4-11	119.6	121.8	118.6	121.3
		(1.0)	(1.0)	(1.4)	(1.7)
2	2, aged 11-17	119.6	121.8	127.3	130.0
		(1.0)	(1.0)	(1.6)	(1.6)
2	2, aged 18-24	119.6	121.8	119.7	122.6
		(1.0)	(1.0)	(1.2)	(1.1)
2	3, aged 0-3	126.7	129.8	121.9	119.8
		(1.3)	(1.4)	(3.5)	(4.0)
2	3, aged 4-11	126.7	129.8	125.7	129.2
		(1.3)	(1.4)	(2.0)	(2.4)
2	3, aged 11-17	126.7	129.8	137.6	140.8
		(1.3)	(1.4)	(2.3)	(2.3)
2	3, aged 18-24	126.7	129.8	126.8	130.9
		(1.3)	(1.4)	(1.7)	(1.6)

Notes: (1) All standard errors calculated with Jack-knife method (see text for details).
(2) Scale with weights 1.0 for the first adult, 0.5 for other adults, and 0.3 for children aged 0-17.

Table 5.13 (continuation)

Family composition		Selective model		Adjusted
Adults:	Children:	mu	logYmin	OECD (2)
2	0	100	100	100
		0	0	
2	1, aged 0-3	107.1	106.8	120
		(1.6)	(1.6)	
2	1, aged 4-11	108.8	110.2	120
		(0.9)	(1.1)	
2	1, aged 11-17	112.7	114.4	120
		(1.1)	(1.1)	
2	1, aged 18-24	115.2	118.4	133.3
		(1.4)	(1.4)	
2	2, aged 0-3	112.4	111.8	140
		(2.8)	(2.9)	
2	2, aged 4-11	115.6	118.1	140
		(1.7)	(2.1)	
2	2, aged 11-17	122.6	125.8	140
		(2.0)	(2.1)	
2	2, aged 18-24	127.3	133.4	166.7
		(2.6)	(2.7)	
2	3, aged 0-3	116.8	116.0	160
		(3.8)	(4.0)	
2	3, aged 4-11	121.1	124.7	160
		(2.3)	(2.9)	
2	3, aged 11-17	130.9	135.5	160
		(2.8)	(3.0)	
2	3, aged 18-24	137.6	146.4	200
		(3.6)	(3.9)	

Source: Estimates shown in table 5.12, based on Belgian SEP, amalgamated waves 1985, 1988 and 1992.

Some differences between the subjective equivalence scales may be noted. Compared with the simple model, the two more sophisticated models lead to lower equivalence factors for families with babies or toddlers (children aged 0-3), and higher factors for families with teenage or older children (11-17 and 18-24). According to the selective model, financial needs of families are affected as much by the age of children as by their number; the equivalence factors for a family with only one child aged 18-24 is about equally high as that of a family with three pre-school age children. The equivalence factors of the Kapteyn-Muffels model indicate that the costs of children aged 18 to 24 are smaller than those of children aged 11 to 17, while the reverse is true for the selective model. This result is mainly an artifact of the specification of the Kapteyn-Muffels model, which does not distinguish between university age children and other adults. Finally, it can be remarked that the logYmin equations produce somewhat steeper equivalence scales than the μ ones. (The difference is statistically significant for all models.) Nevertheless, all these differences are rather minor, compared to the gap between the subjective equivalence scales and the adjusted OECD scale.

LPL and SPL income thresholds

Choices in the calculation of the LPLs and SPL – The calculation of Leyden Poverty Lines (LPLs) and Subjective Poverty Lines (SPLs) from the μ and logYmin regression results involves a number of choices. The most important one is the classification of the variables in the μ and logYmin equations into cost variables and reference variables. Cost variables are assumed to influence the costs that households face when maximizing their standard of living. Reference variables on the other hand, are assumed not to have a direct effect on the material standard of living, but to influence the aspirations of persons. Since we have defined poverty as a concept related to the material standard of living of households and persons, income thresholds should be differentiated according to cost variables and not according to reference variables. That is, income thresholds should be higher for household A than for household B only if household A must spend more than household B to reach a certain material standard of living. Income thresholds should not be higher for household A than for household B if A says it needs more money than B because A has higher aspirations than B, e.g. because A has wealthier friends. This distinction is fairly clear on the theoretical level, but does not provide straightforward guidance on the problem of which variables used in the models above are to be regarded as cost variables and which ones as reference variables. Lacking a direct and accurate measure of the material standard of living (if we had one, the subjective approach to measuring poverty would be largely superfluous), this choice is to some extent a matter of a-priori judgments. Moreover, many empirical variables can have both cost and reference effects, of course[20].

I have chosen to regard the number of adults, the number and the ages of children, and home tenure status as cost variables. Age of head, education of head and region are treated as reference variables. This decision is motivated by the following considerations. The cost effect of the number of family members - adults and children - is beyond doubt. It appears rather plausible that the monetary costs of children increase with their age; some traditional equivalence scales increase with the age of children (Whiteford, 1985). Also, it is not easy to see how children's ages could have a reference effect, when controlling for the age of the respondent. Tenants and mortgage-paying home owners have housing costs that mortgage-free owners do not have. One might argue that in a life-time perspective, total housing costs may not depend on the home tenure status. Whether this is true or not, it seems that respondents use a time perspective of a few years at the longest when answering the income evaluation questions.

Age and education of head are treated as proxies for an individual's reference group. As we have seen above (section 4.5) in the literature about reference groups and subjective income evaluations, both variables are often used for this purpose. One might argue that age of head might also have a cost effect since the need for some kinds of expenditures varies with age. The elderly do not have employment-related costs, and may have to invest less in durable goods and home furnishings. On the other hand, the elderly may have to spend more on health-related goods and services. Since the direction of the cost effect of age of head is therefore unclear, I have chosen to neglect it. Similarly, regarding education of head, it might be argued that obtaining higher education involves costs, due to direct expenditures as well as foregone earnings. However, in Belgium almost all of the direct costs are borne either by the state, or by the parents, not by the person receiving the education. (Taking up loans to finance ones higher education is very rare in Belgium.) Anyway, if respondents do not take a life-time perspective, but a much shorter one, expenditures as well as foregone earnings in one's early adulthood will have mostly a very limited effect on subjective income evaluations. Furthermore, since education presumably widens one's options as a consumer, it may also enable persons to reduce the costs needed to reach a certain level of welfare. E.g. persons with higher education may be able to read English-language books instead of more expensive Dutch ones, or look at foreign TV-channels instead of hiring video cassettes.

The treatment of region is a more difficult matter. As we have seen in section 5.3, there is a large and (in the case of the MIQ) increasing gap between the subjective income evaluations of the Flemish speaking population on the one hand, and the French speaking one on the other. As regional price indices are not available, it is impossible to ascertain to which extent this gap is due to cost differences. There is no evidence which would suggest that prices diverge as much as the IEQ and MIQ results seem to indicate. Also, it is possible that the Dutch and French wordings of the IEQ and MIQ are not quite equivalent. Given these uncertainties, I have decided not to differentiate the SPLs and LPLs according to region, which in effect means that region is regarded as a reference variable. However, I will also show what happens when the income thresholds are calculated for each region separately.

Having decided that the variables age of head, education of head and region are to be regarded as reference variables, and therefore should be set at a fixed value when calculating income thresholds, the question is which value should be assigned to these variables. Hagenaars (1985: 107) uses the average value. Kapteyn, Kooreman et al. (1985: 41-45) calculate income thresholds with a 'poor' reference group and a 'median' reference group. In our case, using the average value in the sample for the reference variables seems to be the least arbitrary.

The income perception bias correction term (logC) and the Heckman non-response bias correction term (Mill's ratio) have been included in the regressions in order to avoid distortions in the parameter estimates. For the calculation of income thresholds they are set at values corresponding to no income perception bias (logC = 0) and no non-response (Mill's ratio = 1). Somewhat arbitrarily, the effect of the mail survey in 1988 is also regarded as a distortion; therefore the dummy variable representing 'mail survey' is set at zero.

A final decision concerns the welfare levels for which LPLs are to be calculated. LPLs can be calculated for any welfare level. However, as shown in the review in section 4.3, welfare levels 0.4 and 0.5 are the most popular ones, and will also be used here. Level 0.5 corresponds to μ, or the midpoint between 'sufficient' and 'insufficient', while level 0.4 is situated slightly below 'insufficient' on the WFI-scale. As equation (5-11) shows, the LPLs for welfare levels other than 0.5, say δ, involve a term $\sigma \cdot q_{\delta}$, where q_{δ} is the δ-th quantile of the standard normal distribution ($q_{0.4}$ = -

0.253), and σ is the parameter describing the slope of the WFI-curve. Since σ has been found to be hardly or not related to family income or family size (see section 5.2), I have used the (weighted) sample average of σ in each year to calculate all LPLs at the 0.4 level; in this I follow most other studies. The values are as follows:

	1985	1988	1992
'full' sample	0.406	0.389	0.407
'restricted' sample	0.394	0.383	0.399

The full sample is the sample use for the simple model and the Kapteyn-Muffels model. The restricted sample is the one used for the selective model.

Level and evolution of the LPLs and SPL – Table 5.14 shows the resulting income thresholds for two-adult households; LPLs and SPLs for other family types can be derived using the equivalence scales in table 5.13. The LPL-0.4 is in all models and all years about 15 percent below the LPL-0.5. The LPL-0.5 and the SPL are always at about the same level. With the simple model, the SPL generally exceeds the LPL-0.5, while with the Kapteyn-Muffels model and the selective model, the SPL is below the LPL-0.5 for single persons, and above the latter for larger families, due to the SPLs steeper equivalence scale. Comparing across models, the simple model yields the lowest LPLs, and the Kapteyn-Muffels model the most generous ones, with the selective model in between. More or less the same pattern is found for the SPL, though the differences are smaller. In general, the subjective income thresholds seems rather generous for single persons and childless couples; in 1992 even the LPL0.4 considerably exceeds the guaranteed minimum income for those family types (18,700 and 25,000 BF per month, respectively). For families with several children, the LPLs and SPL are more strict; the LP0.4 is actually below the guaranteed minimum income.

The most interesting feature of the income thresholds is their evolution over time, where all models produce the same pattern. Between 1985 and 1988 the level of the LPLs. and SPL has dropped: by 6 percent using the simple model, by 2 or 3 percent according to the more sophisticated models (the latter figure is not significantly different from zero). Taking price changes into account, the decrease is larger: 10 percent with the simple model, 6 or 7 percent using the other models. Between 1988 and

1992 there has been a substantial increase in the level of the income thresholds. After adjustment for price changes, the rise is limited, though: between 2 and 4 percent for the LPL, depending on the model, while the level of the SPL is stable. Also, both the SPL and the LPL remain some distance below their 1985 levels in real terms. Relative to the evolution of average disposable income or average equivalent income, the SPL and LPL fall even more behind.

Table 5.14
LPL and SPL income thresholds derived from three models, Belgium, 1985, 1988 and 1992

	Simple model		
	1985	1988	1992
LPL 0.4 for two adults	25,330	24,020	28,270
	(490)	(560)	(490)
LPL 0.5 for two adults	29,790	28,060	33,260
	(540)	(600)	(520)
Change in LPLs relative to 1985 (%)	-	-5.8*	+11.6**
	-	(2.3)	(2.3)
Change in real terms (%)(1)	-	-9.9**	-5.7*
SPL for two adults	31,230	29,370	33,440
	(610)	(580)	(650)
Change in SPL relative to 1985 (%)	-	-6.0*	+7.1*
	-	(2.7)	(3.0)
Change in real terms (%)(1)	-	-10.1**	-10.2**
Average equivalent income (2)	31,220	33,860	41,160
Change in real terms (%)(1)	-	4.4	14.5

Notes: Standard errors between parentheses.
* significant at the 5 percent level.
** significant at the 0.1 percent level.
(1) I.e. adjusted for price changes.
(2) Using 'modified OECD' equivalence scale, with weights 1.0 for first adult, 0.5 for other adults, 0.3 for children.

As explained above, the interpretation of the large differences between regions is ambiguous. It is therefore interesting to see what happens to the income thresholds when the regions are regarded as separate countries. For this purpose, the simple model was re-estimated for each of the three regions. For the Kapteyn-Muffels model and the selective model the 'national' model estimates (as shown in table 5.12) were used for the calculation of income thresholds, together with regional averages of the reference variables. That is, the working assumption is that although Flanders, Wallonia and Brussels are separate countries, the models that apply in all three differ only in their intercepts and in the coefficients for the year dummies, but are otherwise exactly the same. This implies that the income thresholds vary across regions only as regards their levels, but incorporate exactly the same equivalence scale.

Table 5.14 (continuation)

Kapteyn-Mufels model			Selective model (3)		
1985	1988	1992	1985	1988	1992
26,700	26,290	30,340	26,130	25,450	29,560
(510)	(610)	(550)	(610)	(680)	(680)
31,620	30,910	35,930	31,080	30,130	35,230
(560)	(660)	(600)	(650)	(710)	(720)
-	-2.2	+13.6**	-	-3.1	+11.6**
-	(2.1)	(2.0)	-	(2.1)	(2.0)
-	-6.3**	-3.7	-	-7.2**	-5.7**
31,820	31,090	35,120	31,680	30,600	34,450
(720)	(640)	(740)	(780)	(730)	(830)
-	-2.3	+10.4**	-	-3.4	+8.8
-	(2.0)	(2.8)	-	(2.2)	(2.9)
-	-6.4**	-6.9*	-	-7.5**	-8.5**
31,220	33,860	41,160	29,850	32,040	39,470
-	4.4	14.5	-	3.2	14.9

Notes: (3) For selective model figures refer to restricted sample.
Source: Belgian Socio-Economic Panel, waves 1985, 1988 and 1992.

Figure 5.4 shows that this assumption results in income thresholds that differ considerably between Flanders and Wallonia. (Results only shown for the Kapteyn-Muffels model; the other models gave essentially the same results.) Both the SPL and the LPL are at a higher absolute level in Wallonia compared to Flanders, even though average income is lower than in Flanders. (Moreover, the average Walloon household is slightly smaller than the average Flemish one.) For the LPL, the difference in 1985 is 8 to 12 percent, depending on the model. It increases in 1988 to between 12 and 16 percent, while dropping to between 7 and 14 percent in 1992. Overall, the trend over time in the LPL does not diverge very much across regions.

In both regions, the LPL decreases in real terms between 1985 and 1992; in Flanders by 4 to 5 percent, in Wallonia by 2 to 6 percent. However, the Flemish LPL falls behind relative to average income more than the Walloon LPL does. By contrast to the LPL, the SPL follows a quite different trajectory across time in the two regions. In 1985, the Walloon SPL exceeds the Flemish one by only 4 to 6 percent. In Flanders the SPL remains at virtually the same nominal level during the period 1985 - 1992, leading to a drop in real terms of 15 to 17 percent. Relative to average price-adjusted income, which increases by 10 to 12 percent in Flanders, the SPL falls behind even more. In Wallonia, by contrast, the SPL rises in real terms by 3 to 7 percent, thus keeping up with the trend in average income. As a result, in 1992 the gap between the Flemish and the Walloon SPL has increased to a stunning 23 to 31 percent.

Figure 5.4
Evolution of regional SPLs and LPLs (Kapteyn-Muffels model)

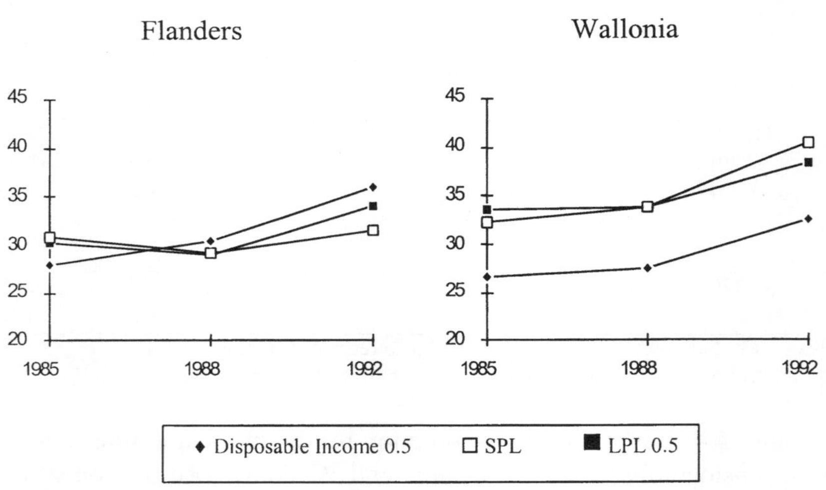

(Amounts in thousands of BF per month for a two-adults family)

Low income rates

Overall levels and trends – How many persons are below the SPL and LPLs? Table 5.15 shows the percentages by year for the simple model and the Kapteyn-Muffels model. (Since the selective model was estimated using a restricted sample of all observations, consistency would require that the resulting low income rates are limited to the same subsample, and in any case, the selective model does not yield income thresholds for certain household types, i.e. 'complex' households.)

Table 5.15
Percentage of households and individuals below LPLs and SPL, Belgium, 1985, 1988 and 1992

Individuals		Simple model			Kapteyn-Muffels model		
		1985	1988	1992	1985	1988	1992
LPL0.4	%	5.8	3.3	3.3	7.2	5.2	5.2
	s.e.	(0.4)	(1.3)	(0.3)	(0.5)	(1.4)	(0.7)
	(1)			**			**
LPL0.5	%	11.1	7.7	7.2	14.5	10.6	9.9
	s.e.	(2.1)	(0.8)	(1.1)	(1.0)	(1.2)	(0.9)
	(1)					*	**
SPL	%	14.2	8.9	7.2	15.4	11.1	8.8
	s.e.	(1.6)	(0.8)	(0.7)	(1.5)	(1.7)	(3.0)
	(1)		**	**		*	*

Notes: (standard errors between parentheses).
(1) Significance of change in percentage below line relative to 1985.
* indicates change is significant at the 5% level.
** indicates change is significant at the 0.1 percent level.

Source: Belgian Socio-Economic Panel, waves 1985, 1988 and 1992.

A number of observations can be made. In the first place, the SPL and LPL0.5 produce fairly high low income rates in terms of households, in particular in 1985. Although the level of the LPL0.4 is only 15 percent below that of the LPL0.5, the number of households and individuals below the LPL0.4 is generally about half of the corresponding number below the LPL0.5; in some cases the proportion is close to 40 percent. Between the SPL and the LPL0.5 there is not much difference; in 1985 and 1988 the low income rates produced by the SPL are slightly higher than the LPL0.5

ones; in 1992 the reverse is true. Secondly, the percentage of individuals below the LPLs and SPL is always much smaller than the corresponding percentage of households. The LPL0.4 individual low income rates come close to those obtained with relative lines at 50 percent of mean income. The much lower individual low income rates compared to the household ones indicate of course that small families, in particular single persons, are more likely to have an income below these lines compared to larger households. Thirdly, comparing across models, the Kapteyn-Muffels model produces the highest low income rates, and the simple model the lowest ones. This reflects the levels of the income thresholds yielded by the models, as discussed in the previous subsection.

The most striking finding is certainly the clear downward trend in the low income rates. According to the results of the Kapteyn-Muffels model, between 1985 and 1992 the LPL0.4 low income rate among all households (full sample) dropped from 12 percent to 9 percent, and the LPL0.5 one from 22 percent to 17 percent. The SPL low income rates fell even more, from 22 percent to 15 percent. Low income rates among individuals decreased by about the same number of percentage-points, but from a much lower initial level.

Are these results in agreement with low income trends based on other income standards? In table 5.16 the trend in low income rates according to the subjective standards (Kapteyn-Muffels model) are compared with low income trends measured with several variants of the relative standard. Variant 0 of the relative standard is the one most commonly used, where the income threshold is set at 50 percent of average equivalent income in each year. This yields low income rates roughly comparable to those obtained with the LPL0.4, but in contrast to the latter, these display a slightly rising trend. As shown in table 5.13, the so-called 'modified OECD' equivalence scale of this line is much steeper than the subjective equivalence scales. When a relative line incorporating an equivalence scale similar to the subjective one is used (variant 1), the results are virtually the same as with variant 0, though. When the line is set at a higher level of 60 percent of average equivalent income (and with a flat equivalence scale, variant 2), the resulting low income rates are in the range of those obtained with the LPL0.5 and the SPL. In contrast to the latter, however, the relative low income rates are practically stable over time.

In the final two variants, the income standard is kept at a constant level across all years (adjusting for price changes). At the 50 percent level, this results in a slightly falling trend in the low income rate; the overall fall during the period 1985 to 1992 (1.3 percent) is comparable to the one measured with the LPL0.4 (2 percent). At the 60 percent standard, the decreasing trend is more marked, and seen over the whole period 1985-1992 is in fairly strong agreement with the trend in the LPL0.5 low income rates. For both levels, it is true though, that according to the LPLs the prevalence of low income fell mostly between 1985 and 1988, remaining stable between 1988 and 1992, while the constant income thresholds indicate a more gradual decline in the incidence of low income. Low income rates obtained with the SPL have fallen more strongly. The overall conclusion, then, of this comparison seems to be that the results of the subjective income thresholds agree well with those based on constant income thresholds in that both measure a downward trend in low income rates. By contrast, relative lines that move in tandem with average household income across years, produce low income rates that are stable or slightly rising.

Table 5.16
Trends in low-income rates, comparing subjective and relative income thresholds, Belgium, 1985, 1988 and 1992

	1985	1988	1992
LPL0.4	7.2	5.2	5.2
LPL0.5	14.5	10.6	9.9
SPL	15.4	11.1	8.8
Relative line at 50 %, OECD equiv. scale	4.9	5.0	5.6
Relative line at 50 %, low equiv. scale	4.6	5.2	5.7
Relative line at 60 %, low equiv. scale	11.6	12.4	12.1
Constant line at 50 %, low equiv. scale	6.0	5.4	4.7
Constant line at 60 %, low equiv. scale	14.1	12.8	9.7

Notes: Relative lines are defined as percentages of average equivalent income in each year.

Constant lines are defined as unweighted averages across years of corresponding relative lines.

OECD equivalence scale is 'Modified OECD' equivalence scale with weights 1.0 for first adult, 0.5 for other adults, 0.3 for children.

Low equivalence scale has weights 1.0 for first adult, 0.25 for other adults, 0.15 for children.

LPLs and SPL are calculated using the Kapteyn-Muffels model.

Source: Belgian Socio-Economic Panel, waves 1985, 1988 and 1992.

Characteristics of persons in low income households – What are the characteristics of the persons below the SPL and LPLs, and how do these compare with those of persons below the relative lines? The flatter equivalence scales of the LPLs and the SPL lead to very high low income rates for single persons (especially when they are not working), and low ones for larger households. Using relative lines incorporating the 'modified OECD' scale, the contrast between the low income risks of small and large households is much less pronounced. This difference in the results of relative and subjective low income standards is reflected in the patterns of low income rates by age, sex and labor force status, since these characteristics of individuals are correlated with the size of the household they live in. (More detailed comparisons can be found in Van den Bosch, 1999.)

Comparison between individual income thresholds and average income thresholds – Another interesting comparison is that between low income status according to the SPL and LPL on the one hand, and the purely subjective income status implied by the answers to the MIQ and IEQ on the other hand. That is, one might define respondents who's perceived household income is below their answer to the MIQ as having a 'subjective low-income status'. In that case, the individual answer to the MIQ serves as a respondent's own, very individual, low-income threshold. (A similar argument applies to the answers to the IEQ, of course.) In the same vein, the standard SPL and LPLs could be called 'average' income thresholds, since the regression procedure in effect takes averages across a number of individual answers.

Table 5.17 shows that the overlap between the two definitions of low-income status is limited. In all cases, more households are below their individual thresholds than are below the average thresholds; the difference varies between 2.5 and 6.6 percentage-points. Partly as a consequence, a large proportion - 43 to 62 percent - of the first group do not have low-income status according to the corresponding average income thresholds. Perhaps more surprisingly, among those who have a low income according to the average SPL or LPL, there is a substantial number - 34 to 45 percent - who implicitly declare that subjectively they do not feel that they have a low income.

Table 5.17
Comparison of low-income status according to 'average' and 'individual' income thresholds

SPL	1985	1988	1992
Below average threshold	22.0	15.8	12.5
Below individual threshold	25.5	22.4	18.1
Below both thresholds	12.7	9.2	6.9
Below individual threshold - not below average threshold	12.8	13.3	11.3
Not below individual threshold - below average threshold	9.3	6.6	5.6
Not below both thresholds	65.2	70.9	76.3
Total	100	100	100

LPL0.5	1985	1988	1992
Below average threshold	21.9	15.6	14.1
Below individual threshold	25.3	20.5	19.4
Below both thresholds	14.5	10.1	9.3
Below individual threshold - not below average threshold	10.8	10.4	10.2
Not below individual threshold - below average threshold	7.5	5.5	4.8
Not below both thresholds	67.3	74.1	75.8
Total	100	100	100
Number of observations	5653	3059	3459

Notes: Average income thresholds are SPL and LPL0.5 according to Kapteyn-Muffels model.

Individual income thresholds are Ymin and EXP(mu), i.e. individual answers to MIQ and IEQ.

'Below individual threshold' means that perceived household income is below Ymin or EXP(mu).

Only cases with adequate answers to MIQ and IEQ. Results are unweighted.

Source: Belgian Socio-Economic Panel, waves 1985, 1988 and 1992.

Age-specific equivalence scales and low income rates among children – Above we have seen that an analysis of the answers to the MIQ and the IEQ suggests that children become considerably more expensive as they get older. As a result, the equivalence factors derived from the Kapteyn-Muffels model and from the selective model were influenced as much by the age of children as by their number. The question can now be asked:

what effect does the use of age-specific equivalence scales have on estimated low income rates among children? For this purpose, I compare the low income rates resulting from the simple model, where the family size specification does not take account of the ages of the family members, with those derived from the selective model. (The selective model was used instead of the Kapteyn-Muffels model, because the former, in contrast to the latter, treats dependent children aged 18 to 25 as a special category and does not count them with the adults. This implies that the restricted sample was used.)

Table 5.18 presents low income rates among dependent children in the age categories that were also used in the estimation of the subjective equivalence scales. Following the simple model, babies and toddlers aged 0 to 3 are clearly more likely to be below the LPLs and the SPL than children in other age categories. Between the other age groups, differences are fairly small. Using the Selective model, low income rates in the youngest age group are slightly lower, while they are considerably higher in the older age categories 12 to 17 years, and 18 to 25 years in particular. The risk of being in a low income household for the latter group now equals, or exceeds that for the youngest age category.

Table 5.18
Percentage of children below LPLs and SPL, using simple model (with no age-specific equivalence scale) and the selective model (with age specific equivalence scale), Belgium, 1985, 1988 and 1992

Age group		Simple model		Freq.
	LPL0.4	LPL0.5	SPL	
0-3	4.4%	8.0%	10.2%	13.4%
4-11	1.6%	5.1%	7.3%	44.4%
12-17	2.0%	4.5%	6.1%	28.2%
18-25	2.8%	5.1%	5.8%	14.0%
		Selective model		
	LPL0.4	LPL0.5	SPL	
0-3	4.0%	8.1%	8.9%	
4-11	1.6%	5.6%	7.0%	
12-17	2.5%	6.7%	9.2%	
18-25	3.9%	8.3%	10.2%	

Note: Only dependent children in restricted sample.
Definition of dependent children: see notes at table 5.6.

Source: Socio-Economic Panel, amalgamated data waves '85, '88 and '92.

These differences in the patterns of low income rates according to the age of children have direct policy implications. In Belgium, the family allowance system provides more generous benefits as children get older. Looking at the results of the simple model (and, also at those of the relative income thresholds), one might conclude that the age-dependent premiums in the family allowance scheme are inefficient from a low income-combat point of view. Considering the results of the more sophisticated selective model, such a conclusion could no longer be drawn.

Precision of estimates using the subjective approach

In this subsection, I want to discuss the somewhat neglected issue of the statistical reliability, or precision, of estimates resulting from the subjective method, focusing on the percentage of persons below the LPLs and the SPL. Subjective income thresholds are arguably more valid than e.g. relative ones, since the former are based on the views and judgments of the population, and are not determined by arbitrary choices of the researcher. However, this advantage would be of little worth if it would turn out that the results of the subjective approach are very unreliable, i.e. if the confidence intervals of the estimates of parameters such as equivalence factors, low income thresholds and below-threshold percentages would be very large. This section looks only at sample variability, i.e. imprecision due to the fact that we are working with samples, and do not have data for the whole population. Imprecision due to measurement error in variables, e.g. household income and the answers to the income evaluation questions, is not discussed.

Standard statistical packages such as SPSSx or SAS routinely report measures of statistical precision, such as standard errors. However, there are two main reasons why the estimates of standard errors as calculated by SPSSx or SAS are incorrect for the parameters at issue. In the first place, those packages routinely work on the assumption that the sample is a simple random one. In fact, the Belgian Socio-Economic Panel, as is true of most surveys used for low income studies, does not have a simple random sample design, but a multistage one, involving both clustering and stratification (see the appendix for details). A clustered sample is typically less efficient (i.e. has larger standard errors) than a simple random sample of the same size, while stratification always enhances the efficiency of the sample (Blalock, 1972: 516-527). Usually, the effect of the clustering predominates, so that standard error estimates based on the assumption of a simple random sample design are biased downwards, i.e. overstate the true reliability of parameter estimates. Moreover, in the SEP (as in many surveys) weights are used to adjust the results for the effects of non-response and panel following rules. These weights are a source of sampling variability which is not always adequately taken into account in the calculations carried out by SPSSx and SAS.

Secondly, the procedures used by SAS or SPSSx to compute standard errors are strictly only applicable to linear statistics. Low income and low-income percentages are a linear function of low income or low-income status on the household level (assuming the sample size is fixed), but low-income status itself is of course not directly observed, but the result of a comparison of household income and the income threshold. The latter is in turn derived in a complex way from the sample data. Since, then, low-income percentages are complex non-linear statistics, their standard errors as computed by SAS or SPSSx are incorrect, even with a simple random sample. The direction of the bias due to this source is difficult to ascertain, but is unlikely to be upwards.

Analytically deriving the standard errors of low-income percentages based on subjective income thresholds is beyond the ambitions of this thesis. Fortunately, pseudoreplication techniques exist which can tackle both complex sample designs and non-linear statistics. Pseudoreplication means that several 'replicates', i.e. synthetic samples are formed from the sample data. The statistic at issue is calculated for each replicate, and the variance of these figures across replicates is used to derive the standard error of the estimate at issue (Kalton, 1983: 79-81; Rao, 1988: 436-444). From the several pseudoreplication techniques that are proposed in the literature, I have chosen the Jackknife, since the Balanced Repeated Replications method does not fit the SEP sample design, while the Bootstrap is computationally more demanding.

The Jackknife procedure works as follows (Kalton, 1983: 80-81; Rao, 1988: 441-442). Suppose one is interested in the standard error of a parameter a, estimated from a stratified and clustered sample with I_h sampled clusters in stratum h, with H strata, and I clusters overall. A replicate is constructed by dropping out a single cluster (at the same time weighting up the other clusters in its stratum to retain the sample distribution across strata). For each replicate the parameter is calculated, resulting in I estimates $a°_{hi}$. A Jackknife estimator of the variance of a is then:

$$var(a) = \Sigma_h((I_h-1)I_h)\Sigma_i (a°_{hi} - a°_h)^2$$

where $a°_h$ is the average of the $a°_{hi}$ in stratum h. Instead of $a°_h$, the overall average $a°$ across replicates can also be used.

Table 5.19 illustrates the impact of the use of various procedures on estimated standard errors of percentages of individuals below the LPLs and the SPL (based on the Kapteyn-Muffels model). Details and formulas are given in appendix. Column (1) gives the standard errors under the extreme assumptions of a single random sample of individuals, and direct observation of low-income status. Since in fact low-income status is of course measured at the household level, households can be regarded as clusters where the intra-cluster correlation is equal to 1. Use of the appropriate number of degrees of freedom in the calculations leads to considerably higher standard error estimates, as shown in column (2). These are the estimates most likely to be reported by a 'naive' analyst using SAS or SPSSx. In column (3) the degrees of freedom are further adjusted to take account of the clustering of the sample, again resulting in larger standard errors. Standard errors reported in column (4) reflect the stratification of the clusters or first-stage sampling units, i.e. municipalities. A comparison with column (3) shows that stratification produces substantial gains in the precision of the estimates of the low-income percentages. The main reason for this is that the important cross-regional variation in those proportions have no impact on the standard errors shown in column (4). The use of stratum weights, which reflect the proportions of the total population within particular strata, also leads to slightly different estimates of the percentages below the LPLs and SPL. This is due to the fact that the weights available in the SEP data-sets do not adjust for small differences in response rates across strata in the 1985 wave.

Table 5.19
Standard errors of LPL° and SPL° poverty percentages, using various estimation procedures

Year	Line	(1) %	(2) %	(3) %	(4) %	(5) %	(6) %
1985	LPL0.4	0.19	0.32	0.40	0.37	0.40	0.54
	LPL0.5	0.26	0.44	0.63	0.56	0.60	1.02
	SPL	0.27	0.45	0.67	0.61	0.65	1.47
1988	LPL0.4	0.21	0.36	0.48	0.39	0.41	1.37
	LPL0.5	0.29	0.50	0.80	0.63	0.65	1.19
	SPL	0.29	0.51	0.83	0.65	0.68	1.66
1992	LPL0.4	0.21	0.36	0.48	0.40	0.42	0.67
	LPL0.5	0.28	0.48	0.66	0.54	0.59	0.95
	SPL	0.27	0.46	0.63	0.49	0.53	2.99

Notes: (1) - (4) Standard errors calculated with the usual variance estimator, using four different models of sample design, assuming that poverty status is directly observed in the survey.

(1) Model: simple random sample of individuals.
(2) Model: simple random sample of households.
(3) Model: unstratified clusters as primary sampling units (PSUs).
(4) Model: Stratified clusters as primary sampling units (PSUs).
(5) Taylor approximation of variance of ratio, with stratified clusters as primary sampling units.
(6) Standard errors calculated with the Jack-knife, 'Jack-knifing' the whole estimation procedure, including the regressions and the calculation of poverty lines; without weighting of clusters, and ignoring stratification.

° SPL and LPLs based on Kapteyn-Muffels model.

Some key statistics about the sample

	1985	1988	1992
Number of clusters:	70	70	116
Number of original strata:	8	8	19
Number of strata after collapsing:	8	8	11
Total number of households	6471	3779	3821

Source: Belgian Socio-Economic Panel, waves 1985, 1988 and 1992.

Since weights derived from sample data are used in the estimation procedures (and, moreover, sample sizes were not fixed), the denominator of estimates of low-income percentages is subject to sample variability. This implies that those percentages are not linear functions of sample data, but are ratio estimates. Standard errors of ratios can be estimated with the Taylor expansion method. An application of this method results in standard errors (column (5)) that are close to the corresponding linear estimates in column (4). However, for the Taylor expansion method to be appropriate, the coefficient of variation (CV) of the weights must be less than 0.2 (Kalton, 1983: 71). In fact the CVs are equal to 0.49, 0.50 and 0.63 in 1985, 1988 and 1992 respectively.

Finally, column (6) shows estimates of standard errors calculated with the Jackknife technique. All steps of the whole procedure necessary for determining the percentages of households below the SPL and LPLs (i.e. estimating regression equations, calculating income thresholds and comparing the latter with household incomes) were carried out for 116 pseudoreplicates, each formed by dropping one cluster at a time from the SEP amalgamated data set. In order to simplify the already complex and laborious computations (which necessitated several computational 'shortcuts'), the stratification of clusters was ignored, and all clusters were given equal weight in the final calculation of standard errors from the pseudoreplicate results. (Also the term $(I_h\text{-}1)I_h$ was omitted.) The procedure yields slightly different estimates of the percentages below the LPLs and SPL (column (c)). The resulting standard errors shown in column (6) are very much larger than those obtained with other methods. The variation or imprecision due to the fact that the income thresholds are themselves derived in a complicated way from the same sample data, is thus shown to be considerable. The reported Jackknife standard error estimates must be seen as approximations, though. As mentioned, the computations have been simplified. More importantly, it is not clear whether the Jackknife method (and other pseudoreplication techniques) is applicable to statistics such the percentage of households below a stochastic income threshold. Rao (1988) considers only non-linear estimators, such as correlation and regression coefficients, that can be computed from (linear) sample totals. This (as far as I can see) is not the case for low-income percentages. The same author also mentions that the Jackknife method is not consistent for median and quantiles. Nevertheless, the results shown in table 5.19 strongly suggest that treating low income or low-income status as if it was directly observed leads to an enormous downward bias in estimated standard errors of the percentages of individuals below the LPLs and the SPL.

Summary

In this section, I have looked at the equivalence scales, income thresholds and low income rates resulting from the three models of μ and logYmin discussed in the previous section. Given the specification of these models, the resulting equivalence scales are the same for all waves of the Belgian Socio-Economic Panel (BSEP). The level of the LPL (Leyden Poverty Line) and SPL (Subjective Poverty Line) income thresholds, as well as the number of households and individuals below these thresholds, varies across years. Here I will limit myself to summarizing the findings reported in this section. The implications regarding the validity and the usefulness of the subjective approach to measuring poverty will be discussed at the end of the next chapter, after we have taken a close look at possible interpretations of the answers to the subjective income evaluation questions.

All models produce equivalence scales that are rather flat, i.e. indicate that as household size rises, the income needed to remain equally well off increases relatively little. A couple with three children requires only about 60 percent more income than a single person. The age-specific equivalence factors following from the Kapteyn-Muffels model and the selective model suggest that older children are much more expensive than pre-school children, and indeed, the costs of children are affected as much by their age as by their number.

LPL and SPL income thresholds were differentiated by the 'cost' variables number of adults, number and ages of children, and home tenure status, while the 'reference' variables age and education of head and region were set at their mean values in the samples in each year. LPLs were calculated for the welfare levels 0.4 and 0.5. The LPL0.5, the SPL and even the LPL0.4 appear to be fairly generous, at least for small and medium-sized families. Due to the flat equivalence scale, the LPL0.4 turns out to be relatively strict for families with several children. Although there are some differences between the LPLs and the SPL and between the three models, the trends over time are essentially the same. Between 1985 and 1988 (adjusted for price changes) there has been a significant drop in the level of the income thresholds. Between 1988 and 1992 the LPL rose only a little, and the SPL did not change at all. As a result, across the period as a whole, the real value of the LPLs fell by 4 to 6 percent, and that of the SPL by 7 to 10 percent. Relative to average equivalent income, which rose by more than 14 percent during the same period, the subjective income thresholds fell even more behind. When the LPLs and SPL are calculated for each region separately, it is found that income thresholds are higher in Wallonia then in Flanders. Furthermore, while the LPLs follow similar trends across time in both regions, the SPL drops precipitously in Flanders and at the same time rises significantly in Wallonia. These differences in levels and developments are not easily explained in terms of reference effects, since average income in Wallonia is smaller than in Flanders, and also has risen less.

In 1992, the number of households below the SPL was 15 percent, while 17 percent were below the LPL0.5 and 9 percent were also below the LPL0.4 (using the Kapteyn-Muffels model). The number of individuals below these income thresholds was much smaller: 9 percent for the SPL, 10 percent for the LPL0.5 and 5 percent for the LPL0.4. Between 1985 and 1988, all low income rates have dropped considerably: about 2 percentage-points for the LPL0.4, 5 percentage-points for the LPL0.5 and 7 percentage-points for the SPL. Most of this drop occurred between 1985 and 1988. This downward trend contradicts slightly rising low income rates measured with relative income thresholds that move in tandem with average income, but is in agreement with the evolution in low income rates according to constant income standards that are adjusted only for price changes. The risk of finding oneself below the LPLs or the SPL is always higher for the Walloon people than for the population of Flanders, even with 'national' income thresholds, and does not decrease as rapidly for the former as for the latter. Using 'regional' income standards, these differences become much more emphasized, and in 1992 subjective low income rates in Wallonia are no less than two (LPLs) or three (SPL) times higher than in Flanders.

Looking at SPL and LPL low income rates across a range of subgroups, I find that persons aged 55 or over, women, unemployed, retired or disabled persons, single persons when not working, persons living in one-parent families, and in general persons living in households where neither head nor spouse are at work, face a higher than average risk of living in a low income household. Comparing these results with those obtained with relative income standards incorporating the modified OECD equivalence scale, I find considerable agreement, but also important differences. In particular, the contrast in low income rates between small and large families is much less marked using the SPL and LPLs with their flat equivalence scales, than with the relative thresholds. As a consequence, children are more likely to be below the relative lines than below the subjective ones, while the reverse is true for the elderly. These differences are also reflected in the patterns of low income rates by other characteristics of individuals. Furthermore, the use of age-specific equivalence scales can lead to different conclusions. When looking at the results of the simple model, which does not take account of age, it was found that babies and toddlers aged 0 to 3 are clearly more likely to be below the LPLs and the SPL than children in other age categories. On the other hand, using the selective model, which produces an age-specific equivalence scale, the results indicate that the risk of being in a low income family among students aged 18 to 25 equals, or exceeds that in the youngest age category.

Popular statistical software packages such as SPSSx and SAS typically calculate standard errors using (implicitly) the assumptions that the sample is a simple random one, and that the estimates in question are linear functions of sample observations. For the low income rates reported above, both assumptions are incorrect, as is likely to be true for most poverty and low income studies. Application of the Jackknife, a pseudo-replication or sample re-use technique, shows that actual standard errors of low income rates are much larger than those routinely calculated by SAS or SPSSx (and most likely to be reported by a 'naive' income analyst). The main reason for this is that the LPL and SPL income thresholds used to identify low income households are themselves non-linear functions of sample data, and therefore subject to sample variability.

Appendix 5.1 Details on sample design and calculation of standard errors

The SEP sample design

The original SEP sample, drawn in 1985, was a two-stage EPSEM (Equal Probability of Selection Method) one, with stratification of the first stage sampling units (municipalities). First, municipalities were stratified according to region (Flanders, Wallonia and Brussels). Within Flanders and Wallonia, municipalities were further stratified according to average taxable income, so that in each of those regions, three strata were formed containing an equal number of households. Furthermore, within Flanders, the city of Antwerp was treated as a separate stratum. In each of the several strata except Antwerp, ten municipalities were selected with probability proportional to size, and with replacement. In the selected municipalities (i.e. sampled clusters), as well as in Antwerp, systematic samples of households were drawn from municipal registers. Since sample sizes in the strata were proportional to population, the procedure followed implies that cluster size varied across regions: it was 116 in Flanders, 86 in Brussels and 75 in Wallonia. Below this sample will be called the *panel* sample.

In 1992 an *additional* sample of 1000 households was drawn, again following a two-stage EPSEM design. Municipalities were stratified by region, and within Flanders and Wallonia, according to a socio-economic typology of municipalities, resulting in a total of 11 strata. The sample size for each cluster was fixed at 20. The total of 50 clusters to be drawn were distributed across strata proportional to the total population in each stratum. Municipalities were selected with probability proportional to size, and with replacement. In the selected municipalities (i.e. sampled clusters) systematic samples of households were drawn.

Before actual calculations were carried out, some adjustments were necessary. The panel sample in the city of Antwerp was arbitrarily split into three clusters, of approximately the same size as the other clusters in Flanders. Because of (cumulative) non-response and other reasons, some clusters contained very few households, especially in 1992 in Brussels. Therefore a few clusters (within a single stratum) were joined together, leaving a total of 70 clusters in the panel sample, and 46 in the additional sample. Furthermore, since several of the strata in the additional sample contained only one or two clusters, strata were collapsed, so that each region (Flanders, Wallonia, Brussels) constituted a single stratum.

Further comments

The *ultimate cluster approximation* is used for variances (3) to (6), which implies that the variance resulting from the second-stage sampling of households within clusters is neglected. Since clusters were selected *with* replacement, and the second stage sampling fraction was small (five percent at the maximum, most often much less), this approximation seems entirely appropriate (Kalton, 1983: 35).

The *stratum weights* for 1985 and 1988 are equal to p'_h i.e. the proportions of the population living in the strata. For 1992 the combination of the panel sample and the additional sample made things a little more complex. The stratum weights are products of the population proportions p'_h and sample weights p_s, s = *panel, additional*. The sample weights are proportional to the realized sample sizes in terms of households. Thus, p_{panel} is equal to (3821-924)/3821, $p_{additional}$ is equal to 924/3821. This choice of sample weights is motivated by the fact that when combining samples, the optimal weights are inverse to the variances in the constituent samples. With simple random sampling, those variances are proportional to the sample sizes. Since in fact the samples were clustered, and clusters were smaller in the additional sample than in the panel sample, the weights used deviate somewhat from the optimal ones for the design at hand. This deviation will not materially affect the results, however.

Notes

1 μ represents the logarithm of the geometric average of the answers to the six levels of the IEQ, logYmin is the logarithm of the answer to the MIQ. See section 4.2 for details.

2 Social scientists with some experience in attitude measurement and factor analysis will appreciate that this stability becomes even more impressive when they consider that the model was developed on the 1985 data, and then applied to the 1988 and 1992 data in a single run, without any modification to the model, or to the selection of observations.

3 The standard WFI measurement model incorporates two main elements the EIA and the lognormal distribution function. Dropping the EIA means that the positions of the IEQ-levels on the welfare scale become indeterminate. However, if the lognormal distribution function is dropped, the translation of positions on the welfare scale into the income dimension is indeterminate. Therefore, in practical terms, dropping any of these assumptions implies that the relative distances of the IEQ income amounts from each other (as indicated by the q_j coefficients) are unconstrained. Rejection of model (5.2) does not therefore unambiguously prove that the EIA does not apply to SEP respondents. See section 6.2 for further discussion.

4 Below, I will use the hyphenated symbols μ' and σ' for the latent variables corresponding to the measured (calculated) variables μ and σ.

5 Given model 5.5,

$$\mu_i = \mu'_i + 1/6\, \sigma'_i\, \Sigma_j\, q_j + 1/6\, \xi'_i\, \Sigma_j\, v_j + 1/6\, \Sigma_j\, e_{ij}\,,$$

but since, by assumption, $\Sigma_j q_j = \Sigma_j v_j = 0$, the second and third terms drop out. Therefore, as the error terms e_{ij} are uncorrelated with each other and with μ',

$$\mathrm{Var}\,(\mu) = \mathrm{Var}\,(\mu') + 1/36\ \Sigma_j\ \mathrm{Var}(e_j).$$

In words, the variance of μ is equal to that of the latent variable μ' plus 1/36 times the sum of the error variances. It is also immediately clear that the covariance of μ' and μ is equal to the variance of μ'.

6 An attractive way to fix the scale for σ' would have been to set $\Sigma q_i^2 = 5$. In that case, (neglecting ξ and the error-terms) σ' would be equal to the standard deviation of the log-

answers to the IEQ. Unfortunately, this turned out to be impossible due to technical difficulties.

7 In 1985, the 'very bad', 'bad', 'sufficient' and 'very good' incomes (but not the 'insufficient' one) had a significant effect, of which that of the 'sufficient' level was by far the most important.

8 The two estimates are not wholly independent, since the errors of the 'insufficient' and 'insufficient' amounts are likely to be correlated. As the effects of the error-correlation on the two estimates are of opposite sign, it will depress the correlation between the two σ-estimates. In fact, though, the error-correlation is fairly limited (for 1985 I obtained an estimate of 0.32, using the standard IEQ-model), so this effect is not likely to be large.

9 The correlations across time of the latent variables μ', σ' and ξ were estimated using a fairly straightforward extension of model (5.5), in which these correlations were the only additions, i.e., no other cross-year correlations were allowed. Equality of the q_j's and v_j's across years was not imposed. This model did not fit the data particularly well: Chi-square = 263.4 for df = 111, AGFI = 0.959, RMR = 0.0062. Allowing the errors to be correlated across time did not improve the fit markedly: a drop in Chi-square of 31.7, for 12 degrees of freedom. In fact, the bad fit seems to be the result of a bad fit of the model *within* each year. This is possibly due to selection effects in the small subsample used.

10 These figures probably overestimate true reliabilities, since they are based on the assumption that μ and logYmin are independent measures, which is not likely to be realistic.

11 Since the SEP question asked for an amount, the econometrics used here are much simpler than those applied by Kapteyn et al. (1988) and Tummers (1994), who had to work with a rough indicator of the respondent's perception of income made up of seven income brackets. Where the respondent in the SEP refused to give an exact amount, he was given the opportunity to answer the question by giving a letter, corresponding to one of fifteen income brackets. Since less than 20 percent of respondents chose this possibility, and the income brackets were fairly narrow, amounts were interpolated for these cases, by taking the midpoints of the brackets.

12 Formally, the model:
$\mu = \beta_0 + \beta_{11}\log Yp + \beta_{12}\log Ym + \beta_x X + e$,
where Yp represents perceived income, Ym measured income, X a vector of other characteristics, β_0, β_{11} and β_{12} parameters to be estimated, and β_x a vector of such parameters, is equivalent to:
$\mu = \beta_0 + \beta_1(\eta\log Yp + (1-\eta)\log Ym) + \beta_x X + e$.

13 The corresponding Durbin-Watson test statistic was the only one below the Durbin-Watson upper bound, indicating inconclusive evidence for serial correlation.

14 It is possible to generalize the equation further, by allowing different transformations for the dependent and independent variables. This possibility has not been considered.

15 Since we are still using a log-log specification (i.e. all income amounts are in logarithmic form), it would in a sense be more correct to call this specification the multiplicative one, in contrast to the logarithmic and linear models, which are exponential in form.

16 Results for the separate years revealed that the overall differences in parameters across years are generally statistically significant, although the gains in R-square by taking account of those differences were quite small (always below 0.003). However, since the differences did not appear substantial or meaningful, I have chosen to ignore most of them. The exception are the effects of region, which change fairly dramatically across time. Also, in order to correct for the slightly different response patterns in the 1988 mail survey, a dummy is included in all models which indicates that a respondent is surveyed by mail, as well as an interaction term of that dummy and log-household income.

Amalgamation also has the advantage of producing smaller standard errors than estimation on data from each single year. To some extent, this advantage more apparent than real, since in many cases two or three observations involving the same household are used. The implied assumption is that observations of the same household separated by three or four years are essentially independent of each other, i.e. can be regarded as observations of different households. In more technical terms, the error terms of those households are assumed to be uncorrelated. However, as shown in section 5.2, there is in fact some serial correlation between observations of μ and logYmin for the same household across years, even after accounting for the influence of income and family size. This means that the reported standard errors are underestimates of the true standard errors. Moreover, the program used for the computations ignores the two-stage clustered design of the sample. This also induces a downward bias in calculated standard errors.

17 However, the differences between Brussels and Wallonia in the logYmin equation were clearly significant; the F-test statistic was equal to 6.9 and 15.1 for 3 degrees of freedom in the selective model and the Kapteyn-Muffels model respectively.

18 These values are derived in the following way. Suppose that in the base year b (1985) the following equation holds:

$$\log(Ymin_b) = \alpha_0 + \alpha_1 \log(Y_b) + \alpha_2 X_b$$

where X represents a vector of variables that are unaffected by inflation, and α_2 is a vector of regression parameters. If we assume that respondents evaluate their income in real terms and do not suffer from money illusion, than in a later year t, the following equation should hold (assuming the structural relationships do not change):

$$\log(Ymin_t/P_t) = \alpha_0 + \alpha_1 \log(Y_t/P_t) + \alpha_2 X_t$$

where P_t is the consumer price index in year t relative to the base year. Some rearrangement yields the following equation:

$$\log(Ymin_t) = \alpha_0 + (1-\alpha_1)\log(P_t) + \alpha_1 \log(Y_t/P_t) + \alpha_2 X_t.$$

In words, in order to keep up with rising prices, the fixed term needs to increase by less than the price index itself, depending on parameter α_1. Note that in this way, the poverty line Ymin* remains at the same real level since

$$\log(Ymin_t^*) = [\alpha_0 + (1-\alpha_1)\log(P_t)\ \alpha_2 X_t] / (1-\alpha_1),$$

and thus:

$$Ymin_t^* = P_t \mathrm{EXP}[(\alpha_0 + \alpha_2 X_t) / (1-\alpha_1)].$$

The consumer price indices for 1988 and 1992, relative to 1985 are 1.041 and 1.173, respectively. Using the estimate of α_1 reported in table 5.12 (selective model), these yield the values mentioned in the text. A similar calculation was made for the μ equation.

19 A parameter often used to characterize an equivalence scale is its elasticity with respect to household size. However, given the specification of the Kapteyn-Muffels model and my model, the equivalence scale elasticity is not a unique value, but depends on the composition of the household in terms of adults and children of various ages. Elasticities evaluated at the mean of the relevant variables were considered less informative than equivalence factors.

20 In her discussion of this problem, Hagenaars (1985: 107) takes the view that this choice is a political one. In her presentation of poverty lines (p. 240) she uses only the number of adults, the number of children, and the number of working persons in a household. However, probabilities of being poor are (implicitly) based on poverty lines that are differentiated according to all variables that were found to influence μ. (p. 249).

6 Interpretation, Validity and Usefulness of the Income Evaluation Method

1 Introduction

This chapter consists of two parts. In the first part (sections 2 to 5), I will discuss in detail possible interpretations the income evaluation approach, i.e. answers to the question: what are the responses to the Minimum Income Question (MIQ) and the Income Evaluation Question (IEQ) supposed to measure? The most prominent interpretation is the one put forward by Van Praag, who claims that the IEQ provides a cardinal and interpersonally comparable measure of welfare. If this claim were correct, the IEQ would also be the ideal measure of poverty, provided of course that poverty can be defined with reference to the concept of welfare that is measured by the IEQ. The following two sections are therefore devoted to Van Praag's interpretation. The next section looks at the claim that the IEQ results have cardinal properties, using theoretical as well as empirical arguments from the relevant literature, supplemented by new empirical results from the Belgian Socio-Economic Panel (SEP). Section three is about the question whether the IEQ can be regarded as an interpersonally comparable measure of welfare. Both aspects of this issue will be discussed: whether it is interpersonally comparable, and whether it can be regarded as a measure of welfare. Section four considers an alternative interpretation of the MIQ, viz. that the answers are indicators of a consensual income threshold. In section five, I will introduce the interpretation of the income evaluation approach favored in this thesis.

Having determined what the income evaluation approach is supposed to measure, we are in a position to assess its validity, i.e. how successful it is in measuring what it is supposed to measure. This is the subject of the second part of the chapter (sections six to eight). Section six reviews the results of chapter 5, focusing on those which can tell us something about the reliability and validity of the method. Section seven looks at the equivalence scales produced by the income evaluation method, considering a number of possible explanations why they are so flat. Section eight evaluates the Subjective Poverty Line (SPL) and the Leyden Poverty Line (LPL), answering the questions: are these income thresholds truly poverty lines? Are they comparable across time and countries? Which is the better one, the SPL or the LPL? Section nine concludes.

2 Is the IEQ a cardinal measure of welfare?

Introduction

Cardinality of a measure implies that ratios have meaning. If welfare is measured with a yardstick that has cardinal properties, it makes sense to say, for instance that this year my welfare is twice as large as five years ago, or that an income of £30,000 a year provide fifty percent more welfare than an income of £10,000. By contrast, in mainstream welfare economics the standard assumption is that cardinal welfare measurement is either impossible or unnecessary or both; it is maintained that welfare can only be measured on an ordinal scale, enabling us to say only that £30,000 gives more welfare than £10,000 to the same person. Whether the welfare difference between £30,000 and £10,000 is larger or smaller than that between £10,000 and £9,500 is impossible to say with an ordinal measure of welfare. This inability of course will in many cases make it impossible to evaluate whether a particular income redistribution scheme has positive or negative welfare consequences.

How are the answers to the IEQ transformed into a cardinal measure of welfare (i.e. welfare derived from income)? Essentially, two steps or assumptions are involved. In the first place, a certain functional form is chosen for the relationship between welfare and income. According to Van Praag (1968, 1971) this relationship has the form of a cumulative lognormal distribution function. The main characteristics of this function are that it is bounded between zero and one, that it is monotonously increasing and that it has an S-form, i.e. that it is convex in its first part. See figure 4.3 for a graphical representation. The partial convexity of the lognormal distribution function implies that at low incomes marginal utility increases with income. A lognormal distribution function is fully defined by two parameters, μ and σ. When a lognormal distribution function is transformed into the corresponding normal distribution function, by taking logs, μ and σ refer to the mean and standard deviation of the latter function. Formally: $W(y) = \Lambda(y| \mu, \sigma) = N(\log(y)| \mu, \sigma)$, where W(y) is the welfare derived from income y, Λ the lognormal distribution function and N the normal distribution function.

In the second step, the labels used in the IEQ are mapped onto the welfare scale. This mapping is done using the equal interval or equal quantile assumption, introduced by Van Praag (1971). This assumption says that the labels 'very bad', 'bad' and so on correspond to the midpoints of intervals of equal length that partition the zero-one welfare scale. Thus, if there are six labels, the boundaries of the intervals are at 1/6, 2/6, 3/6 etc., and the midpoints of those intervals are 1/12, 3/12 and so on.

Given a set of responses to the IEQ by a respondent, we can now draw the corresponding Welfare Function of Income (WFI) of that respondent, linking each income level to a cardinal welfare value. The lognormal distribution function (LDF) establishes the general form of the function, and because of the equal interval assumption we can identify a number of points on it. In fact, six points, corresponding to the six levels of the IEQ, overdetermine the WFI, as it has only two parameters, μ and σ. This makes it possible to evaluate the empirical fit of the LDF, as we will see below.

In practice, the complete WFI is not drawn for every respondent, but only its two parameters μ and σ are estimated. This is done in the following way. Given the assumptions set out above, we know that: N (log of 'bad' amount| μ, σ) = 3/12; i.e., the WFI, taking the form of the (log)normal distribution function, with parameters μ and σ, translates the income amount corresponding to the 'bad' label to a value of 3/12; similar translations can of course be carried out for the other IEQ-amounts. In general:

$$N_S [(\log A_i - \mu) / \sigma] = (Z_i - 1) / 12, \qquad (6.1)$$

where A_i is the answer to the i-th level of the IEQ (i = 1...6), and N_S the standard normal distribution function ($N_S[(\log A_i - \mu) / \sigma] = N(\log A_i| \mu, \sigma)$). Taking the inverse of the standard normal distribution on both sides of (6.1), and rearranging, we obtain:

$$\log A_i = \mu + \sigma.q_i \qquad (6.2)$$

where $q_i = N_S^{-1}((2\,i - 1) / 12)$, or, in words, the 1/12-th, 3/12 th, and so on quantiles of the standard normal distribution. Adding a disturbance term to (6.2), this equation can be estimated for every respondent, yielding estimates of μ and σ. Because the sum of the q_i is zero by definition, μ is equal to the average of the logarithms of the IEQ amounts, if all six have been given by the respondent.

In summary the procedure used to estimate his or her WFI from a respondent's answers to the IEQ, relies on two assumptions: the assumption that the WFI has the form of a log-normal distribution function, and the equal interval assumption. In the following subsections we will have a close look at the arguments pro and contra each of those assumptions.

The log-normal distribution function of welfare: theoretical arguments

The assumption that WFIs have the shape of a lognormal distribution function (LDF) is the outcome of an elaborate theory developed by Van Praag (1968). It is impossible to describe this theory here completely. The following brief sketch is based upon Kapteyn and Wansbeek (1985). A basic assumption is that the welfare derived from a set of goods is a multiplicative function of the welfare derived from each relevant characteristic incorporated in those goods. The welfare functions themselves satisfy a number of conditions; in particular they are bounded between one and zero and they are independent of each other. Furthermore, the budget constraint in terms of characteristics, as perceived by the consumer is multiplicatively separable in functions of the characteristics. The question is, then, what level of welfare will the consumer attach to a certain budget? The neoclassical answer is, the welfare that can be derived from the most preferred combination of characteristics that can be obtained with the given budget. Van Praag's answer is that ex-ante, when the consumer has not yet found out which combination of characteristics she prefers, the consumer evaluates the budget by the welfare associated with *all* the characteristics that might be bought with the budget (Hartog, 1988: 245). This answer is an overestimate, compared with the welfare that the consumer will experience when she actually spends the budget, and it implies that she is not entirely rational. Now, given these assumptions, as well as a number of other ones, Van Praag (1968) shows that the welfare evaluation of a particular budget has approximately the mathematical form of a lognormal distribution function. The approximation will be better if the number of characteristics is larger, i.e. for broad commodity groups. The broadest commodity group is the one that includes all commodities; the most comprehensive budget is total expenditure, or, taking savings as postponed expenditure, total income (Van Praag, 1971: 340).

No other aspect of the WFI-approach has been more often discussed and criticized than the assumption of lognormality. The empirical evidence will be discussed in the next subsection. At the theoretical level, two features of the lognormal distribution function have drawn the critics' fire: first, the fact that it is bounded from above, and secondly its S-shape, i.e. its partial convexity. Both aspects will now be considered in more detail.

Ratchford (1985) and Seidl (1994) both object to the boundedness of the WFI from above. According to Ratchford (1985: 370-371), the boundedness of the WFI may create scaling problems. He thinks that most people can imagine increasing the welfare they derive from their income several times over, which, if the WFI is bounded, is only possible if they are at a bottom of the welfare scale. In fact, the incomes of most respondents are above EXP(μ), implying that they are on the upper half of the welfare scale. If these respondents were asked what amount of money would double their welfare, they ought to answer: "No amount of money, however great it is, can double my present welfare" (Seidl, 1994: 1641).

Kapteyn and Wansbeek (1985b) and Van Praag and Kapteyn (1994) have reacted to Ratchford's (1985) and Seidl's (1994) criticisms, respectively. Regarding boundedness Kapteyn and Wansbeek (1985b: 379) remark that on a-priori grounds, it is hard to decide whether or not utility is bounded from above. In neoclassical economics, where welfare is an ordinal concept, the question is meaningless. However, it appears that a strong theoretical argument for the boundedness of the utility function emerges from the study of decisions under uncertainty: if the utility function is not bounded, it is not possible to order all probabilistic outcomes of options in terms of expected utilities (Van Praag and Kapteyn, 1994: 1821). Otherwise, the matter appears to be rather elusive and insubstantial. At first sight, it may seem implausible that a person with an average income would be unable to imagine being twice as well off, no matter how high his income would become. On the other hand it is quite conceivable that, on reflection, people might consider that an income situation where one can get along fairly easily is indeed more than halfway between the point of starvation and the maximum level of welfare, and that once one is above the median, additional income makes a relatively small contribution to welfare. As a final remark, note that the boundedness of the utility function does not imply that there is a satiation point (Van Praag and Kapteyn, 1994: 1821). Since the lognormal function approaches its upper bound asymptotically, there is no income level where additional income does not increase welfare any more. In fact, because the welfare function shifts with income itself, it is possible that even the welfare evaluation of their own income by the very richest people may not approach the upper boundary very closely.

Another problem is the S-shape of the WFI. As mentioned above, this means that the marginal welfare of income rises gradually with increasing income, until the point of inflection of the WFI is reached, which is located at $EXP(\mu - \sigma^2)$. According to Seidl (1994: 1645) increasing marginal welfare of income contradicts economic intuition, as codified in Gossen's first law. Because he regards boundedness and the S-shape as implausible, Seidl (1994) rejects the hypothesis of log-normality for the shape of the WFI. According to Seidl, empirical research on the so-called 'psychophysical law', which describes the relationship between a physical stimulus and the magnitude of the subjective sensation, has shown that this law has the form of either a power function or a logarithmic function. Both functions are unbounded from above and (provided the parameters of the functions are in the usual range) concave.

Seidl (1994: 1650-1656) recognizes that empirical analyses of the answers to the IEQ show a remarkably good fit for the lognormal function (see below). But he argues that this happens only because the answers to the IEQ are the result of a welfare evaluation process superimposed on the welfare function of income proper. In other words, respondents experience welfare from income according to a logarithmic or power function; when they evaluate this experience in terms of 'good', 'bad' and so on, they implicitly use a welfare evaluation function which is S-shaped. Seidl shows that, e.g. a logarithmic welfare function combined with a normal distribution welfare evaluation function is observationally equivalent to a lognormal welfare function on its own.

Against the criticism that the lognormal function is convex in its first part, thus violating Gossen's first law, Kapteyn and Wansbeek (1985: 341-342) retort that the concavity of the utility function of income is just an assumption, which is never empirically tested. According to these authors, increasing marginal utility at the lower income range seems quite plausible. "If income is below subsistence level, each extra dollar brings one closer to the point where survival is possible, and hence each extra dollar carries a higher marginal utility" (p. 342). However, results from the

BSEP (wave 1985) show that the actual incomes of more than 13 percent of all respondents are below the inflection point (EXP(μ - σ^2)) of their own WFI, as estimated from the answers to the IEQ. It is unlikely that such a large number of people in Belgium are below the subsistence threshold. (They should be dead, strictly speaking.)

In his original book Van Praag (1968) hints very briefly at an economic rationale for postulating increasing marginal utility of a single commodity group. He writes (p. 81): "One can imagine that there is a critical quantity such that a smaller quantity of the commodity concerned is practically worthless". Seidl (1994: 1645-46) finds this argument convincing for a narrow commodity group, but not for total expenditure where the consumer can choose among a large set of different commodities. The argument might be saved, however, if we assume that there is certain commodity that is valued so much that an individual would be willing to sacrifice all other consumption in order to acquire it. Following Lewis and Ulph (1988), we might assume that certain goods are valued not so much for the direct consumption benefits they yield, but mainly because they enable the consumer to participate in certain social activities. If those goods are indivisible, or if a certain minimum expenditure is required to gain access to those activities, it follows that there are discrete changes or "jumps" in the welfare function of income, as Lewis and Ulph (1988) show.

Such a discrete change does imply that the welfare function is not concave, but not necessarily that it is S-shaped. An S-shape might follow, though, if we extend Lewis and Ulph's (1988) theory by assuming that there is not a single minimum level of expenditure giving access to social participation, but rather a range of expenditure thresholds for participating in a variety of activities, or associating with different kinds of people. Especially if the level of those thresholds is related to the incomes of the people involved, an S-shaped welfare function of income might result. (In fact, this is an informal restatement of Kapteyn's (1977) theory that a person's welfare function of income is equal to the income distribution in his reference group.)

In contrast to the question whether the welfare function is bounded from above, the S-shape issue can in principle be settled by empirical evidence, since partial convexity of the welfare function of income has some behavioral implications that are independent of the WFI-framework. One such implication is that low income persons spend money on lottery tickets. If someone is on a convex part of his utility function, the net expected utility of the purchase of a lottery ticket might be positive, even if in monetary terms the net expected return is negative. Casual observation suggests that this implication might well find empirical support. Another implication of convexity is that low income persons do not smooth consumption over time, but, by contrast, bunch all their consumption in certain periods, and consume nothing (or only so much as to survive physically) in others (Tummers, 1992: 35-40). If a person has an income below the inflection point of his WFI, in two subsequent periods of time, he can increase total welfare across the two periods by saving in the first period and spending in the second one, so that his consumption level in the second period reaches the inflection point. This implication seems to be less likely to be confirmed in empirical research. While such bunching may occur at certain occasions and for certain people (holiday, weekends), it does not seem to be a very common sort of behavior for periods like a month or a year, which are the typical reference periods in the IEQ.

The conclusion must be that the arguments in favor of partial convexity of the WFI are not very convincing. It may be true that Gossen's first law is nothing more than a postulate, but the fact that so many economists share this conviction must carry some weight. (See e.g., the discussion following Van Praag, 1977b.) The defenders of the WFI argue that contrary to Gossen's first law, the lognormal welfare function of income stems from a well-developed theory. However, this result depends on the assumption that consumers systematically and repeatedly overestimate the welfare yielded by a certain amount of expenditure. As Hartog (1988: 247) writes, it is likely that consumers will learn from past mistakes, and bring their *ex-ante* evaluations closer to *ex-post* realities. Therefore, the theoretical basis of the lognormal shape of the welfare function does not look very strong. As suggested above, in some circumstances and given certain assumptions, convexity of the initial part of the welfare function of income may be less implausible than it seems at first sight. However, before a theorem that goes against the intuition of many economists can be accepted, those theoretical arguments must be supplemented by empirical evidence, that is independent of the IEQ-approach.

Empirical results on the shape of the WFI

An empirical investigation into the form of the WFI has been carried out by Van Herwaarden and Kapteyn (1981). Using answers to several different variants of the IEQ, as given in seven Belgian and Dutch surveys, they compare the performance of the lognormal distribution function (LDF) with that of twelve alternative functions. The comparison is based on Theil's residual variance criterion. The conclusion is that the logarithm gives a better fit than the LDF, whereas all other functions produce a worse fit (Van Herwaarden and Kapteyn, 1981: 282). In several surveys, the difference between average residual variance of the logarithm and that of the LDF is statistically significant. The logarithmic function differs from the LDF in two crucial respects: it is unbounded, and it does not have a convex part. Since its unboundedness violates the 'finite bliss, finite agony assumption', Van Herwaarden and Kapteyn (1981: 284) are of the opinion that the logarithmic function can "only reasonably be interpreted as a local approximation to some unknown true function".

I have replicated Van Herwaarden and Kapteyn's (1981) analysis, using the Belgian data at hand. Only the two most promising contenders were looked at here, viz. the log-normal distribution function and the logarithmic function. The former is specified in (6.2), the latter is specified as follows:

$$\log A_i = a + b\,((2i - 1)12) + e_i\ ,\ \ i = 1..6, \tag{6.3}$$

where A_i is the amount for IEQ-level i, *a* and *b* are parameters to be estimated for each respondent, and e_i is a disturbance term. Following Van Herwaarden and Kapteyn (1981), I also use Theil's (1971: 543) residual-variance criterion; i.e. the model of which the disturbance term has the lowest variance is regarded as the best approximation to the true model[1]. Only observations where all IEQ-amounts had been given were taken up in the analysis; furthermore a small number of cases (always less than 0.3 percent of the sample) were excluded where either the 'very bad' amount was below 5,000 BF, or where the ratio of two subsequent IEQ-amounts exceeded 4.5. The reason for their exclusion was that they had very high residual variances for both functions.

The results, shown in table 6.1, confirm those of Van Herwaarden and Kapteyn (1981). In all surveys, the logarithmic function has lower residual variance than the log-normal distribution function. Moreover, the difference is statistically significant at any conventional significance level[2]. Nevertheless, both functions perform very well in terms of R-square. Moreover, the log-normal distribution function produces a better fit than the logarithmic one in about a third of all individual cases. The present analysis cannot reveal whether this reflects sampling error, or whether respondents are actually not homogeneous as regards the 'true' form of the WFI. The 1988 results are shown separately for respondents that were interviewed face-to-face, and those that completed a mailed questionnaire. R-square statistics as well as residual variances are higher for the mail respondents than for the face-to-face interviewers. However, as the assignment of respondents to the mail survey or to the face-to-face survey was not at all random, this difference does not necessarily reflect an effect of the data-gathering method. (Elderly respondents and those with a low level of education were never approached by mail.) In 1992, R-square statistics are lower and residual variances are higher than in the other years. This indicates that in 1992 respondents were less careful when answering the IEQ than in the preceding surveys.

Some caution is needed when considering the average R-square statistics. Wierenga (1978) has simulated random answers to the IEQ, and found that they produce the same fit as actual answers from real respondents. In their rejoinder, Van Praag, Kapteyn and Van Herwaarden (1978) argue that the simulation procedure used by Wierenga is less random than it seems, due to a number of constraints he imposes, and that it is in fact equivalent to a data-generating process governed by a linear welfare function. According to Van Praag et al (1978) a proper comparison shows that Wierenga's procedure produces data that fit much worse than actual answers: the residual variance of the former is more than two times larger than that of the latter. Yet, the average correlation of the simulated data is 0.97, indicating that a high R-square is not necessarily evidence that a particular functional form is the 'true' one.

Table 6.1
Comparison of competing functional forms for the WFI, using the residual variance criterion

		1985	1988, mail	1988, face	1992
Lognormal distribution function	Mean R-square	0.9616	0.9634	0.9604	0.9535
	Mean residual var.	0.0093	0.0094	0.00769	0.0119
	St. error of mean	0.00018	0.00035	0.00028	0.0003
Logarithmic function	Mean R-square	0.9658	0.9690	0.9654	0.9575
	Mean residual var.	0.0084	0.0079	0.00678	0.0109
	St. error of mean	0.00018	0.00033	0.00028	0.0003
Difference between residual variances (1)	Mean	0.00095	0.00148	0.00091	0.001
	St. error of mean	0.00006	0.00013	0.00009	0.00009
	T-value	15.8	11.4	10.1	11.1
	Proportion > 0	0.639	0.664	0.659	0.614
Number of cases		5354	1341	1542	3385

Note: (1) Residual variance of lognormal distribution function minus residual variance of logarithmic function.

Source: Belgian Socio-Economic Panel, waves 1985, 1988 and 1992.

As noted above, an essential difference between the logarithmic function, and the lognormal distribution function is that the latter is convex in its lower part, while the former is concave everywhere. Because of the theoretical objections leveled against the convexity of the WFI, it is of some interest to look at this issue independent of any particular functional form incorporating a convex part. Given the equal quantile assumption, an unambiguous indicator of convexity in the lower part of the WFI is that the difference between the 'insufficient' and the 'bad' amounts is smaller than that between the 'bad' and 'very bad' amounts. In 1985 this was true for 25 percent of all respondents (same subsample as was used for table 6.1). The significance of this result is, however, much reduced by the finding that the answers of 35 percent of these respondents would seem to indicate that their WFI is partially convex in its *upper* part[3]. This result suggests that a seemingly convex part in a respondent's WFI may, in many cases, represent nothing more significant than measurement error, perhaps due to rounding off of amounts.

The equal quantile assumption

In the previous subsection we have seen that empirical tests carried out by Van Herwaarden and Kapteyn (1981) and by myself have rejected the hypothesis that the Welfare Function of Income has the shape of a lognormal distribution function (LDF). Instead, the logarithmic function yields a better fit. A crucial assumption in these tests is that the labels used in the IEQ ('very bad', 'bad', and so on) correspond to the positions 1/12, 3/12 and so on the welfare scale, or, in other words, it is assumed that the equal quantile or equal interval hypothesis is true. Therefore, the finding that the logarithmic function outperforms the LDF may also indicate that the latter hypothesis is not correct. Let us therefore look at the arguments and evidence in favor of the equal interval assumption.

In contrast to the log-normal shape of the WFI, the assumption of equal intervals (EIA) is not central in the WFI-theory. It is an auxiliary assumption, introduced by Van Praag (1971), in order to relate the labels of the IEQ to particular points on the zero-one welfare scale. The EIA is justified by reference to an information maximization argument, developed first by Van Praag (1971), generalized by Kapteyn (1977) and summarized by Kapteyn and Wansbeek (1985).

Briefly and informally, the argument runs as follows. It is assumed that an individual in answering the IEQ, tries to inform us as exactly as possible about his welfare function, i.e. he attempts to maximize the information value of his answers. Suppose that a respondent says that an income of 50,000 BF would be 'sufficient', 80,000 BF would be 'good', and 150,000 BF would be 'very good'. What is then her evaluation of an income of 100,000 BF? Without further information, we might choose the evaluation of the answer that is closest to 100,000 BF, i.e. 'good'. In fact, the respondent would probably evaluate 100,000 BF as somewhat better than 'good', which means that the assignment of the evaluation 'good' to 100,000 BF is somewhat inaccurate. If we could quantify this inaccuracy, and repeat the process for all income levels, we would obtain a measure of the total inaccuracy of the respondent's response pattern, or rather, of the way she uses the IEQ labels to partition the welfare space into intervals. It is clear that some partitions give rise to a greater degree of inaccuracy than others. In fact, it can be shown that total inaccuracy is smallest when the partitioning is done according to the Equal Interval Assumption. Minimizing total inaccuracy is equivalent to maximizing the information value of the answers.

Two remarks can be made about this information maximization argument. In the first place, the assumption that the respondent tries to inform us as exactly as possible about her welfare function, appears to be somewhat *ad-hoc*, since it is unclear what interest she has in doing so. Most respondents probably want to finish the questionnaire as quickly as possible. The finding, reported above, that most amounts are rounded to multiples of 10,000 BF, does not seem to support the information maximization assumption.

Secondly, a remarkable implication of the information maximization argument is that the income amounts mentioned by the respondent will be independent of the verbal labels used in the IEQ (Wierenga, 1978: 393). Under the information maximization assumption, one would get the same income level responses with the descriptions currently used as with the following list: "adequate", "just sufficient", "insufficient", "rather bad", "extremely bad", "starvation". Ratchford (1985: 369) is of the opinion that "This does not seem reasonable: it would seem very likely that consumers would respond to the labels rather than adjusting their responses to provide an equal interval scale." Ratchford's comment is borne out by empirical results: Van Praag and Flik (1992: 8, 457) report that in a French survey, the original wording of the IEQ was modified, and that the resulting LPL was "quite sensitive to the wording of the IEQ". They stress "that the original wording of [the IEQ] has to be maintained" (p. 85).

Despite the weaknesses of the information maximization argument, we might still accept the Equal Interval Assumption (EIA), at least as an approximation, provided the descriptive labels in the IEQ have been well chosen. It is therefore interesting to look at the results of empirical tests of the EIA. These tests are of two kinds. In the first place, the EIA is tested on the basis of the answer7s to the IEQ themselves, by means of an analysis of variance technique (Buyze, 1982; Vander Sar et al., 1988; Tummers, 1992; results reported above in section 5.2 also constitute an indirect test of the EIA). Secondly, there are direct tests, where respondents have to order the IEQ-labels on a numerical scale (Antonides et al., 1980; Van Doorn and Van Praag, 1988; Van Praag, 1991).

In the *indirect tests* carried out by Buyze (1982) and Tummers (1992), the following model is used (an adaptation of 6.2):

$$\log A_{in} = \mu_n + \sigma_n q_i + e_{in} \tag{6.4}$$

where A_{in} is the answer to the i-th level of the IEQ by the n-th respondent, μ_n and σ_n are individual parameters, the q_i are quantiles, and e_{in} is an error term with the usual properties. In contrast with the usual procedure, the quantiles are not fixed by the equal interval assumption, but estimated from the data. For this purpose, a few identifying restrictions have to be imposed on the q_i; for further details about the estimation I refer to the papers cited. Note that (6.4) implies that the q_i are the same for all respondents.

Using data from a written survey, conducted in the Netherlands in 1971, Buyze (1982) finds that all estimated quantiles are well within a standard error from those under the equal interval assumption. However, a joint test of the hypothesis that all quantiles are equal to those under the EIA results in a rejection of this hypothesis. Furthermore, according to Tummers (1992), standard errors are probably overestimated by Buyze. Nevertheless, the differences between estimated and EIA-quantiles are quite small: 0.07 at most.

Tummers (1992) uses data from the October 1985 wave of the Dutch Socio-Economic Panel survey. He finds that the estimated quantiles differ significantly from the quantiles under the EIA. Moreover, the differences are larger than those found by Buyze (1982): 0.21 at maximum. This may be due to the fact that different versions of the IEQ were used: the one used by Buyze included nine different welfare levels. Tummers also reports that whether estimated or EIA quantiles are used does not at all affect estimates of μ_n (due to an identifying restriction), while estimates of σ_n are affected very little.

Van der Sar et al. (1988) follow a slightly different procedure to estimate quantiles. They use a model similar to (6.4), in which the q_i are also indexed by respondent, i.e. the assumption that the quantiles are the same for all respondents is dropped. Estimates of μ_n and σ_n are computed as respectively the mean and the standard deviation of the amounts given by each respondent. From these, it is a relatively easy matter to calculate the quantiles for each respondent. A problem with this procedure is that σ_n is only equal to the standard deviation of the amounts if the EIA is true, but generally not otherwise (cf. Tummers, 1992). In other words, the estimation procedure presupposes that the hypothesis to be evaluated is true. Average quantiles are reasonably close to those under the EIA, the maximum difference is 0.17. The standard deviation of quantiles about their means is about 0.21, which suggests that there is considerable variation across respondents. Although Van der Sar et al. do not perform a formal statistical test of the EIA[4], it is clear from the reported values and standard deviations, that the EIA would be rejected by any conventional test. (The IEQ in the survey which Vander Sar et al. used was phrased in an unusual way; the labels were the same as those used by Dubnoff (1985) to describe living levels; see section 2.2.)

Finally, an indirect test of a model incorporating the EIA and the log-normal distribution function was carried out using the structural equations with latent variables approach and the SEP data. As reported in section 5.2, this test resulted in a clear rejection.

In *direct tests* of the EIA, respondents are confronted with the welfare labels used in the IEQ, and are asked to associate a number (e.g. between 0 and 10) with each of the labels. In table 6.2, results of direct tests which have used the most common set of IEQ-labels are summarized. (Values have been standardized to the 0-1 interval. Note that the reported figures refer to the welfare level W_i , not to the quantiles q_i; $Wi = N_S(q_i)$ where N_S is the standard cumulative normal distribution function.)

From the results of such a direct test, Antonides et al. (1980: 32) conclude that "the estimates are significantly different from the values implied by the equal interval assumption". The evaluations of their respondents always exceed those implied by the EIA, although the difference is smaller at higher welfare levels. In fact, the differences between the average evaluations are all virtually the same (0.15 or 0.16); the IEA is rejected only because the series starts at a value that is too high. Antonides et al. (1980) also report that if the empirical evaluations would be used instead of the equal interval values in the calculation of the WFI-parameters, the estimates of μ would be lower, and those of σ would be higher.

Roughly the same pattern can be observed in the results of Van Doorn and Van Praag (1988), although there is more variation across respondents in their results, perhaps because the six labels were presented to the respondents in a random order. In addition to the numerical evaluations, Van Doorn and Van Praag (1988) also asked respondents to represent the six welfare labels in terms of line segments of varying length. They do not report average lengths of the line segments, but from the published results it is possible to derive that the correlation between the numerical evaluations and the line lengths is about 0.9, on average[5].

Table 6.2
Results of tests of the Equal Interval Assumption for IEQ-labels

A: Most common set of six labels

Label	Direct tests				Indirect test	Equal interval values
	Antonides et al., 1980		Van Doorn et al., 1988		Tummers, 1992	
	Average	St..Dev.	Average	St..Dev.		
Very bad	0.17	0.13	0.22	0.14	0.12	0.08
Bad	0.32	0.10	0.31	0.14	0.22	0.25
Insufficient	0.47	0.07	0.38	0.15	0.34	0.42
Sufficient	0.62	0.06	0.58	0.12	0.56	0.58
Good	0.78	0.06	0.70	0.12	0.77	0.75
Very good	0.93	0.07	0.86	0.09	0.93	0.92
Number of subjects	314		28		3026	

B: Set of five labels

Label	Direct tests in Van Praag, 1991				Equal interval values
	Numbers		Line segments		
	Average	St..Dev.	Average	St..Dev.	
Very bad	0.09	0.09	0.07	0.06	0.10
Bad	0.20	0.12	0.18	0.09	0.30
Not bad, not good	0.47	0.11	0.40	0.11	0.50
Good	0.67	0.12	0.60	0.12	0.70
Very good	0.87	0.09	0.82	0.12	0.90
Number of subjects	364		364		

Note: Direct tests consist of letting subjects assign numbers to the labels used in the IEQ; in Van Praag (1991) labels were also evaluated in terms of line segments. Numbers have been standardized to the range 0 to 1. Indirect tests are based on an analysis of the covariance matrix of the answers to the IEQ. See text for details.

Source: See references in table.

Panel B of table 6.2 shows results of an exercise reported by Van Praag (1991), where respondents had to evaluate five descriptions of welfare levels, both in terms of numbers and in terms of line segments. As Van Praag (1991: 78) observes, there appears to be a downward bias in all evaluations. Treating each pair of evaluations (number and line segment) corresponding to a particular label by a particular respondent as an independent observation, Van Praag regresses the numerical evaluations on the line segment evaluations, and finds a regression coefficient of 0.97, with an R-square of 0.85. Van Praag (1991: 79) concludes that the verbal labels are "rather similarly understood by different respondents", that the translations of these labels into numbers or line segments are consistent with each other, and that "the verbal evaluations are translated on a bounded scale in accordance with the Equal Interval Assumption".

These conclusions are not unjustified, but they seem to be based on the most positive reading of the results. Given the (symmetric) choice of labels, and the context-free setting, one would naturally expect respondents to spread out the labels across the whole range of the scale. In a way, the last sentence is an informal restatement of the information maximization argument, and in this limited sense the findings confirm the equal interval hypothesis. Beyond this, however, it is not clear that much has been proven. It is clear from the reported means and standard deviations that any formal statistical test of the equal interval hypothesis would result in a rejection. Also in an absolute sense, the differences between the average empirical evaluations and those following from the EIA appear to be fairly large, in particular for the label 'bad'; it seems likely that this is due to respondents' reactions to the meaning of the label.

Another importance qualification of Van Praag's conclusions is that there appears to be considerable variation in the individual evaluations. If the numbers assigned to the label 'not bad, not good' are normally distributed, the reported standard error implies that the interval in which 95 per cent of all answers are contained runs from 0.25 to 0.70. This interval seems quite wide, and it overlaps to a considerable degree with corresponding intervals for the labels 'good' and 'bad'. Secondly, the number evaluations and the line segment evaluations are consistent with each other only on the level of aggregate values in the sample as a whole. The high R-square in the regression mentioned above is mainly due to the fact that any two monotonously increasing series will be highly correlated. In fact, calculations on the basis of the published results indicate that the correlation between the evaluations of any particular label in terms of line segments and of numbers is on average probably no higher than 0.40. This moderate correlation suggests that most of the variation across respondents in the evaluation of labels is pure white noise, and does not reflect possible differences in the meaning of the labels for different respondents.

The *conclusion* of this review of tests of the equal interval assumption (EIA) must be that in its formal sense, this assumption must be rejected.

Nevertheless, provided the descriptive labels have been well chosen, the equal interval assumption will be a reasonable approximation to the true values on the welfare scale. In practical work, where empirical evaluations of IEQ-labels on a 0-1 scale are generally not available, use of the EIA-values seems to be justified.

The findings regarding the EIA give rise to a brief reconsideration of the hypothesis that the welfare function of income has the shape of a *lognormal distribution*. The reader may recall that empirical tests of this assumption show that the logarithmic function fitted the data better than the lognormal distribution function. However, these tests rely on the equal interval assumption, while in indirect tests of the EIA, the lognormal distribution function hypothesis is assumed to be true. In fact, both are tests of the joint hypothesis of lognormality and equal intervals (Kapteyn and Wansbeek, 1985b: 378). Therefore, the lognormality assumption (which is central in the WFI-theory) might be saved, if the equal interval assumption would be dropped. Of course, the lognormal distribution function can be made to fit any empirical data, by choosing the proper welfare values for the labels. In a sense, this is exactly what Tummers (1992) has done. It is therefore interesting to compare the welfare values estimated by Tummers (1992) with those found in direct tests with the same set of labels. As table 6.2 shows, the differences between the two series of values are as great, or greater than those between the estimated values and the equal interval ones. (Of course, the results of Antonides et al., 1980 and those of Tummers, 1992 are based on different samples, though in both cases the language was Dutch). It appears, therefore, that substitution of the empirical values of IEQ labels found in direct tests for those based on the EIA, cannot save the hypothesis that the welfare function of income has the shape of a cumulative lognormal distribution function.

Conclusion

Does the IEQ provide a cardinal measure of welfare? We have seen that the measurement procedure rests on two assumptions: first that the welfare function of income has the shape of a lognormal distribution function (LDF), and secondly, that the IEQ-labels - 'very bad', 'bad' and so forth - correspond to the midpoints of intervals of equal length on the welfare scale. For both assumptions there are theoretical arguments as well as empirical tests. The LDF assumption stems from an elaborate theory developed by Van Praag (1968). One implication of the assumption is that the welfare function of income is partly convex, contradicting Gossen's first law. It is not clear whether the empirical implications of this aspect of the WFI are borne out by the actual behavior of low-income consumers. Moreover, the theory assumes that consumers are in a particular sense systematically irrational. The theoretical justification of the equal interval assumption (EIA) is that respondents try to maximize the information content of their answers to the IEQ. This argument is ingenious but also a little *ad-hoc*, and there is little evidence that respondents actually have this goal in mind.

Where the theoretical arguments are inconclusive, the results of the empirical tests are less ambiguous. The IEQ answers themselves allow strictly speaking only a test of the joint hypothesis that both assumptions (LDF and EIA) are correct. When the EIA is assumed, it is found that the logarithmic function has a better fit than the LDF. When the LDF is supposed to be true, the EIA is rejected by formal tests. Also, the EIA fails in direct tests, where respondents evaluate the IEQ-labels in terms of numbers or line segments. Moreover, as reported in section 4.2, at least three, instead of two, parameters are necessary to describe fully answers to the IEQ. This implies that the LDF (as well as any other two-parameter function, such as the logarithmic one) can only be an approximation of the complete welfare function of income, even when the EIA is dropped.

Faced with this evidence, proponents of the IEQ maintain that the assumptions of LDF and EIA are reasonably well met by empirical answers. This is in itself correct, and when estimating μ and σ, there is no reason to discard the procedure based on these assumptions. The claim that the IEQ provides a cardinal measure of welfare, however, is reduced in credibility. The claim rests on a theory and a measurement procedure. From the theory follow certain implications regarding the outcomes of the measurement procedure. These implications turn out not to be true. Of course, this does not necessarily mean that the theory is refuted. The proponents of the IEQ, in effect, blame the measurement procedure, which, they argue, is not yet perfect (e.g. Van Praag, 1991). In the end, cardinal measurability is a matter of faith, as Hartog (1988: 264) has written. But for non-believers, the results provide little reason to change their opinion.

The importance of this conclusion should not be exaggerated, though. We are interested here in a method to identify the poor. Supposing poverty can be defined as situation of low welfare, identification of the poor requires only ordinal comparisons of welfare, i.e. whether persons or households are above or below a certain welfare threshold. What is crucial for this purpose is that the welfare measure derived from the IEQ is comparable across persons (cf. Osmani, 1993: 388). This subject is taken up in the next section.

3 Interpersonal comparability of the answers to the income evaluation questions

The crucial question regarding the WFI-approach is, of course, whether the answers to the IEQ and the MIQ, and the individual parameters derived from these answers, such as μ and $\log Y_{min}$, provide an interpersonally comparable measure of welfare. If the answer were no, the derivation of poverty lines and equivalence scales from these answers would, at the very least, be problematic. In view of its evident importance, this question has been discussed surprisingly rarely in the WFI-literature. For instance, it is not addressed in Van Praag (1971), where the IEQ was introduced. Hagenaars (1985: 57) devotes only a few sentences to this problem. It is not touched upon at all by Kapteyn and Wansbeek (1985) in their review of research within the WFI-approach. Only in Van Praag (1993) is the question discussed at some length. The main reason for this apparent neglect seems to be that following Van Praag (1968: 1), utility is regarded as a primitive concept, which cannot usefully be defined in terms of other concepts. Therefore, "utility is in fact defined by means of a measurement method" (Hagenaars, 1985: 5). Welfare is, then, whatever is measured by the WFI. If this basic assumption is accepted, the statement that WFIs are interpersonally comparable is essentially a tautology, and further arguments are pointless. Below, we will return to this point of view, after having discussed the more substantive arguments in favor of interpersonal comparability of WFIs.

According to Van Praag (1993: 366, 370), the basic issue regarding interpersonal comparability is "whether different people assign the same emotional value to the same verbal label". Three pieces of evidence are given in favor of a positive answer to this question. In the first place, Van Praag refers to the psychometric experiments described in section 6.2, in which individuals were asked to translate verbal labels into figures on a 0-10 scale or into line segments. Van Praag states that "A consistent response pattern was found which suggests that those verbal labels have roughly the same connotation for most individuals". The second piece of evidence comes from the IEQ itself. Different people have different opinions on what is a 'good' income, but this does not imply that 'good' has a different meaning for those persons. Van Praag argues that "if the proportional deviation pattern were constant, say 'good' always corresponds to 20 per cent above the mean and 'bad' to 20 per cent below the mean, then this regularity would strongly suggest that people translate the verbal labels on the same emotional scale" (p. 368). Actually, as Van Praag recognizes, the strong variation in empirical measurements of σ means that this hypothesis has to be rejected as well. However, Van Praag states that the standardized response $((\log A_i - \mu) / \sigma)$ is practically constant across respondents. This means in effect that the second-order differences of the log-IEQ-amounts are constant[6], or in other words, that the answers can be fully described by two parameters (one for location and one for dispersion). According to Van Praag, "This predictability is evidence that the emotional content of the set of stimuli is about the same for all respondents" (p. 369). The third argument is of a more general nature. Within any language community, words must have more or less the same meaning for all, or at least most, individuals. Otherwise, communication is impossible (Van Praag, 1993: 367).

How convincing are these arguments? A first remark is that the evidence is perhaps not as strong as Van Praag makes it appear. As we have seen, there is in fact considerable variation in the ratings by respondents of IEQ labels on a numerical scale, or in terms of line segments. As reported in section 4.2, actually three parameters are needed for a complete characterization of the IEQ answers. Also, the approximate equality of second-order differences in the answers of respondents to the IEQ may well be an artifact of the question format, rather than the result of anything more substantial. Everyday communication may not be much hampered by some leeway in the meaning of words. However, these objections turn on the degree of precision that is implied by the words like "about" and "more or less", and are similar to a discussion whether a bottle is half full or half empty. They are not fundamental, but can, at least hypothetically, be met by additional questions, training of respondents, etc.

Perhaps a more basic objection is that Van Praag ignores, or glosses over some important distinctions. As its name suggests, the IEQ asks for income *evaluations*, which are cognitive acts. Yet, Van Praag and others often seem to imply that the IEQ measures how *satisfied* the respondent feels with her income (e.g., Van Praag, 1993: 364). Satisfaction seems to be a concept of a more affective nature than evaluation is. A person's evaluation of something and the same person's feelings about it need not at all go in the same direction. The statement "I can see it is a good movie, but I don't like it" is after all perfectly comprehensible and such statements are commonly made. Similarly, people may *feel* unsatisfied with their standard of living, while at the same time *recognizing* that it is quite good in comparison with that of others.

A related problem is that income evaluations can be made from several different points of view. People are assumed to evaluate their income in terms of the standard of living it allows them to have, i.e. the amount of consumption per person in the household that it yields. Alternatively, they could evaluate their income from the point of view of whether it is a sufficient compensation for the amount of work they perform, taking into account their qualifications and the working conditions. The two evaluations may differ markedly; for the second kind of evaluation the number of children does not seem as relevant as it is for the first one. Again, these problems should not be exaggerated. If cognitive evaluations and affective feelings of satisfaction diverge, it may be better to look at the former, since they are likely to be based on a considered appreciation of the household's situation, and also to be more stable than feelings. Also, empirically, how a respondent feels about her income, and how she evaluates it, are likely to be strongly correlated. The point of view from which respondents answer the IEQ is a matter that is amenable to empirical study. If it is found that an appreciable number of people do not take the appropriate point of view, the question could be reformulated to remedy this problem. However, the fact that the answers to the IEQ are strongly related to the number of children, and not so much to the level of education, indicates that most respondents do not misunderstand the IEQ in this respect.

It is important to keep in mind that Van Praag (1993: 370) does not claim that the evidence shows beyond any doubt that the IEQ yields an interpersonally comparable measure of welfare. Rather, he regards this proposition as a primitive assumption, which is maintained as long as it does not run counter to empirical evidence. According to Van Praag, equating an empirical measure with a theoretical concept like welfare is always a convention. Such conventions must be accepted if we want to make scientific progress. In this perspective, the objections mentioned above are insufficient to reject this convention, since they merely show that the IEQ may not be a very reliable instrument, or that it may not work in certain cases, or under certain conditions. The appropriate response to such problems is to improve the measurement instrument, not to discard it.

However, there is one fundamental problem that, in my view, undercuts the WFI-approach. Van Praag appears to think that the main issue is whether the IEQ labels have the same meaning for all people, or, whether they have the same emotional content for everyone. But in fact, the main problem lies elsewhere. Implicitly, Van Praag makes another assumption, which is harder to justify. In the words of Osmani (1993: 390), commenting on Van Praag's (1993) paper:

> "He takes it for granted that the same emotional content means the same *level* of welfare. It is this final step which enables him to equate verbal labels with welfare levels, and this equation in turn allows him to declare that welfare is relative and that his utility numbers reflect interpersonally comparable welfare levels." [Italics in original.]

Osmani then goes on to argue that

> "there is no a-priori reason why the emotional content of verbal labels should be seen in terms of *levels* of welfare. In other words, when you and I describe the respective income levels X and Y as 'good', we may have the same emotional perception of these income levels, but the perception need not be that of equal welfare levels. Other interpretations are also possible. [...] [I]f we start from the conventional premise that the level of welfare depends on the absolute level of income [, ...] the verbal labels as well as the utility numbers constructed by Van Praag are seen to reflect ratios rather than levels of welfare. [.. Thus,] X and Y may yield different levels of welfare to you and me respectively, but Y may give me the same welfare *relative* to what I consider to be the average norm, as X does to you *relative* what you consider to be the average norm. [...] Van Praag's utility numbers can, therefore, be seen to represent the proportionate difference between the welfare derived from a given level of income and the welfare derived from some notion of average income. In other words, these utility numbers reflect some notion of relative welfare." [Italics in original.]

Van Praag might answer that, although there is no a-priori reason why the IEQ-labels should have the same meaning in terms of levels of welfare for everyone, Osmani does not mention any particular objection to this assumption either, other than that it contradicts the premise that the level of welfare depends on the absolute level of income. This premise may well be conventional, but in Van Praag's view may have little else to recommend it. After all, in the mainstream economic approach only ordinal welfare comparisons are possible, and even those can be made only for persons who are equal in all respects, other than their level of income. On the other hand, the WFI-method offers a cardinal measure of welfare, which can be used for comparisons across many different kinds of situations. Therefore, although utility numbers derived from the IEQ *can* be seen as reflecting some notion of relative welfare, there is no particular reason to do so.

Below, I will extend Osmani's points and argue that there are in fact good reasons to *reject* the assumption that the IEQ-labels have the same meaning for everyone in terms of levels of welfare, even though they may have the same meaning in terms of emotional content. The argument consists of two, complementary, parts. In the first place, I will argue that evaluations are always made within a certain context, and that evaluations made within a particular context cannot be carried over to another context just like that. The second point I want to make is that welfare comparisons are not just a scientific exercise, but are (at least implicitly) used to guide public policy, e.g. for the setting of minimum income standards. Welfare is not just a metaphysical concept waiting for a measurement procedure. This puts certain constraints on the way these welfare comparisons are made, and I will suggest that the WFI approach, as it is applied by Van Praag, violates these constraints.

The fact that evaluations are always context-dependent, and the implications of this fact, are perhaps best grasped through an example. Imagine a professor talking to a student about a paper the latter has submitted. In the course of the conversation, the professor might say: "Your paper is excellent; [...] however, you should have a look at the excellent paper by Samuelson on this subject." Suppose that afterwards we ask her: "You just used the word "excellent" twice. Did it have the same meaning in those two instances?" The answer will probably be a somewhat puzzled "yes". Suppose that we then ask her: "So you think that the student's paper and Samuelson's paper are of the same academic quality?" The answer will almost certainly be "Of course not", followed by (if she is of a somewhat pedantic disposition): "What I meant was that this student's paper is very good, given the standards that are used to evaluate papers by students. In other words, it is one of the best papers by a student that I have ever seen. Samuelson's paper, on the other hand, is excellent by the standards that are used to judge the writings of leading economists. Those standards are of course much higher than the ones we employ to grade student's papers. Therefore, one might perhaps say that the papers are equally excellent within their own distinct domains, but I never implied that they are of equal quality."

I think that it is fairly self-evident that *all* evaluations are made with certain standards in mind (implicitly or explicitly), and that these standards change from one context to another. Any individual evaluating a person or a thing always takes into account what the circumstances are, what reasonably can be expected, etc. Therefore, depending on the context, any evaluative label can refer to many different degrees of the desirable or undesirable characteristic in question. To give another example, a 25-year old man may rate his health as only passing, while a 85-year old woman may declare that she is doing fine, while *at the same time both* may recognize that the young man is much healthier than the older woman. Both persons may base the evaluations of their health on comparisons with other people of the same age, and with their own situation in the recent past. There is no particular reason why the evaluation of income levels should be an exception to this general rule. Since respondents live in different situations, have different income histories, and associate with different people, it would be strange indeed if all would use the same standards when evaluating income amounts; particularly so since the IEQ *invites* them to take their own situation into account when making these evaluations. The variation in standards is not likely to be random. People with large incomes now or in the past, or whose family and friends are well-off, probably have higher standards than poorer persons. This implies that the level of welfare associated with the label 'good' is not the same for all respondents, but varies systematically over the income distribution.

The answer of Van Praag to the above argument might be that it is nothing else than a description in other words of the preference and reference processes (see section 4.5). The evaluation of income levels shifts according to a person's (recent) income history and reference group. However, Van Praag will maintain that this is not a matter of different welfare levels being evaluated by the same verbal label, but, rather, that the level of welfare that can be derived from a certain amount of income itself changes. Distinguishing welfare and the evaluation of welfare is an unnecessary complication. Should we accept this? In other words, suppose that a man who has always been poor evaluates his income of £200 per week as 'good', while another man, now living in similar circumstances and with the same income, but with a prosperous background, regards £200 per week as 'insufficient'. Should we then conclude that the welfare level of the second man is lower than that of the first one?

This question brings us to the second point. Is Van Praag's definition of welfare acceptable, or, in other words, does it conform sufficiently to the theoretical concept of welfare? As we have seen above, Van Praag regards welfare as a purely subjective phenomenon. E.g. Van Praag (1968: 3): "someone's welfare experience is a *mental* thing, and not an objective concept. The individual's welfare is exactly what the individual experiences as his welfare" [italics in original]. Otherwise, welfare is regarded as a rather vague and evasive concept (Van Praag, 1968: 1) and defined by the measurement method, which is accepted as a convention or working assumption.

As a scientific position, this is of course perfectly acceptable, since any concept can be defined in any way one likes, as long as the definition is maintained consistently. However, there are serious conceptual and normative objections against the 'mental state' conception of welfare (Sen, 1985; Griffin, 1986). This has motivated a number of writers to abandon the 'mental state' account of welfare in favor of more objective accounts of welfare. One of the more attractive conceptions is the one based on the notions of functionings and capabilities, formulated by Amartya Sen (Sen, 1985). According to Sen, a person's welfare is measured by an index of his or her capabilities. Mental states like satisfaction are at best indicators of that index of capabilities. An implication of this concept is that if two persons are in the same circumstances, have the same handicaps and skills, and earn the same income, they have the same level of welfare, even if one is more satisfied than the other[7].

As a matter of public policy (or even of private charity), I think few persons would consider an income transfer in favor of the less satisfied person to be justified, even when we believe that he is sincere when he says that he is unsatisfied with his income. That is, the welfare comparisons that are made in the context of public policy are not based on how individuals feel about or evaluate their incomes. The reason for this is not that it is difficult to acquire reliable information on how people really feel about their economic situation, or the presence of other more or less practical problems. The reason is that a different conception of welfare lies behind public policy as it is in fact pursued. The way that income transfers, support for the handicapped etc., are organized seems consistent with the capabilities conception of welfare. The obvious goal of these policy measures is to ensure that people are able to do certain things, that they can buy certain amounts of food, clothes and other consumption goods, that they can participate in certain activities. Achieving a certain level of income satisfaction does not appear to an important objective in itself.

In conclusion, the answers to the IEQ do not directly provide an interpersonally comparable measure of welfare, unless welfare is defined as a mental state. However, the welfare conception that is relevant for public policy is not a mental state one, but a more objective one, which focuses on people's 'functionings and capabilities', i.e. on what they can do and what they are. Different people make income evaluations from within different contexts, using different standards, and therefore the same (measured) level of mental or subjective welfare may correspond to different levels of actual welfare.

4 Income evaluations as indicators of a social consensus

Some authors regard the income evaluation approach as a variant of the consensual income method discussed in Chapter 2. Thus, Veit-Wilson (1987: 190) writes about the Leyden approach: "[T]he principle is clear - to try to discover if a consensus can be achieved within a country on the level of net cash income required to 'make ends meet'." In this view, the answers to the income evaluation questions are not so much seen as indicators of the respondent's level of welfare, but as expressions of his opinion about a social issue, viz. the poverty line, or the income needed to make ends meet in a certain community. In this perspective, an advantage of the income evaluation question over e.g. the Gallup question is that persons do not have to make judgments about household situations with which they may not be familiar. Furthermore, since respondents with high incomes may have only a hazy notion of how much income is needed to make ends meet, "the best approximation of a consensual poverty line achievable using this survey method is the level of income at which respondents on average claim that they are only just able to make ends meet" (Veit-Wilson, 1987: 191). Although Van Praag never uses the word 'consensual', he also compares the SPL and LPL favorably with the CSP-method (cf. chapter 8) on the grounds that the latter uses the answers of only a small subset of respondents. Flik and Van Praag (1991: 322-323), argue that "it is not democratic to discard the opinion of the richer and especially of the poorer part of the population from the information set. The whole population determines the social norm". These citations also suggest a consensual perspective.

The consensual interpretation of the income evaluation method is problematic for a number of reasons. In the first place, since the MIQ and the IEQ ask respondents about their own situation, it seems a little forced to say that any summary statistic based on these answers could reflect a consensus. As argued in section 2.1, talking about a consensus can, strictly speaking, only make sense in the context of publicly-oriented evaluations, using Barry's (1990b: 12-13) terminology. The income evaluations prompted for by the MIQ and the IEQ are clearly privately-oriented, i.e. refer only to the respondent and his or her household. Since the answers of different respondents are about different matters, it is a little beside the point to investigate whether is a consensus or not.

Secondly, it could be misleading to say that in the SPL and LPL procedures, the opinions of all respondents are taken into account. This could create the impression that, although the views of some respondents (those close to the poverty line) are taken more seriously than those of others, everyone's opinion gets some weight in the resulting SPL and LPLs. It is probably more correct to say that the SPL "reflect[s] in effect the views of a sub-set of those in the sample" (Callan et al., 1989: 91). The answers of all respondents are used in the computations, but the reason for this is that at the outset of the analysis it is of course not known at which income level there is no misperception of the poverty line. This was already phrased succinctly in the original paper by Goedhart et al. (1977: 514): "[W]e need all observations in order to find out which people's opinion on minimum income we should honor."

This point can perhaps be further elaborated, by looking at the influence that individual respondents have on the poverty threshold, e.g. the SPL. In technical terms, this influence could be defined as the first derivative of the SPL with respect to the answer to the MIQ of an individual respondent. Words like 'consensual' and 'democratic' could suggest that even when not all respondents have the same influence, they all have an influence that is at least greater than zero. That is, when a single respondent gives a higher income to the MIQ, the SPL should always increase as well, and vice versa. Actually, it can be shown that this is not true for some respondents. When a respondent with a sufficiently elevated level of income decides to give a more generous answer to the MIQ, the SPL will *decrease* a little. This is not just a theoretical possibility, or something that happens for a few outlying cases. For the 1992 SEP survey, calculations (using the simple model) show that the MIQ answers of 14.1 percent of all respondents have this seemingly perverse kind of influence on the SPL[8]. The precise level of income at which the influence becomes negative depends on a number of parameters; for a couple with no children, this occurs when their income exceeds 96,000BF per month, about 1.5 times the average income. Looking at figure 4.1, this effect can be understood intuitively by noting that when a high income respondent increases his or her income to the MIQ, the regression line (A-B) becomes steeper, and crosses the line logY = logYmin at a lower level.

Furthermore, it is easily shown that when *every* respondent gives a 1 percent higher answer to the MIQ, the SPL does not increase by 1 percent, as one might intuitively expect, but by $1/(1-b_y)$ percent, where b_y is the regression coefficient for household income in the logYmin equation. Given empirical estimates of b_y, this value amounts to 1.6 - 1.7 percent. This fact is also difficult to make sense of when the income evaluation method is seen as an adaptation of the consensual method.

In conclusion, the consensual interpretation of the income evaluation method, at least when taken rather literally, is hard to maintain. First of all, the formulation of the IEQ and the MIQ is at odds with this interpretation, since they ask explicitly for the respondent's evaluation of his own private income situation. Secondly, the SPL (as well as the LPL) does not behave as one would consensual income thresholds to do. In particular, they can go down when the answer of a single respondent increases.

5 Income evaluations as indirect measures of welfare

Having rejected the original interpretation of the income evaluation approach, according to which it provides a cardinal and interpersonally comparable measure of welfare, as well as the consensual one, the question is, what are we left with? That is, how should we interpret the income evaluation method? In my view, Osmani (1993) has suggested the most plausible account. This account starts from the premise that welfare is defined as something like the material standard of living, and thus depends only on 'objective' circumstances and income. When a person's income increases, and he gives higher answers to the IEQ and MIQ, this is not seen as an indication that his actual income needs (i.e. the income required to reach a certain level of welfare) are rising, but rather that his *perception* of his needs is changing. The preference and reference processes can no longer be regarded as descriptions of the way in which the welfare derived from a certain income level shifts when circumstances change. Instead, they are interpreted as descriptions of the way in which the perception or the experience of a certain level of welfare is colored by circumstances, including one's own welfare now and in the past, and that of one's reference group. In other words, the preference effect is reinterpreted as a perception effect. There may be some persons who do not misperceive the income they need to make ends meet, but identification of those persons will always be uncertain.

This account of the income evaluation approach has some similarities with the consensual one. But in contrast to the consensual interpretation, the answers to the MIQ and the IEQ are still regarded as respondent's private views on the income needs of his or her own household. Also, this account accepts that those views, apart from the 'perception effect' of income, are subject to a host of influences, some of which ought to be reflected in the poverty threshold (e.g. ages of children), while others should not (e.g. a rich neighborhood). In other words, there is no assumption that there is a social consensus on this matter.

This point can perhaps be further clarified by considering a slightly different but equivalent interpretation of the income evaluation approach. Here the difference, or distance, between the respondent's household income and her answer to the MIQ or the IEQ is regarded as a measure of the subjective level of welfare of the respondent. The latter is seen as a biased indicator of the real level of economic welfare, i.e. the material standard of living. The bias is due to variables such as reference groups, income history as well as more idiosyncratic factors. When estimating income thresholds and equivalence scales, it must be shown or assumed that the effects of those variables are, on average, nil or negligible. If that is not the case, the distorting factors should be included in the regression models, so that the resulting income thresholds and equivalence factors can be adjusted appropriately[9].

The difference between the interpretation put forward here and the consensual one can perhaps be clarified in the following way. In the consensual perspective, the income evaluation approach seems to be regarded as a kind of referendum or opinion poll on the issue of the poverty line (although not all opinions get the same weight in the final result). In the interpretation suggested here, the income evaluation method is more like a statistical simulation of an experiment in social psychology.

The experiment would consist of letting an individual experience a number of income levels, and recording his subjective welfare or sense of economic frustration. Where the latter reaches a certain threshold, the corresponding income level is set down as (an estimate of) the poverty line. By systematically varying other relevant characteristics and circumstances, unbiased estimates of a range of poverty lines and equivalence factors could be obtained. Repeating the exercise for a number of individuals would reduce the effects of random errors.

The procedure that is followed empirically can be seen as an attempt to achieve the same objectives through comparisons *across* individuals, i.e. through a 'natural' or ex-post facto experiment. It therefore has all the disadvantages of ex-post facto experiments, in particular that there is no guarantee that all relevant variables are adequately controlled for, possibly resulting in biased estimates[10].

The interpretation favored here can be formalized as follows: Suppose that welfare W is defined as the ratio of household income Y and household needs N, where needs N are measured by $\alpha_0 FS^{\alpha 2}$, with FS as usual standing for household size. What we want to find are estimates of the coefficients α_0 and α_2, which would enable us to make correct welfare comparisons across households of different sizes. In order to do that, we ask a sample of households the MIQ, which can be interpreted as a question after household needs N. However, a respondent's perception of her needs is biased or colored by her level of welfare, in such a way that $Y_{min} = NW^{\alpha 1}$, where Y_{min} is the answer to the MIQ. This equation incorporates the assumption that people whose income is equal to their needs have an unbiased perception of their needs, since when Y = N, it follows that $W^{\alpha 1} = 1$, and therefore $Y_{min} = N$. (Of course less primitive specifications of the 'perception process' are possible, but that would not change the basic argument.) If we now apply the usual SPL-methodology, the estimated regression equation will be:

$$\log Y_{min} = \alpha_0'(1-\alpha_2) + \alpha_1 \log Y + \alpha_2(1-\alpha_1)\log FS, \qquad (6.5)$$

where $\alpha_0' = \log(\alpha_0)$, and the estimated set of poverty lines Y^*_{min} will be: $Y^*_{min} = \alpha_0 FS^{\alpha 2} = N$. This shows that even under the new interpretation, the SPL methodology yields the 'true' poverty lines and equivalence scales. Of course, the same line of argument can be applied to the LPL.

Which interpretation is preferred has no implications for the estimation procedures that are used actually. Therefore, one might ask, is this discussion not very academic? The crucial difference between the interpretation outlined above and that of Van Praag is that subjective welfare is seen as an imperfect indicator of economic welfare, instead of as the essence of the latter. According to the WFI-approach, an individual's welfare W_i' was measured as W_i' = CNDs [log Y_i - μ_i) / σ_i], where CNDs represents the standard normal cumulative distribution function. Provided that the IEQ yielded correct estimates of μ_i and σ_i, W_i' was an unbiased measure of welfare, no matter how the values of μ_i and σ_i had come about. Consequently, the results of the income evaluation method were valid almost by definition, even if they seemed implausible. The income evaluation method could be used as a yardstick to assess the validity of other approaches to measuring economic welfare and poverty (e.g. Van Praag and Flik, 1992: 69).

In the present interpretation, this is no longer possible. Using the SPL and LPL methodology, we can still derive an interpersonally comparable measure of welfare $W_i = Y_i / N_i$ (whether this measure has cardinal or only ordinal properties is debatable), but in the new interpretation we need to assume that the bias in the perception of needs is adequately described by $W^{\alpha 1}$. If this assumption is not correct, the estimates of welfare W_i are biased. This implies that the income evaluation approach becomes one fallible method among others to measure economic welfare and poverty. Whether the results can be accepted as valid depends on whether the assumptions on which it relies are sufficiently credible. To some extent, those assumptions can be tested empirically. Ultimately, however, it is a matter of judgment, in which, inevitably, the empirical performance of the method plays an important role. When the results are inconsistent or simply very implausible, i.e. are in sharp conflict with the outcomes of other approaches, the validity of the method is called into question.

An advantage of the interpretation suggested here is that it resolves an inconsistency in the income evaluation method. If welfare can be measured by the distance between income and the answer to the MIQ or to the IEQ, then poverty is recorded when household income is below those amounts. The SPL and LPLs calculated in the usual way indicate, strictly speaking, only the average income levels below which households tend to fall into poverty. It is not clear, in the Van Praag interpretation, why they should be used to identify the poor. The logic of that interpretation seems to require that individual poverty lines (i.e. the individual answers to the MIQ or IEQ) are used for that purpose (Cf. O'Higgins, 1980, part 2: 6-7). In fact, that method is followed by Hagenaars (1985: 249); however, in most studies 'average' SPL and LPLs are used for the identification of the poor. As shown in section 5.4, the two methods produce quite different results. A large proportion of those below individual poverty lines are not below the average poverty lines, and to a lesser extent the reverse is also true. In the interpretation proposed here, the use of 'average' SPL and LPLs is no longer inconsistent, since the answers to the MIQ and IEQ are not seen as direct measures of the respondent's income needs, but only as perceptions of those needs, which are prone to systematic and random errors. The procedure followed, including regression and averaging, is supposed to cancel out those errors.

6 Reliability and validity of the answers to the MIQ and IEQ

Having concluded that the validity of the income evaluation approach must at least partly be assessed by how the method works in practice, let us review the empirical results, focusing on those results that can tell us something about the reliability and validity of the method. In the first place, response rates to the MIQ and IEQ in the SEP are quite high. In face-to-face interviews, almost all respondents give answers to the MIQ and IEQ, and relatively few of those answers are inconsistent or outside of reasonable bounds. However, in a mail survey, i.e. when unprompted by interviewers, a substantial minority of respondents do not answer the IEQ, or only for one level. By contrast, response to the MIQ drops only a little in the mail survey, suggesting that respondents find the MIQ easier to answer than the IEQ. More than half of the amounts given are multiples of 10,000 BF (per month, equivalent to about £200), most of the rest are multiples of 5000 BF. This degree of rounding suggests that the average SEP respondent does not have a very precise idea of the income amounts asked for in the MIQ and IEQ.

The reliability of logYmin (the logarithm of the answer to the MIQ) and of μ (the logarithm of the geometric average of the IEQ amounts) is quite high. This is indicated by the high correlation between μ and logYmin at a single point in time, and also by the substantial correlations (0.5 - 0.7) between observations of μ and logYmin in subsequent waves of the SEP (which are separated by three or four years). Reliability estimates are higher for μ than for logYmin, but the difference is small. On the other hand, results suggest that the reliability of σ, which measures the dispersion of the IEQ amounts around μ per respondent, is quite low. In the original 'Van Praag' interpretation of the IEQ, σ is supposed to measure the sensitivity of subjective welfare to income changes. However, the results suggest that most of the variance of σ is random error.

How valid are the answers to the MIQ and IEQ? In other words, do they measure what they are supposed to measure, which is an evaluation of income levels from the point of view of the standard of living they would allow the respondent's household to have? The distance between those answers and household income can be seen as a measure of the subjective welfare of the respondent. Though, ultimately, it is perhaps a matter of faith, to a certain extent the validity of a measure can be tested by looking at its correlations with other variables. If those correlations are in the expected directions, a measure is said to have construct validity. In the case of the answers to the MIQ and the IEQ, we expect them to be related both to cost variables and reference variables. Cost variables are variables that affect the material standard of living (real welfare) than can be achieved with a given amount of income, such as household size, ages of children and home tenure. Reference variables (perhaps better called perception variables) are variables that influence the perception of the income needs for a particular standard of living. Foremost among these is household income itself, but incomes in the social environment could also be important.

These expectations are fulfilled to a considerable extent. The empirical analysis has shown that the main determinants of the answers to the MIQ and the IEQ are household income, the number of adults, the number and ages of children, home tenure, and region. Otherwise, perhaps the most significant and surprising result of the detailed investigations is that few other variables have much of an effect. Employment status, i.e. whether the adults in the household are in paid employment, which could be regarded as both a cost and a reference variable, was found to have no impact whatsoever. Other variables which could serve as proxies for the income in the social environment, such as education and age of the head of household, had very limited and unstable effects. Also, the effect of home tenure is much smaller than expected. The answers of tenants and mortgage paying homeowners are higher than those of mortgage-free homeowners, but the differences are fairly small, and do not match by far the actual expenses on rent or mortgage payments.

Part of the explanation of the unsatisfactory results regarding home tenure lies no doubt in the ambiguity of the phrase 'in your circumstances' which appears both in the MIQ and the IEQ. Does this mean 'living in your present home' or does the respondent have to consider moving to other (cheaper) housing? This points to the wider ambiguity of the income evaluation questions. Do they ask for the income amounts that are 'sufficient' or are needed to 'make ends meet' given the current lifestyle of the household, or for the most Spartan style of life feasible in present society, or for something else yet? No doubt, respondents have different understandings of the MIQ and IEQ in this respect (cf. Garner and De Vos, 1995).

Another problem with the income evaluation questions in their present format is that a single respondent acts as spokesperson for the whole household. The possibility that members of the same household may hold different views about its income needs appears never to have been considered. A basic assumption is that all persons within the same household have the same level of welfare, since the income evaluation approach breaks down if there is unequal distribution of welfare within households. Moreover, even if all members enjoy the same level of welfare, they may still have different perceptions of need, for instance if they have different income histories. To some extent, these worries are relieved by the finding for the 1992 wave of the SEP that the answers to the MIQ and IEQ were not systematically related to the sex of the respondent. This means that results are probably not seriously biased by the choice of respondent. A related problem is the demarcation of the household in the mind of the respondent. An analysis of the answers to the MIQ and IEQ in households where one or more adult children were living with their parents produced inconsistent results, suggesting that the costs and incomes of those children are taken into account insufficiently by the respondent.

Other problems are raised by the important effect of the region in Belgium where the household lives. Flemish respondents give lower answers to the MIQ and IEQ than their Walloon counterparts living in otherwise similar circumstances, and in the case of the MIQ the difference increases over time. The most plausible interpretation is that the words and phrases used in the French and Dutch versions of the income evaluation questions have slightly different meanings. This suggestion is reinforced by the fact that the Dutch, but not the French wording of the MIQ in the SEP questionnaire was changed between 1985 and 1988. The IEQ remained unchanged in both versions. A first implication of this interpretation is that it highlights the importance of keeping the wording of the MIQ and IEQ exactly the same if one wants to obtain comparable results. At the same time, the comparability of the results of the income evaluation approach across different languages is put into doubt. More fundamentally, the finding that seemingly insignificant changes in the wording of the question can have a large impact on the answers, raises questions about the meaning and validity of the results of the income evaluation approach. These issues will be taken up below.

7 Validity of the equivalence scales produced by the income evaluation approach: why are they so flat?

Introduction

In section 5.4 we have seen that the answers to the MIQ and IEQ in the Belgian SEP produce equivalence scales that are rather flat, i.e. the income needs of families do not increase much with rising family size. This is a general feature of the income evaluation method, though it is important to note that it does not always occur. In some countries, such as Ireland and Italy, but also in Denmark and Sweden, and, according to some studies, even in Belgium and The Netherlands (see section 4.3), the method results in fairly steep equivalence scales. Nevertheless, most other equivalence scales, whether derived from data on consumption behavior or proposed by experts, are much steeper than those based on answers to the MIQ and IEQ.

The question whether the equivalence scales from income evaluation method are valid, that is whether they correctly indicate the income levels where households or families of various sizes enjoy the same standard of living, is obviously of great importance. The distribution of poverty risks in the population depends strongly on the equivalence scale of the poverty line. Given the interpretation put forward in the previous sections, which says that the income evaluation questions do not provide a direct measure of welfare, but only an indirect and potentially biased one, we cannot take the position that the income evaluation approach is inherently superior to other methods.

Unfortunately, there is no secure yardstick against which to assess the validity of the MIQ and IEQ equivalence scales. While other methods usually result in steeper scales, each has its own problems and uncertainties. Budget standards rely on normative judgments and choices by researchers, and the results are not necessarily in agreement with the actual behavior and preferences of households. Equivalence scale estimates derived from actual consumption behavior of households appear to be rather sensitive to the specification that is used. 'Political' equivalence scales that are incorporated in income transfer programs are often of obscure origins, and moreover, are influenced by policy considerations of various kinds. The motivation for 'expert' equivalence scales, such as the OECD-scale, is often no better than that they seem reasonable.

By contrast with the budget, political and expert methods, the income evaluation approach has the advantage that it is based on the views of a random sample of the population. Compared with the analysis of consumption behavior, the income evaluation approach has the advantage that it is technically simple and straightforward, and also that the results are remarkably stable over time, and also across different model specifications[11].

Yet, nagging doubts remain, and many observers find that it simply contradicts plain common sense to maintain that the costs of a child of primary school age are less than one-eighth of those of a single adult, as implied by the SPL and LPL scales. It is therefore useful to consider possible reasons why the income evaluation method produces equivalence scales that are so much flatter than other ones. In the next subsection, I will discuss hypotheses which focus on shifts in preferences regarding household consumption of various kinds. The third subsection considers the hypothesis that the results of the income evaluation method are distorted by reference group effects. The fourth subsection discusses the possibility that respondents do not include family allowances in their answers to the MIQ and IEQ. Subsection five is about the hypothesis that those answers are 'regressed to the mean' because respondents are influenced by what they regard as a reasonable income. Subsection six sums up.

Shifts in preferences regarding household consumption

Under this heading I want to discuss a number of explanations which focus on the possibilities of changes and shifts in household consumption, which are presumably taken account of in the equivalence scale produced by the income evaluation method but not in other ones. In the first place, it could be argued that traditional equivalence scales, like the so-called 'Oxford scale' appear to be mainly based on food consumption, where economies of scale are rather low. Modern households may spend a larger part of their budget on housing, energy and transport by car, where there is greater scope for economies of scale. Yet, modern budget standards, which also reflect those changes in budget shares, still result in much steeper equivalence factors than the income evaluation method. (E.g. Bradshaw, 1993: 176: "The couple with two children aged 10 and 16 needs to spend 43 percent more than a couple if child care costs and housing costs are excluded." If those costs are included, they must spend 52 percent more.)

A second explanation focuses on shifts in preferences and life-style consequent on changes in family size. It is expressed well by Goedhart et al. (1977: 516):

> "Although we recognize that the life-style and preferences change drastically when a family size changes from one to two or from two to three, our small estimates of the increase in needs reflect the fact that the preferences within the family shift in such a way that material needs do not increase very much. For example, a two-person family (husband and wife) may be accustomed to a life-style which includes relatively high holiday expenditures. When the first child is born, the parents decide to spend their holidays at home, thus saving money which may be used to compensate for the additional expenditures caused by the increase in family size. In our opinion, substitution possibilities of this kind are not fully taken account in current literature on the family equivalence scale."

It is clear that such changes in consumption behavior are very common. However, assuming for the moment that those substitution effects are indeed responsible for the flatness of the income evaluation equivalence scales, it is less clear what this means for the interpretation of those scales. At least two interpretations are possible. In the first one, the birth of a child changes the relative prices of consumption goods (e.g. holidays abroad vs. holidays at home), and also involves some direct expense. The increase in income indicated by the MIQ or IEQ equivalence scale is sufficient to bring the parents back to the indifference curve in the consumption goods space where they were before the child was born. To state this otherwise, suppose that the total consumption of the family with a child could be split up between consumption of the child and consumption of the parents. Then, if the consumption package of the parents (after an increase in income according to the MIQ or IEQ equivalence factor) were to be given to the childless couple, the latter would not feel worse off than before. This implies that their material welfare has not changed. This is probably the interpretation that Goedhart et al. had in mind.

Another interpretation of the change in consumption behavior, which in my view is no less plausible, is that the couple with the child ends up on a lower indifference curve (in the space of consumption goods and services), but that the pleasure derived from spending time with their child compensates for the loss in material welfare. Thus, in an indirect way the contribution of children to well-being is endogenized (Bradbury, 1989), i.e. the presence of children itself increases the respondent's feeling of well-being. Because they have found other sources of well-being, people with children can be satisfied with a lower level of material welfare[12]. In fact, such a dampening of material aspirations could happen even without substitution effects. The level of income needed to make ends meet is after all a matter of social expectations. Perhaps people are simply prepared to give up part of their material welfare in order to have children. A third interpretation might be that the care for the child simply robs the couple from time and opportunities to spend money. In that case too, their material welfare decreases, although there may not be a compensating increase in child-derived well-being[13].

Which interpretation is the correct one has important implications for the validity of the MIQ and IEQ equivalence scales. If the increase in income indicated by the MIQ or IEQ equivalence factor allows the parents to reach the same level of material welfare as they were on before the birth of the child, those scales are valid. However, if they partially reflect a dampening of aspirations, the SPL and LPL equivalence factors do not represent the same level of material welfare for all household types, and in that sense they would be biased. This does not make them necessarily invalid for all purposes, however. The rejection of a subjective, or 'mental' concept of welfare was at least partly motivated by the idea that changes in aspirations are often unconscious processes, caused by influences beyond the individual's control. People should not be 'punished' by being assigned a lower income threshold, just because their subjective needs have diminished as a result of living in a poor social environment. This objection loses at least some of its force when people voluntarily adjust their income needs, as result of a deliberate choice, and being fully aware of the consequences. The latter description (hopefully) now often pertains to the decision to get children. If people genuinely feel that their own material needs are less great while they are caring for children, it may not be inappropriate to use an equivalence scale which reflects those feelings.

A final point is that the scenario sketched by Goedhart et al. may be realistic for well-to-do couples, but that those kind of adjustments are probably more difficult or impossible for low-income couples. If that supposition were correct, one would expect that among low-income families, the answer to the MIQ is more sensitive to differences in family size than is the case for high income families, resulting in a steeper equivalence scale for the first group. In technical terms, this implies that there is interaction between the household size variables and household income in regressions of the answers to the MIQ and IEQ. As we have seen, however, (section 5.3) the results of analyses using such interaction terms indicated that, if anything, the opposite was true: the effect of children increased with household income.

A third explanation brings up the possibility of substitution of consumption between different periods in life. It could be argued that the flat equivalence scale reflects the saving behavior patterns of families over the life-cycle. Assuming that earnings can be expected to rise moderately during a person's working life, it makes sense for families to save before children are born, to dissave and/or borrow while they are raising children, and to save again after the children have left home, in order to maintain as much as possible a constant material standard of living across the life-cycle. Assuming those savings are seen as necessary expenses, they would be included in the answers to the MIQ and IEQ. The estimated equivalence scales would then reflect only unanticipated costs of children. (This might explain why older children are apparently so much more expensive than babies and toddlers.) This argument is ingenious, but perhaps presupposes more long-term planning by families than is realistic. At present, empirical data, which could confirm or falsify it, are lacking.

Distortions due to reference group effects

Bradbury (1989: 400) argues that the equivalence scales resulting from the income evaluation method are distorted due to reference group effects. He writes: "equivalence scales derived using these attitudinal methods will only be valid if reference group effects are independent of family composition." Reference group effects are supposed to include a variety of extraneous influences upon people's answers. He goes on:

> "Such effects may well be responsible for the discord between the equivalence scales generated by the attitudinal approach and those attained by other means. The overall lack of responsiveness of the

> attitudinal scales to family size may reflect some tendency for families to judge their standard of living relative to other families of the same composition. If this were entirely the case, the equivalence scale would be equal to unity for all groups."

The latter statement, however, is true under only exceptional circumstances. In fact, given the actual distribution of income across families, reference groups consisting only of families of the same composition would more likely lead to an *upward* bias in the estimated equivalence scale.

This can be shown as follows. Suppose that the 'true' model of μ can be written as (an adaptation of equation 4.18):

$$\mu_i = \beta_0 + \beta_1 \log Y_i + \beta'_2(1 - \beta_1)\log FS_i + \beta_3(\log M_i - \beta'_2 \log HS_i) + \varepsilon \qquad (6.6)$$

where β'_2 is the elasticity of the 'true' equivalence scale with respect to household size, M_i is the geometric mean of the incomes in the reference group of household i, HS_i is the geometric mean household size in the reference group, and thus $(\log M_i - \beta'_2 \log HS_i)$ represents average welfare in the reference group. Suppose that we can formalize Bradbury's hypothesis as follows:

$$HS_i = FS_i$$
$$\log M_i = h \log FS_i$$

where h is an auxiliary coefficient. The formalization is restrictive only in that it imposes a log-linear relation between average income and household size. If we would then estimate the following regression equation:

$$\mu_i = b_0 + b_1 \log Y_i + b_2 \log FS_i + e,$$

The expected values of the regression coefficients are:

$$E(b_1) = \beta_1$$
$$E(b_2) = \beta'_2(1 - \beta_1 - \beta_3) + \beta_3 h,$$

and the estimated value of the equivalence scale elasticity is (ignoring sample variance):

$$b_2/(1 - b_1) = \beta'_2 + \beta_3(h - \beta'_2) / (1 - \beta_1), \qquad (6.7)$$

where the term after the + sign on the right hand side indicates the bias. This bias can be both upwards or downwards, depending on the relative sizes of h and β'_2. The estimated equivalence scale becomes a constant across family types (i.e. the equivalence scale elasticity is zero) only if $h <= 0$[14]. In fact, in Belgium (as is true for most OECD countries), income is strongly and positively related to family size. This would imply that the reference group mechanism posited by Bradbury induces an upward bias into the equivalence scales produced by the income evaluation method, i.e. those scales are too steep rather than too flat. In other words, because the average standard of living increases with rising family size, a situation where reference groups are composed only of people living in families with the same composition would inflate the answers of respondents with large families, and deflate the answers of those with small families.

Of course, even if the particular hypothesis of Bradbury cannot explain the flatness of the SPL and LPL equivalence scales, it remains true that reference group effects may distort those scales. However, it is difficult to think of a scenario where they could produce a serious downward bias in estimated costs of children. Furthermore, in a study where empirical measures of reference group incomes were used, the estimated equivalence scales were not steeper than usual (Muffels et al., 1990: 170; cf. table 4.A1, rows 20i-j). It seems therefore unlikely that reference group effects can be an important part of the explanation of why the income evaluation method results in flat equivalence scales.

Discounting of family allowances by respondents

O'Higgins (1980) has proposed an explanation of a more technical nature, which focuses on the way people take account of family allowances when answering the MIQ and IEQ. O'Higgins (1980: 19), commenting on results in Van Praag et al. (1980), noted that:

> "countries with the most generous levels of child support (Belgium, France and the UK) have the lowest equivalence scales implied in their national poverty lines [SPL and LPLs]. Conversely, Italy and Ireland, with the lowest levels of child support, have the highest equivalence scales."

O'Higgins argues that these results:

> "strongly suggest that the equivalence scales implied in people's responses to the poverty question reflect a discounting by respondents of existing levels of state child support provision."

That is, respondents in effect do not regard them as part of net household income, but as a partial refunding of the costs of children. (In the same way that, at least in Belgium, reimbursements of medicine bills are not seen as part of net income.) In order to obtain the 'true' households minimum income needed to make ends meet, according to the income concept used by researchers, family allowances should be added to the recorded answer to the MIQ.

In Belgium, where child allowances are quasi-universal, this hypothesis is hard to test empirically with the available data. (A way would be to ask additional questions after the MIQ, such as 'Did you take account of child allowances in your answer?') Nevertheless, excluding child allowances from the answers to the MIQ and IEQ is unlikely to be a general phenomenon. Before the MIQ and IEQ are asked, respondents are reminded that family allowances are part of net household income. The regression results for perceived income show that most respondents do indeed include them in their estimate of total household income.

Furthermore, results of the income evaluation method obtained in later studies do not display the clear pattern in the equivalence scales that emerged in the results of Van Praag et al. (1980), as noted by O'Higgins. For instance, in Hagenaars (1985), the equivalence scale elasticities are as follows: Ireland: 0.24, Italy: 0.25, France: 0.22, Belgium: 0.21. More generally, comparing the results on equivalence scales reported in table 4.A1 with the ranking of countries in terms of the generosity of the child benefit package according to Bradshaw et al. (1993: 265), does not reveal any clear pattern. Certainly, the equivalence scales in countries where child benefits are meager or absent (the USA, Ireland, Italy) are not systematically steeper compared with those in countries with generous child benefits (Belgium, France, Luxembourg).

'Regression to the mean' of answers to the MIQ

Another hypothesis which could explain the flatness of the equivalence scale resulting from the income evaluation method is that respondents are influenced by what they regard as a 'reasonable' income level. That is, suppose that the 'true' minimum income of a single person is 30,000 BF per month. Then, if one were to follow the modified OECD equivalence scale, the 'true' minimum income of a two-adult family with three children would be 72,000 BF. A respondent in the latter kind of family might feel that 72,000 BF per month is an unreasonably high amount for a minimum income, and state '60,000' in answer to the Minimum Income Question. At the same time, a single person may regard 30,000 as a rather low income, and give '35,000' as an answer.

To put this more generally, the assumption is that respondents have a conception of what constitutes a 'reasonable income', which is independent of the size of the household that has to live from it, and that this conception affects their answers to the MIQ and the IEQ. What people regard as a reasonable income will be influenced by their own income history, as well as by the incomes in the wider social environment. I have called this (hypothetical) effect 'regression to the mean', since it will tend to draw all responses towards the mean value (although otherwise it has little relationship with the statistical phenomenon known as regression to the mean). The hypothesis clearly has similarities with the reference group effect hypothesized by Kapteyn (1977) and others (see section 4.5). The important difference is that here it is assumed that respondents only consider other people's incomes and not the sizes of their families, thus ignoring the actual standard of living those income allow people to have.

What are the implications of regression to the mean for the estimated equivalence scale? In order to be able to see those, I use the following formalization of the hypothesis:

$$\begin{aligned} Ymin &= Y^*min(Yr/Y^*min)^{\phi}\,\varepsilon && 0 < \phi < 1 \\ Y^*min &= \alpha_0(Y/FS^{\alpha_2})^{\alpha_1}\,FS^{\alpha_2} && 0 < \alpha_1 < 1, 0 < \alpha_2 < 1 \\ Yr &= \eta_0 Y^{\eta_1} M^{(1-\eta_1)} && 0 < \eta_1 <= 1 \end{aligned} \qquad (6.8)$$

where Ymin represents the actual answer to the MIQ, Y*min the 'true' value of minimum income, Yr the income level regarded as reasonable, Y actual household income, FS household size, M average income in the population and ε a random disturbance term. Thus, a respondent's conception of what constitutes a reasonable income is supposed to be a weighted function of his own income and average income in the population. Taking logarithms and substituting for Y*min and Yr, we obtain the following equation:

$$\log Ymin = (1 - \phi)\alpha_0 + \phi\log\eta_0 + [\alpha_1 + \phi(\eta_1 - \alpha_1)]\log Y$$

$$+ (1 - \phi)(1 - \alpha_1)\alpha_2 \log FS + \phi(1 - \eta_1)\log M + \log\varepsilon. \qquad (6.9)$$

Suppose we would estimate the standard regression equation logYmin = $a_0 + a_1\log Y + a_2\log FS$. Then (ignoring sampling variation), a_1 could both be biased upwards or downwards as an estimate of α_1, depending on the relative sizes of η_1 and α_1. By contrast, a_2 is unambiguously biased towards zero as an estimate of $(1 - \alpha_1)\alpha_2$. The estimate of the equivalence scale elasticity would be

$$a_2/(1 - a_1) = \alpha_2\{[(1 - \phi)(1 - \alpha_1)/[1 - \alpha_1 - \phi(\eta_1 - \alpha_1)]\}. \qquad (6.10)$$

The expression between curly brackets represents the proportional size of the bias in $a_2/(1 - a_1)$ as an estimate of α_2 (the 'true' equivalence scale elasticity). Given the assumptions about the parameters, the numerator of that expression is always smaller than the denominator, unless $\eta_1 = 1$. Thus, the bias is always downwards, unless respondents' conception of a reasonable income is influenced only by their own incomes. In the latter case, the coefficient for household income is overestimated, and that for household size is underestimated, but the estimate of the equivalence scale is unbiased. Otherwise, the bias can be substantial; e.g. when $\eta_1 = \alpha_1$, its proportional size is simply $(1 - \phi)$.

Unfortunately, at present there are no data which would allow an empirical test of the regression to the mean hypothesis. In any case, it might be difficult to distinguish regression to the mean from a reference group effect.

Provisional conclusion

The income evaluation approach tends to produce equivalence scales that are rather flat, i.e. the income needs of families do not increase much with rising family size. Most other equivalence scales, whether derived from data on consumption behavior or proposed by experts, are much steeper. The distribution of poverty risks in the population depends strongly on the equivalence scale of the poverty line, and it is therefore crucial that the latter is valid and unbiased. However, none of the other methods to estimate equivalence scales provides a secure yardstick against which to assess the validity of the MIQ and IEQ equivalence scales; each has its own problems and uncertainties. In some respects the income evaluation method is arguably superior to the other ones. By contrast with those derived from the budget, political and expert methods, the MIQ and IEQ equivalence scales have the advantage that they are based on the views of a random sample of the population. Compared with the analysis of consumption behavior, the income evaluation approach has the advantage that it is technically simple and straightforward, and also that the results are remarkably stable over time, and also across different model specifications.

Yet, doubts about the MIQ and IEQ equivalence scales remain. It is therefore important to try to understand why those scales are so much flatter than other ones. The preceding subsections discussed four hypotheses: substitution effects, reference group effects, discounting of family allowances and regression to the mean. Empirical and analytical results indicate that it is unlikely that reference group effects are responsible for the flatness of the MIQ and IEQ equivalence scales, while discounting of family allowances does probably not occur on an extensive scale. There are no data which could confirm or otherwise the 'regression to the mean' hypothesis. At this point in the analysis, substitution effects in conjunction with dampening of aspirations regarding the material standard of living concurrent with the birth of children, seem the most likely explanation of the low cost of children according to the income evaluation method.

As noted, this might imply that the SPL and LPL equivalence factors do not represent the same level of material welfare for all household types, and in that sense would be biased. It was argued, though, that if people genuinely feel that their own material needs are less great while they are caring for children, it may not be inappropriate for some purposes to use an equivalence scale which reflects those feelings. However, when one wants to compare the material standard of living of households of various sizes, the equivalence scales produced by the income evaluation method may be misleading, and they should be used with caution in poverty studies.

This conclusion is preliminary, since in chapter seven we will see that the seemingly related income satisfaction method leads to very steep equivalence scales. Reasons for this discrepancy will be discussed in that chapter, and final conclusions will be drawn in the concluding chapter 8.

8 Validity and usefulness of the SPL and LPL income thresholds

Introduction

The income thresholds that are derived from the income evaluation method are called Subjective Poverty Line (SPL) and Leyden Poverty Line (LPL). In the previous section I have discussed the question whether the equivalence scales incorporated in these thresholds are valid and unbiased. In this section the focus is on the level of the thresholds. The first issue considered is whether these income thresholds are valid as poverty lines (subsection two). The third subsection deals with the question of the comparability across time and across countries of the SPL and LPL. Finally, there is a brief discussion of the question which method is to be preferred (if one has to make the choice): the SPL or the LPL?

Validity

Regarding the level of the thresholds, the issue of validity boils down to the question whether these income amounts can properly be called (Subjective or Leyden) Poverty Lines. Two objections can be made to that assertion. The first is that the MIQ and IEQ do not ask for the income needed to stay out of poverty. It is not self-evident that the level of income needed to make ends meet (SPL), or that is midway between the income levels that are insufficient and sufficient (LPL0.5), is equal to the poverty line. It is possible that when asked, many people would put the income required just to escape poverty somewhere below the income needed to make ends meet. The second, and related, objection is that the SPL and LPL0.5 income thresholds are in most cases simply too generous to be realistically called poverty lines. Even in the richest countries of the E.U., the percentage of persons below the SPL or LPL0.5 can be as high as 15 or 20 percent or even more. It is straining the meaning of the word to maintain that all those persons are living in poverty. As argued in chapter 1, poverty cannot be defined in any way one likes. Its technical definition in research should not stray too far from the everyday meaning of the word.

Both of these points are valid objections, but on the other hand, not too much should be made of them. For many people, the word poverty evokes images of total distress and deprivation. The social scientific use of the word does not have to follow those connotations. What is necessary is that it is applied to situations that are generally regarded as in some way problematic, and that we as a community would want to change through some form of public policy, at least in principle if not immediately here and now. In that sense the SPL and LPL0.5 income thresholds used in the Belgian SEP are probably not too generous, although they are on the border. Few persons would deny, I think, that most households below those thresholds have a difficult time making ends meet. Also, a comparison with income thresholds derived from the budget method shows that the difference is not very large. It is of course possible to use a less charged term, such as 'low income', instead of 'poverty', but that seems to me to be a bit insipid. Implicitly or explicitly, research on so-called low income situations addresses itself to the normative concerns associated with poverty. Without those concerns the research would probably not have been undertaken (and would certainly attract less attention). In my view it is more honest to face up to the challenge of developing an operational definition of poverty. Such operational definitions can of course never be perfect. They always remain conventions, research instruments used to reveal certain social conditions, and discarded when something better is found. Thus, it does not seem inappropriate to call the SPL and LPL poverty lines, as long as their limitations are kept in mind.

The SPL and LPL cannot be regarded as *the* poverty line, if only because results suggest that the level of those income thresholds can be strongly influenced by small changes in the wording of the MIQ or IEQ. As reported in chapter 5, in Flanders the real value of the SPL dropped by 10 percent, relative to the LPL0.5, between 1985 and 1992, and this was probably caused by some seemingly insignificant changes in the wording of the Dutch version of the MIQ. While 10 percent may not seem very dramatic, the resulting drop in the poverty rate approaches 20 percent. Also, in actual income transfer policy, a 10 percent rise or drop means a great deal. Presenting a particular outcome of the SPL as 'the income level that the population says is needed to make ends meet' (let alone as *the* poverty line) seems a little rash when the addition or deletion of little words like 'just' or 'minimum' to the MIQ would produce a significantly lower or higher income threshold.

Comparability across time and countries

Does the income evaluation method produce income thresholds and low income rates that, even if they cannot always be described as poverty lines and poverty rates, are at least comparable across time and across countries? Let us consider the issue of cross-time comparability first.

An obvious, but important remark is that it is absolutely crucial that exactly the same wording of the income evaluation questions is maintained over time. Some empirical results suggest strongly that seemingly insignificant changes in the wording of the MIQ can have a substantial impact on the results. However, even when the wording of the questions is unchanged, the evolution in the thresholds is sometimes difficult to make sense of. For instance, I found a fairly small but significant drop (before adjustment for prices) in the LPL0.5 in the SEP between 1985 and 1988, producing a 27 percent decrease in the number of persons below that threshold. It is hard to think of any technical or substantive reason for this drop. Also, Aalbers et al. (1990: 16), using five waves of the Dutch Socio-Economic Panel, find that the most advanced models "produce poverty lines [SPL and LPL] which vary with time in an implausible manner". Similar drastic changes in the SPL are reported by Van den Bosch et al. (1993: 241-242) for Luxembourg (from 66 to 55 percent of median income between 1985 and 1986) and Ireland. Extended time-series for the SPL and LPL are unavailable, unfortunately, so nothing can be said about the behavior of the SPL or LPL in the long term.

A more theoretical problem is that even when strange jumps are absent, SPLs and LPLs that are calculated or each year separately will not, in general, represent the same material standard of living in all years (unless by accident they were to move parallel with the consumer price index). One could argue that the deviations of the SPL and LPL from the consumer price index reflect changes in the material aspirations of the population. Even supposing that movements in the SPL and LPL are reliable indicators of those changes (which is supposing a great deal), it is doubtful that one wants to use poverty lines which are sensitive to shifts in aspiration levels.

The problems of cross-time comparability are compounded for cross-country comparisons of the results of the income evaluation method. In most cases, different organizations are responsible for the surveys, leading to deviations in questionnaire design, and interviewing procedures, and making it difficult to make sure that the wording of the MIQ and IEQ is exactly the same in all countries (cf. Garner and De Vos, 1995). Most importantly, of course, different countries mostly use different languages, making the goal of exact equivalence of wording rather elusive. Assuming that 'making ends meet', 'de eindjes aan elkaar knopen' (Dutch) and 'joindre les deux bouts' (French) have the same meaning in standard-of-living terms seems rather heroic. Of course, they will mean roughly the same thing in all countries. The question is at which point roughly becomes too rough. The finding that in 1985 the SPL in The Netherlands was almost 20 percent below the Belgian SPL (Van den Bosch et al., 1993: 240), even though median disposable household income in The Netherlands was higher, producing a 16 percent-point difference in low income rates, suggests that that point is sometimes exceeded.

According to Van Praag et al. (1982: 357) poverty ratios based on the income evaluation method "do not merely reflect income differences, but differences in aspiration levels between countries as well." One might add that they are also influenced by differences in the meaning of words, questionnaire design, etc.. More importantly perhaps, it is totally unclear what kind of factors are behind those differences in aspiration levels. History, the level of collective services, the importance attached to material possessions in the popular culture, the degree at which current norms prescribe modesty in one's demands, and a host of other variables may play a role. Even where the results are less implausible than in the Belgo-Dutch example just quoted, the uncertainty about the interpretation of the changes across time and the differences across countries which makes the SPL and LPL income thresholds difficult to use. By contrast, relative standards (e.g. 50 percent of median income) may be less valid in principle, but the transparency of the method makes it much easier for the researcher to explain changes and differences in the results of that method. The SPL and LPL could be used for the limited goal of making comparisons of what income is regarded in various countries as the level below which households tend to start to have financial difficulties. However, for this purpose the consensual income method, e.g. the Gallup question is better suited, since it is conceptually and computationally much more straightforward.

SPL or LPL?

Suppose a researcher wants to use the income evaluation approach to estimate a poverty line, but because of constraints on interviewing time can only add a single question to the questionnaire, i.e. either the MIQ or the IEQ. Should she choose the former or the latter, i.e. opt for the SPL or for the LPL? Flik and Van Praag (1991: 321) argue that the LPL is superior to the SPL. First of all,

> "the SPL is likely to be more subject to random response fluctuations and more sensitive to varying interpretations of the one level. The answers to several ordered verbal labels may be expected to be much more carefully selected and calibrated as one has to rank several levels than when the respondent is offered just one level, i.e., 'make ends meet'."

Also, in a summary measure like μ (the log of the geometric mean of an individual's answers to the IEQ) any remaining random response errors will tend to cancel each other out. In short, the LPL is much more reliable than the SPL. A second argument of Flik and Van Praag is that the LPL method is more flexible, since it enables the researcher to set poverty lines at any welfare level, while the SPL is limited to a single income threshold.

Regarding the reliability argument, we have seen that reliability estimates for μ based on the Belgian SEP are somewhat higher than those for logYmin (the logarithm of the answer to the MIQ). Also, standard errors of the LPL were smaller than those of the SPL. In both cases, the difference was not large, though. In favor of the SPL is the finding that response rates are higher for the MIQ than for the IEQ, in particular in the mail survey, indicating that respondents find the first question easier to answer.

The LPL methodology is more flexible than the SPL one, in that income thresholds can be calculated for any welfare level. According to Van Praag, the welfare level to which the poverty lines should correspond is in principle a political choice, to be made by politicians. To my knowledge, no politician has ever publicly indicated his or her preference for a particular welfare level in terms of a number between zero and one. Perhaps, not being well versed in the underlying theory, politicians find those WFI numbers too abstract. In practice, LPLs have been mostly calculated for welfare levels 0.5 and 0.4. The LPL0.5 seems an obvious choice, not only because it is located at the midpoint of the scale, but mainly since it is in the middle between the incomes regarded as 'sufficient' and 'insufficient', respectively. In words, the LPL0.5 might be described as the income level that is 'just barely sufficient'. The LPL0.4, by contrast, is some distance below the income deemed 'insufficient', which, in my view, is an odd choice for a poverty line. How far the LPL0.4 is below the LPL0.5 in income terms depends on the parameter σ, which measures the dispersion of the individual's responses around their average μ. As suggested above, however, it is doubtful whether σ points to any substantive characteristic of respondents. Moreover, the use of the number

0.4, suggesting that the LPL0.4 represents 80 percent of the welfare of the LPL0.5, makes sense only when the IEQ provides a cardinal measure of welfare. The claim of cardinality rests upon two more specific assumptions, which were consistently rejected in empirical tests (cf. section 6.2). Therefore, calculating an LPL at the welfare level 0.4 is at best only a little less arbitrary than simply taking 75 or 80 percent of the LPL0.5 as a rough indicator of a 'more strict' poverty line.

Overall, then, the hypothetical researcher mentioned above might be inclined to adopt the IEQ because of the greater reliability of the LPL. However, not much would be lost if the greater simplicity of the MIQ would make her choose that question instead.

9 Conclusion: interpretation, validity and usefulness of the income evaluation approach

Interpretation

The original interpretation of the income evaluation approach is that it provides a cardinal and interpersonally comparable measure of welfare. Since in this interpretation poverty is defined as a situation of low welfare, the income evaluation method is also eminently suitable for measuring poverty. Welfare is measured as a function of the proportional difference between household income and the answer to the IEQ[15]. Empirically, it turns out that the answers to the IEQ rise strongly with increasing income; estimated elasticities vary from 0.3 to 0.7. In Van Praag's terminology, this finding reflects the 'preference effect': as income rises, so do one's standards, and some of the income gain is not transformed in an increase in welfare. A person's welfare, in this perspective, depends not only on her objective circumstances, characteristics and income, but also on her aspirations, which are shaped by her income history and also by the incomes in her reference group. This would imply that two persons living in the same situation and having the same income, may enjoy quite different levels of welfare, even though their material standard of living is the same.

This concept of welfare is clearly inconsistent with the welfare conception implicit in public policy. A feeling of being subjectively worse off while the material standard of living is the same, even when this feeling is quite sincere, is not generally perceived as a justification for an income transfer. For this reason, many writers have argued against a mental state account of welfare, and in favor of more 'objective' ones, such as the one developed by Sen, using the notions of functionings and capabilities. In this conception, welfare is an index of what a person is and does, or of what she could be and do. Her feelings regarding the adequacy of her income are at best one of many elements in this, and probably a rather minor one. The income evaluation approach does not provide a measure of this more material or objective concept of welfare, at least not in a simple direct way.

An alternative, but less developed interpretation of the income evaluation method sees it as an adaptation of the consensual income approach. The answers to the IEQ and the MIQ are regarded as opinions of respondents on the poverty line. Taking into account that persons with high incomes may have only a hazy, and biased, notion of how much income is needed to escape poverty or to make ends meet, the LPL and SPL are interpreted as estimates of a poverty line reflecting a social consensus. As argued in section 6.4, this interpretation is difficult to maintain. In the first place, the IEQ and the MIQ do not ask for an opinion about a social issue, but for an evaluation of one's own income situation from one's own private point of view. Secondly, the procedure used to derive the SPL and LPL has some implications that seem to clash with a consensual interpretation of those income thresholds. In particular, more generous answers by high income respondents will lead to *lower* LPL's and SPL.

I have argued for an interpretation which starts from the premise that welfare is defined as something like the material standard of living, and thus depends only on 'objective' circumstances and income. When a person's income increases, and he gives higher answers to the IEQ and MIQ, this is not seen as an indication that his actual income needs (i.e. the income required to reach a certain level of welfare) are rising, but rather that his *perception* of his needs is changing. In other words, the preference and reference processes are reinterpreted as perception effects. A respondent's answers to the MIQ and IEQ provide only colored or biased estimates of his 'true' income needs. In order to obtain unbiased estimates of income thresholds and equivalence scales, we must make certain assumptions about the perception process, i.e. that the effects are nil or negligible, or that they are adequately captured and adjusted for in the estimation procedure.

Which interpretation is preferred has no implications for the estimation procedures that are used actually. However, in the interpretation favored here the income evaluation method can no longer be used as a yardstick to assess the validity of other approaches to measuring economic welfare and poverty, but becomes one fallible method among others. The results can be accepted as valid only when the assumptions on which it relies are sufficiently credible. To a considerable extent, this is a matter of judgment, in which, inevitably, the empirical performance of the method plays an important role. The latter will be reviewed in the balance of this concluding section.

Reliability and validity of the answers to the MIQ and IEQ

From a technical perspective, the MIQ and IEQ appear to be quite successful measures of the subjective evaluation of incomes. In face-to-face interviews, almost all respondents give answers to the MIQ and IEQ, and relatively few of those answers are inconsistent or outside of reasonable bounds. The reliability of the answers to the MIQ and the IEQ is quite high, as evidenced by the high correlation between those answers at a single point in time, and also by the substantial correlations across subsequent waves of the SEP. On the other hand, the results also suggest that the reliability of σ, which measures the dispersion of the IEQ answers of each respondent around their average, is quite low.

The finding that variables such as household income, number and ages of children and home tenure status all have effects on the MIQ and IEQ answers that are in the expected direction confirms the validity of those answers. Otherwise, perhaps the most significant and surprising result of the detailed investigations is that a number of variables which could serve as proxies for reference groups, such as labor market status, education and age of the head of household, were found to have no, very limited and/or unstable effects.

However, there are also a number of ambiguities and problems with the approach. In the first place, it is not entirely clear what the phrase 'in your circumstances' which appears both in the MIQ and the IEQ, is supposed to mean. E.g., are people supposed to continue living in their present home, or not? No doubt, respondents have different understandings of the MIQ and IEQ in this respect. This ambiguity may be partly responsible for the unsatisfactory results regarding housing costs. A second problem with the income evaluation questions in their present format is that a single respondent acts as spokesperson for the whole household, with the implicit assumption that all members of the household share the same view about its income needs. A related problem is the demarcation of the household in the mind of the respondent. An analysis of the answers to the MIQ and IEQ in households where one or more adult children were living with their parents produced inconsistent results.

The finding that Flemish respondents give considerably lower answers to the MIQ and IEQ than their Walloon counterparts living in otherwise similar circumstances do raises another problem. In the case of the MIQ the difference increased over time. The most plausible explanation of these results is that the French and Dutch versions of the income evaluation questions are not quite equivalent, in combination with slight changes in the Dutch version of the MIQ in the SEP questionnaire. The suggestion that rather subtle differences and changes in the wording of the MIQ and IEQ can have a large impact on the answers, raises questions about the meaning and validity of the results of the income evaluation approach.

Validity and usefulness of the SPL and LPL income thresholds

Does the income evaluation approach provide a valid way to measure poverty? A first, very obvious but important point is that the income evaluation method works quite well. The resulting income thresholds are reasonable, i.e. neither absurdly high (e.g. above average income) or absurdly low (e.g. way below the statutory minimum income). The equivalence scale conforms to the basic requirement that income needs increase with the size of the household[16]. The conclusion that it works does not mean that it works perfectly. There are a number of problems, which cluster around the following three questions: Can the SPL and LPL income thresholds be regarded as poverty lines? Is the equivalence scale incorporated in these lines valid, i.e. unbiased? Are the SPL and LPL comparable over time and across countries?

For some observers, the SPL and LPL are a bit too generous to be properly called poverty lines. In their view, it is straining the meaning of the word 'poverty' a little too much to assert that 15 to 20 percent of the Belgian population is living in poverty, as use of the SPL and LPL indicates. However, when the word poverty is not supposed to refer exclusively to situations of total distress and deprivation, but also to people having a hard time to meet the social requirements and expectations of an affluent society, it becomes more acceptable to use the SPL and LPL as poverty lines. In any case, one must keep in mind that there is not likely to be such a thing as a single valid poverty line, existing somewhere in society and waiting to be found by the most clever and diligent researcher. The SPL and LPL are only operational definitions of poverty, research instruments used to reveal certain social conditions. They certainly cannot be regarded as *the* poverty line, if only because results suggest that the level of those income thresholds can be strongly influenced by small changes in the wording of the MIQ or IEQ.

If the SPL and LPL are research instruments, what is important is that they allow us to identify correctly groups and categories of persons and households at relatively high risk of poverty. Since the distribution of poverty risks in the population depends strongly on the equivalence scale of the poverty line, it is evidently crucial that the latter is unbiased. The equivalence scale incorporated in the SPL and LPLs tends to be rather flat, i.e. the income needs of large families appear to be not much greater than those of small families. However, none of the other methods used to estimate equivalence scales provides a secure yardstick against which to assess the validity of the MIQ and IEQ equivalence scales; each has its own problems and uncertainties. Arguably, in some respects the income evaluation method is superior to the other ones. By contrast with those derived from the budget, political and expert methods, the MIQ and IEQ equivalence scales have the advantage that they are based on the views of the population. Compared with the analysis of consumption behavior, the income evaluation approach has the advantage that it is technically simple and straightforward, and also that the results are remarkably stable over time, and also across different model specifications. A number of hypotheses about the flatness of the MIQ and IEQ equivalence scales were reviewed, and the conclusion was that substitution effects, in conjunction with dampening of aspirations regarding the material standard of living concurrent with the birth of children, seemed the most likely explanation. This would imply that the SPL and LPL equivalence factors do not represent the same level of material welfare for all household types. In this sense comparisons of living standards based on those income thresholds could be misleading, and they should be used with caution in poverty studies.

This brings us to the third question: does the income evaluation method produce income thresholds and low income rates that, even if they cannot always be described as poverty lines and poverty rates, are at least comparable across time and across countries? Obviously, comparability across time can only be assured when exactly the same wording of the income evaluation questions is maintained. However, even when the formulation of the questions is unchanged, the evolution in the thresholds is sometimes characterized by inexplicable jumps and fluctuations. More generally, there is the problem that SPLs and LPLs that are calculated at each point in time separately will not represent the same material standard of living in all years. One might argue that the trends in the SPL and LPL also reflect changes in the material aspirations of the population, in addition to the evolution in the consumer price index. Supposing that to be true, it is doubtful that it would enhance the validity and usefulness of the SPL and LPL poverty thresholds, when the reasons for those shifts in aspirations are very unclear.

The problems of cross-time comparability are compounded for cross-country comparisons of the results of the income evaluation method. Not only will survey organizations and questionnaires differ, but most importantly of course, different countries often use different languages, making the goal of exact equivalence of wording of the MIQ and IEQ rather elusive. Empirical results confirm that those problems are not just theoretical: one finds that the pattern in the poverty rates across countries following from the income evaluation approach is not at all in agreement with the outcomes of other methods. One might argue that poverty ratios based on the income evaluation method do not merely reflect income differences, but differences in aspiration levels between countries as well. However, this makes those results rather hard to interpret, since it is totally unclear what kind of factors lie behind those supposed differences in aspiration levels. This opaqueness robs the results of the income evaluation method of much of their potential usefulness.

Notes

1 Strictly speaking, one can only say that if the true model is among those tested, it will, on average, have the lowest residual variance. Given that both models have the same dependent variable, and the same number of parameters, the residual-variance criterion is equivalent to the maximum R-squared criterion.

2 Van Herwaarden and Kapteyn (1981: 282), find that the difference is only significant at the 5-percent level. Possibly they did not take the substantial covariance between the residual variances across respondents into account.

3 I.e., $A_{vg} - A_g < A_g - A_{sf}$ or $A_g - A_{sf} < A_{sf} - A_{if}$, where A_{vg}, A_g, A_{sf} and A_{if}, represent the 'very good', 'good', 'sufficient' and 'insufficient' amounts, respectively.

4 Somewhat puzzlingly, they state that "Formal testing seems to be too dependent on the statistical model and the confidence limits accepted to be of much practical use" (p. 84).

5 Van Doorn and Van Praag (1988) use the LISREL approach to model the relationship between the evaluations of the welfare labels and the answers to two versions of the IEQ. When the individual empirical evaluations are replaced by the values implied by the equal quantile assumption, the fit of the model does not worsen appreciably, and the R^2 improves slightly. The authors interpret this result as a confirmation of the EIA.

6 I.e., if respondent A thinks that 'good' is 20 per cent above the mean and 'very good' 50 per cent above the mean, then respondent B, who is of the opinion that 'good' is 30 per cent above the mean, will state that 'very good' is 62.5 per cent above the mean.

7 A complication is that one might argue that the level of felt satisfaction is part of a person's total situation, and therefore an element in the index of functionings or capabilities. Similarly, one could also maintain that the situation of the two individuals in the example is not the same, since the person with the rich background has a smaller ability to gain satisfaction from a certain amount of income. Even when this is granted, however, the level of felt satisfaction will only have a relatively small weight in the total index of welfare, instead of being the sole criterion.

8 This was done by increasing the answer to the MIQ of each respondent in turn by 1 percent, each time repeating the regression and the calculation of the SPL for the household size of the respondent. The simple model was used to limit the computational burden.

9 It might seem that this interpretation is not wholly in accordance with the actual procedure used in empirical work, since what is regressed on household income and other variables is not subjective welfare as measured by the distance between household income and the answer to the MIQ or to the IEQ, but those answers themselves. However, as shown in section 4.2, the two procedures are formally equivalent, and lead to exactly the same results.

10 It might also be noted that in this interpretation, compared with the consensual one, respondents are reduced from the status of citizens taking an interest in social issues, to that of guinea pigs.

11 Moreover, demand data are insufficient to identify equivalence scales, cf. Kapteyn (1993).

12 In this vein, one might interpret the finding that the costs of children increase strongly with their age as partly a reflection of parents getting bored with their children and wanting to go on holiday abroad again, or of older children being less pleasant to care for and to have around.

13 The finding by Kapteyn (1993, cf. section 4.4) in a test of the equivalence of direct (IEQ) and indirect (demand behavior) measures of cost functions, that the coefficient for log-household size is reduced but does not wholly disappear, might perhaps be interpreted as an indication that both interpretations (i.e. substitution while remaining on the same indifference curve, and dampening of material aspirations) are partially true.

14 Also assuming that $\beta_1 + \beta_3 <= 1$, i.e. that the answers to the income evaluation questions are partly or wholly relative, but not more than relative.

15 Formally, welfare W_i of respondent i is defined as:

$$W_i = N((\log Y_i - \mu_i) / \sigma_i)$$

where N is the standard cumulative normal distribution function, Y_i household income of respondent i, μ_i the logarithm of the geometric average of her answers to the Income Evaluation Question, and σ_i an indicator of the spreading of those answers.

16 This may not seem much to boast of, but in fact it is not uncommon for seemingly valid methods to produce rather implausible results. The econometric literature on equivalence scales derived from consumer behavior provides several examples. Tellingly, the income satisfaction method (see chapter 7), which is closely related to the income evaluation approach, produces quite implausible income thresholds.

7 The Income Satisfaction Method

1 Introduction

In what I will call income satisfaction methods, respondents are asked to rate their own income or standard of living on a particular scale, consisting of ordered categories. A typical question is: "How do you feel about your standard of living?", to which answers can be given on a seven point scale, ranging from "Terrible" to "Delighted". Another question often used is "With your current household income, how can you make ends meet?", with six possible answers, ranging from "very difficultly" to "very easily". (For further details and exact formulations, see table 7.A1.) While the answers to such questions can be used for a number of purposes (see, e.g., Andrews and Withey, 1976), I will only look at their application in the context of the study of living standards in general, and poverty in particular. Here they have been used mostly for the estimation of equivalence scales and poverty lines.

The chapter is organized as follows. In section two I explain how equivalence scales and income thresholds are derived from the answers to the income satisfaction questions. Section three provides an overview of studies in this field, concentrating on the empirical determinants of income satisfaction, and on the resulting equivalence scales and income thresholds. In section four I consider the specification of the relationship between income satisfaction and its most important determinant, household income, using both published results and original analysis. The technical quality and reliability of the answers to the income satisfaction question is the subject of section five. Using data from the 1988 wave of the Belgian Socio-Economic Panel (BSEP), it also addresses the question whether feelings of overall income satisfaction must be seen as aggregates or averages of feelings about specific areas of consumption (bottom-up model) or whether, conversely, feelings about specific areas are no more than instances of overall income satisfaction (top-down model).

In section six results are presented of a probit model of the answers to the Making Ends Meet Question (MEMQ), which is asked in the BSEP, waves 1985, 1988 and 1992. Equivalence scales and income thresholds based on the probit estimates are discussed in section seven. It turns out that these equivalence scales are much steeper than those derived from the income evaluation method (cf. chapter 5, 6 and 7). The remaining sections are devoted to various hypotheses about the reason or reasons for this discrepancy. Section eight looks at the 'rosy-outlook' effect, i.e. the hypothesis that answers to the income satisfaction questions are coloured by how the respondent feels about his or her life as a whole. The effects of possible random error in household on estimated equivalence scales are analysed in section nine. Section ten considers the hypothesis that respondents have different (implicit) notions of the 'reference welfare level', i.e. use different standards when answering the MEMQ. The implications for estimated equivalence scales are investigated, as well as the question whether the answers to the Minimum Income Question (MIQ) and Income Evaluation Question (IEQ) can be regarded as measures of the reference welfare level. Section eleven considers the possibility that the income evaluation questions and the income satisfaction questions in fact do not refer to the same concept, but to different ones, and discusses one particular hypothesis about the way in which those concepts could differ. Section twelve summarises and concludes.

2 Derivation of equivalence scales and poverty thresholds

Equivalence scales

The form of the regression equation most often used to explain the answers to the direct question is as follows:

$$S_i = \gamma_o + \gamma_1 \log Y_i + \gamma_2 Z2_i \ldots + \gamma_n Zn_i + \varepsilon_i \tag{7.1}$$

where S_i represents the income satisfaction score of household i, Y_i the household's income, $Z2_i$ ... Zn_i other characteristics of the household which are thought to have an effect on S, $\gamma_o \ldots \gamma_n$ are parameters to be estimated, and ε_i is a disturbance term.

Suppose that we have two households, a reference household with characteristics $Z2_r \ldots Zn_r$, and a second household with characteristics

$Z2_a \ldots Zn_a$. (Both households can be seen as representing types of household.) Then the equivalence factor of the second household, relative to the reference household, is defined as the ratio of incomes Y_a/Y_r, such that both households are equally well off. In the present context, equally well off means, of course having the same feelings about the household's income or living standard, or finding it equally easy or difficult to make ends meet. (More formally, it means that the expected value of S is the same.)

This implies that we have to find the solution to:

$$\gamma_o + \gamma_1 \log Y_a + \gamma_2 Z2_a \ldots \gamma_n Zn_a = \gamma_o + \gamma_1 \log(Y_r) + \gamma_2 Z2_r \ldots \gamma_n Zn_r$$

which is:

$$\log(Y_a/Y_r) = (1/\gamma_1)[-\gamma_2(Z2_a - Z2_r) \ldots -\gamma_n(Zn_a - Zn_r)] \qquad (7.2)$$

Equation (7.2) can often be simplified. In many cases, the aim is to estimate equivalence scales for households of various sizes. Replacing Z2 by logFS, where FS represents the number of household members, assuming that other characteristics are the same for households *a* and *r*, (so that the other terms in Z are eliminated), and getting rid of the logarithm, we obtain:

$$Y_a/Y_r = (FS_a/FS_r)^{-\gamma_2/\gamma_1} \qquad (7.3)$$

The term $-\gamma_2/\gamma_1$ is, then, the elasticity of the equivalence scale with respect to household size. Another possibility is to use a series of dummy variables, each representing a particular household type. If Z2 is the dummy variable representing household type *a*, while the variable representing reference household type *r* has been left out of the equation, then the equivalence factor is simply:

$$Y_a/Y_r = \exp(-\gamma_2/\gamma_1), \qquad (7.4)$$

where exp() stands for the number e raised to the power of what is between brackets.

Both in (7.3) and (7.4) the equivalence factor depends only on family size (and the parameters γ_1 and γ_2), but not on income, or on any other characteristic of the household. This convenient result is, of course, due to the specific form of equation (7.1), in particular to the fact that it is additive, and that income is entered in a logarithmic transformation. It is possible to test whether this specification is in accordance with the data, as we will see below. One alternative is to assume that the relation between S and income is linear, instead of log-linear. In that case, the equivalence factor is not an income ratio, but a fixed amount. That is, at each income level, household *a* needs a fixed extra amount of income to be equally well off as the reference household.

Income thresholds

The calculation of income thresholds, including poverty lines, is even more straightforward than that of equivalence scales. First, one has to choose a particular level on the income satisfaction measure, with which the poverty line is to correspond. This level will typically, but not necessarily, be equal to a particular answer to the income satisfaction question. Let us call this level S*. The poverty line for household *a*, called Y^*_a, can then easily be solved from (7.1):

$$Y^*_a = \exp\left[(S^* - \gamma_0 - \gamma_2 Z2_a \ldots - \gamma_n Zn_a) / \gamma_1\right] \quad (7.5)$$

It is immediately seen that the level of the poverty line, in contrast to the equivalence scale, depends on all variables that are included in the regression equation.

In some cases one may have normative reasons for not differentiating the poverty lines according to certain variables, such as level of education, even though these have been found to have a significant effect on income satisfaction. In that case, the level of that variable has to be kept constant across the set of poverty lines, for instance at the average value in the sample.

3 Overview of other studies

Introduction

In this section I will give an overview of the fairly limited number of studies that have used the direct or scale method to estimate equivalence scales, and in some cases, income thresholds. (The term "income thresholds" is used, because in some cases it is doubtful whether these income amounts can be interpreted as poverty lines.) The most important results of the several studies, together with their most relevant characteristics, are reported in table 7.A1. Below I will not discuss these studies one by one, but I shall raise a number of issues that come up in the literature, or are suggested by the results.

Empirical determinants of income satisfaction

The most important overall result is certainly that the method seems to work. Most variables entered into the regressions have statistically significant effects in the expected direction. The higher the *income*, the more satisfied the respondent is with it, or the more easy he finds it to make ends meet. Unfortunately, because of the different scales used, the parameters are not directly comparable across different studies. In order to make the coefficients for household income somewhat comparable, I have calculated for each study by what factor household income must be multiplied in order to raise income satisfaction by an amount equal to half the range (the range is defined as the highest possible score minus the lowest possible score)[1]. The results reported in table 7.1 show that, according to the studies by Dubnoff et al. (1981), Vaughan (1984) and Poulin (1988), income has to increase by an absurdly high factor to make people substantially more satisfied with their income. Conversely, household income could be reduced by a very considerable amount without a very strong effect on measured satisfaction. The factors for the other studies are more realistic, but still quite high. This shows that the relation between income satisfaction and household income is weaker than one might have expected, or, as Poulin (1988: 17) calls it, rather "horizontal".

As one might have anticipated, the larger the *size of the household*, the less satisfied one is with one's income, or the more difficult it is to make ends meet. Again, the coefficients as such are not comparable across studies; the comparison is best made by looking at the resulting equivalence factors (see below). In some studies family size is entered into the equation as the log of the number of household members, while other studies use a series of dummy variables, each dummy variable representing a particular household size or household type. The dummy variable specification has the advantage that it is more flexible; the log-household size specification has the advantage that if it is correct, it leads to more precise estimates.

Table 7.1
Relationship between household income and measured income satisfaction in a number of studies

Study	Regression coefficient for log-income	Proportional increase in income needed to raise income satisfaction by one point	Range of income satisfaction scale	Proportional increase in income needed to raise income satisfaction by half of the range
Dubnoff a.o. (1981)	4.66	1.24	12	3.6
Vaughan (1984)	0.0628	3.77 (1)	1	2,869.2
Poulin (1988)	0.760	3.73	6	51.8
Bradbury (1989)	0.48	8.03	9	11,789.9
Melenberg and Van Soest (1996) (3)	-	2.86	9	112.5
Stanovnik (1992) (2)	1.108	4.22	4.785	8.7

Notes: (1) Proportional increase needed for 1/12 point rise.
(2) Stanovnik has used probit regression to estimate the model. Stanovniks's income satisfaction scale has four categories, and so there are three thresholds. The estimates were communicated to me by personal letter. They are: -6.078; -5.124 and -2.888 respectively. The average distance between subsequent thresholds on is regarded as a distance of 'one point' on the income satisfaction scale. Total range is calculated as three times the average distance.
(3) Figures estimated from figure 4 in source.

Only Poulin (1988) presents results for both specifications. Judging by the proportion of variance that is explained, the dummy variable specifications does not perform much better than the log-family size one. The difference in R^2 may be statistically significant (due to the large sample size) but seems very small. An implication of the log-family size specification is that the larger the family size, the smaller the effect of an additional person. The coefficients for the dummy-variable specification do not always follow this pattern, though. For instance, the results of Dubnoff et al. (1981) seem to indicate that the fourth child in a family has a much greater effect on income satisfaction than the other ones. Poulin's (1988) results show an anomaly at family size four. But not too much should be made of these differences, as they may well be due to peculiarities in the data. Finally, it is noteworthy that in studies that differentiate between one-parent and two-parent families (Bradbury, De Coster), it is mostly found that the income satisfaction of one-parent families is, ceteris paribus, relatively low.

All studies which take account of *age* find that the elderly, compared with the middle aged, are more satisfied with their income, or find it easier to make ends meet. While this effect is fairly limited according to the Slovenian study, it appears to be quite strong in the American, Canadian and Australian samples. In the latter studies, this leads to equivalence factors for elderly families, relative to similarly-sized non-elderly families, that are very low. Vaughan (1984: 499) expresses the opinion that the income satisfaction equivalence factor for the elderly that he finds (0.30) "is too low to be taken seriously". For this reason, he has tested a number of additional elements in the model, that could possibly account for the low equivalence factor for the aged. These are: 1) an interaction term for family size and income, 2) a dummy variable for one-person aged units, 3) a number of variables thought to be related to aged/non-aged differences, viz. home tenure, number of earners, value of durables and amount of other fungible assets, 4) a crude approximation of after-tax income (in the original model the income measure was before-tax income). Only the addition of the dummy variable for one-person aged units had an important effect on the aged/non-aged equivalence ratios, but even this was fairly limited: the aged/non-aged equivalence ratio for two-person units increased from 0.30 to 0.37, while it fell to 0.22 for single persons. Vaughan concludes that aged singles apparently confront different conditions from aged couples, but this phenomenon cannot explain away the large effect of age per se. Other authors did not report any further analyses relevant to this issue.

A remarkably consistent finding across studies is that home tenure status has an important effect on income satisfaction measures. *Ceteris paribus*, owners who have to pay off a mortgage are less satisfied with their income than non-mortgaged owners, while people who rent their home feel even worse off than the former. In order to be able to compare the estimates across studies, 'equivalence factors' for owners with a mortgage and for tenants, relative to non-mortgaged owners have been calculated, and are shown in table (7.A1). These equivalence factors must be interpreted with considerable caution, because the decision to rent or to buy is not independent of the (subjective) financial situation of the household, and also because these scales are averages across households with very different mortgage or rent amounts to pay, in different housing situations, and with possibly different preferences. The results of Bradbury (1989) are way out of line, and together with his very steep household size equivalence scale, this leads to the suspicion that something is wrong with Bradbury's estimate of the relation between household income and income satisfaction. But the two other studies (Poulin, Stanovnik) produce factors that are remarkably close to each other, especially for tenants: in all countries they appear to need on average 24% to 30% more income to feel as much income satisfaction as non-mortgaged home owners in otherwise similar circumstances. This estimate seems rather high, both in itself, and in comparison with the factor for mortgaged owners. Perhaps mortgage-paying households perceive this outlay in part as a saving or an investment, or they may feel that they get better value for their money than tenant households do.

Another consistent finding across several studies is that people who report that their *financial situation has improved* in the recent past enjoy higher income satisfaction than people in otherwise similar circumstances who perceive no change, while the reverse is true for people who say that they have experienced a change for the worse. This suggests that a person's satisfaction with his or her income is affected by comparisons with his or her situation in earlier periods. It is not immediately clear what this does imply for the interpretation and validity of equivalence scales based on income satisfaction data. A striking result is that a deterioration of the financial situation has a much stronger effect than an improvement. This is noted both by Dubnoff et al. (1981) and Vaughan (1984) but neither gives an interpretation of this asymmetry. Dubnoff et al. find that, in addition to perceived financial change in the past year, perceived financial change in the past five years also has a significant effect on income satisfaction. Vaughan reports that income satisfaction is also influenced by prospects for the future: those who expected their financial situation to change in the year following the survey, whether for better or for worse, are considerably less satisfied than others. The latter, at first sight perhaps puzzling finding might reflect a tendency on the part of persons who undergo strong fluctuations in income to be less satisfied with their incomes, ceteris paribus, than those whose incomes are more stable. Uncertainty about future income may have to be compensated by a higher level of expected income for people to be equally satisfied. Such a tendency might also explain part of the asymmetry in the effects of recent improvements or worsenings in the financial situation. Possibly many improvements in income are foreseen before they occur, because they form part of a normal professional career for instance, and are already discounted for in people's minds. Conversely, deteriorations in the financial situation may often be unpredictable, because they result from unemployment, sickness, or unexpected expenditures.

A number of other variables were included in the regression equations of one or more studies, the results of which are not shown in table 7.A1. Three studies have looked at possible *regional differences*. Dubnoff et al. (1981) do not find any significant differences between the main regions of the USA. Poulin (1988) finds that people in the western regions of Canada are less satisfied than those in the eastern regions, while the inhabitants of Quebec are more satisfied, ceteris paribus, than those of Ontario. It is suspected, though, that the latter effect is due to a problem with the translation of the Delighted-Terrible scale from English into French. Poulin (1988) also reports that persons in rural areas and small cities are more satisfied than the inhabitants of large cities.

A few studies have looked at the impact of *education*. Poulin (1988) finds that people with higher education are considerably more satisfied with their income than those with lower levels of education (holding income constant). Bradbury (1989) finds no effect of the age at which respondents finished education (a rough indicator of level of education). De Coster et al. (1984) finds that Belgian couples where both partners work are considerably less satisfied than couples where only the husband or wife works, given the same income and number of children.

Equivalence scales and income thresholds

In contrast to the regression coefficients, the resulting equivalence factors, being dimensionless, have the advantage that they are comparable across studies. In the studies by Dubnoff et al. (1981) and Vaughan (1984), which use USA data, the equivalence scale is rather flat, indicating that the effect of family size is rather limited, compared to that of income. The authors of these studies note that this is a common result in research working with subjective income evaluations, although it is not very clear why this is so. Yet, all other studies produce equivalence scales that are very much steeper. Those obtained by Poulin (1988) for Canada, by Stanovnik (1992) for Slovenia and by Melenberg and Van Soest (1996) for The Netherlands are within the range of equivalence scales used for statistical purposes (e.g. the one recommended by the OECD, 1982; cf. Buhmann et al., 1988). Poulin (1988: 24) observes that the equivalence scale based on income satisfaction is steeper than that incorporated in Statistics Canada's LICO s (Low Income Cut-Offs), which are based on a food-ratio methodology[2]. Estimates of the equivalence scale by Bradbury (1989) and by Doughitt et al. (1992) appear implausibly steep. However, in the case of Bradbury, due to the large standard errors of the regression coefficients, most of the equivalence factors are not significantly different from each other. In studies which differentiate between one-parent and two-parent families, the relatively low level of income satisfaction of one-parent families leads to high equivalence factors for this type of family.

The reason for these differences in equivalence scales are not immediately clear. Poulin and Dubnoff et al. obtain very different results, despite using very similar data and models. Whether a dummy-variable, or a log-linear specification for family size was used, does not make much difference. Bradbury attributes his disappointing results to the effects of unmeasured variables, such as the reference groups of respondents. Note that a steep equivalence scale may be the result of a strong impact of family size on income satisfaction, but also of a *small* effect of household income. This issue will be further explored below.

Only Poulin (1988) and De Coster et al. (1984) have used the regression results to calculate income thresholds corresponding to various income satisfaction levels[3]. Thresholds for a family consisting of two non-aged adults[4], as reported in Poulin (1988: 16), recalculated as a percentage of average household income in the sample, are as follows:

Terrible	Unhappy	Mostly dissatis-fied	Mixed	Mostly satisfied	Pleased	Delighted
1.0	3.8	14.3	53.4	198.9	741.2	2762.4

Thresholds for other household types can be derived from those for two-adult households, by using the equivalence factors reported in table 7.A1. According to De Coster et al. (1984: 78) the income threshold for the border between 'somewhat difficultly' and 'fairly easily' is 76.1 percent of average sample income for a one-earner couple and 94.0 for a two-earner couple. The corresponding income thresholds for the border between 'fairly easily' and 'easily' are 131.6 and 178.6.

As Poulin (1988: 17) remarks "the income levels associated with the extreme levels of satisfaction appear ridiculously high or low". She attributes these unreasonable results to the fact that the relationship between satisfaction and income is "very horizontal". She finds more plausible thresholds by an alternative method, viz. average income by level of satisfaction and family size. The relationship between income and satisfaction will be studied in detail in the next section.

4 Specification of the relationship between household income and income satisfaction

While the results of the several studies show that the income satisfaction approach to estimate equivalence scales is at least promising, there are a number of methodological problems which need looking into. One of these is the specification of the relationship between income satisfaction, household income and household size and composition. Most studies use a linear-log specification, where the scores of the income satisfaction measure are untransformed, while income is entered in logarithmic form. For household size both logarithmic and dummy variable specifications have been used. The question may be asked whether the relationship between satisfaction and income is adequately described by a linear-log type of curve. The same question can be posed regarding household size. Furthermore, it is conceivable that the relation between satisfaction and income varies according to household type or other characteristics of the respondent; in more technical terms, there is the possibility of interaction.

Several authors have investigated the relationship between household income and satisfaction measures. Vaughan and Lancaster (1979) have looked at the relationship between ratings of family income on the seven point "delighted-terrible" scale, and net household income before taxes (measured in brackets) in a sample of about 900 parents with dependent children living in the USA. They tested three specifications: a linear model, a log-linear one, and a two-segment model, in which two linear equations are estimated for different income ranges linked by an intersection point. The authors conclude that the segmented model is the most successful one in terms of R-square (proportion of variance that is explained). Yet, though both the log-model and the segmented model perform much better than the linear one, the log model has a higher R-square value than the segmented model in four of the eight possible comparisons, and in the other ones, its R-square value is only slightly lower.

Poulin (1988: 10) mentions that she examined many variants, but she presents results for only one alternative to the linear-log model, viz. the log-log model, where income satisfaction is also entered in logarithmic form. Compared with the linear-log model, the log-log specification has a worse R-square (0.172 vs. 0.192), while the regression coefficient for log-income (0.228) does not indicate that the relationship becomes stronger in the log-log model. To raise income satisfaction by half of the range, income would have to be multiplied by a factor of 71.5 (instead of 51.8 in the linear-log model).

Melenberg and Van Soest (1996) present results of a nonparametric (quartic kernel) regression of satisfaction with household income (10-point scale) on log-family income. The specification allow the relation to take any form. The resulting curve has some peculiar bends in the lower range of incomes, but at realistic income levels (Dfl. 18,000 to Dfl. 100,000) it is virtually a straight line, indicating that the relationship between income satisfaction and household income has approximately a linear-log form.

A related issue is the possibility of interaction effects between household income and household size. That is, the effect of changes or differences in household income on income satisfaction could differ according to the size or composition of the family or household. (If that would the case, the converse would also be true: the effect of household size would vary according to household income.) This would imply that different equivalence scales apply at different income levels, which does not seem implausible: children in rich families may cost proportionally less (though more in absolute amounts) than children in poor families.

One analyst who considers this possibility is Vaughan (1984). He introduces a multiplicative term between log-household size and log-household income into the model. He finds that the coefficient for this term is positive and just significant at the 5% level in one variant of the model, indicating that at lower income levels, children (and other persons) cost proportionally more than at higher income levels. (The elasticity of the equivalence scale with respect to family size varies from 0.49 for the average family living in poverty to 0.19 for families with incomes at twice the median level.) But the magnitude of this effect is not very stable when other variables are added to the model.

Models used by Melenberg and Van Soest (1996) allow non-linearities and interactions (or 'cross terms') in the specification, but those authors do not report the regression results. The equivalence scales resulting from those models are not much different from those where linearity is imposed, but the standard errors are much larger.

Finally, an important matter is the estimation technique used. As table 7.A1 shows, most studies use regression (presumably Ordinary Least Squares or OLS) to estimate the model. De Coster et al. (1984), Stanovnik (1992) and Melenberg and Van Soest (1996) recognise that the answers on the scales used have ordinal properties[5], so that ordinary regression is inappropriate - or, at least, they are the only ones to take this problem seriously enough to turn to a more suitable technique, viz. logistic or probit regression.

Bradbury (1989) circumvents this problem by asking his respondents to give their ratings directly in the form of a number. Whether these answers really constitute a variable on an interval level (i.e. whether the difference in satisfaction between 10 and 9 is equal to the difference between 2 and 1, or 6 and 5) is debatable. In any case, Bradbury's results do not inspire confidence in the validity of this way of measuring satisfaction with income. Unfortunately, no analyst reports both OLS and probit or logistic regression results, so we cannot ascertain whether the choice of technique has an important effect on the results. In section 7.6 results of a probit model of the answers to the MEMQ in the Belgian SEP will be presented. I will then also take a brief look at the question whether the results differ much from those obtained with OLS regression.

5 Quality, reliability and validity of income satisfaction measures

Introduction

An apparently somewhat neglected issue in the literature on income satisfaction (at least in the context of equivalence scale estimation) is the reliability of the income satisfaction measures. Reliability is the consistency of measurement (Bollen, 1989: 206). It can be understood as the extent to which repeated applications of the same instrument produce the same result. Independent repeated measurements with the same instrument on the same object would be expected to fluctuate more or less, because of random errors. Therefore, reliability is that part of a measure that is free of purely random error (Bollen, 1989: 207).

Reliability needs to be distinguished from validity. 'Validity is concerned with whether a variable measures what it is supposed to measure' i.e., whether a measure corresponds to a theoretical concept (Bollen, 1989: 184-185). Therefore, a valid measure cannot be totally unreliable (because random disturbances are generally not what one wants to measure), but a reliable measure can be perfectly invalid. In more technical terms, the validity of a measure can be defined as its correlation with the latent true state variable. Its reliability can be measured by its correlation with a parallel measure (Andrews and Withey, 1976: 180).

Why is it important to consider the reliability of the income satisfaction measures? In the first place low reliability leads, ceteris paribus, to less precision in the estimates of model parameters. Though the estimates remain unbiased in the presence of random measurement errors in the dependent variable, large standard errors mean that in any single sample the estimates can deviate considerably from the true population values. Secondly, we have seen that in all studies that have been reviewed, a very large part of the variance of the income satisfaction scores remains unexplained. This could be the result of the omission of important variables from the model, or of low reliability of the income satisfaction measure. If relevant variables have been omitted from the model, the estimates of parameters that are in the model may well be biased.

Therefore, depending on whether the reliability of the income satisfaction measures is low or high, rather different strategies must be pursued to get better parameter estimates: if reliability is low, better measures of income satisfaction must be devised; if reliability is high, we must search for omitted variables.

Earlier studies on reliability and validity

In the literature that uses income satisfaction measures to estimate equivalence scales or income thresholds, no attention appears to have been given to the reliability of the measures that are used. But, fortunately, information about this issue is available from other sources.

In particular, Andrews and Withey (1976) provide a great deal of evidence about the reliability and validity of the income satisfaction measures used by Dubnoff Vaughan and Lancaster (1981), Vaughan (1984) and Poulin (1988). Dubnoff et. al. (1981) use the unweighted sum of two items: "How do you feel about the income you (and your family) have?" (the income question) and "How do you feel about your standard of living - the things like housing, furniture, recreation and the like?" (the standard of living question), with answers on the Delighted-Terrible scale.

Based on data from a national survey in the USA in May 1972 (N = 1297), Andrews and Withey (1976: 55) report that the correlation between the answers to the two questions is 0.66. This is among the highest of correlations between any life concerns. Within various subgroups (according to age, race, Socio-Economic Status) similar correlations were found (Andrews and Withey, 1976: 394-402).

Using a structural model and various kinds of methods, including graphical ones, Andrews and Withey (1976: 192-194) have further analysed the reliability and validity of these measures. The variance of each observed measure is assumed to come from three distinct and uncorrelated sources: the respondents' 'true feelings' about the relevant aspect of well-being, the 'method effects', and residual random error (Andrews and Withey, 1987: 185). They call the correlation between the measured variable and the true feelings the 'validity coefficient' of the former. Andrews and Withey (1976: 188) estimate that the validity coefficient of the Delighted-Terrible measure of standard of living is 0.79. The method effect is 0.28. The Delighted-Terrible measure performs better than most other ones. Andrews and Withey (1976: 190) conclude that, in general, using Delighted-Terrible scales yields measures with about 65% valid variance, 8% variance induced by the method, and 27% residual (random error) variance. For a single-item measure, this appears to be quite good.

An analysis of questions similar to the Making Ends Meet Question used by De Coster et al. (1984) and me has been carried out by Dickes (1987b). He uses data from a Luxemburg survey in 1985, in which the following questions were asked (Dickes, 1987b: 148-150; my translation):

1. "With your monthly income does your household/group live, very difficultly, difficultly, somewhat difficultly, somewhat easily, easily or very easily?"
2. "Within your household/group do you experience difficulties to make ends meet?" Answers on a six-point scale going from "enormous number of difficulties" to "no difficulties".

3-9: Questions were asked about difficulties in repaying loans and in paying for food, health care, clothing, rent or mortgage, utilities, and heating.

Dickes (1987b: 123-129) evaluates a number of psychometric models, using these data. For our purposes, it is important to note that (in the Luxembourg survey) the correlation between the general items 1 and 2 is

0.84, which is quite high. The correlation of these general items with the 'difficulties of paying' items is also reasonable, ranging from 0.30 to 0.67.

Comparison of the Making Ends Meet Question with a replicate and with difficulties in paying items

In most of the Belgian SEP surveys only a single income satisfaction question was asked. But the data of the 1988 wave provide an opportunity to assess the reliability and validity (as defined above) of the Making Ends Meet Question (MEMQ). In addition to the latter question, which was situated in the first half of the questionnaire, the following questions were asked at the very end of it:

> "During the past year, did you encounter difficulties in paying for the following charges:
> - paying the bills for gas, water and electricity.
> - paying the heating costs.
> - buying food.
> - making ends meet with my total income."

The same response categories were used as for the first MEMQ. Although the phrasing is somewhat different, it seems reasonable to regard the last item on this list as a replication of the first MEMQ. The most important difference is that in the second question the time frame is clearly the past year, while in the first question a reference was made to monthly income.

The cross-tabulation of the answers to the two versions of the MEMQ is given in table 7.2. It is clear that there is close correspondence between the answers to the two questions: more than half of all respondents give the same answer; the great majority provide the same or an immediately adjacent answer. The Pearson correlation of 0.706 can be interpreted as a measure of the reliability of both measures (Bollen, 1989: 210).

A reliability coefficient of 0.71 for a single item appears to be quite high. There are two reasons why it might be an overestimate. In the first place, it is possible that respondents remember their answers to the first MEMQ when responding to the second one, and try to be consistent. It is rather difficult to assess to which extent this may have happened. Because of complicated skip patterns in the questionnaire, the time that has elapsed between the two questions may have varied a great deal across respondents. It might be expected that memory effects would be particularly important for those respondents who were surveyed by mail questionnaire (who were after all able to look up their first answers). However, while the correlation is higher among the mail respondents than among the face-to-face respondents, the difference is not very large: 0.751 versus 0.686.

Table 7.2
Comparison of answers to Making Ends Meet Question with a replicate, Belgium 1988 (percentages)

	Answer to MEMQ 1						
Answer to MEMQ2	Very difficultly	Difficultly	Somewhat difficultly	Fairly easily	Easily	Very easily	Total
Very difficultly	55	19	5	1	0	3	7.3
Difficultly	22	34	11	4	3	1	9.8
Somewhat difficultly	16	34	54	11	2	0	22.5
Fairly easily	2	9	21	49	14	4	24.3
Easily	1	4	7	26	61	26	24.0
Very easily	4	1	3	9	19	65	12.2
Total	100	100	100	100	100	100	100
(row perc.)	(6.1)	(11.1)	(26.2)	(29.7)	(20.2)	(6.8)	(100)
N	213	385	911	1032	702	236	3479

Notes: Number of missing values: 300 gamma 0.757
Chi-square: 3609.5 (df = 25) tau-b 0.633
phi 1.019 tau-c 0.602
Cramer's V: 0.456 Pearson correlation coefficient: 0.706
Respondents with identical answers on both questions: 52.4 %.
Respondents with identical or immediately adjacent answers: 87.4 %.

Source: Belgian Socio-Economic Panel, wave 1988.

A second reason why 0.71 might be an overestimate of the reliability of the MEMQ is that the random error components of the two versions might be correlated. Some short-lived influences, which are irrelevant from the point of view of the study, may persist during the time it takes to complete the questionnaire. For instance, a respondent may temporarily feel that she has difficultly making ends meet, because she received a larger than expected electricity bill that day[6].

In Van den Bosch (1999) I have developed two models, which have been labelled "top-down", and "bottom-up". In the top-down model, it is assumed that the two MEMQs, and the three Difficulties-in-Paying items are all indicators, on an equal footing, of the same concept, which I have called 'Subjective Financial Situation', i.e. the respondent's view about how she is able to make ends meet. The central feature of the top-down model is the assumption, that the respondent first makes an overall assessment of her financial situation (success in making ends meet), and that the judgements about specific areas of the budget are derived from this overall assessment. The bottom-up model incorporates the reverse hypothesis: it is assumed that the respondent first assesses his financial situation in specific areas. An overall assessment of the financial situation is made on the basis of these specific judgements. It is assumed that the Difficulties-in-Paying items measure the specific judgements, and that the MEMQ items are indicators of the overall assessment. The results indicated that both models fit the data about equally well.

Conclusion

In this section the technical quality, the reliability and the validity of income satisfaction measures have been investigated, summarising results from the literature, as well as presenting new findings from the BSEP. In the first place, I considered the distribution of answers across categories in the scales predominantly used in the measurement of income satisfaction, i.e. the Delighted-Terrible scale and the 'Difficultly-Easily' scale used in the MEMQ. This turned out to be quite good; in particular the performance of the latter scale is close to ideal, having no dominant category, and relatively few observations in the extreme categories. Secondly, simple models suggested that the use of categories (instead of a continuous measure) in itself does not introduce important amounts of measurement error. Thirdly, estimated reliability coefficients for income satisfaction measures are fairly high for a single question: 0.66 to 0.84. The correlation of answers to the MEMQ with those to a replicate in the BSEP 1988 wave is 0.71. Fourthly, the validity of the answers to the income satisfaction question also appears to be quite satisfactory. Andrews and Withey (1976) modelled correlations between measures of various kinds and estimated the validity coefficient for the Delighted-Terrible measure of the standard of living is 0.79. Using answers to the MEMQ replicate and to questions about whether respondents experience difficulties in paying the bills for three budget components, I found that answers to the MEMQ contain at least 81 percent valid variance, which is very high for a single question. Fifthly, two different models were evaluated using to the two MEMQuestions and the Difficulties-in-Paying items. In the bottom-up model feelings of overall income satisfaction are seen as aggregates or averages of feelings about specific areas of consumption, while in the top-down model feelings about specific areas are regarded as instances of overall income satisfaction. Both models fitted the data about equally well.

The corollary of the finding that most income satisfaction measures have high validity and reliability is that measurement error is not the reason why in all studies reviewed in section 7.3 exogenous factors account for only a rather small proportion of the variance of income satisfaction measures. Thus, it appears that statistically important explanatory variables have been left out of the regression equations. Not all of these variables are necessarily of much substantive interest, though. For instance, fluctuations in mood, or the effects of recent events, that persist during the time of the interview may play a role. Perhaps more fundamentally, it may be naive, as Andrews and Withey (1976: 215) write, "to think that a person's feelings about various aspects of life could be perfectly predicted by knowing only the characteristics of the person's present environment". Nevertheless, the fact that at best only half of the valid variance is explained implies that the estimates of parameters of interest must be regarded with some caution, as these estimates might be biased due to the omission of relevant variables.

Of course, many aspects of the objective circumstances of a person could be relevant. We will look at some of them in the next section 7.6. In sections 8 and 10, however, I will discuss variable of a somewhat subjective nature. Section 7.8 looks at a person's appreciation of his or her life as a whole (the 'rosy outlook effect'), while in section 7.10 I will consider the possibly varying standards used - implicitly or explicitly - by respondents in the evaluation of their standard of living and financial situation.

6 A probit model of income satisfaction

Introduction: an ordinal response model

Several authors have used Ordinary Least Squares regression to produce the estimates shown in table 7.A1. But, in fact OLS regression is not an appropriate technique for the income satisfaction data. The main reason for this is that the scoring of the income satisfaction variable - i.e. the assignment of numeric values to the several categories - is to some extent arbitrary. Usually, consecutive integer numbers are used. But it is not self-evident that the distance between 'delighted' and 'pleased' is equal to the distance between 'mostly dissatisfied' and 'unhappy', or that the difference between making ends meet 'very easily' and 'fairly easily' is twice as large as that between 'fairly easily' and 'somewhat difficulty'. With as much justification, one might assign scores -5, -3, -2, 0, 1, 3, 7 to the "delighted-terrible" scale. Obviously, a different scoring procedure might well yield different regression results. In other words, the income satisfaction measures used have ordinal properties: while a higher score indicates a greater degree of income satisfaction, differences between scores have no real meaning. Fortunately, techniques exist for the analysis of such variables. These are extensions of models used for the analysis of qualitative (binomial or multinomial) variables, such as probit and logit (an introduction into these models is provided by Aldrich and Nelson, 1984). In the balance of this subsection I will introduce these ordinal response models in a general way.

It is assumed that the answers to the income satisfaction question are determined by a continuous latent variable, which will be called S°. The position of household i on this latent variable (S°_i) is assumed to be determined by a linear model:

$$S^{\circ}_i = \alpha + \gamma' \mathbf{X}_i + \varepsilon_i \tag{7.6}$$

where α is a parameter, γ' a vector of parameters, $\mathbf{X}_i$ a vector of values on a number of explanatory variables, and ε_i a disturbance term. It is also assumed that the latent variable S° can be divided into a number of intervals, such that if the position of the household on S° falls within a certain interval, the household will choose a particular answer to the income satisfaction question. These intervals are divided by threshold values μ_k (k = 1.. J-1); the lowest and highest intervals are open-ended.

Now, given a value for $\alpha + \gamma'\mathbf{X}_i = Z_i$, and values for the thresholds μ_k, the probability that S°_i will fall within a certain interval depends on the disturbance term ε_i, or, more formally:

$$
\begin{aligned}
P(S_i = j) &= P(\mu_{j-1} {}^{3} S^{\circ}_i < \mu_j) \\
&= P(\mu_{j-1} - Z_i {}^{3} \varepsilon_i < \mu_j - Z_i) \\
&= P(\varepsilon_j < \mu_j - Z_i) - P(\varepsilon_i < \mu_{j-1} - Z_i) \\
&= \text{CDF}\,(\mu_j - Z_i) - \text{CDF}((\mu_{j-1} - Z_i) \qquad (7.7)
\end{aligned}
$$

where CDF stands for the Cumulative Distribution Function of ε_i . (For μ_o one has to read minus infinity, and for μ_j, infinity.)

The parameters α and γ, and the thresholds μ_k in this model can be estimated with Maximum Likelihood procedures, if a particular form for the CDF is chosen. The most popular ones are the logistic and normal CDFs. The logistic CDF is defined by: CDF(X) = exp(X) / (1 + exp(X)); the normal CDF is the standard cumulative normal distribution. Both define so-called sigmoid curves: they are symmetric about zero, they are positive for all values of X, they increase monotonously with X, and approach 1 or -1, if X goes to infinity or minus infinity, respectively. In fact, the logistic and normal CDFs are very similar.

Empirical determinants of income satisfaction

In order to develop a model for the answer to the Making Ends Meet Question, I have looked at the variables that were also considered with regard to the models for the answers to the income evaluation questions in chapter 5. These include almost all of the variables that are used in the literature (cf. section 7.3). Also, as in chapter 5, the selective subsamples were used to estimate the model. This subsample includes only single family households of single persons or couples, with or without dependent children. Households with children with an income of their own, or other relatives or non-relatives are excluded. Also excluded are households where one or both of the adults is or has been self-employed. Within thus subsample non-response on the MEMQ was very small: 1.7 percent in 1985, 2.4 percent in 1988 and 1.8 percent in 1992. Therefore, no attempt was made to correct for possible sample selection bias.

Table 7.3 reports the parameter estimates for the selected model. Table 7.4 shows results of tests of various alternatives to the selected model. In the remainder of this section, I will discuss the results, indicating what considerations have lead to the final model. In contrast to the μ and logYmin models, the hypothesis that the same model applied to all years - i.e. equality of all coefficients, except the intercept - was clearly rejected (line A of table 7.4). Even when the effects of the independent variables were allowed to vary across years (through the introduction of interaction terms), but the threshold values were assumed to be constant, a high chi-square test statistic was obtained (line C of table 7.4).

Unsurprisingly, *household income* is the main determinant of income satisfaction. In itself, the coefficient is difficult to interpret. A useful perspective is gained by calculating the proportional rise in income needed to increase measured income satisfaction by half the range[7]. According to the 1985 results, household income must be multiplied by a factor of 5.2 to make the average respondent so much more satisfied. The corresponding figures for 1988 and 1992 are 4.1 and 5.1, respectively. Given the distribution of household incomes in Belgium, these increases in income amount to jumps from the first decile to the eighth or ninth decile. These figures are more realistic than some of those derived from the results of other studies (see table 7.1). Yet they indicate that the relationship between household income and income satisfaction is weaker than one might have expected.

Somewhat surprisingly, the *income perception bias correction term* has an important effect on the answer to the MEMQ. The positive coefficient seems to imply that of two respondents having the same income, the one who perceives his income more correctly finds it easier to make ends meet. Supposing that the answer to the MEMQ reflects the subjective gap between the needs and wants of the respondents and the standard of living that is actually achieved with the current income, it is not easy to see how misperception of income can have such an important effect. As explained in section 5.3, income perception bias is defined as the ratio of perceived income to total household income, perceived income being the answer to a single question about total household income, while total household income is calculated by summing across answers to a large number of questions about individual income components. Part of the explanation of the effect may be that perceived income is not just an inadequate measure of total household income. Possibly both perceived income and the sum of income components are both imperfect measures of the income concept that is relevant for the respondent. While the sum of income components may measure accurately total household income in the particular month, perceived income may more adequately capture the income level across a longer period. When both income measures are entered into the probit regression equation (in logarithmic form), perceived income turns out to have the greater effect, although the ratio of the coefficients varies across years: 3.5 to 1 in 1985, 1.1 to 1 in 1988 and 2.9 to 1 in 1992.

Table 7.3
Results of ordered probit model of answer to Making Ends Meet Question

Predictor	1985		1988		1992	
	Esti-mate	St. error	Esti-mate	St. error	Esti-mate	St. error
logY	1.623	0.056	1.670	0.081	1.519	0.074
logC	1.265	0.188	0.891	0.185	1.133	0.207
logFSA	-0.579	0.067	-0.483	0.097	-0.169	0.091
logFSCh3	-0.792	0.119	-0.849	0.167	-0.701	0.156
logFSCh11	-0.689	0.078	-0.890	0.105	-0.845	0.103
logFSCh17	-1.005	0.085	1.175	0.119	0.901	0.110
logFSCh25	-1.132	0.104	-1.524	0.129	-1.295	0.153
Tenant	-0.315	0.041	-0.238	0.058	-0.325	0.056
Mortgagee	-0.205	0.048	-0.221	0.063	-0.334	0.064
Owner outright*	0		0		0	
Head is working	0.097	0.049 °	0.323	0.071	0.331	0.069
Head is not working*	0		0		0	
Head below 25	0.253	0.085	0.071	0.195 °	0.168	0.112 °
Head above 64	0.245	0.052	0.286	0.072	0.199	0.070
Head 25-64°	0		0		0	
University education	0.227	0.074	0.013	0.100 °	0.209	0.104 °
No univ. educ.*	0		0		0	
Senior employee	-0.037	0.066 °	0.298	0.073	0.214	0.073
Other profession*	0		0		0	
Wallonia	-0.321	0.036	-0.389	0.048	-0.253	0.048
Brussels	-0.176	0.060	-0.564	0.117	-0.369	0.104
Flanders*	0		0		0	
Mail survey * logY	0		-0.035	0.008	0	
Intercept	-10.748	0.304	-11.084	0.441	-10.876	0.411

Table 7.3 (continuation)

	1985	1988	1992
Log Likelihood	-5805.60	-3309.45	-3285.83
Chi-square model (df)	1513.32 (16)	986.22 (17)	1029.98 (16)
Pseudo R2	0.263	0.298	0.299
N of cases	4249	2325	2410

Notes: * Reference category.
- Subsample used includes only non-complex households, where neither head nor partner are or were self-employed (see text).
- logC: Income perception bias correction term.
- logFSA: log(Number of adults + 1).
- logFSCh3: Number of children aged 0-3, weighted by rank.
- logFSCh11: Number of children aged 4-11, weighted by rank.
- logFSCh17: Number of children aged 12-17, weighted by rank.
- logFSCh25: Number of children aged 18-25, weighted by rank.
- 'University education' and 'Senior employee' refer to characteristics of head of household.
- All parameters are significantly different from zero at the 1 percent level, except those marked with °.
- Chi-square of model calculated as -2*(Log-likelihood of model - Log-likelihood of model with intercept only).
- Pseudo R2 calculated as Chi-square of model / (Number of cases + Chi-square of model) (Aldrich and Nelson, 1984).

Source: Belgian Socio-Economic Panel, waves 1985, 1988 and 1992.

The effects of the *family size* variables all have the expected negative sign: at equal income levels, the larger the household, the more difficult it is to make ends meet. As was the case for the answers to the income evaluation questions, the effect of children on feelings of being able to make ends meet increases strongly with their age. As shown in table 7.4, line D, the age effect is highly significant. Remarkably, the effect of the (rank-weighted) number of adults seems smaller than that of children, especially in 1992. This partially reflects the size of the rank weights, which are higher for adults than for children in two-adult families. However, even when this is taken into account, it turns out that in 1988 and 1992 children of all ages have a greater impact on feelings of being able to make ends meet than adults, while in 1985 this is true for children older than 12.

The limited effect of the number of adults does not appear to be a distortion induced by the specification. When running the model on a subsample of childless families, the following estimates were obtained of the effect of the number of adults (*fsv*): 1985: -0.55; 1988: -0.55; 1992: -0.12 (since complex families are excluded, these figures are in fact estimates of the effect of childless couples vs. single persons). These results are very close to the estimates reported in table 7.3. Also, further analysis showed that the effect of the number of adults does not vary much by age.

Table 7.4
Chi-square tests of modifications of the ordered probit model

			1985	1988	1992	Total
A.	Equality of models across years	Chi^2				148.30
		Df.				38
		Signif.				***
B.	Equality of effects of variables across years	Chi^2				82.36
		Df.				30
		Signif.				***
C.	Equality of thresholds across years	Chi^2				65.94
		Df.				8
		Signif.				***
D.	Ages of children	Chi^2	21.94	29.06	12.84	63.84
		Df.	3	3	3	9
		Signif.	***	***	**	***
E.	Special effect of one-parent families	Chi^2	0.84	0.96	3.32	5.12
		Df.	4	4	4	12
		Signif.	-	-	-	-
F.	Interaction of effects of family size and income	Chi^2	13.20	5.36	11.78	30.34
		Df.	5	5	5	15
		Signif.	*	-	*	*
G.	Effects of rent and mortgage payments	Chi^2	17.12	48.66	33.24	98.92
		Df.	6	6	6	18
		Signif.	**	***	***	***
H.	Effect of employment of persons other than head	Chi^2	2.80	1.22	1.24	5.26
		Df.	3	3	3	9
		Signif.	-	-	-	-

Table 7.4 (continuation)

			1985	1988	1992	Total
I.	Age categories other than 16-24 and 65+	Chi²	4.96	11.42	8.64	25.02
		Df.	5	4	5	14
		Signif.	-	*	-	*
J.	Education categories other than university	Chi²	15.38	4.18	5.52	25.08
		Df.	6	6	6	18
		Signif.	*	-	-	-
K.	Professional categories other than senior employee	Chi²	2.04	1.52	12.74	16.30
		Df.	3	3	3	9
		Signif.	-	-	**	-
L.	All reference variables other than selected ones	Chi²	26.08	20.94	15.84	62.86
		Df.	14	13	14	41
		Signif.	*	-	-	*
Number of observations			4249	2325	2410	8984

Notes: Selective sample used (see table 7.3).
* significant at 5 percent level.
** significant at 1 percent level.
*** significant at 0.1 percent level.

Source: Belgian Socio-Economic Panel, waves 1985, 1988 and 1992.

Since children in one-parent families have lower rank and therefore higher rank weights, compared to children in two-adult families, the specification used implies that the former have a stronger impact on the answer to the MEMQ than the latter. In order to test whether this implication is supported by the data, four variables representing the weighted number of children in the four age categories in one-parent families were added to the model. As shown in table 7.4, line E, the resulting improvement in the fit of the model was not significant at all. Moreover, in each year the signs of three out of four coefficients for these additional variables were negative (not always the same ones), instead of positive, as had been expected. Thus, the effect of children in one-parent families on feelings of making ends meet is certainly not overestimated by the results reported in table 7.3.

The possibility was considered that the effect of family size varies by income level. The introduction of the appropriate interaction terms into the model yields a limited improvement in the fit, that (summed across years) is just significant at the 5 percent level (see table 7.4, line F). The coefficients of the interaction terms displayed a rather erratic pattern across years, being negative in one year, and positive in another. Only the interaction term of income and the number of adults had consistently a negative sign, though it was statistically significant only in 1992. Because of the limited improvement in explanatory power and the erratic pattern of the coefficients, interaction between household size and household income was not retained for the final model.

Home tenure has an important effect on feelings of being able to make ends meet. As expected, tenants and mortgage-paying owners find it more difficult to get by - in otherwise similar circumstances - than those who own their home outright. The difference between the coefficients for the two home tenure statuses is small and not statistically significant.

Somẹ time and effort has been spent in exploring the impact of rent and mortgage payments on the answer to the MEMQ. As shown in table 7.4, line G, potentially the impact is substantial, especially in 1988 and 1992. (The reported improvements in fit were obtained through the introduction of six variables: the amounts of rent and mortgage payments themselves, interaction terms of these amounts with household income, and interaction terms of the home tenure dummy variables with household income.) A number of specifications were tried, but all yielded inconsistent results. Estimated coefficients were highly variable across years, and even worse, in some cases the compensating variation which could be estimated from the results was either negative, or exceeded the amounts actually paid in rent or for the mortgage. (The compensating variation is the increase in income needed to make a rent-paying or mortgaged household feel equally well off as a household that owns it home outright.) As argued in section 5.3 with regard to the effects of rent and mortgage payments on the answers to the MIQ and IEQ, these unsatisfactory results are probably due to the ambiguous nature of housing costs, which may reflect both differing circumstances, as well as variation in preferences regarding housing. In the final model only the home tenure dummies are retained. The other parameter estimates were hardly or not affected by the inclusion of rent and mortgage payments and related variables in the probit regression equation.

In contrast to income evaluations, feelings of being able to make ends meet are influenced by the *employment* of family members. Surprisingly, however, only the employment of the head has any effect. (The head is either a single adult, or the man in couples.) As shown in table 7.4, lines H, whether the woman in couples has paid work does not make any difference. Couples where both partners work feel equally well off as those where the wife stays at home. When *only* the woman is employed, the answer to the MEMQ is not significantly different from answers in households where no one works. Also, the effect of employment is the same, whether the head is single or married or cohabiting.

Perhaps even more surprisingly, the effect of employment the head is positive, implying that in otherwise similar circumstances and at the same level of income, households where the head is working find it more easy to make ends meet than households where the head is unemployed, retired or otherwise out of work. In 1988 and 1992 the effect is equivalent to a rise in income of 21 percent and 24 percent, respectively. Since there are work-related costs, and also because the social environment of working persons will tend to include more high-income people than that of non-working persons, one would have expected the opposite. The positive effect could reflect monetary or non-monetary benefits from work, which are not reported in the SEP, such as a company car, meals eaten at work, etc.. It could also be a result of the 'rosy-outlook' effect (see section 7.8). Persons at work may feel better about their life as a whole than persons without paid work, and this may make them more satisfied with their income as well.

Supposing that paid work is more important for men than for women in the total evaluation of life, the 'rosy-outlook' effect (see section 7.8) could explain the finding that for couples only the employment of the man has an impact on the answers to the MEMQ. The 'rosy-outlook' effect refers to the finding that people who feel better about their life as a whole are also more satisfied with their income. A test of this hypothesis was carried out by looking at single persons. If the sex-specific 'rosy-outlook' interpretation of the effect of employment is correct, we should find that among single persons, employed men find it easier to make ends meet than men without work, while there is no difference for women. Using a sample of single persons between 25 and 65 years old, and a model incorporating all variables in the selected model (except the family size variables), the following coefficient estimates were obtained:

	1985	1988	1992
men not at work	0	0	0
men at work	-0.00	0.44	0.02
women not at work	-0.02	0.11	-0.24
women at work	0.20	0.44	0.28
number of cases	400	157	233

Even disregarding the fact that none of the coefficients is statistically significant, the results do not al all confirm the hypothesis. In 1985 and 1992, the effect of employment is larger among single women than among single men. The interpretation of the positive effect of employment remains unclear.

Possible effects of a number of *other background variables* were explored. These are age of head (ten-year brackets), education of head (seven categories) and professional category of head (four categories). Effects that stood out more or less consistently across years were taken up in the final model. In some cases, some other categories had statistically significant effects (see table 7.4, lines I, J, K, and L), but these seemed too limited and too erratic across years to retain. Even the variables that are included are not consistent in their effects (table 7.3).

Young (below 25) and elderly (above 64) householders find it easier to make ends meet than middle-age respondents. (Though for the young the coefficient is not statistically significant in 1988 and 1992.) The most likely interpretation of this finding is that it represents a reference effect. In 1985, households where the head has had a university education are more satisfied with their income than others. In 1988 and 1992, where the effect of the latter variable is not significant, senior employees say they are better able to make ends meet than other persons in similar circumstances. A reference group interpretation is not very plausible for the latter two findings, since both categories of households will tend to live in social environments with a higher standard of living than average. As in the case of employment, non-monetary benefits or the 'rosy-outlook' effect might be parts of the explanation.

Respondents in the *regions* of Wallonia and Brussels find it more difficult to make ends meet than their counterparts in Flanders. The effect for Wallonia is equivalent to a difference in income of 18, 21 and 15 percent in 1985, 1988 and 1992, respectively. Again, a reference group interpretation is not likely, since Wallonia has a lower average income than

Flanders. The possibility cannot be excluded that the words used in the French and Dutch versions of the MEMQ are not quite equivalent[8].

Some methodological points regarding the probit model

An important question is whether the retained model fits the data. A formal lack-of-fit test was not feasible here, due to the total number of groupings (i.e. the total number of combinations of values of the independent variables) being of the same order of magnitude as the number of observations in the sample. A 'score test for the equal slopes assumption' has been applied, however. This is a test whether the effects of the independent variables are the same for each of the five binary variables which can be constructed from the answers to the MEMQ, i.e. 'very difficultly' vs. the other ones, 'very difficultly' and 'difficultly' vs. the other ones, and so on. This test evaluates whether $\gamma_i = \gamma$. The results are as follows:

Year	1985	1988	1992
Chi-square	133.4	77.6	117.5
Degrees of freedom	64	60	64
Significance	< 0.0001	> 0.05	< 0.0001

In 1985 and 1992, the 'equal slopes assumption' is clearly rejected. Inspection of the results of probit models for the separate binary variables showed that the main point on which these models differ is that for all independent variables the size of the estimates is smaller when the distribution of the dependent binary variables is unbalanced (i.e. when one of the two categories contains relatively few observations). This is of course particularly true for the 'extreme' binary variables, 'very difficultly' vs. the all higher answers to the MEMQ, and 'very easily' vs. the other MEMQ answers. Otherwise, the results revealed no systematic differences across the binary probit models. The *relative* size of the coefficients was always more or less the same. For this reason, I have retained the ordered probit model.

Table 7.5 lists the estimates of the threshold values resulting from the probit model. These threshold values (the μ_j of equation 7.7) indicate the boundaries of the intervals corresponding to the six categories of the MEMQ on the latent continuous variable supposedly underlying the recorded answers. Use of the probit model implies that the latent variable is assumed to have a standard normal distribution. The reported estimates of the threshold values are arbitrary in the sense that they shift up and down collectively according to the values of the independent variables. (In fact, the estimates of the effects of those variables can be interpreted as the amount by which these thresholds are shifted when the independent variable changes one unit.) Since the lowest threshold (between 'very difficultly' and 'difficultly') has been arbitrarily set equal to zero, what is significant are not the absolute values of the thresholds, but their differences, which indicate the width of the intervals. With the exception of the bottom and top interval, which are unbounded on one side by definition, all intervals appear to be of approximately equal size. Only the second interval, corresponding to the 'difficultly' category, is systematically somewhat smaller than the other ones.

Table 7.5
Thresholds estimates from probit model

Threshold	1985		1988		1992	
	Estim.	St.error	Estim.	St.error	Estim.	St.error
Very difficultly / difficultly	0		0		0	
Difficultly / somewhat difficultly	1.38	0.04	1.08	0.05	1.36	0.05
Somewhat difficultly / fairly easily	2.45	0.05	2.04	0.05	2.41	0.05
Fairly easily / easily	3.46	0.05	3.04	0.06	3.27	0.06
Easily / very easily	4.28	0.06	3.83	0.07	3.94	0.07

Notes: See table 7.3.

Source: Belgian Socio-Economic Panel, waves 1985, 1988 and 1992.

The similarity of the intervals suggests that the usual simple scoring scheme, which assigns consecutive numbers 1, 2, 3, 4, 5 and 6 to the MEMQ answers, may be fairly appropriate. If that would be true, simple OLS regression results for those answers may not be too misleading. A more formal test of this notion was carried out by replacing all independent variables in the probit model with the predicted value of the answer to the MEMQ obtained from an OLS regression model with the same predictors. The value of the resulting Chi-square test statistic summed across years was a totally insignificant 3.9 at 46 degrees of freedom. This shows that the OLS regression estimates differ only by a scaling factor from the probit estimates.

7 Equivalence scales and income thresholds

The *equivalence factors* resulting from the probit models are shown in table 7.6. Although the factors differ somewhat by year, the general pattern is quite similar. Also shown are the weighted averages of the equivalence factors across years, making the somewhat doubtful assumption that the factors are drawn from the same population. The most striking aspect is of course that the equivalence scale rises quite steeply with the number and age of children. Especially children aged 18 to 25 appear to be rather expensive. The resulting factors for couples with children are in fact quite close to those of the modified OECD-scale (with weights 1.0 for the first adult, 0.5 for other adults and 0.3 for children; children aged 18 to 24 are here counted as adults). At the same time they are of course much higher than those resulting from the income evaluation methods (see table 5.13). The difference is unexpected and remarkable, taking into account that the MEMQ and the MIQ seem closely related in their wording, and at first sight would appear to be two ways to measure the same thing. Possible reasons for the discrepancy are explored in the following sections.

It is important to note that while children are apparently expensive, adults are not. The equivalence factor for single persons is quite close to that of two-adult families, and much higher than the corresponding factor according to the modified OECD-scale. As discussed in the previous section, this result is not a distortion induced by the model, but appears to reflect the actual answers to the MEMQ of singe persons and childless couples.

The equivalence factors for one-parent families seem excessive: those for a single person and one child exceed those for two-adult families by a considerable amount, while the factor for single persons with two children are as high or higher as those for couples with two children. This is a result of the strong effect of children in general, of the fact that the equivalence factor of single persons without children is already high to begin with, and of the greater weight that children in one-parent families get in the specification used, compared with children in two-adult families. Nevertheless, as reported in the previous section, statistical analysis revealed that, if anything, the specification leads to an underestimation rather than an overestimation of the effect of children in single adult families on the answers to the MEMQ. Therefore, the very high equivalence factors for one-parent families reported in table 7.6 appear to reflect the answers to the MEMQ of those families.

Table 7.6
Equivalence scales, resulting from answers to Making Ends Meet Question

Number of adults	Number of children	Age of children	1985		1988	
			Estimate	Stand. error	Estimate	Stand. error
1	0	-	78	2.2	82	2.8
1	1	0-3	110	6.5	116	9.2
1	1	4-11	105	4.6	118	5.9
1	1	12-17	120	6.1	133	8.8
1	1	18-24	126	6.9	153	11.1
1	2	0-3	134	12.6	142	18.0
1	2	4-11	124	7.6	146	11.2
1	2	12-17	154	10.6	176	16.3
1	2	18-24	168	13.2	220	22.8
2	0	-	100	0	100	0
2	1	0-3	122	3.7	122	5.0
2	1	4-11	119	2.5	124	3.6
2	1	12-17	129	2.4	132	3.6
2	1	18-24	133	3.4	144	6.2
2	2	0-3	140	7.8	141	8.8
2	2	4-11	134	4.4	144	6.2
2	2	12-17	154	5.2	161	7.4
2	2	18-24	162	7.2	186	10.7
2	3	0-3	156	10.8	158	14.0
2	3	4-11	148	7.7	162	9.1
2	3	12-17	176	8.5	188	12.7
2	3	18-24	189	10.5	227	17.7
Tenant°			121	3.3	115	4.3
Mortgagee°			113	2.9	114	4.4

Notes: * Weighted average across years, with weights inversely proportional to variances, such that the variance of the average is minimised.

° Equivalence factors relative to owner without mortgage.

Table 7.6 (continuation)

Number of adults	Number of children	Age of children	1992		Average*		OECD scale
			Esti-mate	Stand. error	Esti-mate	Stand. error	
1	0	-	93	4.0	82	1.6	67
1	1	0-3	128	9.0	116	4.6	87
1	1	4-11	136	9.1	114	3.4	87
1	1	12-17	140	8.7	128	4.3	87
1	1	18-24	167	12.5	140	5.3	100
1	2	0-3	154	18.8	140	9.0	107
1	2	4-11	171	16.7	136	5.9	107
1	2	12-17	178	19.3	164	8.1	107
1	2	18-24	236	30.8	188	10.7	120
2	0	-	100	100	100	0	100
2	1	0-3	121	5.4	122	2.6	120
2	1	4-11	125	3.6	122	1.8	120
2	1	12-17	127	3.6	129	1.8	120
2	1	18-24	141	6.2	137	2.5	133
2	2	0-3	138	9.9	140	5.0	140
2	2	4-11	147	7.2	139	3.2	140
2	2	12-17	151	7.8	155	3.8	140
2	2	18-24	181	13.4	172	5.5	167
2	3	0-3	153	14.5	156	7.4	160
2	3	4-11	167	10.3	157	5.1	160
2	3	12-17	172	11.7	178	6.0	160
2	3	18-24	218	19.0	203	8.2	200
Tenant°			124	4.4	120	2.2	160
Mortgagee°			125	5.7	115	2.2	200

- Standard errors calculated with numerical simulation, using estimated variances and covariances of probit coefficients.
- OECD scale is modified OECD scale, with weights 1.0 for first adult, 0.5 for other adults (i.e. all persons 18 or older), and 0.3 for children.

Source: Probit model estimates, reported in table 7.3.

Income thresholds for childless couples, derived from the probit results using equation 7.5 are shown in table 7.7, panel A. Income thresholds for other family types can be calculated from those, using the equivalence factors in table 7.6. Because of the particular specification of probit models, income thresholds are given corresponding to the threshold values shown in table 7.5. The income amounts shown in table 7.7 can therefore be interpreted as the points on the income scale where the average couple without children makes a jump from one answer to the MEMQ to the next one.

The results make clear that before the average childless couple is going to say that it can make ends meet 'very difficultly', its income must fall to an unrealistically low level. (This does not mean that the number of childless couples saying that they can make ends meet 'very difficultly' is very small, but rather that at all realistic income levels, those households are a fairly small minority.) Conversely, only when income rises to a very high level can that type of household be expected to make ends meet 'very easily'. These income thresholds are less implausible than those obtained by Poulin (1988: 16), but still give evidence of the weak or 'horizontal' relationship between income and income satisfaction.

Table 7.7
Income thresholds resulting from answers to the Making Ends Meet Question, and percentages below those thresholds

A. Income thresholds for childless couples (1)			
Threshold	1985	1988	1992
Very difficultly / difficultly	19	23	18
Difficultly / somewhat diffic.	32	37	28
Somewhat diffic. / fairly easily	60	67	49
Fairly easily / easily	116	117	99
Easily / very easily	271	221	242
B: Percentage of all households below income thresholds (selective subsample)			
Threshold	1985	1988	1992
Difficultly / somewhat difficultly	1.8	5.1	2.1
Somewhat difficultly / fairly easily	30.9	44.7	23.8
Fairly easily / easily	87.7	89.3	77.3

Notes: (1) As a percentage of geometric average income in the sample.
Source: Belgian Socio-Economic Panel, waves 1985, 1988 and 1992.

Across years, the income thresholds are rather unstable. Between 1985 and 1988 the lowest income threshold rises by about 24 percent, while the top one falls by 16 percent. Between 1988 and 1992 those changes are partly reversed, though the resulting income amounts are generally some distance below the corresponding 1985 ones, both in absolute and in relative terms. As a result, the percentage of households below those thresholds (table 7.7, panel B) fluctuates rather strongly across years.

Income thresholds calculated following an alternative method proposed by Poulin (1988: 17) are shown in table 7.8. Here, the (geometric) average income of childless couples making ends meet 'very difficultly', 'difficultly' and so on, is used as an income threshold. The resulting income amounts appear much more realistic, and are also more stable over time. It can be noted that the income thresholds corresponding to the three lower levels ('very difficultly', 'difficultly', 'somewhat difficultly') are close together. The persons finding it 'very difficult' or 'difficult' to make ends meet are not found in the bottom income categories only, but are a significant minority across a fairly wide income band.

Table 7.8
'Average' income thresholds resulting from answers to the Making Ends Meet Question

Level	1985		1988		1992	
	(1)	(2)	(1)	(2)	(1)	(2)
Very difficultly	34200	61	39300	68	36600	61
Difficultly	39100	70	36500	63	40400	67
Somewhat difficultly	41800	74	43400	75	43700	72
Fairly easily	51100	90	51200	88	56300	93
Easily	60300	107	63100	109	66200	109
Very easily	73100	130	75700	131	82600	137

Notes: (1) Amounts in BF / month; 1985 and 1988 amounts inflated to 1992 prices.
(2) As a percentage of geometric average income in the sample.

Source: Belgian Socio-Economic Panel, waves 1985, 1988 and 1992.

In Van den Bosch (1997) the validity of the 'average income method' as well as a related method used for some time by the Centre for Social Policy, was examined in detail. The conclusion was that the income thresholds produces by those methods were mainly determined by the level and distribution of actual household income. Selecting a group of respondents giving a particular answer to the MEMQ produces in fact nearly a cross-section of the whole population. For this reason the equivalence scale is to a great extent a replica of the actual distribution of income across household types. These findings imply that the validity of the average income method is very questionable.

Conclusion

The most important and most surprising finding reported above is that the income satisfaction method produces equivalence scales that are much steeper than those obtained with the income evaluation method. This is the case for the Making Ends Meet Question used in the Belgian Socio-Economic Panel, but, as the review of the literature revealed, also for other measures of income satisfaction. In the following sections, I will discuss a number of possible reasons for this discrepancy. In the next section (7.8), I consider the 'rosy-outlook' effect, i.e. the hypothesis that answers to the income satisfaction questions are coloured by how the respondent feels about his or her life as a whole. The effects of possible random error in household on estimated equivalence scales are analysed in section nine. Section ten considers the hypothesis that respondents have different (implicit) notions of the 'reference welfare level', i.e. use different standards, when answering the MEMQ. The implications for estimated equivalence scales are investigated, as well as the question whether the answers to the Minimum Income Question (MIQ) and Income Evaluation Question (IEQ) can be regarded as measures of the reference welfare level. Section eleven considers the possibility that the income evaluation questions and the income satisfaction questions do in fact not refer to the same concept, but to different ones, and discusses one particular hypothesis about the way in which those concepts could differ.

8 The 'rosy-outlook' effect

Introduction

The 'rosy-outlook' effect refers to the finding in some studies on happiness that "the appreciation of a life-as-a-whole affects evaluative perceptions of various aspects of life" (Heady and Veenhoven, 1989). This includes satisfaction with the standard of living or with income. It means that people who are happy express greater satisfaction with e.g. their income than unhappy people in objectively similar circumstances. The idea of a 'rosy-outlook effect' is incompatible with the usual view that domain satisfactions determine the overall evaluation of life. According to this view, people first evaluate how well they do in specific areas of life, and then make up their minds about their life as a whole. If this would be true, a reverse 'top-down' effect is not possible: the overall appreciation of life cannot influence the appraisal of its constituent domains.

Heady and Veenhoven (1989) have empirically investigated this matter, using data from four waves of the Australian Quality of Life Panel Study. They find that there are indeed significant 'top-down' effects for a number of domain satisfactions. For satisfaction with the standard of living, the standardized estimate of the top-down effect is 0.17. Remarkably, there is no significant, 'bottom-up' effect of standard of living satisfaction on satisfaction with life as a whole. Heady, Hempel and Meyer (1990), using data from four waves (1984-1987) of the German Socio-Economic Panel (SOEP) find considerable reciprocal effects between Income Satisfaction and Life Satisfaction (controlling for household income itself). The top-down effect is 0.27, and the bottom-up effect is 0.32 (standardized coefficients).

What is the interpretation of this top-down effect? Heady and Veenhoven (1989) suggest that greater happiness may really improve satisfaction with income, because happy people are more active, are more motivated, set themselves more realistic goals, and have greater resistance to stress. Yet, they conclude that "the data convey the suggestion that the perceptual effects are strongest" (p. 122). Thus, the 'rosy-outlook' effect would be the most important explanation of the top-down effect. Heady, Hempel and Meyer (1990) regard life satisfaction as a proxy for the range of personality and mood variables that could influence satisfaction scores.

What are the consequences of reciprocal causation between life satisfaction and income satisfaction for the estimates of the parameters in the income satisfaction regression equation? When life satisfaction is not included in the equations, these parameters could be biased because of the omitted variables problem. Consequently, estimated equivalence scales and income thresholds might also be biased. The direction of the bias depends on the relationship between family size and life satisfaction. Unfortunately, the effect of household size on life satisfaction is no clear-cut affair. One of the outstanding results of the happiness research is that single people are typically less happy than people who married or cohabiting (Veenhoven, 1989b: 44). On the other hand, the presence of children appears to have no, or a slightly negative effect on reported happiness (Veenhoven, 1984: 249-251). The results of Plug and Van Praag (1994/95) seem to point in the same direction[9].

It can be shown (Van den Bosch, 1999) that this implies that the 'rosy-outlook effect could be responsible for the relatively high equivalence factors for single persons and one-parent families, reported in section 7.7. The interpretation would be that single persons, being rather unhappy in general, are less satisfied with their income than one would expect when looking at their material standard of living. The equivalence factors for couples with children (relative to childless couples) should be relatively unaffected. The discrepancy with the MIQ and IEQ equivalence factors therefore remains.

9 Random measurement error in household income

Introduction

Until this point all analyses have been based on an implicit assumption that household income is measured without error. In this section, I will look at the effects of possible measurement error in household income. Such error could distort the estimates of parameters in the (probit) regression equations for the answers to the MEMQ, the MIQ and the IEQ. I will focus in particular on the question whether measurement error in household income can explain the divergence between the equivalence scales obtained with the income satisfaction method and the income evaluation method. Below, I will first derive analytically expressions for the bias in relevant parameter estimates resulting from measurement error in household income. In a second step, I will present empirical results bearing on this issue.

Possible bias in equivalence scales: analytical results

In order to be able to assess the consequences of measurement error in household income, it will be assumed that the true model is as follows:

$$\begin{aligned} S &= \gamma_0 + \gamma_1 \log Y^\circ + -\gamma_1(\Sigma_j \gamma_{2j} \log FS_j) + es \\ \log Ymin &= \alpha_1 + \alpha_1 \log Y^\circ + (1 - \alpha_1)(\Sigma_j \alpha_{2j} \log FS_j) + em \\ \log Y &= \log Y^\circ + u \end{aligned} \qquad (7.8)$$

Here S represents the answer to the Making Ends Meet Question, logYmin the answer to the Minimum Income Question, Y household income-as-measured, Y° the 'true' value of household income, $logFS_j$ the j-th element in a vector of background variables, measuring household size and composition, home tenure, etc. without error, while *es* and *em* are disturbance terms, and *u* represents measurement error in household income. γ_{2j} and α_{2j} stand for (row vectors of) equivalence scale parameters, indicating the steepness of the equivalence scales resulting from S and logYmin respectively, with respect to $logFS_j$. For the moment at least, those equivalence scales are allowed to be different. Measurement error *u* in household income will be assumed to be unrelated to household income itself, S, logYmin and to any of the variables $logFS_j$, and to have a normal distribution with constant variance.

Suppose we now estimate the following system of equations:

$$
\begin{aligned}
S &= g_0 + g_1 logY + -g_1 \Sigma_j g_{2j} logFS_j + es' \\
logYmin &= a_0 + a_1 logY + (1-a_1)\Sigma_j a_{2j} logFS_j + em' \\
logY &= h_0 + \Sigma_j h_j logFS_j + ey \qquad (7.9)
\end{aligned}
$$

where roman letters instead of Greek ones represent regression parameters to be estimated. h_0 and h_j are parameters in an auxiliary regression of measured household income on the background variables logFS, and *ey* represents the corresponding disturbance term. Then, using the results of Judge et al. (1985: 708) on the inconsistency in least square regression estimates due to errors in the independent variables, the following expressions the biases in the estimates of the equivalence scale parameters g_{2j} and a_{2j} can be derived (ignoring sampling variance).

$$
\begin{aligned}
g_{2j} - \gamma_{2j} &= (\gamma_{2j} - h_j)k/(1-k) \\
a_{2j} - \alpha_{2j} &= \alpha_1 k(h_j - \alpha_{2j})/[1 - \alpha_1(1-k)] \qquad (7.10)
\end{aligned}
$$

where k = VAR(u) / VAR(ey). Since k/(1-k) is always positive, the direction of the bias in g_1 depends on the sign of $(\gamma_{2j} - h_j)$. If the true equivalence scale parameter with respect to variable $logFS_j$ exceeds the parameter for the same variable in the auxiliary regression of logY, the estimate g_{2j} of the former derived from the S-equation is biased upwards, and vice versa. Interestingly, the reverse is true for the corresponding estimate a_{2j} of the equivalence scale parameter from the logYmin equation. If $0 <= \alpha_1 <= 1$, the term $\alpha_1 k/[1 - \alpha_1(1-k)]$ is always positive, and therefore if the true equivalence scale parameter α_{2j} is higher than the corresponding auxiliary regression parameter h_j, the estimate a_{2j} is biased downwards.

Empirical results

A test of this hypothesis was carried out, by estimating a model incorporating the assumptions that the 'true' equivalence scale parameters in the S and logYmin equations are equal (except those for the region dummies), and that there is random error in household income. The model thus is as follows:

$$\begin{aligned} S &= g_0 + g_1 \log Y' + -g_1 \Sigma_j g_{2j} \log FS_j + g_{31} Bru + g_{32} Wal + es' \\ \log Ymin &= a_0 + a_1 \log Y' + (1-a_1)\Sigma_j g_{2j} \log FS_j + a_{31} Bru + a_{32} Wal + em' \\ \log Y' &= c_0 + \Sigma_j c_j \log FS_j + c_{31} Bru + c_{32} Wal + + ey \\ \log Y &= \log Y' + u \end{aligned} \tag{7.11}$$

where Y' is the unobserved 'true' value of household income, and Y the observed value incorporating a random error component *u*. *Bru* and *Wal* represent the region dummies.

Results about the fit of this model are shown in table 7.9, panel A, columns (a). With the partial exception of 1992, the model fits rather poorly according to all indicators. Remarkably, in 1985 and 1988 the R^2's for logY (observed household income) exceed 0.98, implying that the model that is best able to account for the measured covariances, given the constraint of equality of equivalence scale parameters, involves very little random error in logY. Closer inspection of the results revealed that those high reliability estimates for logY were 'forced' by two variables, viz. *Head is at work* and *Head is working as senior employee*.

Table 7.9
Results for *S* and *logYmin* models incorporating error in household income and equality of equivalence scale parameters

A: Goodness-of-fit indices and R-square statistics

	1985		1988		1992	
	(a)	(b)	(a)	(b)	(a)	(b)
AGFI	0.919	0.959	0.9133	0.976	0.963	0.979
RMR	0.006	0.001	0.0063	0.001	0.004	0.001
Partial RMR	0.024	0.001	0.0195	0.006	0.013	0.004
Chi-square	184.1	74.8	99.3	22.2	48.5	22.0
Degr. of freedom	11	9	11	9	11	9
N of observations	3796		1917		2213	
R^2 S	0.284	0.404	0.344	0.414	0.366	0.397
R^2 logYmin	0.560	0.616	0.602	0.632	0.545	0.561
R^2 logY (reliability)	0.985	0.840	0.982	0.899	0.962	0.917

B: Estimates of coefficients for logY' ('true' value of household income)

	1985		1988		1992	
	(a)	(b)	(a)	(b)	(a)	(b)
S-equation (1)	1.56	2.49	1.77	2.41	1.68	1.97
logYmin equat'n (2)	0.38	0.60	0.46	0.62	0.46	0.54

Table 7.9 (continuation)

C: Estimates of equivalence scale parameters resulting from model (b) (3)

	1985		1988		1992	
	Estimate	St. error	Estimate	St. error	Estimate	St. error
logFSa	0.36	0.02	0.35	0.04	0.21	0.04
logFSCh3	0.33	0.04	0.31	0.07	0.27	0.07
logFSCh11	0.31	0.03	0.43	0.05	0.42	0.04
logFSC17	0.42	0.03	0.55	0.05	0.45	0.05
logFSCh25	0.52	0.04	0.68	0.06	0.68	0.07
Tenant	0.08	0.02	0.10	0.03	0.14	0.03
Mortgagee	0.08	0.02	0.13	0.03	0.15	0.03

Notes: (a) Model where equivalence scale parameters for all variables except the region dummies were constrained at the same value in S-equation and logYmin equation.

(b) Model where equivalence scale parameters for variables 'Head is at work' and 'Head works as senior employee' were NOT constrained at the same value.

- Subsample used includes only non-complex households, where neither head nor partner are or were self-employed, and with adequate answers to the MIQ and the IEQ.
- Also included in models were dummies for region and whether head has paid job.
- AGFI: Adjusted Goodness of Fit Index.
- RMR: Root Mean Square Residual.
- Partial RMR: Root Mean square of residual covariances of S with household size and home tenure variables.
- logFSA: log(Number of adults + 1).
- logFSCh3: Number of children aged 0-3, weighted by rank.
- logFSCh11: Number of children aged 4-11, weighted by rank.
- logFSCh17: Number of children aged 12-17, weighted by rank.
- logFSCh25: Number of children aged 18-25, weighted by rank.

(1) In columns (a) standard error < 0.08; in columns (b) standard error < 0.16.

(2) In columns (a) standard error < 0.024; in columns (b) standard error < 0.031.

(3) Standard errors of equivalence scale parameters calculated with numerical simulation, using estimated variances and covariances of model parameter estimates.

Source: Belgian Socio-Economic Panel, waves 1985, 1988 and 1992.

Not constraining the equivalence scale parameters for both variables resulted in a considerable improvement in the fit of the model in all years, as shown in columns (b). Certainly in 1988 and 1992, the model thus modified fits quite adequately. The R^2 statistics for S and logYmin also go up. The R^2's for logY, however, fall to as low a level as 0.84 in 1985, implying that in that year random error would account for 16 percent of the total variance of log-household income. Panel B of table 7.9 shows that the larger estimates of the amount of random error in household income in model (b) lead to much higher estimates of g_1 and a_1. Panel C presents estimates of the equivalence scale parameters g_{2j}. As could be expected, they lie approximately midway between the corresponding unconstrained estimates from the S and logYmin equations.

Thus, the modified model 7.11 has good fit, and produces a kind of 'compromise' agreement between the equivalence factors from the S and logYmin equations. It must be stressed, however, that the model is completely *ad-hoc*. We would need independent estimates of the proportion of random error in household-income-as-measured, confirming those resulting from the model. Such estimates are lacking, at present. In addition, a justification should be found for not constraining the equivalence parameters for the variables *Head is at work* and *Head is working as senior employee*. Until such results are forthcoming, we cannot accept the hypothesis that random error in household income is the cause of the divergent equivalence scale results.

In *conclusion*, the analytical results have shown that the measurement error in household income can in certain circumstances produce the observed discrepancies between the MEMQ equivalence scale and those based on the MIQ and IEQ, even when the true values of those scales are the same. To a certain extent, those circumstances are empirically the case according to the data of the Belgian Socio-Economic Panel. However, a formal test of the hypothesis resulted in a rejection, unless special *ad-hoc* assumptions were made. Moreover, the implications that measurement error accounts for between 8 and 16 percent of the total variance of household income would need to be confirmed by independent estimates.

10 Income satisfaction and reference income

Introduction

In this section I will look at possible differences in the reference point that people - consciously or not - use when answering the Making Ends Meet question. Up to this point, it has been assumed - implicitly - that all respondents use approximately the same yardstick or standard when expressing their satisfaction with their household income. But, of course, it is quite conceivable and even plausible, that different respondents employ different standards. Below, I will call this standard or yardstick that a respondent uses his or her 'reference income' or 'reference welfare level', depending on the context, hoping that these terms will cause little confusion. In the following subsection, it will be shown analytically that differences in reference income can lead to a bias in the estimated equivalence scale. The third subsection reports empirical results on the question whether the answers to the MIQ and/or the IEQ can be regarded as measures of the reference income. Subsection four sums up.

Bias in equivalence scales due to differences in reference income

In what circumstances can differences in reference income lead to a bias in the equivalence scale estimated using the income satisfaction method, and what is the likely direction and the possible size of the distortion? In order to explore this issue, I use the following simple model:

$$\mathrm{EXP(S)} = \gamma_0 \, (\mathrm{W}/\mathrm{R_w})^{\gamma_1} \, \varepsilon \tag{7.12a}$$

$$\mathrm{W} = \mathrm{Y} / \mathrm{FS}^{\gamma_2}. \tag{7.12b}$$

Taking logarithms, the model becomes:

$$\mathrm{S} = \gamma_0' + \gamma_1(\log\mathrm{W} - \log\mathrm{R_w}) + \varepsilon' \tag{7.12c}$$

$$\mathrm{W} = \log\mathrm{Y} - \gamma_2\log\mathrm{FS} \tag{7.12d}$$

where S represent the level of income satisfaction (EXP is the anti-logarithm), W actual household welfare, R_w reference household welfare, Y household income and FS household size (since there can be no confusion, individual subscripts have been omitted). γ_0', γ_1, and γ_2 are parameters ($\gamma_0' = \log\gamma_0$), and ε' represents a random disturbance term ($\varepsilon' = \log\varepsilon$). This model (7.12) incorporates the following notions. Income satisfaction is a function of the ratio of the actual standard of living and reference welfare. (Parameter γ_1 is the elasticity of income satisfaction with respect to the ratio). The standard of living W is defined as household income per equivalent adult; γ_2 is the elasticity of the equivalence scale with respect to household size, which translates the latter into the number of equivalent adults. The precise nature of the reference standard of living is left open for the moment; it can be assumed that it is related to the standard of living of the respondent in the past, or as the average standard of living in the reference group. Reference income is the income that would enable the respondent's household to enjoy the reference standard of living. (Formally $R_y = R_w FS^{\gamma 2}$.)

Now, estimates of the parameters could be obtained if we had one or measures of reference income or reference welfare, but this is not necessarily the case. (Whether the answers to the MIQ and IEQ can be regarded as such measures is the subject of the following section.) Usually, regression equations of the following form are estimated:

$$S = g_0 + g_1 \log Y + g_2 \log FS + es$$

and γ_2 will be estimated by $-g_2 / g_1$. We are then clearly in a situation where the estimates are subject to bias due to omitted variables. The size and direction of the bias can be assessed with the following method (Fomby, Hill and Johnson, 1988: 404). In general, if the true regression equation is:

$$Y = \Sigma_i b_i X_i + \Sigma_j d_j Z_j + e \ (i = 1.. I, j = 1..J),$$

but we estimate:

$$Y = \Sigma_i a_i X_i + e' \ (i = 1..I),$$

thus omitting relevant variables Zj, the expected value of a_i is:

$$E(a_i) = b_i + \Sigma_j h_{ij} d_j,$$

where h_{ij} is the regression coefficient in the auxiliary regression equation:

$$Z_j = \Sigma_i h_{ij} X_i + e'$$

of omitted variable Z_j on all included variables. Thus, the bias in the estimated regression coefficients depends both on the true coefficients of the omitted variables and the relation between the omitted and the included variables.

Applying this method, and using (7.12) and the auxiliary regression equation:

$$\log R_W = h_1 \log Y + h_2 \log FS + e_W$$

the following expressions for the expected values of the coefficients in the regression equation are obtained:

$$E(g_1) = \gamma_1 (1 - h_1),$$

$$E(g_2) = -\gamma_1 (\gamma_2 + h_2).$$

Provided the sample is large enough, it will be approximately true that

$$-g_2/g_1 = (\gamma_2 + h_2) / (1 - h_1). \qquad (7.13)$$

This shows that in general the estimate of the equivalence scale elasticity will be biased. Two factors are involved: $(1 - h_1)$ and h_2. It seems reasonable to assume that reference welfare is positively related to household income and negatively to household size, and that the absolute size of both elasticities h_1 and h_2 is below one. Thus $0 < h_1 < 1$ and $-1 < h_2 < 0$. In that case, the distortion induced by h_2 is downward, while the larger h_1, the more $-g_2/g_1$ is biased upwards as an estimate of γ_2. In general it is difficult to say which effect will predominate, so the direction of the net bias is ambiguous. If $h_2 > -h_1\gamma_2$, it is upwards. The size of the bias can be substantial. For example, supposing that $\gamma_2 = 0.5$, $h_1 = 0.4$ and $h_2 = -0.05$, $-g_2/g_1 = 0.75$, an upward bias of 50 percent.

There is an interesting case when reference welfare depends only on the households own welfare, i.e.

$$\begin{aligned} \log R_W &= \gamma_3 \log W + e_W \\ &= \gamma_3 \log Y - \gamma_3\gamma_2 \log FS + e_W \end{aligned} \qquad (7.14)$$

and e_W is uncorrelated with logY and logFS. In that case (disregarding sample fluctuations) $g_1 = \gamma_1(1 - \gamma_3)$ and $g_2 = -\gamma_1\gamma_2(1 - \gamma_3)$, so that $-g_2/g_1 = \gamma_2$. Thus, both regression coefficients are attenuated, relative to the true ones γ_1 and $g1\gamma_2$, but the estimate of the equivalence scale elasticity is unbiased, implying that the estimated equivalence factors are not distorted. This is important, since it shows that a weak relationship between household income and income satisfaction does not necessarily imply that the resulting equivalence scale is biased.

Income thresholds – In section 7.7 we have seen that thresholds corresponding to the extreme categories of the MEMQ are implausibly high or low. As discussed there, this a result of the relatively weak relationship between income and income satisfaction. Because large differences in income produce only rather small differences in income satisfaction, a moderately low expected level of income satisfaction corresponds to an extremely low level of income. Differences in the reference welfare level can explain the weak relationship between income and income satisfaction. If a rise in income is accompanied by a rise in the reference welfare level, then it is to be expected that the net increase in income satisfaction is relatively small. Assuming that cross-sectional differences in income satisfaction are the result of such a dynamic process, a weak correlation between income and income satisfaction follows.

Another way to express the same insight may be useful. Substituting 7.14 into 7.12c, we obtain:

$$S = \gamma_0 + \gamma_1(1 - \gamma_3)\log W + \gamma_1 ew + \varepsilon'. \qquad (7.15)$$

This shows that, to the extent that γ_3 is close to one, income satisfaction is mainly a function of the fluctuations ew. This implies that at any particular standard of living, we can expect to find a wide variety of income satisfaction scores (as is, of course, empirically the case), resulting in a weak relationship between income or the actual standard of living on the one hand, and income satisfaction on the other.

The argument is illustrated in figure 7.1. The horizontal axis represents the actual, current standard of living (W), and the vertical axis stands for the reference standard of living (Rw). Each point in the plane corresponds to a particular combination of values of these variables, and therefore (following 7.12c and ignoring the disturbance term) also to a particular level of income satisfaction (S). The cloud of dots, which is supposed to resemble a bivariate normal distribution with a correlation of about 0.7, represents observations on these three variables. Since income satisfaction is a positive function of actual welfare W and a negative one of reference welfare Rw, points more to the right or downwards correspond to higher levels of income satisfaction. The parallel 'iso-satisfaction' lines S=a and S=b connect points with equal levels of income satisfaction. The line A-A represents the regression line of logRw on logW. Since for any given level of W, income satisfaction is uniquely determined by Rw, line A-A also indicates the expected level of income satisfaction S, given W. Therefore, welfare thresholds corresponding to a particular level of income satisfaction are situated where the iso-satisfaction lines cross the regression line A-A. For S=a and S=b they are indicated by logW*(a) and logW*(b), respectively. It can be observed that logW*(a) lies almost outside the actual range of observations, even though a substantial number of dots lie on or above the line S=a. *Mutatis mutandis*, the same mechanism explains why the threshold W*(b), corresponding to income satisfaction level S=b, is situated at an extremely high point in the distribution of W.

Figure 7.1
Income satisfaction (S), actual welfare (W) and reference welfare (Rw) (for explanation see text)

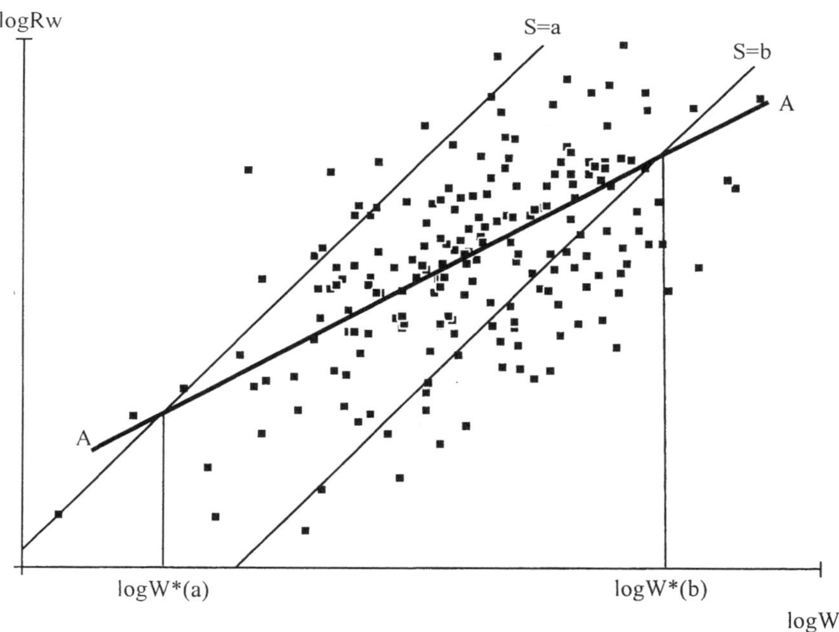

Income satisfaction and income evaluations

In the previous section we have examined the effects of differences in the reference welfare levels that people use when answering the MEMQ on estimates of relevant parameters. It was shown that when these differences are not taken into account, these estimates, including those of equivalence factors, are likely to be biased. An obvious strategy to obtain unbiased estimates of parameters of interest is to introduce measures of the reference welfare levels into the income satisfaction regression equation. A promising candidate for this is surely the answer to the minimum income question (MIQ, cf. chapters 4 and 5). This question asks for the amount that the respondent thinks her household needs in order to just make ends meet. Note that 'making ends meet' is also the key phrase in the MEMQ used in the Belgian and other surveys. Moreover, the MEMQ immediately follows the MIQ in the BSEP questionnaire. Other possible measures of the reference standard of living could be deduced from the answers to the Income Evaluation Question (IEQ, see chapters 4 and 5), which asks what levels of income the respondent in her circumstances would consider very bad, bad, insufficient, sufficient, good and very good, respectively.

Below I will investigate whether the answers to the MIQ or the IEQ, or a combination of these, indeed constitutes an adequate measure of the reference incomes used by respondents when answering the income satisfaction questions (in this case, the MEMQ). I will review a number of models, that range from the very simple to the less simple. In all models, the 'true' model of income satisfaction will be assumed to be 7.12c. A complication is that there R_W is in terms of the standard of living, while the answer to the MIQ (Ymin) is an income amount. The most straightforward solution is to assume that the respondent translates the reference standard of living into an income amount by multiplying the former with the appropriate equivalence scale factor. This income amount is called naturally reference income Ry, and is defined as follows:

$$\log R_Y = \log R_W + \gamma_2 \log FS. \tag{7.16}$$

The models are distinguished by the assumptions made about the relation between the unobserved reference income used by respondents, and the measured answers to the MIQ and the IEQ.

Some of the models used below cannot be estimated with Probit regression, at least not with the software available to me. For this reason, regression-like methods using the covariance matrix will be applied, where the assumption is that the answer to the MEMQ is measured on an interval scale. While this is strictly speaking incorrect, in section 7.6 it was shown that on the basis of the usual coding scheme (1 to 6) of the answers to the MEMQ, OLS regression produces the same estimates as probit regression, except for a scaling parameter. Throughout the section, the selective subsample will be used, while observations with inadequate answers to the MIQ or IEQ are also excluded (cf. section 5.3). This reduces the number of observations by up to 15 percent, compared with the subsample used in section 7.6.

Model 1: no error

The most simple model results when it is assumed that the answer to the MIQ, called Ymin, is an error-free measure of the reference income. Thus:

$$\log Y\min = \log R_y. \tag{7.17}$$

Rearranging (7.17) and substituting for $\log R_w$ in (7.12c) yields:

$$S = \gamma_0 + \gamma_1(\log Y - \log Y\min) + es'. \tag{7.18}$$

The error-free model of Ymin implies that household size, as well as other variables measuring differences in subjective needs, drop out of the income satisfaction equation after the introduction of logYmin. This result provides an easy test whether the error-free model is an adequate description of the data: we only have to take up logYmin in the income satisfaction regression and observe whether the coefficient for household size becomes insignificant.

The results (not tabulated) reveal that the coefficient for logYmin is large and has the expected sign, and that the inclusion of this variable leads to a sizeable improvement in R-square. This suggests that there are indeed differences in the reference income that respondents use when answering the MEMQ, that these are important determinants of income satisfaction scores, and that the answer to the MIQ is an indicator of reference income. However, the coefficients for the household size variables are somewhat closer to zero after the inclusion of logYmin, but the change is not very large, and the estimates remain very far from insignificant. A test of the hypothesis that the coefficients for the household size variables are equal to zero, when logYmin is included, yielded the following values for the F test-statistic: 1985: 37.4, 1988: 21.6, 1992: 19.6, which at 5 degrees of freedom are significant at any conventional level of significance. The conclusion must be that the very simple error-free model is very inadequate as a description of the data.

Model 2: Random error in Ymin

A second model results when it is assumed that the answers to the MIQ measure reference income with some error. Thus, a measurement error term *emin*, with the usual properties, is added to (7.17):

$$\log Ymin = \log R_y + emin. \quad (7.19)$$

Under this assumption, the validity of model (7.12) cannot be assessed through the inclusion of the household size variables in the regression equation. The measurement error in Ymin leads to inconsistent estimates (cf. Pindyck and Rubinfeld, 1991: 160), and the regression coefficients for the household size variables could be significant, even when they are zero in the 'true' equation.

In order to perform a test of the model, I have turned to the Structural Equations Approach, using multiple indicators of reference income. As mentioned above, the most obvious candidates as measures for R_y, apart from the answer to the MIQ (Ymin) are the answers to the Income Evaluation Question, where the respondent has to provide six income amounts, which in her circumstances she would consider, 'very bad', 'bad', 'insufficient', 'sufficient', 'good', or 'very good', respectively. As shown in section 5.2, the ones that seem closest in meaning to Ymin are the 'sufficient' amount Ysuf and the 'insufficient' amount Yinsuf. For Ysuf and Yinsuf models similar to 7.19 are specified. The disturbance terms in the Ysuf and Yinsuf equations are assumed to be correlated with each other, but to be uncorrelated with emin. Moreover, dummies for region are included in the Ysuf and Yinsuf equation, in order to adjust for possible language differences. In this model, reference income R_y is a latent variable, which is supposed to be determined by household income, household size and other background variables.

Two versions of the random-error model were evaluated. In the 'restricted' version the equation for S is:

$$S = g_0 + g_1 \log Y + g_2 \log C + g_3 \log R_y + es'. \quad (7.20)$$

where logC is the household income perception bias correction term. In the 'unrestricted' version, the household size variables and other background variables were added to the S-equation. The restriction following from

7.12c, that $g_1 = -g_3$, was not imposed at this point, but evaluated in a separate step (see below).

The results of a comparison of the restricted and unrestricted models are shown in table 7.10. In addition to the conventional measures of fit, I also report the Partial Root Mean square Residual, which is a summary measure of the residual covariances between income satisfaction and the household size and home tenure variables. If model 7.12c would be correct, those residual covariances would be equal to zero. This is done because a model may have adequate fit overall, while certain parts perform relatively badly. By all criteria, the unrestricted version fits the empirical covariances much better than the restricted one. The unrestricted model fits quite well in 1985 and 1992, though somewhat less so in 1988. As indicated by the Partial RMRs, the restricted model resulted in large and significant residual covariances between S and the household size and home tenure variables. In the unrestricted model, the largest residual covariances were situated in the measurement model of R_y, and even these were in no instance statistically significant.

Finally, the hypothesis that $g_1 = -g_3$ was evaluated. Imposing this constraint on the restricted version of the model produced the following increases in the chi-square statistic: *1985*: 7.2; *1988*: 0.7; *1992*: 26.6. While being acceptable according to the 1985 and 1988 data, the hypothesis is clearly inconsistent with the 1992 data. The reason for this is unclear.

Table 7.10
Income satisfaction and reference income: results for multiple indicators model

Comparison of Goodness-of-fit indices and R-square statistics

	1985		1988		1992	
	Restr. model	Unrestr. model	Restr. model	Unrestr. model	Restr. model	Unrestr. model
AGFI	0.9619	0.9874	0.9422	0.9610	0.9652	0.9884
RMR	0.0055	0.0007	0.0052	0.0025	0.0044	0.0005
Partial RMR	0.0265	0	0.0228	0	0.0242	0
Chi-square	301.7	70.1	228.8	109.9	163.9	37.3
Degrees of freedom	35	25	35	25	35	25
N of observations	3747		1888		2195	
R^2 S	0.372	0.397	0.466	0.485	0.415	0.443
R^2 logRy	0.687	0.677	0.714	0.704	0.630	0.626

Notes:
- Subsample used includes only non-complex households, where neither head nor partner are or were self-employed, and with adequate answers to the MIQ and the IEQ.
- Also included in models were dummies for region and whether head has paid job (Ry equation in restricted model; S and Ry equation in unrestricted model).
- AGFI, RMR, Partial RMR: Seen table 7.9.

Source: Belgian Socio-Economic Panel, waves 1985, 1988 and 1992.

Model 3: Non-random error in Ymin

Answers to the MIQ (and to the IEQ) could not only be affected by random error, but also by non-random error. However, in contrast to random error, there are many different kinds of non-random error (cf. Namboodiri et al., 1975: 574-609). Depending on the specification chosen, one can obtain almost any result. In this section I will look briefly at two particular possible sources of non-random error. The first hypothesis is that model 7.12c is wrongly specified in that feelings of income satisfaction or making ends meet are not an exponential function of the ratio of actual welfare and reference welfare, but of a particular transformation of that ratio. The second possible source of non-random error is that respondents are not equally sensitive to differences between the actual standard of living and the reference standard of living. That is, some persons may feel very satisfied, or may find it very easy to make ends meet, when the ratio between the former and the latter is two, while other persons may reach this level of satisfaction only when the ratio is three (even though they live in similar circumstances and have the same reference standard of living).

The WFI-theory provides more specific hypotheses on both points. According to Van Praag (1991: 84), the function CND[(logY - μ)/σ] describes the welfare evaluation of an individual of his own current income, where CND represents the cumulative standard normal distribution function, μ represent the average of the IEQ-amounts, and σ welfare sensitivity. Welfare sensitivity is measured by the dispersion of the answers to the IEQ. If those answers are wide apart, then the respondent is presumably less sensitive to changes income than when the amounts are close together, i.e. he needs a larger income rise to gain a certain amount of subjective welfare.

The hypothesis is therefore that 7.12c is replaced by

$$
\begin{aligned}
S \quad & = \gamma_0' + \gamma_1 \mathrm{CND}[(\log Y - \log R_y) / \sigma] + \varepsilon'' \\
& = \gamma_0' + \gamma_1 \mathrm{CND}(\log YR) + \varepsilon'' \qquad (7.21)
\end{aligned}
$$

where YR represents household income relative to reference income, adjusted according to the degree of welfare sensitivity. Two questions are of interest here. First, do these additions improve the explanatory power of the model? Secondly, do they have the effect of making the coefficients for the household size variables insignificant?

The results, fully reported in Van den Bosch (1999) are somewhat ambiguous regarding the first question posed above. The CND-transformation of YR (actual income relative to reference income) appears to produce to a significant improvement in the explanatory power of the model. This may be due to the fact that this transformation reduces the impact of measurement errors by truncating extreme values, though. Taking account of variable welfare sensitivity does seem to improve the performance of the model, but only when the assumption is made that the resulting measures contain substantial measurement error. The findings are rather unambiguous, however, regarding the second question. Even with the CND-transformation and variable welfare sensitivity, there remains important residual covariance between income satisfaction and the household size and home tenure variables. In other words, the latter variables continue to have an independent effect on income satisfaction. Model 7.21 must therefore be rejected.

I also reconsidered the hypothesis of random measurement error in household income within a model incorporating (indicators of) reference income. I used a modified version of model 7.20, where the observed variable household income in the S and logRy equations is replaced by a latent variable, supposedly representing 'true' household income. The results for this version were essentially the same as those for the restricted multiple-indicators model with no random error in household income, which were reported in table 7.10.

Conclusion

In this section I have considered the hypothesis that respondents answering the Making Ends Meet Question use different standards, or, as I have called them, different reference welfare levels. In the first place, it was shown that such differences can produce substantial bias in the estimated equivalence scales, though the direction of the bias is ambiguous. In the second place, I have investigated whether answers to the MIQ (*logYmin*) and to the IEQ (μ) are measures of reference income. If that were the case, household size, as well as other variables measuring differences in subjective need, should drop out of the income satisfaction equation after the inclusion of *logYmin* and μ. Various models were used, incorporating random error in the answer to the MIQ, a non-linear transformation of logYmin, differential welfare sensitivity and measurement error in household income. The results made clear that the answer to the MEMQ is indeed strongly related to *logYmin* and μ. Yet, in all models residual covariances between income satisfaction on the one hand and the household size variables and other indicators of need on the other hand remained substantial. Thus, we have to reject the hypothesis that the answers to the MIQ and IEQ are measures of the income or standard of living to which respondents refer when answering to the MEMQ.

11 Satisfaction from income and the evaluation of income: different concepts?

In the previous two sections I have tried to find a technical or econometric reason for the discrepancy between the equivalence scales produced by the income satisfaction method and by the income evaluation method. These attempts were largely unsuccessful. So now we must consider the possibility that those methods are not two ways to measure essentially the same thing, but in fact refer to two different concepts. The obvious question is, then, in what manner can those concepts differ? In a personal note (dated October 1997), an interesting idea has been proposed by Vera Hoorens.

Hoorens notes that an implicit assumption in both methods is that the person answering the Making Ends Meet Question (MEMQ) and the Minimum Income Question (MIQ) has full information about the needs and preferences of the other members of her household, and that there is no disagreement about which or who's needs take precedence. Alternatively, the assumption could be that the respondent has full control over the household's budget, so that it does not matter if other members would have different preferences. These assumptions are not very realistic. It seems more reasonable to assume that there is only partial agreement and partial control. The extent of agreement and control will be smaller the more people there are in the household. Especially teenagers and children in their early twenties may have preferences that differ from their father's and mother's. Moreover, even if they have no income of their own, these children may have ways to coax their parents into giving money for purposes that the latter do not necessarily regard as very worthy. As a result, the household may not spend money on things the parents regard as more important. E.g., a fifteen-year old son may obtain money to buy training shoes of a fashionable brand, even though his parents would prefer him to buy a decent raincoat. The parents may even be of the opinion that their own need for shoes is greater than their son's.

What are the implications of imperfect agreement and less than full control for the answers to the MEMQ and the MIQ? In order to make this link, the assumption is that the respondent regards a certain basket of goods and services as necessary. We can divide all consumption items deemed necessary into those that are actually purchased and those that are not. *Mutatis mutandis*, among consumption items actually bought, we can distinguish between those that are seen as necessities and those that are not. Perfect agreement or full control implies that as long as there remain some necessary items that are not bought, there will be no purchases of non-necessities. Partial agreement and imperfect control, however, mean that a household can purchase some non-necessities, while at the same time still lacking some necessities (as perceived by the respondent). In this sense, imperfect agreement and less than full control introduce inefficiencies into the process of allocating the total budget.

Hoorens proposes that the answer to the MIQ reflects the total cost of the basket of consumption items regarded as necessities. The size and content of the basket will be influenced by the actual standard of living, and therefore will be correlated with actual total expenditure. It is not directly affected by the allocation of the budget across necessities and non-necessities, however. By contrast, that allocation does have an immediate impact on the answer to the MEMQ. More precisely, feelings of being able to make ends meet are supposed to be a function of the proportion of all necessities that are acquired. Thus, given the total budget, a less efficient allocation will make the respondent feel that she has more difficulties to make ends meet.

An example may clarify Hoorens' hypothesis further. Suppose that we have two respondents, Anne and Barbara. They share the same views regarding what goods and services are necessarily for their family, and their total budgets are also equal. This implies that they will give the same answer to the MIQ. Now suppose that Barbara's husband spends much of their joint income on CDs, which Barbara doesn't care for, while Anne and her husband agree on every matter. Then Barbara can spend less money on things she regards as necessary than Anne, and consequently she will feel that she has more difficulties to make ends meet.

As suggested above, it is probable that there will be less agreement in preferences and less control over total expenditure as the household includes more children in their teens or twenties. As a result, the degree of inefficiency will increase, and parents with older children will feel they have more difficulties to make ends meet, compared to childless couples, than one would expect after considering the total budgets and the incomes deemed necessary of those two types of family. This phenomenon is of course exactly what we have found empirically, and which leads to the differences in equivalence scales.

Hoorens' ideas can be formalized in the following way. Let X_n represent total expenditure needed to obtain consumer items regarded as necessary, X_a total actual expenditure and X_{na} total actual expenditure on necessary items. Furthermore, we define $p_n = X_{na}/X_n$, the proportion in which the actual budget includes the items regarded as necessary (i.e. the degree to which the actual budget covers the necessary expenses), and $p_a = X_{na}/X_a$, the proportion of the actual budget spent on necessities. Hoorens' hypothesis can then be expressed in the following model:

$$
\begin{array}{lcll}
Ymin & = & X_n e_m & \\
X_n & = & \alpha_0 X_a^{\alpha_1} FS^{\alpha_2} e_n & 0 < \alpha_1 < 1, 0 < \alpha_2 < 1 \\
EXP(S) & = & \gamma_0 p_n^{\gamma_1} e_s & 0 < \gamma_1 < 1, \\
p_a & = & \delta_0 X_a^{-\delta_1} FS^{-\delta_2} e_a & 0 < \delta_1 < 1, 0 < \delta_2 < 1
\end{array}
\qquad (7.22)
$$

where Ymin is the answer to the MIQ, S the answer to the MEMQ, e_m and e_s represent measurement error, and e_n and e_a are random disturbance terms representing unknown factors. Taking logarithms and substituting for X_n, p_n and p_a, we obtain the following equations:

$$
\begin{array}{lcl}
\log Ymin & = & \alpha'_0 + \alpha_1 \log X_a + \alpha_2 \log FS + e'_n \\
S & = & \gamma'_0 + \gamma_1(1 - \delta_1 - \alpha_1)\log X_a + \gamma_1(-\delta_2 - \alpha_2)\log FS \\
 & & + e'_s
\end{array}
$$

where $\alpha'_0 = \log(\alpha_0)$, $e'_n = \log(e_n) + \log(e_m)$, $\gamma'_0 = \log(\gamma_0) + \gamma_1\log(\delta_0) - \gamma_1\log(\alpha_0)$ and $e'_s = \log(e_s) + \gamma_1\log(e_a) + \gamma_1\log(e_n)$.

If we would equate actual expenditure X_a to total household income Y and would estimate the standard logYmin and S equations:

$$
\begin{array}{lcl}
\log Ymin & = & a_0 + a_1\log Y + a_2\log FS + e''_m \\
S & = & g_0 + g_1\log Y + g_2\log FS + e''_s
\end{array}
$$

the following values for the equivalence scale parameters would result (disregarding sample fluctuations):

$$
\begin{array}{lcl}
a_2/(1 - a_1) & = & \alpha_2/(1 - \alpha_1) \\
g_2/-g_1 & = & (\alpha_2 + \delta_2)/(1 - \delta_1 - \alpha_1).
\end{array}
$$

Given that all parameters in model 7.22 are supposed to lie between 0 and 1 (and assuming $g_1 > 0$), $g_2/-g_1$ is unambiguously larger than $a_2/(1 - a_1)$. This shows that under Hoorens' hypothesis, the income satisfaction (S) method will indeed produce steeper equivalence scales than the income evaluation method (logYmin).

The question can now be asked, if we have two equivalence scales referring to different concepts, which is the correct one? (Or, perhaps more to the point, which one is to be used for what purpose?) It is clear that from the point of view of the respondents, the logYmin equivalence scale is the best one, since it reflects their views of the needs of their respective households[10]. However, according to Hoorens, persons have a tendency to find their own needs and preferences more important than those of others. (Or, one might say, they tend to regard what they want as needs, and what others want as preferences.) Preferences that differ strongly from their own, as may be the case for those of children, are more likely to be discounted. Thus respondents may underestimate the budget required to satisfy the needs of other members, relative to the same for themselves. If this hypothesis were correct, the logYmin equivalence scale would underestimate the aggregate needs of large households, relative to those of single persons, and in particular those of households with children, relative to those of childless families.

The S - equivalence scale is not necessarily more correct, in the sense of being a better reflection of the relative total needs of various household types. It is assumed that income satisfaction is a function of the proportion of total needs that are met, as perceived by the respondent. This proportion depends not only on the size of the total needs of the household relative to resources, but also on the extent to which the preferences of the several household members converge or diverge, and on the degree of control the respondent or another household member has on the allocation of the household's budget. The latter factor points to the possible impact of the intra-household distribution of power on feelings of being able to make ends meet. For instance, the finding that equivalence factors rise strongly with the age of children may not reflect the greater needs of older children, but rather the greater ability of the former to assert their preferences.

It may be useful to place the issues raised by Hoorens' hypothesis into the wider perspective of economic thinking on the costs of children. Browning (1992, p.140) argues that the literature in this domain addresses four distinct questions:

> "(i) The positive question: how do children affect the expenditure patterns of a household?

(ii) The needs question: how much income does a family with children need compared to a childless family?

(iii) The expenditure question: how much do parents spend on their children?

(iv) The iso-welfare question: how much income does a family with children require to be as well off as a family with no children?"

The logYmin equivalence scale appears to be an answer to a question of the second kind. As Browning notes, assessments of the needs of children are usually made by experts. In this case, the experts are the parents. The S-equivalence scale, on the other hand, appears to be more closely related to the positive question. The wording of the MEMQ suggests that it is related more closely than the MIQ to the actual spending patterns of households, although at one remove. That is, one could say that the MEMQ registers differences in expenditure patterns through their effect on the subjective experience.

Another important question is, of course, whether Hoorens' hypothesis can be confirmed on the basis of empirical data. A direct test would probably involve detailed research into the way expenditure decisions are arrived at, as well as asking household members about their own preferences and their perceptions of those of others. Here I will present some material from the SEP data that is admittedly only suggestive, but nevertheless interesting. Included in the SEP questionnaire is a question whether the respondent is able to save or not. Deliberately avoiding the difficult questions of what determines a household's saving decisions, and to what extent people's understanding of the term 'saving' agrees with its economics textbook definition, I assume that the perceived ability to save is closely related to a respondent's experiences in managing his or her budget.

In table 7.11, panel A, the percentage of respondents saying their households is able to save are shown, according to the answer to the MEMQ. Clearly, the correlation between these two variables is very strong: almost no one among the people saying they can make ends meet 'very difficultly' is able to save, while virtually everyone who can make ends meet 'very easily' is saving. The correlation appears to increase over time; it is not clear why this happens.

Table 7.11
Income satisfaction, income evaluation and saving behavior

A. Income satisfaction and saving

Answer to MEMQ	Percentage saying they save			Distribution (%)		
	1985	1988	1992	1985	1988	1992
Very difficultly	18.6	13.4	8.9	4.8	6.1	4.5
Difficultly	28.4	30.7	24.8	11.5	10.9	7.8
Fairly difficultly	37.2	45.4	39.2	26.5	26	19.2
Fairly easily	69.6	77.4	71.1	32.8	29.7	31.8
Easily	85.2	88.2	86.2	21.1	20.5	29.4
Very easily	90.2	93.0	96.2	3.3	6.9	7.4
All	57.8	63.4	64.9	100	100	100

B. Income evaluation and saving

Ratio Ymin / household income*	Percentage saying they save			Distribution (%)		
	1985	1988	1992	1985	1988	1992
below 0.74	31.9	32.3	22.8	8.7	6.1	5.4
0.74 to 0.90	35.4	30.0	27.7	11.4	10.6	8.8
0.90 to 1.11	42.9	46.5	43.2	22.5	23.0	17.9
1.11 to 1.35	63.4	67.6	66.5	22.8	22.1	20.5
1.35 to 1.65	73.3	81.6	79.7	16.4	17.2	17.0
1.65 to 2.01	80.6	87.8	84.9	9.3	10.4	13.9
over 2.01	82.6	88.9	87.9	9.0	10.6	16.6
All	57.8	63.4	64.9	100	100	100

Notes: * Household income as perceived by the respondent; Ymin: Anwer to MIQ
Total number of cases: 5780 in 1985; 3317 in 1988; 3530 in 1992.

Source: Belgian Socio-Economic Panel, 1985, 1988 and 1992.

In panel B, the ratio of the answer to the MIQ and perceived household income is used as an indicator of subjective welfare. The correlation with the answer to the question whether one is able to save is quite strong here as well (and also increasing over time), but less pronounced than is the case of the answer to the MEMQ. This conclusion does not change when the top and bottom categories are broken up into smaller ones (results not shown). Substituting measured household income for perceived household income produced a slightly weaker relationship with the ability to save. Thus the answer to the MEMQ appears indeed to be more closely related to the respondent's experiences in managing their budget than is the case for the answer to the MIQ. Of course, as evidence towards Hoorens' hypothesis these results are only suggestive at best; but they do indicate that that hypothesis merits further investigation.

12 Summary and conclusion

In this chapter, I have looked at what I have called the income satisfaction approach to estimating equivalence scales and income thresholds. In this approach, respondents are asked to rate their own income or standard of living on a particular scale, consisting of ordered categories. A typical question is: "How do you feel about your standard of living?", to which answers can be given on a seven point scale, ranging from "Terrible" to "Delighted". Another question often used is "With your current household income, how can you make ends meet?", with six possible answers, ranging from "very difficultly" to "very easily". The working assumption is that these questions ask about income as a means of acquiring a certain standard of living, and refer to a household context. In the following summary, I will try to bring together relevant results from the literature and from my own analyses, even when these were discussed or presented in different sections.

Determinants of income satisfaction

The most important determinant of income satisfaction is household income. The higher the income, the more satisfied the respondent is with it, or the easier he finds it to make ends meet. Yet, the relationship is much weaker than one might have expected. Even at high levels of income one finds a substantial number of people who are not very satisfied. Conversely, many persons with rather low incomes say they do not have much difficulty to make ends meet. This implies that on average, when comparing across respondents, even large differences in income correspond to fairly small increases in income satisfaction. On the other hand, several studies find that (self-reported) changes in income have a strong impact on income satisfaction. There is a peculiar asymmetry in this, in that a deterioration of the financial situation has a much stronger effect than an improvement. Income satisfaction also appears to be negatively affected by prospects for future changes in income in any direction. These results may reflect a negative influence of uncertainty about income.

Size and composition of the household also have an important effect. As expected, at the similar levels of income, large households find it more difficult to make ends meet than smaller households. In the BSEP it was found that children have a fairly strong impact, while the difference in income satisfaction between single persons and couples limited. Yet, the effect of children in their teens or twenties is much greater than that of younger children. Unfortunately, few other studies take account of the age of children. A finding in several studies is that single parents find it very hard to make ends meet.

Both here and in other studies home tenure was found to be an important determinant of income satisfaction. Home owners who have to pay off a mortgage are less satisfied with their income than non-mortgaged owners, while tenants feel even worse off than the former. Analyses using the BSEP data indicated that the amounts of rent or mortgage payments also appear to have an impact, but the results were inconsistent.

In the BSEP, it was found that single persons who are working find it significantly *easier* to make ends meet than non-working persons in the same situation and with the same income. A analogous difference was found between couples where the man is working and couples where the man is not; couples where both partners work feel equally well off as those where the wife stays at home. These findings, and in particular the direction of the effect, are difficult to interpret. Otherwise, analysis of the BSEP revealed few large and/or consistent effects of 'reference group variables' like age, education and profession of the head. By contrast, some other studies found that the elderly are much more satisfied with their income than the non-elderly in similar circumstances.

Several studies, including this one, discovered large differences in income satisfaction between regions, even after controlling for income and other relevant variables. In Belgium, people in the French-speaking regions find it more difficult to make ends meet than the inhabitants of other regions, while for Canada the reverse is reported. In both cases, translations of the relevant survey questions may not have been wholly equivalent.

Equivalence scales and income thresholds

The income satisfaction approach as applied in this study produces a rather steep equivalence scale, which rises strongly with the number of children and also with their age. For couples with children, the equivalence factors relative to childless couples are in fact close to those of the modified OECD-scale[11]. Equivalence factors for single parents are particularly high. On the other hand, the equivalence factor of single adults is not much below that of two-adult families with no children. Very steep equivalence scales are also reported in a number of other studies. Yet, according to two studies (both USA ones), the income satisfaction method led to a rather flat equivalence scale. The reasons for these divergent results are not clear. Another outcome is that income thresholds corresponding to relatively low or high levels of income satisfaction are often absurdly small or large. In the BSEP, the income thresholds exhibited fairly large jumps across time.

Are children really expensive? Validity of the income satisfaction method

The finding that the income satisfaction approach results in a very steep equivalence scale is rather surprising, given that the seemingly related income evaluation method produces a rather flat equivalence scale. Given the importance of the equivalence scale when comparing standards of living of different households and when identifying households in poverty or low income situations, a large part of this chapter was in fact devoted to a common question: are the results of the income satisfaction valid? Sections 7.4, 7.5 and 7.8 to 7.11 each discussed a particular hypothesis or aspect of this question. In this regard, it is important to recognise that the steepness of the estimated equivalence scale may be due to a strong impact of family size on income satisfaction, but also to a weak effect of household income. Therefore, in several sections the relationship between income satisfaction and household income was studied, considering whether estimates of this relationship could be biased for one reason or another.

A first aspect looked at (section 7.4) was the specification of the probit or OLS regression equation of measures of income satisfaction, and in particular at the linear-logarithmic relationship of income satisfaction with household income, which is presumed in most empirical work. Both the results of my own analysis and those of other researchers provide little or no indication that there is much wrong with the specifications used. A lin-log equation is at least a close approximation to the true relationship between income satisfaction and household income. Also, several analysts have experimented with different specifications of the family size and composition variables, and found that all produce essentially the same results.

In section 7.5 I have investigated the technical quality, the reliability and the validity of the answers to income satisfaction questions, summarizing results from the literature, as well as presenting new findings from the BSEP. In each case, the conclusion was that the income satisfaction measure under scrutiny was highly reliable and valid. All income satisfaction measures used for the estimation of equivalence scales have 60 to 80 % valid variance. This is quite high for measures based on a single question. One reason for this is, perhaps, that both the Delighted-Terrible scale and the Difficultly-Easily scale seem to cover well the entire spectrum of feelings of income satisfaction. Furthermore, a simple model suggests that the use of categories (instead of a continuous measure) in itself does not introduce important amounts of measurement error. Furthermore, two different models were evaluated about how answers to the MEMQ are generated. In the bottom-up model feelings of overall income satisfaction are seen as aggregates or averages of feelings about specific areas of consumption, while in the top-down model feelings about specific areas are regarded as instances of overall income satisfaction. Both models fitted the data about equally well.

The rather elevated reliability and validity coefficients are in sharp contrast with the fairly low (pseudo) R-square statistics reported in sections 7.3 and 7.6, indicating that a large proportion of valid variance of income satisfaction measures remains unexplained. This suggests that important variables have not been included in the explanatory equations. It is possible that those omitted variables could also account for the discrepancy between the equivalence scales derived from the income satisfaction approach and those produced by the income evaluation method. In sections 7.8, 7.9 and 7.10, three of these variables were considered: the 'rosy-outlook effect', random error in household income and differences in the reference standard of living.

The 'rosy-outlook' effect (section 7.8) refers to the finding in some studies that the appreciation of life-as-a-whole affects satisfaction with income. This could distort the equivalence scale estimates from the income satisfaction method. It was suggested that the 'rosy-outlook' effect could be responsible for the relatively high equivalence factor for single persons:

their general unhappiness makes them also relatively unsatisfied with their income. However, since there appears to be little or no relationship between the presence of children and the appreciation of life-as-a-whole, the 'rosy-outlook' effect cannot explain the high equivalence factors for families with children.

Measurement error in household income could distort the results of both the income evaluation and the income satisfaction methods (section 7.9). It was shown that under the circumstances prevailing by and large in the BSEP, random error in household income would induce an upward bias in the MEMQ equivalence scale and a downward one in the scales derived from answers to the MIQ and IEQ. However, a formal test of the hypothesis resulted in a rejection, unless special *ad-hoc* assumptions were made. Moreover, the implied estimates of the proportion of measurement error in the total variance of household income would need to be confirmed by independent results.

It seems plausible that respondents answering the Making Ends Meet Question do not all use the same standards but have different reference welfare levels (section 7.10). It was shown that such differences can produce substantial bias in the estimated equivalence scales, though the direction of the bias is ambiguous. Using various models, I have investigated whether answers to the MIQ and/or to the IEQ are measures of the income level to which respondents refer when answering to the MEMQ. If that were the case, household size, as well as other variables measuring differences in subjective need, should drop out of the income satisfaction regression equation after the inclusion of the MIQ and IEQ answers. The results made clear that income satisfaction is indeed strongly related to the answers to the MIQ and IEQ. Yet, the effects of the household size variables and other indicators of need on income satisfaction remained highly significant. Thus, the hypothesis that the answers to the MIQ and IEQ are measures of the reference income or standard of living had to be rejected.

Having failed to find a convincing a technical or econometric reason for the discrepancy between the equivalence scales produced by the income satisfaction method and those derived from the income evaluation method, I considered the possibility that those methods are not two ways to measure essentially the same thing, but in fact refer to two different concepts. A particular hypothesis is that the answer to the MIQ measures normative notions of the respondent about how much income is needed to obtain a basket of necessary goods and services, while the MEMQ reflects respondents' day-to-day actual experiences in trying to manage their budget. If the respondent had total control over the household's budget, or if there was perfect agreement among the household's members about the way it should be spent, the two methods should produce essentially the same results. However, in many households, in particular in those where children in their teens or twenties are living, control will not be perfect, and there will be some disagreement. It was shown that in that case answers to the MIQ and to the MEMQ will deviate, and the MEMQ equivalence scale will be steeper than the MIQ equivalence scale. At present though, there is not much empirical evidence which could support or refute this hypothesis.

Final comments

What general conclusions can we draw about the income satisfaction method? In the first place, although the reliability of the answers to the income satisfaction appears to be quite high, the results of the method seem less stable than those of the income evaluation approach. Within any sample, standard errors of regression parameters are larger, and equivalence scales are estimated with less precision. Across years the results, in particular income thresholds, fluctuate more than do those of the income evaluation approach. The most straightforward interpretation is that the income satisfaction questions are reliable and valid measures of feelings of income satisfaction, but that those feelings themselves are much more changeable than income evaluations. Both on the individual and aggregate levels, feelings of income satisfaction are perhaps subject to influences of a fleeting and momentary nature, while income evaluations, being considered judgements, are more stable and robust. In any case, in the context of poverty measurement, the income satisfaction method is at best useful for the estimation of equivalence scales; it is clearly unsuitable for the determination of income thresholds.

The latter conclusion brings us to the main issue regarding the income satisfaction method: how valid are the steep equivalence scales it produces? The fact that they are fairly close to the modified OECD-scale (at least for couples with children relative to childless couples) does not carry much weight, given the arbitrary nature of the OECD-scale. The finding that they deviate strongly from the equivalence scales derived from the income evaluation method is more worrying, and also exceedingly puzzling. Despite my best efforts, the puzzle has not been solved in this study. Yet, the investigations did yield some useful insights. It is plausible that the equivalence factors for single persons and lone parents are pushed upwards by the 'rosy-outlook' effect. The income satisfaction approach is more sensitive than the income evaluation approach is to bias due to measurement error in household income. It seems likely that respondents have different reference points when answering the income satisfaction questions, and this can easily distort the results. In short, there are a number of reasons to doubt the validity of the income satisfaction equivalence scales.

Perhaps the most important contribution of the income satisfaction approach is the new light it sheds on the income evaluation method. It has become received wisdom that the latter method tends to produce rather flat equivalence scales (e.g. Buhmann et al., 1988). The results of the income satisfaction approach show that this is not a generic feature of subjective approaches. Any hypothesis about why the income evaluation method leads to such low equivalence factors for families with children must also be able to explain why the income satisfaction method does not. This requirement excludes a large number of potential explanations. For instance, Goedhart et al. (1977) argue that preference changes and substitution possibilities within households are the reason for the low estimates of the costs of children implied by the answers to the income evaluation questions, but if that were true, is not easy to see why that mechanism should not have the same effect on the answers to the income satisfaction questions.

Notes

1 Because of the log-linear relationship of the equations, the proportional increase in income needed to go up the income satisfaction scale a certain distance is the same at every income level. The increase in income Y needed to move from point S on the scale to S', everything else remaining the same, can be calculated by solving $S'-S = b[\log(Y')-\log(Y)]$, where b is the estimated regression coefficient. The solution is:

$$Y'/Y = \exp[(S'-S)/b].$$

Because of the peculiar specification used by De Coster et al. (1984), these computations cannot be carried out on the basis of their results in a straightforward way. For this reason, this study does not appear in table 7.1. Another way to make the coefficients comparable across studies would be to use standardized regression coefficients. Unfortunately, the published results generally do not permit the calculation of those parameters.

2 To facilitate this comparison, Poulin has estimated a special model, which closely parallels the one used for the LICOs. The results were very close to those reported in table 7.A1.

3 While it is in principle possible to compute such thresholds from the published results of the other studies, I have not done this, because there is in general some uncertainty regarding the precise scoring of the income satisfaction variable.

4 As expression (7.5) makes clear, the income threshold depends on all characteristics of the household, in so far as these have been included in the regression equation. It is not clear to me what choices Poulin (1988) has made concerning the values of the control variables included in the equation. For the Belgian results, I have always used the reference category (see table 7.A1), except for the age of the head of household, which is assumed to be between 30 and 64 years.

5 Most researchers simply assign the numbers 1 to 6 or 1 to 7 to the several possible answers. But 1, 3, 4, 5, 7, 10 might be an equally plausible scoring scheme, which would, of course, result in different parameter estimates. This arbitrariness cannot be resolved within the regression framework, unless one is willing to make rather strong assumptions regarding the regression model used (such as those used in optimal scaling, cf. Tenenhaus and Young, 1985).

6 It is perhaps interesting to note that the test-retest reliability results for the Making Ends Meet Question just presented are very close to those obtained by Andrews and Withey (1976: 77-80) for the question: 'How do you feel about life as a whole?', with answers on the Delighted-Terrible scale. They found a correlation of 0.68 between two administrations of this item within the same interview, while 54% of all respondents gave identical answers.

7 The range is calculated as $(5/4)*(\mu_5 - \mu_1)$, where μ_5 is the threshold between 'very good' and 'good', and μ_1 is the threshold between 'bad' and 'very bad'. The factor (5/4) is introduced to make the range approximately equal to the distance between 'very bad' and 'very good'.

8 The Dutch version is:
'Kan U met het totale beschikbare inkomen van uw huishouden, zoals het nu is, zeer moeilijk, moeilijk, eerder moeilijk, eerder gemakkelijk, gemakkelijk, zeer gemakkelijk, rondkomen, d.w.z. de eindjes aan elkaar knopen?'
The French version is:
'Avec le revenu total dont dispose votre ménage actuellement, parvenez-vous à vous en sortir, c-à-d joindre les deux bouts, très difficilement, difficilement, plutôt facilement, facilement, très facilement?'

9 They estimate equivalence scales on the basis of the so-called Cantril scale, which is a measure of life satisfaction. The results indicate that at most income levels single persons require considerably *more* income than a two-person household to feel equally good about their life, while for larger households, the equivalence scale is rising only slightly (at lower income levels), or even completely flat (at higher income levels). Doughitt et al. (1992: 415) report a negative effect of family size on a weighted measure of overall life satisfaction. However, this may be the result partly of a selective sample (which excludes all single persons below 40) and partly of a high weight of economic satisfaction in the total index. For a global measure of life satisfaction (i.e. the answer to

the question: 'How do you feel about life as a whole') the coefficient of family size is negative or positive, depending on the specification, but in both cases not significant.

10 Of course, respondents express views on the needs of their own households, and not on those of others, or on the equivalence factors themselves. The implicit assumption here is that all respondents would give the same answer if they were in each other's shoes (which is equivalent to assuming that the model used is correct).

11 This scale has weights 1.0 for the first adult, 0.5 for all other adults and 0.3 for all children.

Table to Chapter 7

Table 7.A1
Overview of studies using the income satisfaction method

Name of Study	Dubnoff, Vaughan and Lancaster (1981)	Poulin (1988)	Bradbury (1989)	De Coster et al. (1984)
Sample (Kind of)	Random sample of American adults, 1972	Sample of Canadian families, 1983	Probability sample of Australians, 1983	Quota sample of Flemish households, 1982
Size of sample used in analysis	1154	37602	919	2030
Measure of Income Satisfaction	Unweighted sum of two items: "How do you feel about the income you (and your family) have?", "How do you feel about your standard of living - the things like housing, funiture, recreation, and the like?" - Terrible - Unhappy - Mostly dissatisfied - Mixed - Mostly satisfied - Pleased - Delighted	"Which of the following categories best describes how you feel about your family income (or your own income if you are living with relatives)?" Answers on seven-point delighted/terrible scale	"How satisfied are you with the financial situation of your household?" Answers in the form of a number in the range from 1 (dissatisfied) to 10 (satisfied)	"With the total family income it is now, can you make ends meet (1): very difficultly, difficultly, somewhat difficultl fairly easily, easily or very easily?"
Measure of Income	Answer to single question about total annual family income before taxes, divided into ten intervals.	Family income before taxes (i.e sum of answers to individual income questions by source)(2).	Gross family income (annual).	Household net income, after taxes calculated as sum of answers about income components
Technique used	Regression (3).	Regression (3).	Regression (3).	Logistic Regression.
Variables in equation (apart from household income and household type/size)	- age head - region - perceived change in financial position since one year and since five years.	- age head - education head - home tenure status - region - urban or rural residence.	- age, gender - age at which finished education - whether main income earner - home tenure status - recent changes in finanial situation.	- whether one-earner or two-earner family.

Table 7.A1 (continuation)

Name of Study	Dubnoff. Vaughan and Lancaster (1981)	Poulin (1988)		Bradbury (1989)	De Coster e.a. (1984)
Regression coefficients (5)		(4)			
- Log-Family Income	4.66*	0.760*	0.749*	0.48*	-
- Family Income	-	-	-	-	0.00597* (14)
- Family type	(6)	(6)		(12)	
1 adult, 0 children (ref.cat.)	0	0	-	0	-
1 adult, 1 child	-1.84*	-0.443*	-	-0.66	-
1 adult, 2 children	-2.08*	-0.667*	-	-2.51*	-
2 adults, 0 children	-1.84*	-0.443*	-	-0.11	-
2 adults, 1 child	-2.08*	-0.667*	-	0.44*	-
2 adults, 2 children	-2.50*	-0.614*	-	-0.56*	-
2 adults, 3 children	-2.87*	-0.803*	-	-0.55*	-
2 adults, 4 children	-4.39*	-0.888*	-	-0.55*	-
3 adults, 0 children	-2.08*	-0.667*	-	-0.57*	-
- Log Family Size	-	-	-0.488		-1.307*
- Family Size					
- Age Head of Household		(9)			
under 30 (ref. cat.)	0	-0.109*	-0.100*	0	
30-64	2.17*	-0.155*	-0.144*	0.46	
65 and over	4.73*	0.320*	0.307*	1.07	
- Home tenure status		(13)			
Owner, no mortgage (ref. cat.)	-	0	0	0	-
Owner with mortgage		-0.038*	-0.027	-0.43*	-
Renter		-0.185*	-0.178*	-0.98*	-
- Perceived financial change in last year					
better	0.98	-	-	0.40	
same (ref. cat.)	0	-	-	0	
worse	-5.03*	-	-	-1.60	
- Constant	8.18	-2.985*	-2.924*	N.A.	N.A.
Proportion of variance explained (R^2)	0.23	0.194	0.192	0.27	N.A.

Table 7.A1 (continuation)

Name of Study	Dubnoff, Vaughan and Lancaster (1981)	Poulin (1988)		Bradbury (1989)	De Coster e.a. (1984)
Equivalence factors	(6) (7)	(4) (6) (7)			(15) (16)
1 adult, 0 child	67	56	64	80	93
1 adult, 1 child	100	100	100	313	127
1 adult, 2 children	105	134	130	14511	148
2 adults, 0 child	100	100	106	100	100
2 adults, 1 child	105	134	130	198	135
2 adults, 2 children	115	125	157	254	157
2 adults, 3 children	124	161	182	249	173
2 adults, 4 children	172 (8)	180	205	249	185
3 adults	105	134	130	260	N.A.
Single elderly relative to single person age 50	58 (10)	45 (11)		25 (10)	N.A.
Elderly couple relative to couple aged 50	58 (10)	45 (11)		25 (10)	N.A.
Homeowner, no mortgage		100	100	100	
Homeowner with mortgage		105	104	244	
Renter		128	127	613	

Table 7.A1 (continuation)

Name of Study	Vaughan (1984)	Douthitt et al. (1992)	Melenberg and Van Soest (1996)	Stanovnik (1992)
Sample (Kind of)	?	Selective Sample of Wisconsin households. 1980 (Wisconsin Basic Need Study)	EPSEM Sample of Dutch households, 1984	Urban households in Slovenia. 1988 (Household Expenditure Survey).
Size of sample used in analysis	5067	765	2455	2383
Measure of Income Satisfaction	As in Dubnoff, Vaughan and Lancaster (1981) (column 1), recoded to represent a zero to one welfare continuum.	'Economic satisfaction' a weighted sum of satisfaction scores on seven economic domains, using Delighted-Terrible scale: - Physical Needs - Government and Economy - Standard of Living - Financial Security - Cost of Basic Necessities - Household Income - Pay & Fringe Benef.	"How satisfied are you with your household income?" Possible answers ranging from 1 (not satisfied at all) to 10 (very satisfied)	"In relation to living costs, our family income is: (1) very insufficient (2) insufficient (3) sufficient (4) amply sufficient"
Measure of Income	Monthly family income gross of tax.	Sum across 30 sources of income, yearly amounts	After tax household income, constructed by adding up all income components for all family members	N.D.
Technique used	Regression (3)	Weighted Least Squares	Semiparametric estimation (20)	Ordered Probit Model - Maximum Likelihood
Variables in equation (apart from household income and household type/size)	- age head - perceived and expected changes in financial situation - home tenure status - number of earners - value of durables - amount of other fungible assets.	- household expenditures - sample selection bias correction term	- gender head - regional dummies - degree of urbanization	- age head - home tenure status

Table 7.A1 (continuation)

Name of Study	Vaughan (1984)	Douthitt et al. (1992)	Melenberg and Van Soest (1996)	Stanovnik (1992)
Regression coefficients (5)			N.A.	
- Log-Family Income	0.0628*	0.174*		1.108*
- Family Income	-			-
- Log Family Size	-0.0224*			-0.613*
- Family Size		-0.119*		
- Age Head of Household				
under 30 (ref. cat.)	0			0
30-64	0			0
65 and over	0.0763*			0.108 (17)
- Home tenure status				
Owner, no mortgage (ref. cat.)	-			0
Owner with mortgage	-			-
Tenant	-			-0.285* (18)
- Perceived financial change in last year				
better	0.0715*			-
same (ref. cat.)	0			-
worse	-0.1139*			-
- Constant	0.140			N.A.
Proportion of variance explained (R^2) (by all variables)				
	0.263	0.098	N.A.	N.A.

Table 7.A1 (continuation)

Name of Study	Vaughan (1984)	Douthitt et al. (1992)	Melenberg and Van Soest (1996)	Stanovnik (1992)
Equivalence factors	(7)	(19)		(19)
1 adult, 0 child	78	50	66	68
1 adult, 1 child	100	100	100	100
1 adult, 2 children	116	200	128	125
2 adults, 0 child	100	100	100	100
2 adults, 1 child	116	200	128	125
2 adults, 2 children	128	392	152	147
2 adults, 3 children	139	778	-	166
2 adults, 4 children	148	1542	194	184
3 adults	116	200	128	125
Single elderly relative to single person age 50	30			91
Elderly couple relative to couple aged 50	30			91
Homeowner, no mortgage				100
Homeowner with mortgage				-
Tenant				129

Notes:

* Starrred coefficients are statistically significant at the 5% level.

(1) The Dutch and French phrases used for 'make ends meet' were 'rondkomen' and 'joindre les deux bouts'.

(2) Deduced from the Income Questionaire, copied in Poulin, 1985, Appendix 2.

(3) Presumably OLS (Ordinary Least Squares) regression.

(4) Left: dummy-variables specification for family size; right: log-family size specification.

(5) Ref. cat.: reference category.

(6) Family types are distinguished only by size.

(7) Recalculated to base of two adults.

(8) Factor for families of size six or more.

(9) More detailed age categories were used. Coefficients shown are for age groups 25-34, 45-54 and 65-69, respectively, with 15-24 as reference age group.

(10) Own computations from regression coefficients.

(11) Recalculated from Poulin, 1988, table 5, p. 25.

(12) Recalculated, to make '1 adult, 0 children' the reference category.

(13) Recalculated, to make 'owner, no mortgage' the reference category.

(14) Family income is measured in thousands of BF, annually.

(15) Equivalence scale at welfare level "3" (close to sample median level), for couples with a single earner.

(16) Equivalence recalculated from the regression coefficients; equivalence scales published in De Coster e.a. (1984, p. 78) were based on preliminary results.

(17) Effect of dummy for head of household >60.

(18) Effect of being a tenant, in comparison to being a house owner with or without a mortgage (recalculated to a different base).

(19) Equivalence scale calculated from regression coefficients (only differentiated by number of family members).

(20) See original paper for details about the estimation technique. In the paper results for various methods are presented. Results shown here are for the method combining the greatest degree of flexibility with reasonably small standard errors.

8 Summary and Conclusions

1 Introduction

This study has been about the question whether and how subjective information can be used for the identification of the poor. Usually, the poor are distinguished from the non-poor by means of income thresholds (or thresholds defined in another measure of the standard of living). There are a number of ways to determine such thresholds. (See e.g. Callan and Nolan, 1991; Van den Bosch, 1993.) This study has focused on those where respondents in sample surveys are asked about their views or feelings on the matter. The relevant survey questions can be of two kinds. One can inquire after people's views on the income or consumption needs of families *in general*, or one can ask how they feel about or evaluate their *own* income situation. As will be seen, these two approaches involve rather different methodological issues.

The focus in this study has been on the problem of how to identify the poor, i.e. how to distinguish the poor from the non-poor. Another issue is how to measure the total extent of poverty in a group or population, taking into account not only the proportion of poor persons, but also how far the poor are below the poverty line. I have given little attention to this issue, since it seems of a somewhat secondary nature, and also because I do not have much to add to the existing literature. (See Zheng, 1997, for a review of poverty indices.)

This chapter is organized as follows. In the next section, I state the definition of poverty chosen in this study. In the following four sections I discuss the four 'subjective' methods analyzed in this study: the consensual income method, the consensual standard of living method, the income evaluation method and the income satisfaction method. Each of these sections consists of a brief introduction, a summary of the main empirical results and an assessment of the validity of the method in terms of the definition of poverty set out in section two. The final section sums up and gives recommendations about the use of subjective methods in empirical work on poverty.

2 The definition and measurement of poverty

I have defined poverty as a situation where people lack the economic resources to realize a set of basic functionings. The identification of basic functionings (or 'needs') is essentially a normative matter. Therefore, the definition of poverty should be based on standards and conventions that exist in the community. I assume that those standards are to some extent incorporated in the welfare state, as the main institution in the struggle against poverty. As income transfers form an important part of the welfare state, this is one reason to focus on income as the measure of economic resources.

Another reason for this focus is the research context in which the problem of identifying the poor is approached, viz. that of socio-economic research where the object is to obtain estimates of poverty for the whole population of a country or region, as well as for subgroups within that population. This goal implies one has to conduct surveys with large samples of households. The scale of these surveys makes it necessary to use standardized questionnaires of limited length with pre-coded answers. Fairly complete information can be gathered about household composition and income, but it is generally not possible to determine the precise living conditions of households in great detail. In other words, any method to identify the poor must not be too information-demanding in order to be feasible. In practice, this means that one has to rely on imperfect indicators of the actual standard of living of families. In empirical work, a person's poverty status is therefore mostly assessed on the basis of her current income and her household situation. The problem then is where to draw the income threshold between poor and non-poor, and how to adjust the threshold according to a person's circumstances (i.e. how to determine the equivalence scale).

None of the current methods to set a poverty line are very satisfactory. The level of the relative and food-ratio standards is largely arbitrary. Use of the official standard begs the question whether the statutory minimum income is sufficient to escape poverty. The budget approach is theoretically more promising, but difficult to implement practically.

This situation creates a demand for a method that is both theoretically valid (in terms of the poverty definition proposed above) and practical. The subject of this book was to evaluate whether subjective or consensual measures of poverty constitute that method. In the following sections I will summarize the results of this evaluation, using the concepts presented in figure 1.1.

3 The consensual income method

The earliest and most simple 'subjective' method is the consensual income approach. A typical survey question in this approach is the so-called 'get along' question, which reads:

> "What is the smallest amount of money a family of four needs each week to get along in this community?"

This question has been asked regularly from 1945 on in surveys in the USA, and a similar one was included in a series of surveys in Australia. Other consensual income questions have been asked in various one-off surveys. Usually, the mean or the median of the answers is used to represent a supposed consensus view on the minimum income needed to get along.

Results

The main results of the approach are as follows. Within any single survey, there is considerable variation in the answers, and very little of this variation can be explained by household income or other background variables. Over time, the average amount answered rises strongly when average income increases, though somewhat less than proportionally (estimated elasticity of around 0.8). Price changes are fully accounted for in the average answer. Asking a 'get-along'-like question for several family types makes it possible to estimate equivalence scales. In some American studies these turn out to be quite flat, in others the equivalence scales are close to the modified OECD one. Finally, results suggest that for most Americans, 'getting along' is not the same thing as just not living in poverty, but refers to a higher standard of living.

Discussion

In terms of figure 1.1, the consensual income approach can be interpreted as an attempt to measure the income requirements for a set of functionings regarded as basic, given a particular family situation. The validity of the approach rests on a number of assumptions. In the first place, respondents should take a general, publicly-oriented point of view when answering consensual questions, and not a privately-oriented one. That is, they should distinguish between what they want for themselves, and what they think should be included in a community minimum standard of living. Evidence of such a publicly-oriented point of view would be that the answers are not much influenced by the personal circumstances of respondents. Secondly, in the minds of respondents, phrases like 'getting along' should evoke a fairly concrete image of a particular material standard of living, in terms of a set of basic functionings. These images should not vary too much across the population. Thirdly, respondents should be able to translate a given standard of living into a cash amount. This means that, implicitly or explicitly, they have to specify the material requirements for the set of functionings in terms of a concrete basket of goods and services, and also have to price the basket.

The first condition seems to be well met: responses to consensual income questions correlate hardly or not with background characteristics, indicating that respondents do indeed take the required publicly-oriented point of view. Regarding the other two assumptions, the results are more ambiguous. If all respondents had the same understanding of the material standard of living corresponding to 'getting along', and were capable of putting the correct price tag on it, all answers should be nearly the same. The empirical results show clearly that this is not true: the variation in the answers to the get-along question and similar questions is quite large.

The problem is that it is not clear where the variation comes from, i.e. which of the assumptions is violated. Do respondents have different sets of functionings in mind, or do they have different images of the precise abilities and circumstances of the reference family, or do they make errors when translating a standard of living into a cash amount? There are empirical indications that the latter factor is certainly not the single source of variation.

Thus, the results of the consensual income approach do not show that there is a consensus on the amount of income needed to 'get along' (or a similar notion), or on the standard of living to which 'getting along' should correspond.

4 The consensual standard-of-living approach

Another consensual method involves asking people which items from a list they think are necessary, in the sense that all adults should be able to afford them and should not have to do without. (See table 3.1 for a list of such items.) This method was introduced by Mack and Lansley (1985) in Britain, and has subsequently been used in Denmark, Ireland, Sweden and Belgium. Items regarded as necessary by at least 50 percent of respondents were included in the list of socially perceived necessities.People were identified as poor, if they lacked at least three of those twenty-six necessities and also said that they did not have the items because they could not afford them.

Results

The main results of the method are as follows. First, in all countries a range of items are classified as necessities by a very large majority (more than 80%). These items do not only include amenities that are needed to maintain health and decency (such as a damp-free home), but also household goods that save time and effort (such as a washing machine). However, there is also a wide range of items about which opinions are divided, in the sense that the proportion of respondents regarding them as necessities varies between 30 percent and 70 percent.

Secondly, across countries, there is a remarkable degree of convergence in perceptions of necessity, which is greater than could have been expected when comparing possession rates across countries. This is an important result for comparative studies of deprivation, as it is often maintained that cultural differences between countries make it difficult to develop deprivation measures that are valid in several countries. This may in fact be less of a problem than one might have thought. Apparently, the material requirements and conditions of modern living are fairly similar across Western European countries. The number of items for which cultural differences are important (such as 'a roast meat joint on Sunday') is limited, and these items seem easy to spot.

Thirdly, we generally find that items for which possession rates are high, are also very often classified as necessities, and vice versa. This seems natural: people will tend to regard things as necessities which are customary in society, and, conversely, they will tend to acquire the items that are socially approved, encouraged or expected. But there are some exceptions to this rule, a colour TV being the most notable example, where normative considerations apparently predominate. The correlation between possession and perceptions of necessity is also found at the individual level. Whether or not the respondent possesses the item is by far the most important variable influencing his or her perception of its necessity. However, the correlation is far from perfect: many people who have an item do not classify as a necessity, and also a substantial number who do not have it out of choice, still say that no-one should have to do without it.

Fourth, correlations of perceptions of necessity with other characteristics of respondents are generally not strong. For the items which are on the top of the list of necessities there are virtually no differences between various social categories, and for the other items they are mostly fairly limited. The largest differences occur between different age brackets, in particular between the elderly and the non-elderly. Whether the respondent lives single or as a couple, and whether he or she has children also exerts an influence. At least in Belgium, most of these differences between social categories are related to differing item possession rates. Britain in 1990 appears to be somewhat of an exception, since here we find fairly large differences in perceptions of necessity for some items by level of education and by social class. Moreover, and in contrast to the situation in 1985, these differences are all in the same direction: persons with more education and from higher social classes are less likely to consider the item as a necessity. Strikingly, in Belgium, it is the reverse that is true.

Fifthly, over time, perceptions of necessity do not much change in the aggregate. That is, the overall proportion of respondents who classify an item as a necessity generally remains fairly stable or it rises only slightly. The Belgian panel data allow us to look at changes in perceptions of necessity at the individual level. There is a range of items which virtually everyone classified as a necessity in both years. For the other items lower down on the list of necessities, however, it is found that although there is a fair amount of correlation across time, many respondents have changed their perceptions of necessity after a few years.

Discussion

The consensual standard-of-living method can be interpreted as an attempt to ask for a set of basic functionings, or rather for a selection from that set. Strictly speaking, most of the items ask about particular goods and services, but it does not seem too far-fetched to regard those goods etc. as standing for certain functionings. E.g. a washing machine is seen as a necessity because respondents are of the opinion that people should be able to wash their clothes with ease; otherwise there is little point in having a washing machine. Presumably, respondents will take if for granted that almost all people have the abilities and the facilities (water, electricity) needed to operate a washing machine, so that the possession of such a machine is the critical condition for the realization of the functioning of being able to wash one's clothes.

This being said, the obvious question is: do the answers give evidence of a social consensus about the minimum standard of living. As was true for the consensual income approach, two conditions must be met before we can say that such a social consensus exists. In the first place, respondents should be able to take a 'publicly-oriented' point of view when considering this matter. Secondly, the views on this matter in society should not be too divergent.

The first condition seems to be reasonably well met. Many people who have an item but say they could do without it, as well as many of those who do not have it and do not want it for themselves, still say that it is a necessity in the sense that everyone should be able to afford it. Conversely, it also happens quite often that respondents who say they themselves could not do without a particular item, still do *not* classify it as a necessity. Even though judgments of necessity are colored, if not largely shaped, by personal circumstances and experiences, respondents *do* make the distinction between their own private wishes and a more public point of view.

The second condition is more of a problem at first sight. While there is near unanimity about the necessity of some items, there is also a range of items about which opinions are more or less evenly divided. However, as I have argued at length in chapter 3, the evidence available suggests that in general respondents do not have strong opinions about the necessity or otherwise of those latter items. Different answers do not seem to reflect disagreements in the community, but rather uncertainty on the part of the individual. Another finding is that people with higher education, with higher-status professions and with large incomes on average do not differ much in their judgments of necessity from persons with less education, with low-status professions and with small incomes. Together, these results suggest the conclusion that there are no clearly conflicting partisan views in society on the set of basic functionings. To call this a consensus seems to me to stretch the meaning of the word too far; it would certainly be a consensus of a rather latent, diffuse and undefined kind.

An important qualification of the above is that fairly substantial differences in perceptions of necessity are often found between different social or demographic groups, such as age brackets and household types. These differences do not seem to be the result of divergent views on how stringent or generous the minimum standard of living should be, but, rather, reflect the fact that some items are more important for some kinds of people than for others. Older people, for instance, have more need for a telephone and a television, and less need for a car, while the reverse is true for younger people. The suggestion is that older people require other goods and services than younger ones in order to realize the same general functionings (such as maintaining social contacts, or relaxing).

Some practical recommendations for poverty research can be made on the basis of the conclusions reached above. Mack and Lansley (1985) put an item on the list of 'socially perceived necessities' if at least 50 percent of respondents thought it belonged there. To measure deprivation they counted the number of items on this list that people did not have because they could not afford them. In view of my conclusion regarding individual uncertainty about judgments of necessity, such a sharp distinction between necessities and non-necessities seems inappropriate. It is much more defensible to follow the method proposed by Halleröd et al. (1994: 9), who give each item a weight based on the proportion of the population that regards it as a necessity. This weight can be interpreted as the likelihood that the average person will regard the item in question as a necessity. In view of the conclusion that differences in responses probably reflect uncertainty rather than disagreement, the weight can also be regarded as an indicator of how certain the average person is about the necessity of the item. An advantage of this method is that we do not need a more or less arbitrary cut-off point to classify items into necessities and non-necessities. Furthermore, the method provides a simple way to take account of differences in perceptions of necessity between different demographic groups. Instead of having the same set of weights for all persons, the weights for each item can be allowed to vary from one group to another.

Such an index of deprivation could be interpreted as an imperfect measure of the extent to which persons are unable to realize basic functionings. The adjective 'imperfect' is used for two related reasons. First, deprivation indices measure realized functionings rather than the ability to realize functionings[1]. Secondly (and in practical terms, more seriously), it takes account of only a selection of functionings. People may have a number of items that are not on the list, and vice versa they may have only the items that are on the list, and lack many others that are equally necessary. This would not be such a problem, if we could be certain that the selection of items was random. In fact, items seem to be chosen rather haphazardly, with an eye towards easy measurement. (Durable goods seem to be especially popular.) Therefore, the selection may be biased towards particular kinds of functionings that are more easily realized by some persons or families than by others. If that is the case, the results would be misleading concerning the social distribution of deprivation.

In order to overcome these problems, it would be necessary to establish the relationships between the presence or absence of each item on the list of necessities on the one hand, and income, individual and household characteristics on the other hand. Though interesting and useful work on this issue has already been carried out (e.g. Callan, Nolan and Whelan, 1993), a lot remains to be done; in fact this seems to be a problem worthy of a study in its own right.

5 The income evaluation approach

In the income evaluation approach, respondents are asked the Income Evaluation Question (IEQ), which reads:

> "Please try to indicate what you consider to be an appropriate amount of money for each of the following cases. Under my conditions I would call an after-tax income per month of
>
> about ... very bad
> about ... bad
> about ... insufficient
> about ... sufficient
> about ... good
> about ... very good."

Another income evaluation question is the Minimum Income Question (MIQ):

> "Which net family income would in your circumstances be the minimum just to be able to make ends meet?"

Empirically, it turns out that rich respondents mention much higher amounts in answers to both questions than poorer ones. Using the MIQ, income thresholds are estimated by identifying the income levels at which the answer is (on average) equal to actual household income. Doing this for several household types or household sizes separately yields an equivalence scale. These thresholds are called the Subjective Poverty Line (SPL). The average of the six IEQ-amounts[2] can be seen as another indicator of minimum income as perceived by the respondent, since normally the average lies midway between the amounts deemed 'sufficient' and 'insufficient'. This average amount can be used in the same way as the answer to the MIQ to estimate income thresholds and equivalence scales. These are called the Leyden Poverty Line (LPL). However, in contrast to the MIQ, the IEQ allows the calculation of income thresholds corresponding to various levels of welfare. In actual empirical work, the relationship between the answers to the MIQ, IEQ, household income, household size and other background variables is usually specified as a log-log equation, the parameters of which are estimated with regression techniques.

Results

The main empirical results are as follows. First of all, answers to the IEQ have a certain structure and can be characterized by three parameters, measuring the average of the six amounts, their dispersion around the average, and their degree of skewness, respectively. The skewness parameter is a new discovery in this study. However, both the measure of dispersion and that of skewness are virtually unrelated to any background variable and are uncorrelated across time. It is doubtful whether they measure anything more substantial than a passing mood or the constraints of the question format. On the other hand, the average of the IEQ amounts[3] is strongly correlated with the answer to the MIQ, with itself over time, and with a number of background variables (see below). The same is true - mutatis mutandis - for the answers to the MIQ. These results indicate that from a psychometric perspective, both answers have high reliability and validity.

Secondly, the main determinant of the answers to the IEQ and MIQ is household income. In the studies reviewed, estimates of the elasticity of the former with respect to the latter vary between 0.3 and 0.8; in this study they were found to be around 0.45. About 50 percent of all variation in the answers to the income evaluation questions is explained by household income. Household size and household composition were also found to have a considerable effect; in the BSEP, amounts in the MIQ and IEQ answers were found to rise strongly with the age of children. The effects of all other variables were surprisingly small in the BSEP. The difference in answers between those who pay rent or pay off their mortgage on their home and those who do not is much smaller than expected, and does not match by far the actual expenses on housing. Employment status, i.e. whether the adults in the household have paid work, was found to have no impact whatsoever. Variables which could serve as proxies for the reference groups of respondents, such as age and education, had very limited and unstable effects. The exception to his rule is region: the amounts mentioned by respondents in French-speaking regions were systematically and substantially higher than those mentioned by their Flemish counterparts. The difference cannot be readily explained by background characteristics; a plausible hypothesis is that the French and Dutch versions of the income evaluation questions are not quite equivalent.

Thirdly, in the BSEP the SPL and LPL thresholds were found to be rather generous: they are considerably above the subsistence minimum income provided in social assistance, and for most families also higher than relative poverty lines typically used in poverty studies (e.g. half of average or median income). However, across the period covered by the BSEP (1985-1992), both the SPL and LPL have fallen in real terms by up to 10 percent (depending on threshold and model), while average equivalent income rose by more than 14 percent. As a result, the proportion of all persons below the LPL dropped from 14.5 percent in 1985 to 9.9 percent in 1992; for the SPL the fall was even stronger: from 15.4 to 8.8 percent.

Fourthly, the equivalence scales incorporated in the LPL and SPL are rather flat, i.e. as household size rises, the income thresholds increase relatively little. The estimated equivalence factors suggest that older children are much more expensive than pre-school children, and indeed, that the costs of children are affected as much by their age as by their number. As a consequence of the flatter equivalence scale, the composition of the group of persons below the SPL and LPL differs from that below relative poverty lines incorporating the modified OECD scale. Single persons are much more likely to be below the former than below the latter, while for large families, the difference in low income rates between subjective and relative thresholds is much smaller. These differences are reflected in the patterns of low income rates by other variables. E.g., following the SPL and LPL it appears that the retired are at greater risk of low income than the unemployed, while the results of the relative lines suggest that the reverse is true.

In other studies, by and large similar findings are reported. Household income and household size have the most clear and systematic effects on income evaluations. In some countries, the age of the head of household is found to have an important impact, in that the elderly mention much lower amounts in the IEQ and the MIQ answers than the non-elderly. Ages of children have been taken into account only in some Dutch studies; as in Belgium, income evaluations tend to increase with the ages of children. Otherwise, few variables appear to have large or systematic effects.

In other countries than Belgium, the SPL and LPL also tend to be rather generous, though there are a number of exceptions to this rule. The equivalence scales incorporated in these thresholds are mostly rather flat, with again a few exceptions. There may be a tendency that equivalence scales are less flat in countries where average income is relatively low and that are traditionally catholic; yet steep equivalence scale estimates are also reported for Sweden. Within any single country, SPL and LPL income thresholds can fluctuate considerably over time, especially when the estimates come from different, independent studies. Also, the ratio of the SPL to the LPL is by no means constant across countries or even across different studies within the same country.

Interpretation

In terms of the conceptual scheme visualized in figure 1.1, two interpretations of the income evaluation method are possible. These interpretations are complementary and do not exclude one another. In the first one, the answers to the income evaluation questions are regarded as estimates by the respondent of the income required to realize a set of minimum functionings[4]. The variation in the answers comes about partly because different respondents have different abilities and live in different circumstances, and therefore need different amounts of income to realize the same set of functionings. However, another (if not the main) reason is that respondents vary in their ideas about the minimum set of functionings. Some respondents may take a broad view, in particular those who enjoy a high standard of living, and include e.g. a four-week holiday in a comfortable hotel. Others may be more frugal in their opinion, and include only a day trip to the seaside. (A third source of variation is that respondents make errors when translating a set of basic functionings into an income amount.)

In the second interpretation, the difference, or distance, between the respondent's household income and her answers to the MIQ or the IEQ is regarded as a measure of the subjective level of welfare of the respondent. The level of subjective welfare depends on the number and extent of realized functionings, but also on the respondent's standards and expectations regarding the latter. Therefore a person's answers to the MIQ and IEQ constitute distorted or biased indicators of his real level of welfare. Moreover, the biases will be systematically connected with variables such as the respondent's income history and reference group.

The two complementary interpretations just proposed differ in subtle but (in my view) important respects from two other interpretations. The first of those is the original one by Van Praag (1971, 1993), according to whom the income evaluation method provides a cardinal and interpersonally comparable measure of welfare. This claim has been rejected in this study. First of all, the cardinality of the measure rests on two more specific assumptions. These are the equal interval assumption, which says that the categories of the IEQ are equally spaced on the welfare continuum, and the assumption that the welfare function of income has the shape of a cumulative log-normal distribution function. These joint assumptions were repeatedly rejected in empirical tests based on answers to the IEQ. Moreover, the dispersion of the IEQ-amounts is at best a very unreliable measure of the true slope of the respondent's welfare function of income (i.e. the sensitivity of his welfare with respect to income). Together, these results imply that the income evaluation approach cannot provide more than an ordinal and partial measure of welfare.

Nevertheless, for the identification of the poverty line this would be sufficient, provided the measure is interpersonally comparable. The main argument in favor of this claim is that in any language community words like 'bad', 'good' and 'sufficient' must have at least roughly the same meaning for all respondents. However, as I have argued at length in section 6.3, depending on the context such evaluative terms may be used for very different amounts or degrees of that which is evaluated. E.g. an A for maths in high school will refer to a different level of knowledge of mathematics than an A for math's in college. Similarly, Ann may rate her income as 'sufficient' and Bill his as 'good', while both may agree that Ann has a higher level of welfare (in any significant sense of the word) than

Bill - but Ann has richer parents, richer friends and lives in a richer neighborhood than Bill, and therefore expects a higher standard of living.

If this point is accepted, it could be argued that the income evaluation method produces an interpersonally comparable measure of welfare in the sense of satisfaction with income. In that case, however, we are back to a mental conception of welfare, which we have rejected as it is inconsistent with actual social policies. If, then, it is granted that satisfaction with income or subjective welfare from income is a biased or distorted measure of 'true' welfare due to differing standards or expectations of respondents, we have in fact reached the second complementary interpretation of the income evaluation approach proposed above.

A second rival interpretation of the income evaluation method is the consensual one (which is suggested rather than explicitly argued for by some writers). In this interpretation, the MIQ and IEQ are seen as more reliable adaptations of the get-along question (see above), since respondents are asked about their own situation, instead of having to consider a hypothetical family. Taking into account that persons with high incomes may have only a hazy, and biased, notion of how much income is needed to escape poverty or to make ends meet, the LPL and SPL are interpreted as estimates of a poverty line reflecting a social consensus. As argued in section 6.4, this interpretation is difficult to maintain. In the first place, the IEQ and the MIQ do not ask for an opinion about a social issue, but for an evaluation of one's own income situation from one's own private point of view. Secondly, the procedure used to derive the SPL and LPL has some implications that seem to clash with a consensual interpretation of those income thresholds. In particular, more generous answers by high income respondents will lead to *lower* LPLs and SPLs. By contrast, in the interpretation favored here there is no presupposition that there is a social consensus - manifest or latent - about minimum incomes.

The rejection of the original 'Van Praag' interpretation of the income evaluation approach does not imply that the procedures used to estimate relevant parameters and to calculate income thresholds have to be changed. However, it does change the perspective on the validity and usefulness of the income evaluation approach. In Van Praag's view, the results of this method were valid almost by definition, and he could therefore use it as a yardstick to assess the validity of other approaches for measuring economic welfare and poverty. This is no longer possible. Since a respondent's answers to the MIQ and IEQ provide only coloured or biased estimates of his 'true' income needs, we must make certain assumptions about the 'perception' process, in order to be able to use estimation and calculation procedures that result in unbiased estimates of income thresholds and equivalence scales. The results can be accepted as valid only when the assumptions on which they rely are sufficiently credible. To a considerable extent, this is a matter of judgment, in which, inevitably, the empirical performance of the method plays an important role.

Let us therefore review the problems and results of the income evaluation method from this more skeptical point of view. In the first place, there are a number of ambiguities and problems with the way the MIQ and IEQ are worded in the BSEP (and in most surveys). It is not entirely clear what the phrase 'in your circumstances', which appears both in the MIQ and the IEQ, is supposed to mean exactly. E.g., are people supposed to continue living in their present home, or not? No doubt, respondents do not always have the same understanding of the MIQ and IEQ in this respect. This ambiguity may be partly responsible for the unsatisfactory results regarding housing costs. Another problem with the income evaluation questions in their present format is that a single respondent acts as spokesperson for the whole household, with the implicit assumption that all members of the household share the same view about its income needs (or that the respondent is a dictator). A related problem is the demarcation of the household in the mind of the respondent. An analysis of the answers to the MIQ and IEQ in households where one or more adult children were living with their parents produced inconsistent results.

A second and fundamental problem remains the possible bias due to reference effects. The working assumption is that some variables have cost effects only (i.e. affect the income requirements for certain functionings), while others are proxies for reference influences and nothing else. Any reference effects not captured by the latter variables are assumed to be orthogonal to (i.e. uncorrelated with) the cost variables. Of course, reality will not be so neat. One of the main problems is that for many variables the estimated parameters in the regression equation will reflect both cost and reference effects in an unknown ratio. In general, it is very hard to say to what extent the assumptions stated are reasonable approximations of reality. In this respect, perhaps the most encouraging finding is that among the variables which are supposed to be indicators for reference influences, few had important effects. Maybe Belgium is a fairly homogeneous society (or at least, each of its regions are), so that after accounting for the respondent's own level of welfare, there are few systematic differences in expectations and aspirations regarding the standard of living.

Equivalence scales

A more specific worry concerns the equivalence scales resulting from the income evaluation method. These equivalence scales indicate that the income needs of a family increase relatively little when the number of family members rises. E.g., estimates from the BSEP suggest that a family with two children aged between 4 and 11 requires only about 20 percent more income than a childless couple. It must be stressed that technically the estimates are very reliable: standard errors of equivalence factors are fairly small, and more importantly, the results are robust across different model specifications, against the inclusion of various control variables and across several waves of the BSEP. Also, most other studies report similar equivalence scale estimates.

Nevertheless, doubts keep nagging for two main reasons. First of all, the low estimates of the costs of children contradict traditional equivalence scales commonly used in research and implicit in child benefit schemes, as well as common sense. However, one should perhaps not attach too much weight to these discrepancies, since the factual basis of those traditional equivalence scales is generally obscure. The same is true for common sense. On the other hand, estimates of equivalence scales which are based on the consumption behavior of families seem to depend crucially on the specification used, and often vary considerably across studies and countries. Therefore, these do not provide a secure yardstick to assess the validity of the income evaluation results.

The second major reason for doubts about the correctness of the equivalence scale estimates resulting from the income evaluation method is that the seemingly closely related income satisfaction method (see chapter 7 and below) produces equivalence scale estimates which indicate that children are expensive. The importance of the latter finding is that it restricts the range of possible explanations for the low estimates of the costs of children according to the income evaluation method. If both approaches are assumed to measure the same concept (i.e. subjective welfare), the reason for the discrepancy between the results can only be technical. A number of such technical hypotheses were reviewed; the most serious contender was measurement error in household income. A moderate degree of random error in measured household income will indeed (in most circumstances) produce an upward bias in equivalence scale estimates from the income satisfaction method, while at the same time having the opposite effect on estimates from the income evaluation method. However, a model incorporating this hypothesis did not fit the data very well, unless special ad-hoc assumptions were made, and one would need independent corroboration of the resulting estimates of the amount of measurement error in household income.

Alternatively, one can assume that the income evaluation questions and the income satisfaction question measure slightly different concepts. Answers to the latter question could be influenced by the 'rosy-outlook' effect, i.e. be colored by the appreciation of life as a whole. This effect could make single persons feel relatively bad about their income, leading to relatively high equivalence estimates for this family type. Also, it is possible that the income evaluation questions measure normative notions of the respondent about how much income is needed to obtain a basket of necessary goods and services, while the answer to the income satisfaction question reflects respondents' day-to-day actual experiences in trying to manage their budget. If the respondent had total control over the household's budget, or if there was perfect agreement among the household's members about the way it should be spent, the two methods should produce essentially the same results. However, in many households, in particular those with children in their teens or twenties, control will not be perfect, and there will be some disagreement. It was shown that in that case answers to the MIQ and the income satisfaction question will deviate, and the MIQ equivalence scale will be flatter than the one based on the income satisfaction question. At present though, there is not much empirical evidence which could support or refute the latter hypothesis.

The hypothesis formulated in the preceding paragraph can explain why the two methods produce different equivalence scales, but not why those of the income evaluation method are so flat. Here, another process may be at work. When the decision to get children is a deliberate and well-considered one, people may at the same time dampen their material aspirations. In essence, they are substituting welfare derived from their children for material welfare. An implication of this hypothesis is that the income evaluation equivalence factors do not represent the same level of material welfare for all household types, at least as far as the adults in those households are concerned. In this sense, comparisons of living standards and poverty status base on the SPL or LPL could be misleading, However, it may not be inappropriate to use relatively low income thresholds for families with children, if a reduced standard of living is a consciously accepted part of the freely chosen social role of being a parent. Again, there are no clear empirical indications that such a process is at work. Nevertheless, its possibility is a reason to use the results of the approach with caution.

Poverty lines

Another problem with the SPL and LPL is that some observers find them a bit too generous to be properly called poverty lines[5]. In their view, it is straining the meaning of the word 'poverty' a little too much to assert that 15 to 20 percent of the Belgian population is living in poverty, as the SPL and LPL would seem to indicate. However, when the word poverty is not supposed to refer exclusively to situations of total distress and deprivation, but also to people having a hard time to meet the social requirements and expectations of an affluent society, it becomes more acceptable to use the SPL and LPL as poverty lines. In any case, one must keep in mind that there is not likely to be such a thing as a single valid poverty line, already existing somewhere and somehow in society and waiting to be found by the most clever and diligent researcher. The SPL and LPL are only operational definitions of poverty, research instruments used to reveal certain social conditions.

Finally, there is the question whether the income evaluation method produces income thresholds and low income rates that, even if they cannot always be described as poverty lines and poverty rates, are at least comparable across time and across countries. Obviously, comparability across time can only be assured when exactly the same wording of the income evaluation questions is maintained. However, even when the formulation of the questions is unchanged, the evolution of the thresholds is sometimes characterized by inexplicable jumps and fluctuations. More generally, there is the problem that SPLs and LPLs that are calculated independently at different points in time will only seldom represent the same material standard of living in all years. One might argue that the trends in the SPL and LPL also reflect changes in the material aspirations of the population, in addition to the evolution in the consumer price index. However, even if accepted, such an argument does not necessarily enhance the validity and usefulness of the SPL and LPL poverty thresholds, since the nature of and the reasons for those shifts in aspirations are very unclear.

The problems of cross-time comparability are compounded for international comparisons of the results of the income evaluation method. Not only will survey organizations and questionnaires differ, but most importantly of course, different countries often use different languages, making the goal of exact equivalence of wording of the MIQ and IEQ rather elusive. Empirical results confirm that those problems are not just theoretical: one finds that the pattern in the poverty rates across countries following from the income evaluation approach is not at all in agreement with the outcomes of other methods. Within Belgium, the use of region-specific income thresholds resulted in poverty rates for Wallonia (in 1992) that were two to three times higher than those for Flanders, instead of being less than 50 percent higher, as is the case with national thresholds. Again, one might argue that poverty ratios based on the income evaluation method do not merely reflect income differences, but differences in aspiration levels between countries as well. However, this makes those results rather hard to interpret, since it is totally unclear what kind of factors lie behind those supposed differences in aspiration levels. This opaqueness robs the results of the income evaluation method of much of their potential usefulness in international comparisons of poverty.

6 The income satisfaction method

In what I have called income satisfaction methods, respondents are asked to rate their own income or standard of living on a particular scale, consisting of ordered categories. A typical question is: "How do you feel about your standard of living?", to which answers can be given on a seven point scale, ranging from "Terrible" to "Delighted". Another question often used is "With your current household income, how can you make ends meet?", with six possible answers, ranging from "very difficultly" to "very easily". The working assumption is that these questions ask about income as a means of acquiring a certain standard of living, and refer to a household context.

In this approach, income thresholds are estimated in essence by determining at which income level the average respondent (given certain characteristics and circumstances) reaches a certain level of income satisfaction, e.g. 'making ends meet with some difficulty'. Estimates of the equivalence scale can be derived by comparing those thresholds across household types. In actual empirical work, the relationship between measures of income satisfaction and independent variables is parametrized, and (probit) regression techniques are used to obtain estimates of parameters, from which equivalence scales and income thresholds can be calculated. Usually, a specification is chosen which implies that the equivalence scale is the same at all levels of income satisfaction.

Results

The main empirical results are as follows. First, reports in the literature as well as new results from the BSEP indicate that most income satisfaction measures in use are highly reliable and valid. One reason for this is, perhaps, that both the Delighted-Terrible scale and the Difficultly-Easily scale seem to cover well the entire spectrum of feelings of income satisfaction. Secondly, the most important determinant of income satisfaction is household income. The higher the income, the more satisfied the respondent is with it, or the easier he finds it to make ends meet. Yet, the relationship is much weaker than one might have expected. Even at high levels of income one finds a substantial number of people who are not very satisfied. Conversely, many persons with rather low incomes say they do not have much difficulty making ends meet. This implies that on average, when comparing across respondents, even large differences in income correspond to fairly small increases in income satisfaction.

Size and composition of the household also have an important effect. As expected, at similar levels of income, large households find it more difficult to make ends meet than smaller households. In the BSEP it was found that children have a fairly strong impact, while the difference in income satisfaction between single persons and couples is limited. Yet, the effect of children in their teens or twenties is much greater than that of younger children. A finding in several studies is that single parents find it very hard to make ends meet. Both here and in other studies home tenure was found to be an important determinant of income satisfaction. Home owners who have to pay off a mortgage are less satisfied with their income than non-mortgaged owners, while tenants feel even worse off than the former.

In the BSEP, it was found that single persons who are working find it significantly *easier* to make ends meet than non-working persons in the same situation and with the same income. A analogous difference was found between couples where the man is working and couples where the man is not; couples where both partners are working feel equally well off as those where the wife stays at home. These findings, and in particular the direction of the effect, are difficult to interpret. Otherwise, analysis of the BSEP revealed few large and/or consistent effects of 'reference group variables' like age, education and profession of the head of household. By contrast, some other studies found that the elderly are much more satisfied with their income than the non-elderly in similar circumstances.

Several studies, including this one, discovered large differences in income satisfaction between regions, even after controlling for income and other relevant variables. In Belgium, people in the French-speaking regions find it more difficult to make ends meet than the inhabitants of other regions, while for Canada the reverse is reported. In both cases, translations of the income satisfaction questions may not have been wholly equivalent.

Analyses using the BSEP show that income satisfaction is strongly related to the answers to the income evaluation questions MIQ and IEQ. Yet, including the MIQ and IEQ answers in the regression equation of income satisfaction did not result in the estimated effects of all cost and reference variables (in particular household size) becoming insignificant. This shows that the feelings of being able to make ends meet are not a function of actual income and the income regarded as necessary only.

Household income, all cost variables and all reference variables combined do not explain more than 30 percent of the total variance of income satisfaction measures. Including the answers to the MIQ and IEQ in the regression equation boosts this percentage considerably, yet it does not come near to the proportion of systematic variance in income satisfaction measures as indicated by reliability coefficients. This suggests that statistically important determinants of income satisfaction have been omitted from the equation.

Finally, the income satisfaction approach tends to produce a rather steep equivalence scale, which rises strongly with the number of children and also with their age. For couples with children, the equivalence factors relative to childless couples are in fact close to those of the modified OECD-scale[6]. Equivalence factors for single parents are particularly high. On the other hand, the equivalence factor for single adults is not much below that of two-adult families without children. In other words, while children are expensive, the second adult in a household appears to be cheap. Very steep equivalence scales are also reported in a number of other studies. Yet, according to two American studies, the income satisfaction method leads to a rather flat equivalence scale. The reasons for these divergent results are not clear. Another outcome is that income thresholds corresponding to relatively low or high levels of income satisfaction are often absurdly small or large. In the BSEP, the income thresholds exhibited fairly large jumps across time.

Discussion

The income satisfaction question cannot reasonably be interpreted as anything else than a measure of the subjective welfare derived from income (or its reciprocal, the presence or absence of stress related to income). Such a measure can be used to estimate equivalence scales and income thresholds only if it can be shown or reasonably assumed that it is not much affected by different standards and expectations of respondents regarding their standard of living, or that the latter factors are adequately controlled for. Unfortunately, the empirical results indicate that the opposite is the case. The weak relationship of measured income satisfaction with household income suggests that as a person's living standard rises, his standards and expectations rise with it. Answers to the income evaluation questions are apparently correlated with those standards, but do not fully capture them. The steep equivalence scale estimates produced by the income satisfaction method are a result as much of the weak effect of household income as they are of the (relatively) strong effect of household size. This implies that there is a real possibility that the income satisfaction estimates of equivalence scales and income thresholds are seriously biased. Other methods using income satisfaction scores, such as the so-called CSP method (Deleeck et al., 1980; Deleeck et al., 1992) and the 'average income' method produce more plausible poverty lines and equivalence scales. However, it can be shown that these methods lack validity, as the results are sensitive to the level and distribution of actual income, rather than to the subjective views of respondents (Van den Bosch, 1999).

There are also other reasons to distrust the results of the income satisfaction approach. It has been shown that the equivalence factors for single persons could be biased upwards because those persons tend to feel bad about their life as a whole (the 'rosy-outlook' effect). Furthermore, the results of the income satisfaction approach are more easily biased than those of the income evaluation method by measurement error in household income. Finally, from a purely technical point of view, the estimates are less reliable (i.e. standard errors are larger) than those derived from the income evaluation approach. Also, across years the former fluctuate more than the latter. While the income satisfaction questions are reliable and valid measures of feelings of income satisfaction, it may be the case that those feelings themselves are much more changeable than income evaluations. Both on the individual and aggregate levels, feelings of income satisfaction are perhaps subject to influences of a fleeting and momentary nature, while income evaluations, being considered judgments, are more stable and robust.

Perhaps the most important contribution of the income satisfaction approach is the new light it sheds on the income evaluation method. It has become received wisdom that the latter method tends to produce rather flat equivalence scales (e.g. Buhmann et al., 1988). The results of the income satisfaction approach show that this is not a generic feature of subjective approaches. Any hypothesis about why the income evaluation method leads to such low equivalence factors for families with children must also be able to explain why the income satisfaction method does not. As discussed above, such an explanation might be of a technical kind. If it is not, it has to clarify in what way the evaluation of income differs from income satisfaction.

7 Concluding remarks

At the end of this study, a final answer must be given to the question whether and how subjective information can be used for the identification of the poor. However, a question that should be answered first is, why do we want to identify the poor? After all, for many research purposes we do not need a poverty line, or we could do with an arbitrarily fixed poverty line. For comparisons across time or across subpopulations the instrument of inverse generalized Lorenz curves can often provide unambiguous conclusions regarding the evolution and the distribution of poverty (Jenkins and Lambert, 1997)[7].

First of all, more precise information about the location of the poverty line is of course useful when such comparisons are ambiguous. Even if we cannot pinpoint its exact level, being able to specify a lower and/or an upper bound between which the poverty line can vary will often be helpful in reaching unambiguous conclusions. Most important in this respect will be a reduction in the possible range of the equivalence scale, since many comparisons of subgroups of poverty across subpopulations are sensitive to the choice of equivalence scale. Secondly, there is a social demand for absolute estimates of poverty. We do not only want to know whether poverty has risen or fallen, and whether poverty is higher or lower among pensioners than it is among the unemployed, but also how many people are affected by poverty. Whether 2 percent, 10 percent or 20 percent of the population is living in poverty is not an unimportant question.

Can subjective information help in answering those questions? The answer is that it can not only help, but is in fact indispensable for this purpose. In my view the defining characteristic of the poor is that they have a material standard of living that is socially regarded as unacceptable; the poor do not share any other characteristic or combination of characteristics that distinguishes them from the non-poor. The poor are not necessarily excluded in the sense of having low status or being restricted in their social contacts. They cannot be identified on the basis of behavior, or any other observable characteristic only. We can measure their standard of living 'objectively', but in order to know what is socially regarded as unacceptable we have to ask people about their views or feelings on this point.

As we have seen, there are various approaches to obtaining people's views or feelings on this issue. I have distinguished and discussed four approaches: the consensual income method, the consensual standard of living method, the income evaluation method and the income satisfaction method. The results and problems of these four approaches were discussed in the previous sections and need not be repeated here. At this point, I would like to consider the question which method is best suited to reveal which standard of living is socially regarded as unacceptable.

In this perspective, asking people about their views on minimum income (whether for themselves or for a standard household type) can be seen as a shortcut. Instead of having to specify a set of basic functionings and to determine its income cost for persons or households with various abilities and in various circumstances, one obtains income amounts immediately. Such a shortcut would be wonderful if it worked, and in fact, the income evaluation method does work quite well, though only up to a point. The SPL and LPL income thresholds are plausible, the equivalence scale does not display inconsistencies[8], and the results are reasonably stable over time. Yet important uncertainties remain. Prima-facie doubts about whether the low estimates of the costs of children are realistic, are reinforced by the divergent results of the income satisfaction method. Also, falls of e.g. 10 percent in the real level of the SPL or LPL over a time period of three years may not seem dramatic in itself, but they have non-negligible effects on the resulting low-income rates. The fact that it is not known whether those changes in income thresholds reflect changed aspiration levels (and if so, why those aspiration levels have moved), slight modifications in survey methods, or something else yet, makes those results hard to interpret, and difficult to use for policy-relevant research.

In my view, more sophisticated econometric techniques and models are unlikely to resolve those uncertainties. What we need to know is what material standard of living - in terms of realized functionings - corresponds to those income amounts, both in the perception of respondents as well as, most importantly, in actual fact. This implies that we cannot rely on the shortcut, but have to follow the long and difficult road of first specifying a set of minimum functionings[9] and secondly determining the income requirements of this set for persons with various abilities and in various circumstances. 'Subjective' or 'consensual' information is likely to be most useful in the first part of this task.

Two research strategies may contribute to this objective. In the first place, in order to know which functionings are regarded as basic or minimal in present society, we should follow and develop further the consensual standard of living method introduced by Mack and Lansley (1985). That is, we should ask what activities, goods and services are regarded as necessary, in the sense that no one should have to do without them. An assumption here is that there is in practice a direct link between the possession of certain commodities and the realization of certain functionings. From this perspective, choice and formulation of the items that are included in the survey questionnaire might be improved.

At the same time, we should try to estimate at which income levels people with various characteristics and in various household situations actually realize those functionings. This is likely to prove the most difficult task. Research in this field suggests that the relationship between indicators of the actual standard of living and household income is fairly weak. This is no doubt partly due to differing preferences, but also to the fact that we do not know and measure all relevant circumstances and abilities of persons. Special in-depth surveys may be needed to uncover the latter. For instance, the social network of people may be an important factor.

Apart from providing rich information about actual standards of living, this strategy also has the merit of potentially opening up the 'black box of the household'. Use of the income evaluation method implies that one assumes that all household members have the same standard of living. By contrast, there seem few practical objections to gathering information about realized or desired functionings on the individual level.

The other research strategy starts from the budget standard approach. Budget standards have the important advantage that they are very specific, but are hampered by two problems. The first is that the choice of goods and services which go into the basket is often quite arbitrary. The second and related problem is that the composition of the resulting budget can deviate substantially from the expenditure patterns of real households[10]. Using subjective information derived from survey questions might reduce the arbitrariness[11]. Perhaps more importantly, following suggestions by Walker (1987), the choices and results of the budget might be discussed in panels or 'focus groups' composed of ordinary but interested members of the public. Their views and comments might make the exercise less arbitrary and also resolve some of the discrepancies between budget standards and actual spending patterns. The two strategies could support each other, and will hopefully converge on the same income amounts.

Clearly, the two strategies just outlined form a program for the long term. What recommendations can be made for poverty research in the shorter term? In order to have a rough estimate of the extent and social distribution of poverty (the second purpose stated in the beginning of this section), the consensual standard of living approach is probably well suited. An important point in its favor is that it appears to have considerable intuitive appeal for a wide audience; it is no coincidence that this method was developed for a television documentary. The modifications suggested in section 8.4 might improve it further, while work should also be done to ensure that the selection of items covers all domains of the material standard of living.

When one of the purposes of the research is to evaluate the success of social income transfers in relieving poverty, Mack and Lansley-like deprivation indices must be supplemented by income-based poverty measures. In this context, however, relative (arbitrary) poverty lines incorporating conventional equivalence scales, together with IGL-curves and similar devices, might be sufficient to answer most questions satisfactorily.

The attentive reader may have noted that these recommendations do not leave much room for the income evaluation and income satisfaction methods. Indeed, it is my impression that these methods have pretty well exhausted their research potential, and have yielded nearly all that they have to offer as regards the problem of identifying the poor. This does not mean that the methods should be discarded and that the relevant survey questions should be scrapped from questionnaires. In the first place, one might pursue the methods (or at least retain the questions) out of scientific interest. E.g. the income satisfaction method might be part of the study of the subjective quality of life. Secondly, the income evaluation method might be helpful in the determination of the income requirements of basic functionings for various household types. Its usefulness in this respect would probably be enhanced if it was preceded or followed by questions probing the mind of the respondent for the standard of living that he or she is thinking of when answering the income evaluation questions.

A case could be made for the SPL and LPL as an estimate of the social perception of the minimum income. As long as the long-term research program proposed above has not delivered (if it ever does), we should perhaps not discard existing and reasonably effective research instruments. The income evaluation method is, after all, cheap in terms of survey time, computer resources and econometric expertise. As long as it is kept in mind that these income thresholds are not really comparable over time and across countries, and that they may even be misleading as regards the social distribution of poverty and low income, the SPL and LPL could be used as rough indicators of the minimum income on which social perceptions converge.

Yet, this purpose might be equally well, if not better served by survey questions in the spirit of the consensual income approach, e.g. *What is the minimum amount of income a family of two adults and two children needs to just make ends meet in this town or village?* In this case, one has only to calculate the mean or median of the answers. In order to avoid people having to express views about situations with which they are totally unfamiliar, one might put the question just quoted to couples with children only. For one-parent families, childless couples and single persons, suitably rephrased variants of this question could be used. The method is technically and conceptually exceedingly simple, and it is totally clear that the average or median of the answers represents nothing else than, indeed, an average or median of social perceptions of the minimum income.

Notes

1 It must be mentioned that researchers have tried to correct deprivation indices for differences in tastes. E.g. Mack and Lansley (1985) count the absence of an item only as deprivation if people say they do not have it because they cannot afford it. Desai and Shah (1988) make the convenient assumption that differences in tastes are random with respect to socio-economic background variables. Both solutions have their problems, however.

2 More precisely, the geometric mean of the amounts.

3 More precisely, the log of the geometric mean of the amounts, typically denoted μ.

4 This interpretation is perhaps more obvious for the MIQ than for the IEQ, where the word 'minimum' does not enter the formulation. However, given that the empirical results for the IEQ parallel those for the MIQ, it seems reasonable to regard the income level in the middle between the 'sufficient' and 'insufficient' income levels in the IEQ as an estimate of the minimum income.

5 It might be maintained that this is true for the SPL and the LPL0.5, but not for the LPL0.4. However, I have argued that while the LPL0.5 has face-validity as a poverty line, as it corresponds to the income level in the middle between the incomes deemed 'sufficient' and 'insufficient', use of the LPL0.4 is only slightly less arbitrary than simply taking 80 percent of the LPL0.5.

6 This scale has weights 1.0 for the first adult, 0.5 for all other adults and 0.3 for all children.

7 Inverse generalized Lorenz curves visualize in a single picture the number of poor, the average income shortfall of the poor relative to the poverty line, and the degree of inequality among the poor.

8 Inconsistencies such as declining factors for families with more children.

9 This set may vary across broadly-defined categories of persons or households, such as single person, families with children, the elderly.

10 E.g. most of the clothing components of the 'modest but adequate' budgets developed by Bradshaw and his collaborators lie above actual average expenditure on clothing in the fourth and fifth quintiles of equivalent expenditure (Bradshaw, 1993: 76).

11 In fact, Bradshaw (1993) used results from the consensual standard of living method to define the basket.

Bibliography

Agresti, A. (1984), *Analysis of ordinal categorical data*. New York: Wiley.

Aguilar, R. and Gustafsson, B. (1988), Public opinion about social assistance in Sweden, *European Journal of Political Research*, vol. 16, pp. 251-276.

Alcock, P. (1993), *Understanding Poverty*. Basingstoke: MacMillan.

Aldrich, J. and Nelson, F. (1984), *Linear probability, logit, and probit models*, Sage University Paper series on Quantitative Applications in the Social Sciences, 07-045, Beverly Hills and London: Sage.

Alessie, R. and Kapteyn, A. (1988), Preference formation, incomes and the distribution of welfare. *The Journal of Behavioral Economics*, vol. 17, no. 1, pp. 77-96.

Allardt, E. (1981), Experiences from the comparative Scandinavian welfare study, with a bibliography of the project, *European Journal of Policitical Research*, vol. 9, pp. 101-111.

Amiel, Y. and Cowell, F. (1997), The Measurement of Poverty: An Experimental Questionnnaire Investigation, *Empirical Economics*, no. 22.

Anderson, M., Bechhofer, F. and Gershuny, J. (1994), *The Social and Political Economy of the Household*. Oxford: Oxford University Press.

Andreß, H.-J. and Lipsmeier, G. (1995), Was gehört zum notwendigen Lebensstandard und wer kann ihn sich leisten? Ein neues Konzept zur Armutsmessung, *Aus Politik und Zeitgeschichte, Beilage zur Wochenzeitung Das Parlament*, B 31-32/95 (28 July 1995).

Andrews, F. and Withey, S. (1976), *Social Indicators of Well-Being: Americans perception of life quality*. New York: Plenum Press.

Antonides, G., Kapteyn, A. and Wansbeek, T. (1980), *Reliability and Validity Assessment of Ten Methods for the Measurement of Individual Welfare Functions of Income*. Unpublished paper.

Antonides, G., Wunderink, S. and Jansen van Rosendaal, E. (1994), *Household Labor Time and Durable Goods in Household Behavior.*

Paper presented at the Aldi Hagenaars memorial conference, Leyden, August 28-29.

Apps, P. and Rees, R. (1996), Labour Supply, household production and intra-family welfare distribution, *Journal of Public Economics*, vol. 60, pp. 199-219.

Apps, P. and Rees, R. (1997), Collective Labour Supply and Household Production, *Journal of Political Economy*, vol. 105, no. 1, pp. 178-190.

Atkinson, A. (1987), On the measurement of poverty, *Econometrica*, vol. 55, pp. 749-764.

Atkinson, A. (1989), *Poverty and Social Security*. Hemel Hampstead: Harvester Wheatsheaf.

Atkinson, A. (1990), Poverty, Statistics and Progress in Europe, in: Teekens and Van Praag (1990), pp. 27-44.

Atkinson, A. (1992), Measuring Poverty and Differences in Family Composition, *Economica*, vol. 59, pp. 1-16.

Atkinson, A., Gardiner, K., Lechêne, V. and Sutherland, H. (1993), *Comparing Poverty in France and the United Kingdom*, Discussion Paper WSP/84, London: Suntory-Toyota International Centre for Economics and Related Disciplines.

Atkinson, A., Rainwater, L. and Smeeding, T. (1995), *Income Distribution in OECD Countries*. Paris: OECD.

Auletta, K. (1982), *The Underclass*. New York: Random House.

Balestrino, A. (1996), *A Note on Functioning - Poverty in Affluent Societies*. Pisa: University of Pisa, mimeo.

Barr, N. (1992), Economic Theory and the Welfare State: A Survey and Interpretation, *Journal of Economic Literature*, vol. 30, pp. 741-803.

Barry, B. (1990a), *Political Argument. A reissue with a new introduction*. New York/London: Harvester Wheatsheaf (first edition in 1965).

Barry, B. (1990b), The welfare state versus the relief of poverty, in: Ware and Goodin (1990), pp. 73-103.

Becker, G. (1965), A Theory of the Allocation of Time, *Economic Journal*, vol. 75, pp. 493-517.

Becker, G. (1981), *A Treatise on the Family*. Cambridge (Massachusetts): Harvard University Press.

Behrman, J. (1997), Intrahousehold Distribution and the Family, in: Rosenzweig, M. and Stark, O. (eds.), *Handbook of Population and Family Economics*. Amsterdam: Elsevier, vol 1A, pp. 125-187.

Berghman, J. and Cantillon, B. (1993), *The European Face of Social Security. Essays in honour of Herman Deleeck*. Aldershot: Avebury.

Berghman, J., Cantillon, B. and Marx, I. (1993), The future of social security in Europe, in: Berghman, J. and Cantillon, B. (1993), pp. 369-395.

Berghman, J., Deleeck, H., De Smet, E., Janssens, P., Marynissen, R., Schulpen, L., Spiessens, E. and Van Hoye, R. (1985), *Sociale Indicatoren van de Vlaamse Gemeenschap*, C.B.G.S. Monografie 1985/2, Brussels: Ministerie van de Vlaamse Gemeenschap.

Berghman, J. and Dirven, H.-J. (1991), *Poverty, insecurity of subsistence and relative deprivation in The Netherlands: Report 1991*. Tilburg: IVA.

Bernelot-Moens, W. (1980), De invloed van de buitenshuis werkende gehuwde vrouw en van de gezinsfase op geld- en tijdsbesteding in het gezin, *Vakblad voor huishoudkunde*, vol. 5, no. 1, pp. 130-147.

Blackburn, M. (1993), *International Comparisons of Income Poverty and Extreme Income Poverty*. Luxembourg Income Study Working Paper, No. 97.

Blalock, H. (1972), *Social Statistics* (second edition). Tokyo: McGraw-Hill Kogakusha.

Blundell, R. and Lewbell, A. (1991), The information content of equivalence scales, *Journal of Econometrics*, vol. 50, pp. 49-68.

Blundell, R. and Preston, I. (1994), *Income or Consumption in the Measurement of Inequality and Poverty*. IFS Working Paper Series No W94/12, London: The Instititute for Fiscal Studies.

Bolderson, H. and Mabbett, D. (1991), *Social Policy and Social Security in Australia, Britain and the USA*. Aldershot: Avebury.

Bollen, K. (1989), *Structural Equations with Latent Variables*. New York: Wiley.

Borooah, V. and McKee, P. (1994), Intra-household income transfers and implications for poverty and inequality in the U.K.., in: Creedy, J. (ed.), *Taxation, Poverty and Income Distribution*. Aldershot: Edward Elgar.

Börsch-Supan, A. and Stahl, K. (1991), Life cycle savings and consumption constraints. Theory, empirical evidence and fiscal implications, *Journal of Population Economics*, vol. 4, no. 3, pp. 233-255.

Bourguignon, F. and Chiappori, P. (1992), Collective models of household behavior. An introduction, *European Economic Review*, vol. 36, pp. 355-364.

Box, G. and Cox, D. (1964), An analysis of transformations, *Journal of the Royal Statistical Society series B.*, vol. 26, pp. 211-234.

Bradbury, B. (1989), Family Size Equivalence Scales and Survey Evaluations of Income and Well-Being, *Journal of Social Policy*, vol. 18, no. 3, pp. 383-408.

Bradshaw, J. (1993), *Budget standards for the United Kingdom*. Aldershot: Avebury.

Bradshaw, J., Ditch, J., Holmes, H. and Whiteford, P. (1993), A comparative study of child support in fifteen countries, *Journal of European Social Policy*, vol. 3, no. 4, pp. 255-271.

Brock, D. (1993), Quality of Life Measures in Health Care and Medical Ethics, in: Sen and Nussbaum (1993).

Broome, J. (1988), What's wrong with poverty?, *London Review of Books*, vol. 10, no. 10, pp. 16-17.

Broome, J. (1991), Utility, *Economics and Philosophy*, vol. 7, pp. 1-12.

Brown, C. and Preece, A. (1987), Housework, in: Eatwell, J., Milgate, M. and Newman, P. (eds.), *The New Palgrave, A Dictionary of Economics*. London and Basingstoke: MacMillan, vol. 2, pp. 678-680.

Browning, M. (1992), Children and Household Economic Behavior, *Journal of Economic Literature*, vol. 30, pp. 1434-1475.

Browning, M., Bourguignon, F., Chiappori, P. and Lechêne, V. (1994), Incomes and outcomes: a structural model of intrahousehold allocation, *Journal of Political Economy*, vol. 102, no. 6, pp. 1067-1096.

Buhmann, B., Rainwater, L., Schmaus, G. and Smeeding, T. (1988), Equivalence Scales, well-being, inequality, and poverty: sensitivity estimates across ten countries using the Luxembourg Income Study (LIS) database, *The Review of Income and Wealth*, vol. 34, no. 2, pp. 115-142.

Buyze, J. (1982), The estimation of welfare levels of a cardinal utility function, *European Economic Review*, vol. 17, pp. 325-332.

Callan, T. and Nolan, B. (1991), Concepts of Poverty and the Poverty Line, *Journal of Economic Surveys*, vol. 5 no. 3, pp. 243-261.

Callan, T., Nolan, B. et al. (1989), *Poverty, Income and Welfare in Ireland*, General Research Series Paper no. 146, Dublin: The Economic and Social Research Institute.

Callan, T., Nolan, B. and Whelan, C. (1993), Resources, Deprivation and the Measurement of Poverty, *Journal of Social Policy*, vol. 22, pp. 141-172.

Cantillon, B. (1990), *Nieuwe behoeften naar zekerheid. Vrouw, gezin en inkomensverdeling*. Leuven: Acco.

Cantillon, B. (1991), Socio-demographic changes and social security, *International Review of Social Security*, no. 4, pp. 399-426.

Cantillon, B., Marx, I., Proost, D. and Van Dam, R. (1993), Indicateurs Sociaux 1985-1992, *Revue Belge de Securité Sociale*, vol. 36, no. 2, pp. 485-535.

Chadeau, A. and Fouqet, A. (1984), Peut-on mesurer le travail domestique?, *Economie et Statistique*, no. 136, pp. 29-42.

Chiappori, P. (1992), Collective Labor Supply and Welfare, *Journal of Political Economy*, vol. 100, no. 3, pp. 437-467.

Chiappori, P. (1997), Introducing Household Production in Collective Models Labor Supply, *Journal of Political Economy*, vol. 105, no. 1, pp. 191-209.

Citro, C. and Michael, R. (1995), *Measuring Poverty. A New Approach*. Washington D.C.: National Academy Press.

Cohen, G. (1993), Equality of What? On Welfare, Goods and Capabilities, in: Sen and Nussbaum (1993), pp. 9-29.

Colasanto, D., Kapteyn, A. and Van der Gaag, J. (1984), Two subjective definitions of poverty: results from the Wisconsin Basic Needs study, *The Journal of Human Resources*, vol. 19, no. 1, pp. 127-138.

Commission of the European Communities (1981), *Final Report from the First Programme of Pilot Schemes and Studies to Combat Poverty*, Brussels: Commission of the European Communities.

Commission of the European Communities (1991), *National Policies to Combat Social Exclusion. First Annual Report of the European Community Observatory* (ed. by Room, G.), Bath: Centre for Research in European Social and Employment Policy.

Coser, L. (1965), The Sociology of Poverty, *Social Problems*, vol. 13, no. 2, pp. 140-148.

Dahrendorf, R. (1990), *The Modern Social Conflict, An essay on the Politics of Liberty*. Berkeley: University of California Press.

Danziger, S., Van der Gaag, J., Taussig, M. and Smolensky, E. (1984), The Direct Measurement of Welfare Levels: How much does it cost to make ends meet?, *Review of Economics and Statistics*, vol. 66, pp. 500-504.

Danziger, S. and Weinberg, D. (1986), *Fighting Poverty: What Works and What Doesn't*. Cambridge: Harvard University Press.

Darian, J. and Klein, S. (1989), Food Expenditure Patterns of Working-Wife Families: Meals Prepared Away From Home Versus Convenience Foods, *Journal of Consumer Policy*, vol. 12, pp. 139-164.

David, M. and Smeeding, T. (1985), *Horizontal Equity, Uncertainty and Economic Well-Being*. Chicago: University of Chicago Press.

Davies, H. and Joshi, H. (1994), Sex, Sharing and the Distribution of Income, *Journal of Social Policy*, vol. 23, pp. 301-340.

De Vos, K. (1991), *Micro-economic definitions of poverty*. Erasmus Universiteit Rotterdam (Academic Thesis).

De Vos, K. and Garner, T. (1991), An evaluation of subjective poverty definitions: Comparing results from the U.S. and the Netherlands, *The Review of Income and Wealth*, vol. 37, no. 3, pp. 267-285.

De Vos, K., Hagenaars, A. and Van Praag, B. (1987), *Armoede, arbeid en sociale zekerheid*. Den Haag: Ministerie van Sociale Zaken en Werkgelegenheid.

De Vos, K. and Zaidi, M. (1994), *Trend analysis of poverty in the European Community. Synthesis of country reports for the United Kingdom, Spain, France, Portugal, Belgium and Greece. Report to the statistical office of the European Community*. Tilburg and Rotterdam: Economic Institute Tilburg and Erasmus University.

Deaton, A. (1992), *Understanding Consumption*. Oxford: Clarendon Press.

Deaton, A. and Mullbauer (1986), *Economics and Consumer Behavior*. Cambridge: Cambridge University Press (sixth printing).

Deaton, A., Ruiz-Castillo, J. and Thomas, D. (1989), The Influence of Household Composition on Household Expenditure Patterns. Theory and Spanish Evidence, *Journal of Political Economy*, vol. 97, no. 1, pp.179-200.

DeCoster, A., Houthuys, D., Nicaise, I., Pacolet, J. and Wouters, R. (1984), *Sociale Zekerheid en Personenbelasting*. Leuven: Katholieke Universiteit Leuven.

Deleeck, H. (1989), The adequacy of the Social Security System in Belgium, 1976-1985, *Journal of Social Policy*, vol. 18 no. 1, pp. 91-117.

Deleeck, H. (1991), *Zeven lessen over Sociale Zekerheid*. Leuven: Acco.

Deleeck, H., Berghman, J., Van Heddegem, P. and Vereycken, L. (1980), *De Sociale Zekerheid tussen Droom en Daad, Theorie, Onderzoek, Beleid*. Deventer and Antwerpen: Van Loghum Slaterus.

Deleeck, H., Cantillon, B., Meulemans, B. and Van den Bosch, K. (1991), Indicateurs sociaux de la securité sociale, 1985-1988, *Revue Belge de Securité Sociale*, vol. 33, no. 10-12, pp. 689-756.

Deleeck, H., Van den Bosch, K. and De Lathouwer, L. (1992), *Poverty and the adequacy of social security in the EC, A comparative analysis*. Aldershot: Avebury.

Delhausse, B., Lutgens, A. and Perelman, S. (1993), Comparing measures of poverty and relative deprivation. An example for Belgium, *Journal of Population Economics*, vol. 6, pp. 83-102.

Desai, M. and Shah, A. (1988), An Econometric Approach to the Measurement of Poverty, *Oxford Economic Papers*, vol. 40, pp. 505-522.

Dickes, P. (1987a), Une mesure alternative pour la mesure de la pauvreté, *Cahiers Economiques de Nancy*, no. 18, pp. 83-116.

Dickes, P. (1987b), Indicateur subjectif de la pauvreté, *Cahiers Economiques de Nancy*, no. 18, pp. 117-151.

Dickes, P. (1988), L'impact des groupes de revenu sur les mesures de bien-être subjectif, *Cahiers Economiques de Nancy*, no. 20, pp. 49-71.

Dickes, P. (1989), Pauvreté subjective et bien-être subjectif: validité de construct, *Cahiers Economiques de Nancy*, no. 22, pp. 21-57.

Donnison, D. (1988), Defining and Measuring Poverty. A Reply to Stein Ringen, *Journal of Social Policy*, vol. 17, pp. 367-374.

Douglas, M. (1976), Relative poverty - relative communication, in: Halsey, A. (ed.), *Traditions of social policy: essays in honor of Violet Butler*. Oxford: Basil Blackwell, pp. 197-215.

Douthitt, R., MacDonald, M. and Mullis, R. (1992), The relationship between measures of subjective and economic well-being: a new look, *Social Indicators Research*, vol. 26, pp. 407-422.

Downs, A. (1957), *An Economic Theory of Democracy*. New York: Harper and Row.

Doyal, L. and Gough, I. (1991), *A theory of human needs*. London: Macmillan.

Dubnoff, S. (1985), How much income is enough? Measuring public judgments, *Public Opinion Quarterly*, vol. 49, pp. 285-299.

Dubnoff, S., Vaughan, D. and Lancaster, C. (1981), Income Satisfaction Measures in Equivalence Scale Applications, *Proceedings of the*

Social Statistics Section, American Statistical Association, pp. 348-352.

Duncan, O. (1975), Does Money Buy Satisfaction?, *Social Indicators Research*, vol. 2, pp. 267-274.

Dworkin, R. (1981), What is Equality. Part 1: Equality of Welfare, *Philosophy and Public Affairs*, vol. 10, no. 3, pp. 185-246.

Dworkin, R. (1981), What is Equality. Part 2: Equality of Resources, *Philosophy and Public Affairs*, vol. 10, no. 4, pp. 283-345.

Ellwood, D. and Summers, L. (1986), Poverty in America: Is Welfare the Answer or the Problem?, in: Danziger and Weinberg (1986), pp. 78-105.

Elster, J. (1989), *Nuts and Bolts for the Social Sciences*. Cambridge (UK): Cambridge University Press.

Elster, J. and Hylland, A. (1986), *Foundations of social choice theory*. Cambridge: Cambridge University Press.

Elster, J. and Roemer, J. (1991), *Interpersonal comparisons of well-being*. Cambridge: Cambridge University Press.

Elster, J. and Roemer, J. (1991a), Introduction, in: Elster, J. and Roemer, J. (1991), pp. 1-16.

Engbersen, G. (1988), De rationele arme. De politieke economie van moderne armoede, *Tijdschrift voor Arbeidsvraagstukken*, vol. 4, no. 4, pp. 23-32.

Engbersen, G. (1990), *Publieke Bijstandsgeheimen*. Leiden: Stenfert Kroese.

Engbersen, G. (1991), Moderne armoede: feit en fictie. *Sociologische Gids*, vol. 37, no. 1, pp. 7-23.

Engbersen, G. and Van der Veen, R. (1987), *Moderne armoede. Overleven op het sociaal minimum: een onderzoek onder 120 Rotterdamse huishoudens*. Leiden: Stenfert Kroese.

Engel, E. (1895), Die Lebenskosten Belgischer Arbeiter-Familiën Früher und Jetzt, *Bulletin de l'Institut International de Statistique*, vol. 9, pp. 1-124.

Esping-Andersen, G. (1990), *The Three Worlds of Welfare Capitalism*. Cambridge: Polity Press.

Eurostat (1990), *Poverty in Figures. Europe in the early 1980s*. Luxembourg: Office for Official Publications of the European Communities.

Findlay, J. and Wright, R. (1996), Gender, Poverty and Intra-Household Distribution of Resources, *Review of Income and Wealth*, vol. 42, no. 3, pp. 335-351.

Fitzgerald, J., Swenson, M. and Wicks, J. (1996), Valuation of Household Production at Market Prices and Estimation of Production Functions, *Review of Income and Wealth*, Series 42, no. 2, pp. 165-180.

Flik, R. and Van Praag, B. (1991), Subjective Poverty Line Definitions, *De Economist*, 139, no. 3, pp. 311-329.

Fomby, Th., Hill, R. and Johnson, S. (1988), *Advanced Econometric Methods*. New York: Springer Verlag.

Förster, M. (1993), *Comparing Poverty in 13 OECD Countries: Traditional and Synthetic Approaches*, Luxembourg Income Study Working Paper, No. 100.

Foster, J. (1984), On Economic Poverty: a summary of aggregate measures, *Advances in Econometrics*, vol. 3, pp. 215-251.

Foster, J., Greer, J. and Thorbecke, E. (1984), A Class of Decomposable Poverty Measures, *Econometrica*, vol. 52, no. 3, pp. 761-766.

Foster, J. and Shorrocks, A. (1988), Poverty Orderings, *Econometrica*, vol. 56, no. 1, pp. 173-177.

Friedman, B. and Warshawsky, M. (1990), The Cost of Annuities: Implications for Saving Behavior and Bequests, *Quarterly Journal of Economics*, Series 105, no. 1, pp. 135-154.

Frohlich, N. and Oppenheimer, J. (1992), *Choosing justice: an experimental approach to ethical theory*. Berkeley: University of California Press.

Frohlich, N., Oppenheimer, J. and Eavy, C. (1987), Laboratory Results on Rawl's Distributive Justice, *British Journal of Political Science*, vol. 17, pp. 1-21.

Gans, H. (1968), Culture and class in the study of poverty: an approach to anti-poverty research, in: Moynihan (1968), pp. 201-228.

Garfinkel, I. and Haveman, R. (1977), *Earnings Capacity, Poverty, and Inequality*. New York: Academic Press.

Garner, T. and De Vos, K. (1995), Income sufficiency versus poverty. Results from the United States and The Netherlands, *Journal of Population Economics*, vol. 8, no. 2, pp. 117-134.

Ghiatis, A. (1990), Low Income Groups Obtained by Enhanced Processing of the Household Budget Surveys in EC - Summary Figures for Italy and the Netherlands, in: Teekens and Van Praag (1990), pp. 117-137.

Gibbard, A. (1986), Interpersonal comparisons: preference, good, and the intrinsic reward of a life, in: Elster and Hylland (1986).

Glorieux, I. (1992), *Arbeid en Zingeving: Een onderzoek gesteund op theoretische logica en tijdsbudgetanalyse.* Brussels: Vrije Universiteit Brussel.

Glorieux, I. (1995), *Arbeid als Zingever: Een onderzoek naar de betekenis van arbeid in het leven van mannen en vrouwen*. Brussels: VUB Press.

Goedhart, Th., Halberstadt, V., Kapteyn, A. and Van Praag, B. (1977), The Poverty Line, Concept and Measurement, *The Journal of Human Resources*, vol. 12, no. 4, pp. 503-520.

Goldthorpe, J. (1980), *Social Mobility and Class Structure in Modern Britain*. Oxford: Clarendon Press.

Goodin, R. (1988), *Reasons for Welfare: The political theory of the welfare state*. Princeton: Princeton University Press.

Goodin, R. (1990), Relative Needs, in: Ware and Goodin (1990), pp. 12-33.

Gordon, D., Pantazis, C., Townsend, P., Bramley, G. and Bradshaw, J. (1994), *Breadline Britain in the 1990's. A Draft Report to the Joseph Rowntree Foundation*. York: Joseph Rowntree Foundation.

Graham, J. and Green, C. (1984), Estimating Parameters of a Household Production Function with Joint Products, *Review of Economics and Statistics*, vol. 66, pp. 277-282.

Griffin, J. (1986), *Well-being: Its meaning, measurement and moral importance*. Oxford: Clarendon Press.

Groenland, E. (1989a), Sociale zekerheid versus welzijnsbeleving en psychologische gezondheid: een contradictio in adjecto?, in: Frinking, G. et al (eds.), *Sociale zekerheid: onderzoek en beleid*. Tilburg: Katholieke Universiteit Brabant, pp. 15-42.

Groenland, E. (1989b), *Socio-economic well-being and behavioral reactions. A panel study of people drawing benefits from the Dutch National Security System.* Tilburg: Tilburg University (Academic Thesis).

Gronau, R. (1988), Consumption Technology and the Intrafamily Distribution of Resources: Adult Equivalence Scales Reexamined, *Journal of Political Economy*, vol. 96, no. 6, pp. 1183-1205.

Gujarati, D. (1988), *Basic Econometrics*. Singapore: McGraw-Hill.

Gustafsson, B. (1995), Assessing poverty. Some reflections on the literature, *Journal of Population Economics*, vol. 8, no. 4, pp. 361-381.

Gustafsson, B. and Lindblom, M. (1993), Poverty Lines and Poverty in Seven European Countries, Australia, Canada and the USA, *Journal of European Social Policy*, vol. 3, no. 1, pp. 21-38.

Hagenaars, A. (1985), *The Perception of Poverty*. Academic Thesis, University of Leyden. Published 1986, Amsterdam: North-Holland.

Hagenaars, A., De Vos, K. and Zaidi, M. (1992), *Statistiques relatives à la pauvreté, basées sur les microdonnées. Resultats pour neuf Etats Membres des Communautés Européennes*. Rapport soumis à l'Office Statistique des Communautés européennes. Rotterdam: Erasmus University.

Hagenaars, A., De Vos, K. and Zaidi, M. (1994), *Patterns of Poverty in Europe*. Paper to be presented at the 23rd General Conference of the IARIW, St. Andrews, Canada.

Hagenaars, A., Homan, M. and Van Praag, B. (1984), Draagkrachtverschillen tussen huishoudens met één, resp. twee kostwinners, *Economisch Statistische Berichten*, vol. 69, pp. 552-559.

Hagenaars, A. and Van Praag, B. (1985), A Synthesis of Poverty Line Definitions, *The Review of Income and Wealth*, vol. 31, no. 2, pp. 139-154.

Hagenaars, J. (1990), *Categorical Longitudinal Data. Log-Linear, Trend and Cohort Analysis*. Newbury Park: Sage Publications.

Halleröd, B. (1994a), *A New Approach to the Direct Consensual Measurement of Poverty*. Social Policy Research Centre Discussion Paper no. 50, Sydney: The University of New South Wales.

Halleröd, B. (1994b), *Poverty in Sweden: a New Approach to the Direct Measurement of Consensual Poverty*. Umea Studies in Sociology no. 106, Umea: Sociologiska Institutionen, Umea Universitet.

Halleröd, B. (1995), Making Ends Meet: Perceptions of Poverty in Sweden, *Scandinavian Journal of Social Welfare*, vol. 4.

Halleröd, B., Bradshaw, J. and Holmes, H. (1994), *Adapting the Consensual Definition of Poverty*, in: Gordon et al. (1994).

Hammond, P. (1991), Interpersonal comparisons of utility: why and how they are and should be made, in: Elster and Roemer (1991).

Harman, H. (1976), *Modern Factor Analysis*. Chicago: University of Chicago Press.

Harris, D. (1987), *Justifying State Welfare. The New Right versus the Old Left*. Oxford: Basil Blackwell.

Harsanyi, J. (1976), *Essays in ethics, social behaviour and scientific explanation*. Dordrecht: Reidel.

Hartog, J. (1988), Poverty and the Measurement of Individual Welfare, *The Journal of Human Resources*, vol. 23, no. 2, pp. 243-266.

Haveman, R. (1993), Who are the nation's "truly poor"? Problems and pitfalls in (re)defining and measuring poverty, *The Brookings Review*, Winter 1993, pp. 24-27.

Haveman, R. and Buron, L. (1993), Escaping poverty through work: the problem of low earnings capacity in the United States, 1973-88, *The Review of Income and Wealth*, vol. 39, no. 2, pp. 141-157.

Headey, B., Hampel, J. and Meyer, W. (1990), *The relationship between objective and subjective indicators: a reciprocal causation model linking changes in income, income satisfaction and life satisfaction.* Arbeitspapier No. 332, Frankfurt: J.W. Goethe-Universität Frankfurt and Universität Mannheim.

Headey, B. and Veenhoven, R. (1989), Does happiness induce a rosy outlook?, in: Veenhoven (1989).

Heckman, J. (1979), Sample Selection Bias as a Specification Error, *Econometrics*, vol. 47, no. 8, pp. 153-161.

Heclo, H. (1986), The political foundations of antipoverty policy, in: Danziger, S. and Weinberg, D. (eds.), *Fighting poverty: what works and what doesn't.* Cambridge (Massachusetts): Harvard University Press.

Hess, F. (1987), Niveau de vie et unité d'analyse, *Cahiers Economiques de Nancy*, 1er semestre 1987, no. 18, pp. 39-82.

Himmelfarb, G. (1985), *The idea of poverty. England in the early industrial age*. New York: Random House.

Hochman, H. and Rodgers, J. (1969), Pareto optimal redistribution, *American Economic Review*, vol. 59 (Sept. 1969), pp. 542-557.

Homan, M. (1988), *The Allocation of Time and Money in One-earner and Two-earner Families: An Economic Analysis*. Rotterdam: Erasmus University (Academic Thesis).

Homan, E., Hagenaars, A. and Van Praag, B. (1986), *Interhuishoudelijke vergelijkingen van consumptie, welvaart en tijdsallocatie. Eindverslag van het onderzoek Kostwinnersproblematiek.* Leiden en Rotterdam: Centrum voor Onderzoek van de Economie van de Publieke Sector and Erasmus Universiteit Rotterdam.

Homan, E., Hagenaars, A. and Van Praag, B. (1991), Income inequality between one-earner and two-earners households: is it real or artificial, *De Economist*, vol. 139, no. 4, pp. 530-549.

Hoorens, V. (1997), *Discrepanties tussen op subjectieve metingen gebaseerde equivalentieschalen. Drie toetsbare hypothesen.* (Unpublished note).

Huston, A. (1991a), Antecedents, consequences and possible solutions for poverty among children, in: Huston, A. (1991b).

Huston, A. (1991b), *Children in poverty: child development and public policy.* Cambridge (Massachusetts): Cambridge University Press.

Jahoda, M. (1982), *Employment and unemployment: a social-psychological analysis.* Cambridge: Cambridge University Press.

Janssens, P. and Schulpen, L. (1985), Het sociaal levensminimum, een vergelijking van twee methodes, *Tijdschrift voor Sociologie*, vol. 6, pp. 107-131.

Jencks, C. (1992), *Rethinking social policy: race, poverty and the underclass.* Cambridge: Harvard University Press.

Jencks, C. and Peterson, P. (1991), *The Urban Underclass.* Washington D.C.: The Brookings Institution.

Jenkins, S. (1991), Poverty measurement and the within-household distribution: agenda for action, *Journal of Social Policy*, vol. 20, no. 4, pp. 457-483.

Jenkins, S. and Lambert, P. (1997), Three 'I's of poverty curves, with an analysis of UK poverty trends, *Oxford Economic Papers*, vol. 49, pp. 317-327.

Jöreskog, K. and Sörbom, D. (1993), *New features in LISREL 8.* Chicago: Scientific Software International.

Judge, G., Griffiths, W., Carter Hill, R., Lütkepohl, H. and Lee, T.-C. (1985), *The Theory and Practice of Econometrics* (2nd edition). New York: John Wiley.

Kalton, G. (1983), *Introduction to Survey Sampling.* Sage University Paper Series no. 35, Beverly Hills: Sage.

Kangas, O. and Ritakallio, V.-M. (1995), *Different Methods - Different Results? Approaches to Multidimensional Poverty.* Paper presented at the ISA RC19 conference on 'Comparative Research on Welfare State Reforms' at Pavía.

Kapteyn, A. (1977), *A theory of preference formation.* Leyden University (Academic Thesis, Ph.D.).

Kapteyn, A. (1985), Utility and economics, *De Economist*, vol. 133, no. 1, pp. 1-20.

Kapteyn, A. (1994), The measurement of household cost functions. Revealed preference versus subjective measures, *Journal of Population Economics*, vol. 7, pp. 333-350.

Kapteyn, A., Kooreman, P., Muffels, R., Siegers, J., Van Soest, A. and Willemse, R. (1985), *Determinanten van bestaansonzekerheid. Een vooronderzoek.* COSZ-reeks no. 10, Den Haag: Ministerie van Sociale Zaken en Werkgelegenheid.

Kapteyn, A., Kooreman, P. and Willemse, R. (1988), Some Methodological Issues in the Implementation of Subjective Poverty Definitions, *The Journal of Human Resources*, vol. 23, no. 2, pp. 222-242.

Kapteyn, A. and Melenberg, B. (1993), Measuring the Well-Being of the Elderly, in: Atkinson, A. and Rein, M. (eds.), *Age Work and Social Security*. New York: St. Martin's Press.

Kapteyn, A., Van de Geer, S. and Van der Stadt, H. (1985), The Impact of Changes in Income and Family Composition on Subjective Measures of Well-Being, in: David, M. and Smeeding, T. (eds), *Horizontal Equity and the Distribution of the TaxBurden*, Chicago: NBER and Chicago University Press.

Kapteyn, A. and Van Herwaarden, F. (1980), Interdependent welfare functions and optimal income distribution, *Journal of Public Economics*, vol. 14, pp. 375-397.

Kapteyn, A. and Van Praag, B. (1976), A new approach to the construction of family equivalence scales, *European Economic Review*, vol. 7, pp. 313-335.

Kapteyn, A., Van Praag, B. and Van Herwaarden, F. (1978), Individual welfare functions and social reference spaces, *Economics Letters*, vol. 1, pp. 173-177.

Kapteyn, A. and Wansbeek, T. (1982), Empirical evidence on preference formation, *Journal of Economic Psychology*, vol. 2, pp. 137-154.

Kapteyn, A. and Wansbeek, T. (1985a), The individual welfare function. A review, *Journal of Economic Psychology*, vol. 6, pp. 333-363.

Kapteyn, A. and Wansbeek, T. (1985b), The individual welfare function. A rejoinder, *Journal of Economic Psychology*, vol. 6, pp. 375-381.

Kapteyn, A., Wansbeek, T. and Buyze, J. (1978), The dynamics of preference formation, *Economics Letters*, vol. 1, pp. 93-98.

Kapteyn, A., Wansbeek, T. and Buyze, J. (1979), Maximizing or Satisficing?, *The Review of Economics and Statistics*, vol. 61, pp. 549-563.

Kapteyn, A., Wansbeek, T. and Buyze, J. (1980), The dynamics of preference formation, *Journal of Economic Behavior and Organization*, vol. 1, pp. 123-157.

Katz, M. (1993), *The Underclass Debate: Views from History*. Princeton: Princeton University Press.

Kerger, A. (1988), La mise-en-oevre sur le terrain de la notion de groupes de revenu: le cas du panel luxembourgeois, *Cahiers Economiques de Nancy*, no. 20 (1er semestre, 1988), pp. 27-36.

Kilpatrick, R. (1973), The income elasticity of the poverty line, *The Review of Economics and Statistics*, vol. 55, pp. 327-332.

Kish, L. (1965), *Survey sampling*. New York: John Wiley.

Layard, R. (1982), Human satisfactions and public policy, *Economic Journal*, vol. 90, pp. 737-749.

Lazear, E. and Michael, R. (1980), Real income equivalence among one-earner and two-earner families, *American Economic Review*, vol. 70, pp. 203-208.

Lazear, E. and Michael, R. (1988), *Allocation of income within the household*. Chicago: University of Chicago Press.

Lewis, G. and Ulph, D. (1988), Poverty inequality and welfare, *The Economic Journal*, vol. 98 (Conference 1988), pp. 117-131.

Lewis, O. (1961), *The Children of Sanchez*. New York: Random House.

Lewis, O. (1966), *La Vida*. New York: Random House.

Lewis, O. (1968), Culture of Poverty, in: Moynihan, D. (1968).

Lipsey, R. (1989), *An introduction to positive economics* (7th ed.). London: Weidenfeld and Nicolson.

Lundberg, S. and Pollak, R. (1996), Bargaining and Distribution in Marriage, *Journal of Economic Perspectives*, vol. 10, no. 4, pp. 139-158.

Lundberg, S., Pollak, R. and Wales, T. (1997), Do husbands and wives pool their resources? Evidence from the United Kingdom Child Benefit, *The Journal of Human Resources*, vol. 32, no. 3, pp. 463-480.

MacDonald, M. and Douthitt, R. (1992), Consumption Theories and Consumer's Assessments of Subjective Well-Being, *The Journal of Consumer Affairs*, vol. 26, no. 2, pp. 243-261.

Mack, J. and Lansley, S. (1985), *Poor Britain*. London: George Allen and Unwin.

Marshall, T. (1950), *Citizenship and Social Class and other essays*. Cambridge: Cambridge University Press.

Marshall, T. (1967), *Social policy in the twentieth century* (second edition). London: Hutchinson.

Matza, D. (1966), Poverty and Disrepute, in: Merton and Nisbet (1966), pp. 619-669.

McCabe, M. and Rose, A. (1993), The clothing budget, in: Bradshaw (1993), pp. 65-79.

McGregor, P. and Borooah, V. (1992), Is low spending or low income a better indicator of whether or not a household is poor: some results from the 1985 Family Expenditure Survey, *Journal of Social Policy*, vol. 21, no. 1, pp. 53-69.

Melenberg, B. (1992), *Micro-econometric Models of Consumer Behavior and Welfare*. Tilburg: Tilburg University (Academic Thesis).

Melenberg, B. and Van Soest, A. (1995), *Semiparametric Estimation of Equivalence Scales Using Subjective Information*. Tilburg: Tilburg University (Unpublished paper).

Menard, S. (1995), *Applied Logistic Regression Analysis*. Sage University Paper series on Quantitative Applications in the Social Sciences, 07-106, Thousand Oaks (California): Sage.

Merton, R. and Nisbet, R. (1966), *Contemporary Social Problems* (second edition). New York: Harcourt, Brace and World.

Meulemans, B. (1993), *Non-respons analyse vermogens en huisvestingsvragen 1992*. Antwerp: Centre for Social Policy (internal note).

Meulemans, B. and Cantillon, B. (1993), De geruisloze kering: de nivellering van de intergenerationele welvaartsverschillen, *Economisch en Sociaal Tijdschrift*, vol. 47, no. 3, pp. 421-448.

Meulemans, B., Geurts, V. and De Decker, P. (1995), *Onderzoek naar de doelgroepen van het woonbeleid*, Antwerp: University of Antwerp, Centre for Social Policy.

Meulemans, B. and Marannes, F. (1993), La répartition des revenus du patrimoine: une étude socio-economique des ménages belges en 1988, *Cahiers Economiques de Bruxelles*, no. 137, pp. 71-107.

Miller, D. (1976), *Social Justice*. Oxford: Clarendon Press.

Miller, S. and Roby, P. (1970), Poverty: changing social stratification, in: Townsend (1970), pp. 124-145.

Miller, S. and Roby, P. (1970), *The future of inequality*. New York: Basic Books.

Mincy, R. (1994), The underclass: concept, controversy and evidence, in: Danziger, S., Sandefur, G. and Weinberg, D. (eds.), *Confronting poverty: prescriptions for change.* Cambridge (Massachusetts): Harvard University Press, pp. 109-146.

Mishra, R. (1990), *The welfare state in capitalist society. Policies of retrenchment and maintenance in Europe, North America and Australia.* New York: Harvester Wheatsheaf.

Mitchell, D. (1991), *Income Transfers in Ten Welfare States.* Aldershot: Avebury.

Moriani, C. (1990), Italian experience of harmonized poverty measures: a summary, in: Teekens and Van Praag (1990), pp. 139-152.

Moynihan, D. (1968), *On understanding poverty: perspectives from the social sciences.* New York: Basic Books.

Muellbauer, J. (1987), Professor Sen on the Standard of Living, in: Sen, A. et al. (1987), pp. 39-58.

Mueller, D. (1989), *Public Choice II.* Cambridge: Cambridge University Press.

Muffels, R., Kapteyn, A., De Vries, A. et al. (1990), *Poverty in the Netherlands: report on the Dutch contribution to an international comparative study on poverty and the financial efficacy of the social security system.* The Hague: VUGA.

Muffels, R., Berghman, J. and Dirven, H.-J. (1992), A multi-method approach to monitor the evolution of poverty, *Journal of European Social Policy*, vol. 2, no. 3, pp. 193-213.

Murray, C. (1984), *Losing ground, American social policy 1950-1980.* New York: Schuster.

Murray, C. et al. (1990), *The emerging British underclass.* London: The IEA Health and Welfare Unit.

Namboodiri, N., Carter, L. and Blalock, H. (1975), *Applied multivariate analysis and experimental designs*. New York: McGraw-Hill.

Nelson, J. (1988), Household Economies of Scale in Consumption: Theory and Evidence, *Econometrica*, vol. 56, no. 6, pp. 1301-1314.

Niemöller, K. and Van Schuur, W. (1983), Stochastic models for unidimensional scaling: Mokken and Rasch, in: McKay, D., Schofield, M. and Whitely, P. (eds.), *Data Analysis and the Social Sciences.* London: Frances Pinter.

Nussbaum, M. and Sen, A. (1993), *The Quality of Life.* Oxford: Clarendon Press.

OECD (1976), *Public Expenditures on Income Maintenance Programmes*, Studies in Resource Allocation, Paris: OECD.

OECD (1982), *The OECD list of social indicators*. Paris: OECD.

O'Higgins, M. (1980), *Poverty in Europe - The Subjective Assessment of Poverty Lines: An Evaluation*. Bath: University of Bath (Unpublished manuscript in two parts).

O'Higgins, M. and Jenkins, S. (1990), Poverty in Europe: estimates for the numbers in poverty in 1975, 1980, 1985, in: Teekens and Van Praag (1990), pp. 187-212.

Orshansky, M. (1969), How poverty is measured. *Monthly Labor Review*, vol. 92.

Osmani, S. and Van Praag, B. (1993), The relativity of the welfare concept, in: Nussbaum and Sen (1993), pp. 386-392.

Oster, S., Lake, E. and Oksman, C. (1978), *The Definition and Measurement of Poverty, Volume 1: A Review*, Boulder: Westview Press.

Pahl, J. (1988), Earning, Sharing, Spending: Married Couples and Their Money, in: Walker, R. and Parker, G. (eds.), *Money Matters. Income, Wealth and Financial Welfare.* London: Sage, pp. 195-211.

Pahl, J. (1989), *Money and Marriage.* London: Macmillan.

Peterson, P. (1991), The urban underclass and the poverty paradox, *Political Science Quarterly*, vol. 106, no. 4, pp. 617-638.

Phipps, S. and Garner, T. (1994), Are equivalence scales the same for the United States and Canada?, *Review of Income and Wealth*, vol. 40, no. 1, pp. 1-17.

Piachaud, D. (1987), Problems in the definition and measurement of poverty, *Journal of Social Policy*, vol. 16, no. 2, pp. 147-164.

Pindyck, R. and Rubinfeld, D. (1991), *Econometric models and economic forecasts* (3rd ed.). New York: McGraw-Hill.

Piven, F. and Cloward, R. (1971), *Regulating the poor.* New York: Vintage.

Plant, R., Lesser, H. and Taylor-Gooby, P. (1980), *Political philosophy and social welfare. Essays on the normative basis of welfare provision*. London: Routledge and Kegan Paul.

Plotnick, R. and Winters, R. (1985), A politico-economy theory of income redistribution, *American Political Science Review*, vol. 79, pp. 458-473.

Plug, E. and Van Praag, B. (1994/95), Family equivalence scales within a narrow and broad welfare context, *Journal of Income Distribution*, vol. 4, no. 2, pp. 171-186.

Pollak, R. (1991), Welfare comparisons and situation comparisons, *Journal of Econometrics*, vol. 50, pp. 31-48.

Pollak, R. and Wachter, M. (1975), The relevance of the household production function and its implication for the allocation of time, *Journal of Political Economy*, vol. 83, no. 2, pp. 255-277.

Pollak, R. and Wales, T. (1979), Welfare Comparisons and Equivalence Scales, *American Economic Review*, vol. 69, pp. 216-221.

Poulin, S. (1985), *Overview of the 'Income Satisfaction Supplement' (1983 Survey of Consumer Finances)*. Ottawa: Statistics Canada, Labour and Household Surveys Analysis Division, Staff Reports.

Poulin, S. (1988), *An Application of Analytic Techniques to Canadian Income Satisfaction Data*. Ottawa: Statistics Canada, Labour and Household Surveys Analysis Division, Staff Reports.

Poulin, S. (1989), *Overview of the 'Income Satisfaction Supplement' (1986 Survey of Consumer Finances)*. Ottawa: Statistics Canada, Labour and Household Surveys Analysis Division, Staff Reports.

Rainwater, L. (1974), *What Money Buys: Inequality and the Social Meanings of Income*. New York: Basic Books.

Rainwater, L. (1990), *Poverty and Equivalence as Social Constructions*. LIS Working paper no. 55, Walferdange: The Luxembourg Income Study.

Ramsey, J. (1969), Tests for specification errors in classical linear least squares regression analysis, *Journal of the Royal Statistical Society*, series B, vol. 31, pp. 350-371.

Rao, J. (1988), Variance estimation in sample surveys, in: Krishnaiah, P. and Rao, C. (eds.), *Handbook of Statistics*, vol. 6. Amsterdam: North Holland, pp. 427-447.

Ratchford, B. (1985), The individual welfare function, *Journal of Economic Psychology*, vol. 6, pp. 365-374.

Rawls, J. (1973), *A Theory of Justice*. Oxford: Oxford University Press (first published 1971).

Rawls, J. (1982), Social unity and primary goods, in: Sen and Williams (1982), pp. 159-185.

Rein, M. (1970), Problems in the Definition and Measurement of Poverty, in: Townsend, P. (ed.), *The Concept of Poverty*, London: Heinemann.

Renard, R. and Pauwels, K. (1971), Eléments de recherche sur le minimum social, *Population et Famille*, no. 25, pp. 117-139.

Rendall, M. and Speare, A. (1993), Comparing Economic Well-Being Among Elderly Americans, *Review of Income and Wealth*, vol. 39, no. 1, pp. 1-21.

Riffault, H. and Rabier, J. (1977), *La perception de lat misère en Europe.* Bruxelles: Commission des Communautés européennes.

Ringen, S. (1987), Poverty in the Welfare State, *International Journal of Sociology*, vol. 16, no. 3-4, pp. 122-138.

Ringen, S. (1988), Direct and indirect measures of poverty, *Journal of Social Policy*, vol. 17, pp. 351-365.

Ringen, S. (1989), *The possibility of politics. A study in the political economy of the welfare state.* Oxford: Clarendon Press (first published 1987).

Ringen, S. (1996), Households, goods and well-being, *The Review of Income and Wealth*, vol. 42, no. 4, pp. 421-431.

Ringen, S. and Halpin, B. (1997), Children, standard of living and distribution in the family, *Journal of Social Policy*, vol. 26, pp. 21-41.

Roach, J. (1965), Sociological analysis and poverty, *American Journal of Sociology*, vol. 71, pp. 68-75.

Rodgers, J. (1974), Explaining income redistribution, in: Hochman, H. and Peterson, G. (eds.), *Redistribution through public choice.* New York: Columbia University Press.

Rossi, P. and Blum, Z. (1968), Class, Status and Poverty, in: Moynihan (1968), pp. 36-63.

Rowntree, B.S. (1901), *Poverty: A Study of Town Life.* London: Macmillan.

Rowntree, B.S. and Lavers, G. (1951), *Poverty and the Welfare State*, London: Longman.

Ruggles, P. (1990), *Drawing the Line, Alternative Poverty Measures and their Implications for Public Policy.* Washington D.C.: The Urban Institute.

Ruggles, P. and Williams, R. (1989), Longitudinal Measures of Poverty: Accounting for Income and Assets over Time, *Review of Income and Wealth*, vol. 35, no. 3, pp. 225-243.

SAS Institute Inc. (1989), *SAS/STAT User's Guide Version 6*, Fourth Edition, vol. 1, Cary (North Carolina): SAS Institute.

Saunders, P. and Bradbury, B. (1991), Some Australian evidence on the consensual approach to poverty measurement, *Economic Analysis and Policy*, vol. 21, no. 1, pp. 47-78.

Saunders, P., Halleröd, B. and Matheson, G. (1994), Making ends meet in Australia and Sweden: A comparative analysis using the subjective poverty line methodology, *Acta Sociologica*, vol. 37, no. 1, pp. 3-22.

Saunders, P. and Matheson, G. (1992), *Perceptions of poverty, income, adequacy and living standards in Australia*, Social Policy Research Centre Reports and Proceedings no. 99, Kensington (New South Wales): The University of New South Wales.

Saunders, P. and Matheson, G. (1993), Politics, Income Perceptions and Living Standards, *Australian Journal of Political Science*, vol. 28, pp. 1-18.

Sawhill, I. (1988), Poverty in the U.S.: Why is it so persistent?, *Journal of Economic Literature*, vol. 26, pp. 1073-1119.

Scanlon, T. (1991), The moral basis of interpersonal comparisons, in: Elster and Roemer (1991), pp. 17-44.

Schokkaert, E. and Van Ootegem, L. (1990), Sen's concept of the living standard applied to the Belgian unemployed, *Recherches Economiques de Louvain*, vol. 56, no. 3-4, pp. 42-450.

Schuyt, C. and Tan, A. (1988), De maatschappelijke betekenis van armoede, *Op zoek naar armoede en bestaansonzekerheid langs twee sporen*. Rijswijk: Nationale Raad voor Maatschappelijk Welzijn, pp. 34-54.

Seidl, C. (1988), Poverty measurement: a survey, in: Bös, D., Rose, M. and Seidl, C. (eds.), *Welfare and efficiency in public economics*. Berlin: Springer.

Seidl, C. (1994), How sensible is the Leyden individual welfare function of income?, *European Economic Review*, vol. 38, pp. 1633-1659.

Sen, A. (1976), Poverty: an ordinal approach to measurement, *Econometrica*, vol. 44, no. 2, pp. 219-231.

Sen, A. (1981), *Poverty and Famines. An essay on entitlement and deprivation*. Oxford: Clarendon Press.

Sen, A. (1983), Poor, Relatively Speaking, *Oxford Economic Papers*, vol. 35, pp. 135-169.

Sen, A. (1984), The living standard, *Oxford Economic Papers*, vol. 36, supplement, November, pp. 74-90.

Sen, A. (1985), *Commodities and capabilities* (Professor dr. P. Hennipman lectures in economics, theory, institutions, policy, 7). Amsterdam: North Holland.

Sen, A. (1985b), A sociological approach to the measurement of poverty: a reply to professor Peter Townsend, *Oxford Economic Papers*, vol. 37, pp. 669-676.

Sen, A. et al. (1987), *The standard of living*. Cambridge: Cambridge University Press.

Sen, A. (1987a), The standard of living: Lecture I, concepts and critiques; Lecture II, lives and capabilities, in: Sen et al. (1987), pp. 1-38.

Sen, A. (1987b), Reply, in: Sen et al. (1987), pp. 103-112.

Sen, A. (1992), *Inequality reexamined*. Oxford: Clarendon Press.

Sen, A. (1993), Capability and well-being, in: Sen and Nussbaum (1993), pp. 30-53.

Sen, A. and Nussbaum, M. (1993), *The Quality of Life*. Oxford: Clarendon Press.

Sen, A. and Williams, B. (1982), *Utilitarianism and beyond*. Cambridge: Cambridge University Press.

Simmel, G. (1965), The poor (translated by C. Jacobson), *Social Problems*, vol. 13, no. 2, pp. 118-140. (Original edition: Der Arme, in: Simmel, G. (1908), *Soziologie: Untersuchungen über die Formen der Vergesellschaftung*. Leipzig: Duncker und Humblot, pp. 454-493.)

Simon, H. (1982), *Models of bounded rationality*. Cambridge (Massachusetts): MIT Press.

Slesnick, D. (1992), Aggregate consumption and saving in the postwar United States, *Review of Economics and Statistics*, vol. 74, pp. 585-597.

Slesnick, D. (1993), Gaining ground: poverty in the postwar United States, *Journal of Political Economy*, vol. 101, no. 1, pp. 1-38.

Smeeding, T., Rainwater, L. and O'Higgins, M. (1990), *Poverty, Inequality and the Distribution of Income in an International Context: Initial Research from the Luxembourg Income Study (LIS)*, London: Wheatsheaf.

Smeeding, T., Saunders, P., Coder, J., Jenkins, S., Fritzell, J., Hagenaars, A., Hauser, R. and Wolfson, M. (1992), *Noncash Income, Living Standards, and Inequality: Evidence from the Luxembourg Income Study*, Working paper 79, Walferdange: The Luxembourg Income Study.

Smeeding, T., Saunders, P., Coder, J., Jenkins, S., Fritzell, J., Hagenaars, A., Hauser, R. and Wolfson, M. (1993), Poverty, Inequality and Family Living Standards: Impacts Across Seven Nations: The Effect of Noncash Subsidies for Health, Education and Housing, *The Review of Income and Wealth*, vol. 39, no. 3, pp. 229-254.

Smith, J. (1979), The distribution of family earnings, *Journal of Political Economy*, vol. 87, no. 5, pp. S163-S192.

Spicker, P. (1993), *Poverty and social security. Concepts and principles.* London: Routledge.

Stanovnik, T. (1992), Perception of poverty and income satisfaction. An empirical analysis of Slovene households, *Journal of Economic Psychology*, vol. 13, pp. 57-69.

Stinson, L. (1997), *The subjective assessment of income and expenses: Cognitive test results*. Washington D.C.: Bureau of Labor Statistics.

Stitt, S. (1994), *Poverty and Poor Relief: Concepts and Reality*. Aldershot: Avebury.

Stitt, S. and Grant, D. (1992), *Poverty: Rowntree revisited*. Aldershot: Avebury.

Strober, M. and Weinberg, Ch. (1978), Some non-differences between working wives and non-working wives, *University Research Papers*, no. 465.

Supplementary Benefit Commission (1979), *Annual report for 1978*, Cmnd 7725. London: HMSO.

Tabard, N. and Clapier, P. (1979), *Influence du travail féminin sur les budget familiaux. Exploitation complémentaire des enquêtes sur les conditions de vie des ménages*. Paris: INSEE.

Tacq, J. (1991), *Van probleem naar analyse: de keuze van een gepaste multivariate analysetechniek bij een sociaal-wetenschappelijke probleemstelling*. De Lier: Academisch Boeken Centrum.

Taylor-Gooby, P. (1985), *Public opinion, ideology and state welfare*. London: Routledge and Kegan Paul.

Teekens, R. and Van Praag, B. (1990), *Analysing Poverty in the European Community*, Eurostat News Special Edition. Luxembourg: Office for Official Publications of the European Communities.

Teekens, R. and Zaidi, A. (1990), Relative and Absolute Poverty in the European Community: Results from Family Budget Surveys, in: Teekens and Van Praag (1990), pp. 213-249.

Theil, H. (1971), *Principles of Econometrics*. New York: John Wiley.

Titmuss, R. (1968), *Commitment to welfare*. London: George Allen and Unwin.

Townsend, P. (1970), *The concept of poverty. Working papers on methods of investigation and life-styles of the poor in different countries*. London: Heinemann.

Townsend, P. (1979), *Poverty in the United Kingdom*. London: Penguin.

Townsend, P. (1985), A sociological approach to the measurement of poverty - a rejoinder to professor Amartya Sen, *Oxford Economic Papers*, vol. 37, pp. 659-668.

Trimp, L. (1985), Eénverdieners en tweeverdieners, 1981, *Sociaal-economische maandstatistiek*, 1985, supplement no. 5, pp. 5-27.

Tullock, G. (1986), *The economics of wealth and poverty*. New York: New York University Press.

Tummers, M. (1991), *The Effect of Systematic Misperception of Income on the Subjective Poverty Line*, Working Paper TEW509, Tilburg University.

Tummers, M. (1992a), *Subjective poverty and earnings: five essays*. Academic thesis, University of Tilburg.

Tummers, M. (1992b), The estimation of the quantiles in the IEQ regression, *European Economic Review*, vol. 36, pp. 1305-1310.

Tummers, M. (1994), The Effect of Systematic Misperception of Income on the Subjective Poverty Line, in: Blundell, R., Preston, I. and Walker, I. (eds), *The measurement of household welfare*, Cambridge: Cambridge University Press, pp. 265-274.

U.S. Bureau of the Census (1987), *Statistical Abstract of the U.S., 1988* (108th ed.). Washington D.C.: U.S. Bureau of the Census.

Valentine, Ch. (1968), *Culture and poverty: Critique and counter-proposals*. Chicago: The University of Chicago Press.

Van de Stadt, H. (1988), *The dynamics of income and welfare*. University of Amsterdam (Academic Thesis).

Van de Stadt, H., Kapteyn, A. and Van de Geer, S. (1985), The relativity of utility: Evidence from panel data, *The Review of Economics and Statistics*, vol. 67, pp. 179-187.

Van den Bosch, K. (1993), Poverty measures in comparative research, in: Berghman, J. and Cantillon, B. (eds.), *The European Face of Social Security, Essays in honour of Herman Deleeck*. Aldershot: Avebury, pp. 3-23.

Van den Bosch, K. (1997), *Wat heeft een gezin nodig om rond te komen? Budgetnormen voor drie type-gezinnen*, UFSIA/Berichten, Centrum voor Sociaal Beleid, Universiteit Antwerpen.

Van den Bosch, K. (1999), *Identifying the Poor, Using Subjective and Consensual Measures*. Antwerp: University of Antwerp (Academic thesis).

Van den Bosch, K., Callan, T., Estivill, J., Hausman, P., Jeandidier, B., Muffels, R. and Yfantopoulos, J. (1993), A comparison of poverty in seven European countries and regions using subjective and relative measures, *Journal of Population Economics*, vol. 6, pp. 235-259.

Van den Bosch, K. and Cantillon, B. (1992), Welfare Comparisons Between One-earner and Two-earner households: an application of the income evaluation method for Belgium, in: De Jong Gierveld, J. and Beets, G. (eds), *Population and Family in the Low Countries*. Amsterdam and Lisse: Swets and Zeitlinger, pp. 121-140.

Van der Haegen, H., Van Hecke, E. and Juchtmans, K. (1996), *De Belgische stadsgewesten 1991*. Statistische Studiën no. 104. Brussels: Nationaal Instituut voor de Statistiek.

Van der Sar, N., Van Praag, B. and Dubnoff, S. (1988), Evaluation questions and income utility, in: Munier, B. (ed.), *Risk, Decision and Rationality*. Dordrecht: Reidel.

Van Dongen, W., Malfait, D. and Pauwels, K. (1995), *De dagelijks puzzel "gezin en arbeid", feiten, wensen en problemen inzake de combinatie van beroeps- en gezinsarbeid in Vlaanderen* (CBGS-Monografie 1995/2). Brussels: Ministerie van de Vlaamse Gemeenschap.

Van Doorn, L. and Van Praag, B. (1988), The measurement of income satisfaction, in: Saris, W. and Gallhofer, I. (eds.), *Sociometric Research, vol. 1: Data collection and scaling*. Basingstoke: Macmillan, pp. 230-246.

Van Herwaarden, F. and Kapteyn, A. (1981), Empirical Comparison of the Shape of Welfare Functions, *European Economic Review*, vol. 15, pp. 261-286.

Van Herwaarden, F., Kapteyn, A. and Van Praag, B. (1977), Twelve thousand individual welfare functions of income: a comparison of six samples in Belgium and The Netherlands, *European Economic Review*, vol. 19, pp. 283-300.

Van Praag, B. (1968), *Individual welfare functions and consumer behavior. A theory of rational irrationality*. Amsterdam: North-Holland.

Van Praag, B. (1971), The Individual Welfare Function in Belgium: An Empirical Investigation, *European Economic Review*, vol. 2, pp. 227-269.

Van Praag, B. (1977a), The perception of welfare inequality, *European Economic Review*, vol. 10, pp. 189-207.

Van Praag, B. (1977b), The perception of income inequality, in: Krelle, W. and Shorrocks, A. (eds.), *Personal income distribution. Proceedings of a conference held by the International Economic Association*. Amsterdam: North-Holland.

Van Praag, B. (1991), Ordinal and Cardinal Utility. An integration of the two dimensions of the welfare concept, *Journal of Econometrics*, vol. 50, pp. 69-89.

Van Praag, B. (1993), The Relativity of the Welfare Concept, in: Nussbaum, M. and Sen, A. (eds.), *The Quality of Life*, Oxford: Clarendon Press.

Van Praag, B. and Flik, R. (1992), *Poverty lines and equivalence scales: A theoretical and empirical evaluation*. Paper presented at the Multidisciplinary Research Conference on Poverty and Distribution, Oslo, November 16-17, 1992.

Van Praag, B., Flik, R. and Stam, J. (1997), Poverty lines and equivalence scales: A theoretical and empirical evaluation, in: Keilman, N. et al. (eds.), *Poverty and economic inequality in industrialized western societies*. Oslo: Scandinavian University Press, pp. 83-122.

Van Praag, B., Goedhart, Th. and Kapteyn, A. (1980), The poverty line - a pilot survey in Europe, *The Review of Economics and Statistics*, vol. 62, pp. 461-465.

Van Praag, B., Hagenaars, A. and Van Weeren, J. (1980), *Poverty in Europe*, Report to the European Community, Center for Research in Public Economics, University of Leyden.

Van Praag, B., Hagenaars, A. and Van Weeren, J. (1982), Poverty in Europe, *The Review of Income and Wealth*, vol. 28 pp. 345-359.

Van Praag, B. and Kapteyn, A. (1973), Further evidence on the individual welfare function of income: an empirical investigation in The Netherlands, *European Economic Review*, vol. 4, pp. 33-62.

Van Praag, B. and Kapteyn, A. (1994), How sensible is the Leyden individual welfare function of income? A Reply, *European Economic Review*, vol. 38, pp. 1817-1825.

Van Praag, B., Kapteyn, A. and Van Herwaarden, F. (1978), The individual welfare function of income: a lognormal distribution function!, *European Economic Review*, vol. 11, pp. 395-402.

Van Praag, B., Spit, J. and Van de Stadt, H. (1982), A comparison between the food ratio poverty line and the Leyden poverty line, *The Review of Economics and Statistics*, vol. 64, pp. 691-694.

Van Praag, B. and Van der Sar, N. (1988), Household Cost Functions and Equivalence Scales, *Journal of Human Resources*, vol. 23, pp. 193-210.

Van Schaaijk, M. (1984), Draagkrachtverschillen tussen huishoudens met één resp. twee kostwinners, *Economisch Statistische Berichten*, vol. 69, pp. 829-830.

Vaughan, D. (1984), Using subjective assessments of income to estimate family equivalence scales: A report on work in progress, *Proceedings of the Social Statistics Section of the American Statistical Association*, pp. 496-501.

Vaughan, D. (1993), Exploring the Use of the Public's Views to Set Income Poverty Thresholds and Adjust Them Over Time, *Social Security Bulletin*, vol. 56, no. 2, pp. 22-46.

Vaughan, D. and Lancaster, C. (1979), Income levels and their impact on two subjective measures of well-being: some early speculations form work in progress, *American Statistical Association, Proceedings of the Social Statistics Section*, pp. 271-276.

Veenhoven, R. (1984), *Conditions of happiness*. Dordrecht: Reidel.

Veenhoven, R. (1989a), *How harmful is happiness?* Rotterdam: Universitaire Pers Rotterdam.

Veenhoven, R. (1989b), Does happiness bind? Marriage chances of the unhappy, in: Veenhoven (1989a).

Veit-Wilson, J. (1986), Paradigms of poverty: a rehabilitation of B.S. Rowntree, *Journal of Social Policy*, vol. 15, pp. 69-99.

Veit-Wilson, J. (1987), Consensual approaches to poverty lines and social security, *Journal of Social Policy*, vol. 16, pp. 183-211.

Vogler, C. (1994), Money in the household, in: Anderson et al. (1994), pp. 225-266.

Vranken, J. (1977), *Armoede in de Welvaartsstaat. Een poging tot Historische en Structurele Plaatsing*, Unpublished doctoral thesis, University of Antwerp.

Vuchelen, J. (1991), De Beleggingen van de Belgische Gezinnen, 1960 - 1988, *Cahiers Economiques de Bruxelles*, no. 130.

Walker, R. (1987), Consensual Approaches to the Definition of Poverty: Towards an Alternative Methodology, *Journal of Social Policy*, vol. 16, pp. 213-226.

Wansbeek, T. and Kapteyn, A. (1983), Tackling Hard Questions by Means of Soft Methods: The Use of Individual Welfare Functions in Socio-Economic Policy, *Kyklos*, vol. 36, pp. 249-269.

Ware, A. and Goodin, R. (1990), *Needs and welfare*. London: Sage.

Watts, H. (1968), An economic definition of poverty, in: Moynihan (1968).

Wedderburn, D. (1974), *Poverty, inequality and class structure*. London: Cambridge University Press.

Weisbrod, B. and Hansen, W. (1968), An Income - Net Worth Approach to Measuring Economic Welfare, *American Economic Review*, vol. 58, pp. 1315-1329.

Whelan, B. (1992), *A Study of the Non-Monetary Indicators of Poverty in the European Community, Final Report*, Dublin: Economic and Social Research Institute.

Whelan, B. (1993), Non-monetary indicators of poverty, in: Berghman, J. and Cantillon, B. (1993), pp. 24-42.

Whiteford, P. (1985), *A family's needs: Equivalence scales, poverty and social security*. Research Paper No. 27. London: Department of Social Security.

Wierenga, B. (1978), The individual welfare function of income: a lognormal distribution function? *European Economic Review*, vol. 11, pp. 387-393.

Wiggins, D. (1985), Claims of need, in: Honderich, T. (ed.), *Morality and objectivity*. London: Routledge and Kegan Paul.

Wiggins, D. (1987), *Needs, values, truth: essays in the philosophy of value*. Oxford: Basil Blackwell.

Williams, B. (1987), The standard of living: interests and capabilities, in: Sen et al. (1987), pp. 94-102.

Wilson, W. (1987), *The truly disadvantaged, the inner city, the underclass, and public policy*. Chicago: The University of Chicago Press.

Wilson, W. (1989a), The ghetto underclass: social science perspectives, *The Annals of the American Academy of Political and Social Science*, vol. 501, January.

Wilson, W. (1989b), The underclass: issues, perspectives and public policy, in: Wilson (1989a), pp. 182-192.

Wilson, W. (1991), Another look at the 'The truly disadvantaged', *Political Science Quarterly*, vol. 106, no. 4, pp. 639-656.

Wolff, E. (1990), Wealth Holdings and Poverty Status in the U.S., *Review of Income and Wealth*, vol. 36, no. 2, pp. 143-165.

Wolfson, M. and Evans, J. (1989), *Statistics Canada's Low Income Cut-Offs: Methodological Concerns and Possibilities*, Research Paper Series, Ottawa: Statistics Canada.

Wolfson, M., Evans, J. and Murphy, B. (1990), Low income statistics, methodological issues and recent experience in Canada, in: Teekens and Van Praag (1990), pp. 335-370.

Woolley, F. and Marshall, J. (1994), Measuring inequality within the household, *Review of Income and Wealth*, vol. 40, no. 4, pp. 415-431.

Year Book Australia (1979, 1988, 1994), Canberra: Australian Bureau of Statistics.

Yu, A. (1993), The low cost budget, in: Bradshaw (1993), pp. 196-215.

Zheng, B. (1997), Aggregate poverty measures, *Journal of economic surveys*, vol. 11, no. 2, pp. 123-162.